FOLLOWING THE SEA

Captain Benjamin Doane (1823-1916)

Following the Sea

By
BENJAMIN DOANE

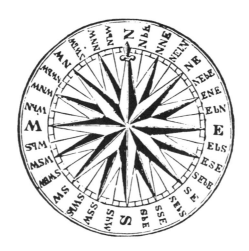

co-published by
NIMBUS PUBLISHING LIMITED
and
THE NOVA SCOTIA MUSEUM
Halifax, Nova Scotia

1987

The Department of Education

Nova Scotia Museum
All rights reserved.

Co-published by Nimbus Publishing Limited and the
Nova Scotia Museum as part of the Education Resource
Services Program of the Department of Education,
Province of Nova Scotia.

Minister: The Hon. Thomas J. McInnis
Deputy Minister: Gerald McCarthy

A product of the Nova Scotia Government
Co-publishing Program.

Printed in Nova Scotia, Canada
Design: GDA, Halifax, N.S.

Typesetting, Printing and Binding:
McCurdy Printing & Typesetting Limited Halifax, N.S.

Canadian Cataloguing in Publication Data

Doane, Benjamin, b. 1823
Following the sea

Co-published by the Nova Scotia Museum.
ISBN 0-920852-88-2 hardcover
ISBN 0-920852-90-4 paperback

1. Whaling — Maritime Provinces. 2. Seafaring
life — Maritime Provinces. 3. Voyages and
travels. I. Nova Scotia Museum. II. Title.

G545.D62 1987   910.4'5   C87-093946-7

DEDICATION

To the memory of three generations of Benjamin Doanes,
whose book this is.

Three generations of the Doane family:
Captain Benjamin Doane (1823-1916), the narrator of the book;
his son, Benjamin Hervey Doane (1863-1947) who wrote the manuscript;
and his grandson, Benjamin Davis Doane (1902-1986)

CONTENTS

PREFACE

BY 1897, Benjamin Doane had retired as a sea captain, and experiences such as those he had known as a young sailor were already slipping from public memory. His recital of his early experiences at sea and his son Benjamin Hervey Doane's recording of them were partly an attempt to keep the spirit of those days alive.

Four successive generations of Benjamin Doanes were involved in this book: The first Benjamin (who had no middle name and has been known in the family as Captain Benjamin), Benjamin Hervey, Benjamin Davis, and Benjamin Knowles, my father. Several times over the years Benjamin Hervey refined the manuscript. It was also read by Captain Ben's grand-nephew, Captain Arthur N. McGray, who affirmed the accuracy of its nautical details. His only criticism was the absence of "sailors' language": "Why was he so afraid to use the word 'damn'?" A longhand draft was typewritten by Mignon Enbree, the fiancée of Robert V. Doane of Plainfield, New Jersey, another grandson of Captain Benjamin. Two drafts were donated to the Cape Sable Historical Society in Barrington, Nova Scotia, and others were retained by various members of the family. Benjamin Hervey never managed to find a publisher for his father's memoir.

Captain Benjamin's grandson, Benjamin Davis Doane, when a boy, lived with the old sea captain in Plainfield and not only looked up to him with respect and admiration but, in his own words, "worshipped him." In his adult years the grandson revised the manuscript to make it more appealing to publishers and even converted some of the material into short stories. His sister Alice Mary Doane Leach, (folklorist Maria Leach) desired as much as her brother to see the work in print but they had no more success than their father in finding a publisher. Eventually, copies of the family treasure were set aside or put into the attic for safe-keeping.

For years I heard the odd mention of the old "manuscript-in-the-attic" in our Nova Scotia home, to which Benjamin Davis's son Benjamin Knowles had returned from the United States to live. It was the same house in Barrington in which Benjamin Doane had courted Maria Knowles, his wife-to-be. An inherited interest in family history led me to investigate the attic where, eventually, I happened upon the manuscript.

I was so impressed and excited by the story that I showed it to Alan Wilson, Professor of History and Canadian Studies at Trent University in Peterborough, Ontario, and to William M. Murphy, Professor of English at Union College in Schenectady, New York (whose wife Harriet is a great-granddaughter of Captain Benjamin). Their enthusiasm proved to be as great as mine, and, happily, the Nova Scotia Museum shared our view.

I am grateful for the help and support of the many other people who have made this publication possible: My father, Benjamin K. Doane; Neal W. Allen, Jr., past Executive Director of the Maine Historical Society; Gerald E. Morris, Director of Publications at the Mystic Seaport Museum in Mystic, Connecticut; Candace Stevenson, Fred Scott and John Hennigar-Shuh from the Nova Scotia Museum; Marven Moore, from the Maritime Museum of the Atlantic, and Mignon and Barbara Doane of Westfield, New Jersey.

My grandfather Benjamin Davis Doane was the greatest help of all, and I am happy that he knew that the manuscript of the grandfather to whom he was so devoted was about to be published. We all regret that his death in January 1986 has made it impossible for him to see the realization of his life-long dream.

HEATHER M. DOANE ATKINSON
Cape Sable Island
June 30, 1987

INTRODUCTION

RARELY does one encounter a manuscript as extraordinary as Benjamin Doane's *Following the Sea*. It combines a vividly-written and gripping adventure story with a tested historical authenticity, and provides a unique insight into mid-nineteenth century life in the forecastles of vessels from the Maritime Provinces.

Benjamin Doane's career was both typical and extraordinary. For young men growing up in the coastal communities of Nova Scotia, going to sea was often an economic necessity which was made more attractive by the lure of adventure. Doane embarked on his career by first sailing in small schooners on coasting voyages. Later he signed on larger vessels which made traditional trading voyages to the West Indies and the United Kingdom. His graduation to deep-water sailing vessels led to his rise from deckhand to second mate, mate and ultimately master. In this respect his life mirrors those of many other Nova Scotian mariners.

The unusual aspect of Doane's career, and a highlight of his memoirs, was his voyage on the whaling ship *Athol* in 1845-48. Whaling, though not prosecuted to the same extent in the Maritime Provinces as it was in New England, was an important fishery, particularly in the 1830s and 1840s. Saint John, New Brunswick, was one of the principal centres of involvement, with a fleet of at least nine whaling ships. All of these were owned by the Mechanic's Whale Fishing Company or by Charles Cole Stewart, who owned and outfitted the *Athol*. In 1850 declining whale stocks and diminishing profits forced the Mechanic's Whale Fishing Company to cease operation and at about the same time Charles C. Stewart gradually began divesting himself of his whaling interests, including the *Athol*.

During his time at sea, Doane kept a journal. Many years later his son, Benjamin Hervey Doane, persuaded his father to recount his experiences. Using his journal to prompt his memory, the elder Doane dictated to his son, who was proficient in shorthand. Benjamin Hervey read it back to his father, who made corrections or added to his accounts as his memory was refreshed by retelling them. Throughout this process Doane's journal provided the hard facts, names, dates and positions at sea which are the historical backbone of the story, and which are corroborated by independent sources, including the logs of other ships.

As editors, we found that the author's literate and vivid style made major alterations unnecessary. In the main, we confined ourselves to correcting occasional misspellings and typographical errors, striving for consistency in nautical terminology, and sometimes streamlining punctuation. A few passages which were not first-person narrative, but digressions on matters having no bearing on Doane's adventures, or which were hearsay accounts of the experiences of others, were deleted. Doane also had a tendency to quote sometimes lengthy poems or song lyrics, with a disclaimer that his memory of them might not be perfect; we deleted all but a few of these. In the original manuscript, the two final chapters recounting his career at sea after his return to Nova Scotia lacked the narrative force of the rest of his memoirs and were omitted, thus ending the story at its emotional climax: his final arrival home and his impending marriage. A summary of the deleted chapters is included in the Epilogue. Those wishing to consult the original manuscript will find a copy of it in the Maritime Museum of the Atlantic in Halifax.

Two other comments about the manuscript are warranted, particularly in view of the period in which it was written. Comparison with an earlier (1899) version in the possession of the Cape Sable Historical Society revealed that Doane had changed the names of several people and one vessel to protect their identities. In view of the lapse of time since the events he chronicled, and in the interests of history, we have reinstated the true names wherever they had been changed. The same comparison also revealed that there were some incidents in the 1899 manuscript which Doane had left out of the latest version, but which fully deserved inclusion. Other incidents were simply described more vividly in the 1899 version than in the latest and have been incorporated. We thank the Cape Sable Historical Society for making this early version available to us.

If the language seems somewhat tame for a sailor, it must be remembered that Doane went to sea when Queen Victoria came to the throne and he was in many ways a Victorian. As his grandson Benjamin D. Doane wrote:

> "If it lacks profanity, where at times profanity would seem to be indicated, that is the way it was told, for though my grandfather may have been a veritable old pirate, and capable of the roughest language that a sailor of his generation could have used, such language, from his point of view, was not for publication . . ."

To supplement the manuscript we have done considerable geographic research in order to include the maps essential to understanding his travels. We have provided a minimum of footnotes to supplement his own footnote on the use of crowsnests on whaleships. We have also made every effort to obtain illustrations of the places Doane saw on his voyages, to show them as they appeared in his day, or as close to it as possible.

In Doane's time aboard whaleships it was common for both officers and seamen who kept logs or journals to make wooden stamps which they used to print images of whales in the margins of their journal pages. A whole whale indicated a successful capture and the flukes of a whale indicated an unsuccessful chase or a whale that escaped after being harpooned. Doane says that he made and used such a stamp. Since his journal apparently has not survived, we have taken two stamps from the journal of an anonymous whaleman aboard the ship *Maria*, Captain Elisha H. Fisher, out of Nantucket, October 1836 to October 1839 (in the collection of the Maritime Museum of the Atlantic).

We have appended available information on vessels Doane sailed on, encountered or mentioned. A glossary of nautical and whaling terms has been included. It provides basic definitions of the terms used by Doane and is not a comprehensive marine glossary. Readers wishing further clarification may consult the comprehensive standard dictionaries as well as nautical dictionaries, particularly *The Encyclopedia of Nautical Knowledge* by W. A. McEwen and A. H. Lewis (Cornell Maritime Press, Cambridge, MD, 1953) and the *International Maritime Dictionary* by René de Kerchove (Van Nostrand Reinhold Company, Toronto, 1961). Charles Scammon's *The Marine Mammals of the Northwest Coast of North America* (facsimile reprint, Dover Press, New York, 1968) contains an excellent description of the North Pacific whale fishery in about 1870. It had not changed substantially by then.

FRED W. SCOTT
Curatorial Assistant,
Natural History Section,
Nova Scotia Museum, Halifax

MARVEN E. MOORE
Curator,
Maritime Museum of the Atlantic
Halifax

Acknowledgements

I N THE enormous task of preparing *Following the Sea* for publication, we received invaluable assistance from many people.

Members of the Doane family have been unstinting in their support for this project and have contributed in a wide variety of ways. Dr. Benjamin Knowles Doane of Halifax provided a number of family portraits and artifacts. His daughter Heather Doane (Mrs. Timothy Atkinson) of Cape Sable Island wrote the preface, located most of the place names in the manuscript so that they could be shown on maps, and provided much supplementary information on the family's history and genealogy. Robert and Mignon Doane, and Barbara M. Doane, of Westfield, NJ, kindly gave us access to artifacts and documents in their possession relating to Captain Doane.

Members of the Coffin family have also provided information, photographs and artifacts. James Doane Coffin's great-granddaughter, Beth Smith of Campbellton, N.B., supplied tintypes of James Doane Coffin, Mary Doane Coffin and James Fernandez Coffin. Her son James Smith and his wife Claire, also of Campbellton, kindly agreed to let us photograph their sperm whale tooth bearing an engraving of the *Athol*. Claire Smith drove from Campbellton to Moncton to deliver the tooth to John Hennigar-Shuh. Other members of the Coffin family, Marie Keen and Eleanor Smith, also provided assistance, as did Marion Robertson of Shelburne, NS.

Niels Jannasch, former Director of the Maritime Museum of the Atlantic, was one of the first to read the manuscript when it was submitted to the Nova Scotia Museum for publication, and his enthusiasm for it has never waned. He has made a large number of valuable suggestions which guided us throughout the editorial process. Tim Brownlow also made some useful editorial comments.

Gathering the illustrations of the places Doane visited was an international task and many persons and institutions joined in the search. In some cases there were no extant illustrations of the right places at the right period of time, and in other cases there was an abundance from which to choose. The List of Illustrations at the back of the book provides full details for those we did use.

In North America, Edward Tompkins, Archivist, Provincial Archives of Newfoundland and Labrador, St. John's, Nfld., searched for illustrations of Labrador and the west coast of Newfoundland. Robert Elliot, Curator, New Brunswick Museum, and Fred Farrell, Archivist, Provincial

Archives of New Brunswick, supplied illustrations of Saint John and Partridge Island, respectively. Scott Robson, Curator, Human History Section, Nova Scotia Museum, assisted with the search for illustrations of Halifax. Neville Elwood of Halifax, Nova Scotia, provided illustrations of Ireland. Gloria MacKenzie, Public Archives of Canada, Ottawa, helped in the search for illustrations of Halifax. On very short notice, Dr. Stuart Frank, Director of the Kendell Whaling Museum, Sharon, MA., provided illustrations of some South American ports and of Sydney, Australia. Richard Kugler, Director, the New Bedford Whaling Museum, New Bedford, MA, kindly provided the cover illustration for the book. Alan Baldridge, Hopkins Marine Station Library, Pacific Grove, CA, allowed us access to the lithographs of whales in their copy of Scammon's monograph. Jay Bluck, Director, Heritage House and Sandra Rouja, Assistant Archivist, Bermuda Archives, both in Hamilton, Bermuda, assisted with the search and provided illustrations of Bermuda Dockyard. Elizabeth Downing, Registrar, the Bermuda Maritime Museum, Somerset, helped in the search for scenes of Bermuda. Deborah Dunn, Curatorial Assistant, Bishop Museum, Honolulu, Hawaii, searched for illustrations of Honolulu. Rebecca Smith, Curator of Research Materials, Historical Association of South Florida, Miami, provided illustrations of Key West. Linda Mainville, Archivist, and Joan Morris, both of Florida State Archives, Tallahassee, provided illustrations of Apalachicola. Eppie D. Edwards, and the Director, National Library of Jamaica, Kingston, assisted with the search for illustrations of Kingston Harbour.

On the other side of the Atlantic, Dr. Alan P. McGowan, Head of the Department of Ships and Antiquities, and Dennis Stonham, Keeper of Historic Photographs, both of the National Maritime Museum, Greenwich, England, on short notice provided illustrations of the *Great Western* and various landmarks along the River Thames. Michael K. Stammers, Curator, Merseyside Maritime Museum, Liverpool, England, provided illustrations of the port of Liverpool. Dr. David Jenkins, Research Assistant, Welsh Industrial and Maritime Museum, Cardiff, Wales, provided scenes of Cardiff and Newport.

In South America, Dr. Coloma, Director, Museo Nacional de Historia, Lima, Peru, searched for illustrations of Tumbez, Payta and Callao, though unfortunately those they found did not arrive in time to be included. We are indebted to Margaret Ann Hamelin of the Education Section, Nova Scotia Museum, who put her fluent Spanish to use in making a number of phone calls on our behalf to institutions in Peru and Chile.

The Australian National Maritime Museum in Sydney searched for illustrations of that city. Unfortunately these also arrived too late to be included in the book.

Five illustrations were drawn especially for the book by Etta Moffatt of the Education Section, Nova Scotia Museum, and the diagrams of vessel rigs were done by Graham McBride, Curatorial Assistant, Maritime Museum of the Atlantic, and enhanced by Etta Moffatt. The final maps were drawn by Derek Sarty of Gaynor/Sarty, Halifax, and lettered by Dirk Kelder of Halifax.

Ron Merrick, Media Services, Nova Scotia Department of Education, did his usual excellent job of photographing a great variety of images and artifacts for us, sometimes at very short notice.

Tracking down information on the vessels Doane mentioned was also a major undertaking and we were greatly assisted by Dr. Stuart Frank, Director of the Kendall Whaling Museum, Sharon, MA, and his staff; and Richard Kugler, Director of the New Bedford Whaling Museum, New Bedford, MA, and his staff, who not only facilitated our research but were gracious hosts during visits to their museums. Ben Fuller, Curator, and Captain Francis E. Bowker, Research Associate, Mystic Seaport Museum, Mystic, CN, provided helpful suggestions and supplementary information on American whaleships. Frank Watson, Volunteer in Maritime History, Peabody Museum, Salem, MA, and Paul Cyr, Librarian, Melville Whaling Room, New Bedford Free Public Library, also contributed information on American whaleships. Robert Elliot, Curator, New Brunswick Museum, and Fred Farrell, Archivist, Provincial Archives of New Brunswick, provided information on the New Brunswick whale fishery. Dr. Charles Armour, Archivist, Dalhousie University Archives, Halifax, was immensely helpful in identifying the New Brunswick and Nova Scotian vessels. Nicholas de Jong, Archivist, Public Archives of Prince Edward Island, Charlottetown, while on a visit to the United Kingdom, gathered information on some of the vessels registered there. Eric Ruff, Curator, Yarmouth County Museum, helped resolve the identity of the vessel Doane called the *Margaret*.

David Crockett, Marine Historian, South Natick, MA, provided background information on the Clyde Steamship Line. Mary Blackford, Librarian, and Stephen Croft, Researcher, Maritime Museum of the Atlantic, assisted respectively with the search for resource material and information on some of the vessels.

Nova Scotia Museum volunteers have also played a significant role. Susan Foshay assisted in the search for illustrations, and also tracked down a number of obscure place names. Minda Oberle reconstructed most of a lost computer database of all the place names, an essential tool for planning the many maps required to illustrate Doane's voyages.

In writing the footnotes we were assisted by Dr. Marie Elwood, Chief Curator of Human History, Nova Scotia Museum, and Dr. Ian Cameron of Halifax, who explained what bluestone water was. Dr. Brian Preston, Curator, Human History Section, Nova Scotia Museum, suggested an explanation for the alleged indebtedness of the Scots to the Duke of Argyle. J. Charles Levesque, Geophysics Division of the Geological Survey of Canada, Ottawa, on 24 hours' notice provided all the information we needed to footnote the Callao earthquake of 1746. It came from a paper by Enrique Silgado F., *Historia de los sismos mas notables occuridos en el Peru (1513-1970)*, published in *Geofisica Panamericana*, vol. 2, pp. 179-243, January 1973.

Tony Crouch, Director, Publishing Section, Nova Scotia Department of Government Services, and his colleague Bonnie Baird, provided useful suggestions and essential administrative support, and Barbara Coldwell of the same section entered the first draft of the manuscript, and all the many subsequent revisions, on the section's word processor. Mary Deagle of the Maritime Museum of the Atlantic typed the first drafts of much of the front and end matter. Dorothy Cooper, Managing Editor, Nimbus Publishing, helped make our co-publishing arrangement another milestone in a fruitful partnership. Steven Slipp of Graphic Design Associates, Halifax, on his first try delighted everyone with his proposed design for the book. Copy editing and proofreading were ably done by Elizabeth Eve and Helen Cook of Halifax. We are grateful for the sense of quality and attention to detail brought to the final production by Doug McCallum of McCurdy Printing, Halifax.

Finally, John Hennigar-Shuh, as chairman of the Nova Scotia Museum Publications Committee, played a crucial role in shepherding *Following the Sea* through all the stages from manuscript to final production.

THE EDITORS

— CHAPTER I —

BEGINNINGS

Plainfield, N.J., September 15, 1897

O<small>N THE SEVENTH OF THIS MONTH I COMPLETED MY SEVENTY-</small>
fourth year. I have lived to see many important events and great
changes, and though my part in them has been small and obscure, I
have had adventures which rubbed close upon some of the epoch-marking
occurrences of my time. For over fifty years I was of "those that go down to
the sea in ships," and if I am not yet worn out, neither am I rusted out. My
earliest memories are of tales of peril and hardship told by my elder brothers
on their return from sea, and as I listened, standing between their knees, I
longed with the impatience of childhood for my turn to come when I could
follow on their adventurous track. A sketch of my life, however roughly
drawn, will be read with interest by my children and grandchildren and other
near friends; it may perhaps be instructive as well, not as furnishing an
example, but serving, like the channel buoys, to help them 'ware shoal.

It is the custom in writing history to begin a long ways back and,
conforming to good precedent, I will briefly account for the presence of my
family in the place where I was born.

John Done (or Doane, as others spelled it), born in Cheshire, England in
the reign of Queen Elizabeth, came to Plymouth in New England in the early
years of that colony, and in 1634 he was chosen Deacon of the Church of
Plymouth. In 1646 he with six others founded a new settlement at Nauset
(Eastham), Cape Cod, where he died in 1685. His grandson Thomas was one
of the first settlers of Chatham, Cape Cod and died at the age of seventy-two
in 1756.

Thomas Doane, my grandfather, a grandson of the above-named
Thomas, also born in Chatham, was left an orphan in early youth. Young
Thomas followed the cod fishing, making voyages to the banks lying off the
shores of Nova Scotia, and often harboring in Barrington, near Cape Sable.
This was before and immediately following the expulsion of the Acadians in
1755, and the settlements along the shore were entirely French until they were
broken up and the inhabitants deported. As is well known, the Indians were
friendly with the French and hostile to the English and New Englanders; so
it behooved the Yankee fishermen, upon seeking shelter in the harbors of
Nova Scotia, to keep a good anchor-watch and look out for night attacks.

When my grandfather was about fifteen years old, while his vessel was
lying at anchor in the Beach Point Channel, Barrington Harbor, he was
awakened one night by a tap-tap-tapping which he heard somewhere, he
could not tell where, about the vessel. Creeping silently out of his bunk and

up on deck, he found the watch asleep and, crawling to the stern whence the sound seemed to emanate, he peeked cautiously over. Through the darkness he saw a canoe lying under the stern, with an Indian in the after end holding a paddle to keep the canoe in position, while in the bow nearer the vessel was another Indian engaged in driving wedges around the rudder-post. Immediately their scheme was apparent. After wedging the rudder they meant to cut the cable and let the vessel drift ashore, kill all hands and carry off the property. As Master Thomas crept back along the rail, his hand seized upon a fish gaff, which is a pole about six feet long with a big iron hook in one end. Thus armed, with a yell he rushed to the stern again and hooked the nearest Indian under the chin. The other Indian instantly paddled off into the darkness. The man who had been asleep on watch, and the men below scrambled on deck at the cry of alarm, to see the boy struggling with the gamest fish he ever encountered, trying to land him, while the Indian on the other end of the gaff was flouncing and jerking and twisting away for dear life, and finally succeeded in wriggling himself clear before anyone else could gaff him.

In 1756 Captain Jedediah Preble, acting under orders from Governor Lawrence, destroyed the French settlements around Barrington and carried away the habitants, and colonists from New England rapidly moved in and occupied their lands. According to a census taken in 1762 there were at that time five hundred families, moved from Cape Cod, settled in Barrington and vicinity. In 1764 my grandfather moved to Barrington, taking up land on an island which had belonged to a Frenchman named Chereaux. It is still known as Sherose Island.

My grandfather died in Barrington in May, 1783. On the day of his funeral the fleet from New York bearing these "United Empire Loyalists," as they loved to be called, was seen passing the mouth of Barrington Harbor on the way to settle Shelburne.

At the close of the American War of Independence in 1783, disbanded soldiers and refugee Tories came to the province in great numbers, about twenty thousand, prinicpally from New York and vicinity, settling at a place theretofore called Port Roseway or New Jerusalem; but the name was changed to Shelburne in honor of a noble English lord. They came with rations for three years, provided by the British government. Through mismanagement, the rations were exhausted by the beginning of the second winter, and the improvident among them, who unfortunately were numerous, were reduced to extreme necessity. Large numbers managed to leave the country. Others wandered about looking for work or begging, as their qualifications fitted them for one calling or the other; and the "old comers" in the scattered settlements, out of compassion for dire suffering, were compelled to shelter whole families of them all winter long.

In a few generations the Loyalist blood intermingled with the old stock. Many of the refugees were eminently respectable people and their descendants are an honor to their Sovereign, whom they hold in great reverence and whose portrait invariably adorns their walls.

In 1799 my father, Nehemiah Doane who was engaged in the coasting trade, making frequent trips to Boston, married Ann Kenney who was born in 1780. Her maternal grandfather was Captain Joseph Godfrey, of

Liverpool, N.S., whose daring adventures while trading to the Spanish Main gained for him the name of "Bold Godfrey."

Isaac Kenney, my mother's father, was born at Chatham, Cape Cod, and grew up in Barrington. He was a merchant, ship owner and captain of the local company of militia, and his father before him had seen much military service against the French. With the following anecdote concerning him, which was told to me by my mother, I will close this chapter of genesis.

As was often the case during the revolutionary struggle, on one occasion an American privateer was at anchor in Barrington Harbor, her captain being ashore at Captain Kenney's house and the crew visiting among their "folks" in the settlement, when a 16-oared barge from a British cruiser outside rowed in and captured her and then headed for shore. A son of Captain Kenney's came running to the house and reported that a "shaving-mill," as boats of that character were called, had landed at the wharf and the men were on the way to the house. The Yankee captain had only time to hide in a bedroom when his pursuers entered the house. Captain Kenney told them to look where they pleased, but when they attempted to enter the bedroom he faced them in the doorway, with the determined words, "The man who enters this room must do so over my dead body."

The leader of the party blusteringly demanded by what authority his search was obstructed. Captain Kenney took down his old sword from its peg, and pointing with it to his scarlet coat hanging on the wall, showing a captain's epaulettes, answered: "*That* is my authority. As captain of His Majesty's militia, I command you to withdraw your men and leave the house!"

"Aha, Captain," laughed the intruder, "I am a Lieutenant in the Royal Navy, and I outrank you. And as you are harboring a rebel and an enemy of the King, I must trouble you to surrender that sword and make no further resistance."

The taunt roused the Kenney fire to white heat, and drawing his blade, Captain Kenney shook it in the face of his inquisitor, saying: "I am a soldier and a gentleman. This was my father's sword, and he who takes it from me must win it!"

The challenge was as delicately declined on the one hand as it was valiantly pressed on the other, and the lieutenant discreetly withdrew himself and his company, but carried off the vessel as a prize. The Yankee captain escaped with a number of his crew through the woods to Yarmouth, where they found willing hands to boat them across the Bay of Fundy. In Boston he fitted out another privateer and, having learned that his old enemy was in Liverpool, Nova Scotia, he sailed there and in the night, with a party of men, broke into the house where the lieutenant was asleep, carried him aboard the vessel and took him to Boston a prisoner.

— CHAPTER II —

CHILDHOOD

1823 to 1837

A PLAIN OLD-FASHIONED ONE-STORY HOUSE, WITH TWO gables and no ells or porches, stood on a hill, a little back from the road that skirts the shores of Barrington Harbor, overlooking the cove back of Sherose Island. Out past the southwest point of the island stretched the broad bay and, beyond its headlands, the ocean was in clear view from out eastern windows. The shores of Cape Sable Island bounded the harbor on the south. Four leagues farther south, hidden from the harbor by the island, lurked the dread Cape Sable, as yet unmarked by any warning beacon. The cape and its treacherous flanking ledges eternally shouldered the Atlantic's surges and had taken heavy toll of ships and lives during the two centuries and more since Champlain had given them their names.

The house faced south, with an apple orchard before the door. The back roof had a longer slope than the front, the eaves in the rear reaching nearly to the ground. Built soon after the war of the American colonies for their independence, the house, like many of its neighbors, was palisaded. That is, between the upright timbers of its heavy frame were set other upright timbers, treenailed together. Thus a solid bullet-proof wall on all sides furnished protection against shore parties from enemy ships if another war should come.

The happy land, however, has been blessed with peace for the past hundred years. A chimney of huge split granite, with fireplaces like small rooms, accounted for the presence behind the house of a pile of wood fully the size of the barn. At the foot of the hill, halfway to the road, was the well with swing-pole and whitewashed curb. The surrounding fields, bounded by stone walls, looked smooth enough while the grass was waiting for the scythe; but when the hay was gathered from them it was a wonder that a horse should dare to roll for fear of smashing all his ribs upon the granite boulders that lay thick scattered over all the land. Indeed, much plowing was out of the question, and the soil, for the most part had to be worked with spade and hoe. In all directions landward stretched sombre forests of spruce and fir, brightened by occasional patches of birch and maple; while seaward, the scene was variable as the weather.

To such surroundings on the 7th of September, 1823, "new to earth and sky," I came, the eleventh and youngest child, and under my parents' loving care; in due time I passed out of the insensibility of babyhood and rounded "to a separate mind from whence clear memory begins."

My first recollections, of course, are of mother, father and the other members of our immediate household. My eldest brother Hervey, and two sisters Maria and Eliza were married before I can remember and keeping house for themselves. Three other brothers Thomas, Isaac and Martin, were away to sea years at a time, and during the brief intervals when they were at home they were more like distinguished guests than everyday members of the family. Next came two younger sisters, Erminie and Irene, and then, my special playmate and companion, next older than I, my brother Nehemiah, who never quarreled or teased, and was obedient, self-commanding and industrious — in short, all that I was not.

One other inmate of the family I must not omit: an old bachelor, Mr. John Wilson, born in Scotland in 1766. For years he made his home at father's, and died there when I was about twelve years old. He and father were congenial spirits. Their favorite secular recreation was to sit together while one listened and the other read Pope's translations of Homer and such other classics as they possessed. On Sundays the heathen poets were shelved, and Harvey's *Meditations*, or the *Gospel Sonnets*, or *Paradise Lost*, took their place.

The last named book (which I now have) was supplied with notes at the foot of the page, referring to chapter and verse in the Bible, or explaining some allusion to ancient mythology. As my father read along, his listener from time to time would interrupt with, "Where does he get the authority for that?" If there was a note, the reference was looked up. If there was none, my father would say, "Well, I don't know, Mr. Wilson; it is certainly not in the Bible." "Ah, that Johnnie Milton!" the old man would say, "he has wrought it out of his own imagination."

The winter of 1828 was a fatal one in our family. The year before, my father had cut timber on his own woodland and hauled it to the shore below the house, and during the summer had built and launched a schooner, named the *Ocean*. My two brothers, Thomas and Isaac, sailed in her to the West Indies. They made two voyages from Halifax, and in February 1828, started upon the third. The night after they left Halifax witnessed one of the severest storms ever known in the history of the Atlantic, and undoubtedly they went down that night. Long months of anxious waiting for their return followed, but they were never seen or heard of again. For years afterwards my mother did not give them up and would watch wistfully anyone coming towards the house, hoping against hope that some word had come at last. More hearts than ours were shadowed with grief at that time, for in the same gale perished many gallant sailors from our little community.

The heavy forests which covered the whole country in my boyhood were the home of numerous moose and bears and other wild game, which are now being steadily pushed back farther and farther and all but exterminated by the remorseless advance of the blueberry industry. Late one winter's afternoon when I was about seven years old, during a heavy northwest gale and snow storm, a moose ran past our windows, down to the shore, and took to the water. My father, who had been in the house reading, grabbed his gun and rushed after him, bareheaded and in his slippers. With the help of a neighbor's son, he launched a boat and sculled after the moose and shot him. I remember watching them from the window. They had only one oar, and with the moose in tow, it took them till dark to scull back to shore.

The Micmac Indians, in my young days, used to come every spring and fall, about fifteen or twenty families, in their canoes, and camp on a point of land covered with woods, known as Charley Point, about a quarter of a mile from our house. Joe Goose was the head of the party.

A fire broke out in the Indian camp one night and it was burned to the ground. Poor Joe was in despair. All that he or his people had in the world was in ashes. Someone trying to condole with him offered the suggestion that Providence meant it all for the best. But such a theory had no place in Indian philosophy. "Oh, no," was the mournful reply, "can't be for the best; it burnt my gun!"

Ghosts were familiar beings to us in my youth. Their chief haunt was Brass's Hill, on the main road between Barrington Passage and the head of the harbor. A book could be filled with stories of the strange sights and sounds that have been seen and heard there—of the groaning, the ringing of bells, the clanking of chains and the jingling of money—underground, and of headless men walking in mid-air. Some of the stories were told by people whose word would go further than that of others. Altogether, it was a place which at night one liked best to pass in company with somebody else.

Charlie Robertson, who was one year older than I, lived down the Passage near me. He was employed by Dr. Geddes at the Head to attend his apothecary shop, and as he was my intimate play-fellow, we were often together on the road at night between the doctor's and his father's house. Charlie was of a most lively, unterrifiable disposition, and if he could have made the ghosts' acquaintance, he would surely have proposed that with his assistance they do something to increase their reputation. Such an alliance, however, never being actually formed, he was forced to avail himself of my poor aid in rendering Brass's Hill more famous, and some marvelous tales that went the neighborhood rounds were founded on nothing but our foolish pranks. But often as, with his moral support, I had played the spectral role, I was once nearly overcome by fear of the supernatural in that uncanny spot.

It was in the winter time when I was about fourteen years of age. A deep snow was on the ground and the weather was clear and very cold. A man came from Cape Sable Island in a great hurry for the doctor, and when he had reached our house he was tired out with wallowing through the snow. The case was urgent, and my father told him to come in, and that I was light of foot and would be glad to go to the doctor's for him. It was within an hour of sundown when I left the house. The doctor lived four miles away. But few vehicles had been over the road since the snow had fallen, and for a great part of the way the snow was hip high. I arrived at the doctor's and delivered the message, and he set out on horseback down the road. I spent the evening visiting with Charlie Robertson, and as we were bidding each other good night he said, "Now, look out for yourself going over Brass's Hill, you may see the man without any head." I made a boasting reply and started for home.

There was no moon, the air was still and frosty, and all that lit the darkness were the stars and the white snow. As I plodded along alone, keeping my eyes about me, the reports of strange apparitions that were current began to work on my mind. When I reached the foot of Brass's Hill, a short distance past the mill stream, my eyes followed the white streak of the road clear to the gap in the trees at the top of the hill. I walked on, and presently saw something right in that gap rising, slowly, black against the sky. I stood still. It looked like the form of a man *without any head*, and with outstretched arms. As I looked, the shape seemed not to touch the ground at all, coming toward me.

"I'm going to turn back," I said to myself. "No, I won't; I've too much pride.—Oh dear, I wish someone was with me.—There's the headless man, sure enough; *I see him.*—Yes, I better go back.—But I've always said I wouldn't be afraid."—There I struggled with pride and fear, while the thing kept coming nearer. Full of terror, I braced forward and walked towards it, thinking with every step my will would give way. In a few seconds I heard the crunch, crunch, of footsteps in the snow.

What a sense of relief as I realized that it was only a human being; and I made out as he approached, a man with white leggings (such as we called "spatlashes") up to his knees, while across the back of his neck, from shoulder to shoulder, he carried a bag, his arms being thrown over it to keep it steady. As he went past me, I said, "Hello, Bob Thurston, is that you? I thought you were the man without any head."

"Oh, you needn't be afraid," he answered; "I've walked over this hill a good many times and never saw anything yet worse looking than myself."

Bob Thurston had been down the Passage, and was returning home with a bagful of provisions. From a distance his white spatlashes could not be seen against the snow which gave him the appearance of walking in the air; and the bag lying across the back of his neck made him appear not to have any head. On reaching home I told my story, and confessed that I had never been so scared in all my life.

Of my days at school I have few agreeable memories—none that I wish to record. Apart from them, my youthful recollections are pleasant and such as I love to dwell upon. In writing these reminiscences, I am carried back heart and soul to the old times and places, and I live over again the years that have passed; but especially my thoughts with affection linger on all that relates to Childhood's Happy Home.

Sketch by Benjamin Doane of the Doane family home in Barrington, N.S.

— CHAPTER III —

COASTING

Fall 1837 to Christmas 1840

*I*N THE FALL OF 1837, I LEFT SCHOOL WITH SUCH slender educational furnishings as I had been able to get from it, and went to work at home. My brothers, Martin and Nehemiah, were both away to sea, and my father was past sixty years old and needed help about the place. We dug potatoes and got things snug for cold weather. Nehemiah's vessel, a coaster, was laid up for the winter, and he came home. When snow came, my father, Nehemiah and I chopped and hauled firewood, and still there was time for skating and other winter sports. Certain evenings in the week through the winter, my father taught, as usual, a night school at home, which Nehemiah and I both were required to attend, and where the young men of the neighborhood who were home from sea came to learn mathematics and navigation.

In the spring of 1838, my brother Nehemiah shipped as mate of the schooner *Favorite*, of Barrington, Thomas L. Crowell, master; and nearly all the boys of my acquaintance left home and went to sea. It was pretty hard on me to stay behind and see them go, but needs must, and I turned to, making fences, digging ground and planting. Oh, it was hard work. My heart was not in it. As I hoed the potatoes, the field looked large and the task interminable; and when haying time came, I could not get the scythe to hang right; and raking, pitching and stowing did not suit me any better. At last the hay was all in the barn, and there was a lull in farm work.

About the end of August, the *Favorite* arrived in Barrington on her way to Halifax with a load of lumber. Nehemiah came home and said they were without a cook. I immediately filed an application for the vacancy. My father knew I was discontented at home and let me go. The vessel remained in harbor for a few days, and in the meantime I took cooking lessons from my mother. On September 1st, 1838, I put my chest aboard and entered on my duties. We did not sail till the next day, so I have time here to describe my new situation.

The *Favorite* was a two-masted schooner of about sixty tons, carrying a square sail on the foremast. She had no forecastle—we all lived aft. In the cabin was a brick chimney and open fireplace, which instead of a crane had a cross-bar with hooks on which to hang a pot and kettle. The cooking outfit consisted of a coffee pot, which was also the tea pot, a tea kettle, an iron pot and a frying pan. The tea kettle was used only to boil water. The frying pan was for baking bread, as well as for frying; the pot, for miscellaneous cooking—stewing, boiling, etc. The dishes were deep plates and yellow

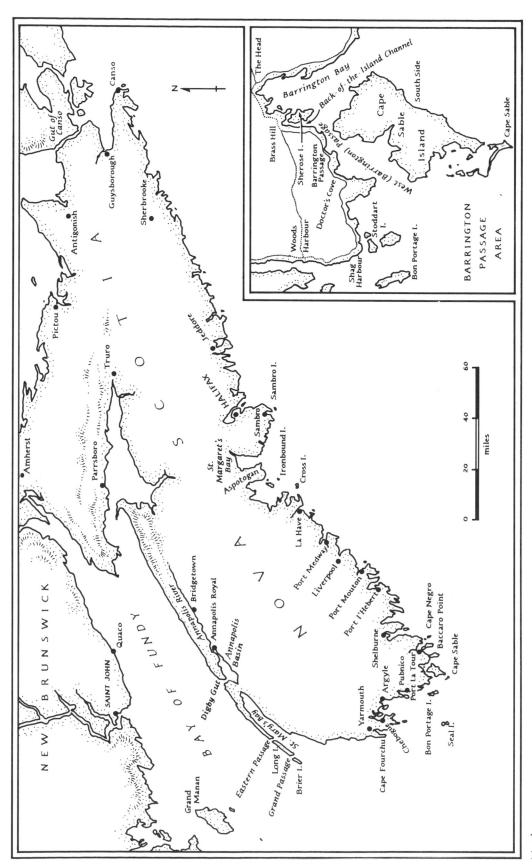

**The mainland of
Nova Scotia**

BARRINGTON PASSAGE AREA

The Head
Barrington Bay
Back-of-the-Island Channel
South Side
Brass Hill
Cape Sable Island
Cape Sable
Sherose I.
Barrington Passage
West (Barrington) Passage
Doctor's Cove
Stoddart I.
Woods Harbour
Bon Portage I.
Shag Harbour

N

Canso
Gut of Canso
Guysborough
Sherbrooke
Antigonish
Pictou
Truro
Parrsboro
Amherst
NOVA SCOTIA
Jeddore
Sambro I.
HALIFAX
Sambro
Ironbound I.
St. Margaret's Bay
Aspotogan
Cross I.
La Have
Port Medway
Liverpool
Port Mouton
Port l'Hebert
Shelburne
Cape Negro
Baccaro Point
Cape Sable
Argyle
Pubnico
Port La Tour
Yarmouth
Cape Fourchu
Chebogue
Bon Portage I.
Seal I.
Bridgetown
Annapolis Royal
Annapolis Basin
Annapolis River
Digby Gut
BAY OF FUNDY
Quaco
SAINT JOHN
NEW BRUNSWICK
Grand Manan
St. Mary's Bay
Long I.
Eastern Passage
Grand Passage
Brier I.

miles
0   20   40   60

mugs, the edges of which were well chipped when I assumed charge of them, and they steadily continued to take on fresh edges. We had no chairs or stools. The sides of the cabin were boxed up level with the lower berths, and made into lockers, where reef gear and such things were kept. The lockers and our chests were the only seats. I have said who the captain was—Captain Crowell. The mate was my brother and when I spoke to him I had to call him "Mr. Doane." The crew was my cousin, Corning Crowell; and I was expected to help on deck when called upon.

At five o'clock in the morning of September 2nd we got underway. Out abreast of Baccaro, I began to be seasick and kept so all day. Now a seasick sailor can be made to do something; but a seasick cook—well, my brother cooked all that day and the next. In the morning of September 4th we passed Sambro. The wind being ahead, we had to beat up Halifax Harbor. At six o'clock we anchored off Fairbanks & Allison's Wharf, and the next day went up to Richmond to discharge. While we were beating up the bay, cannons were firing from the Citadel and from men-of-war in the harbor, and the city was well decked out with bunting, in celebration of the coronation of Queen Victoria.

We next went to Port Medway and back to Halifax again with another load of lumber; and then the captain concluded to take in ballast, run up along the shore and get a load of fish on freight for Halifax. Accordingly, we sailed for Barrington on October 2nd, arrived on the afternoon of the fifth, and anchored in the Back-of-the-Island Channel, hardly two stone's throws from my father's old wharf.

This was my first homecoming, and I looked forward to the end of the day when I should be allowed to go ashore, to be welcomed home by my father and mother as their young sailor hero. But when night came everyone else got ready and left the vessel, and I was ordered to stay aboard all night and keep ship. Oh, how mad I was! It was no trouble to nurse my wrath; it was not only warm itself, but it kept me warm, and I wished all sorts of calamities upon the schooner during the night, which, of course, did not befall. The next afternoon I was permitted to go home for a few hours, but had to come aboard again and stay all night, and the next morning we sailed for Pubnico, to take in fish.

Pubnico is a French settlement, which did not escape the wholesale sacking and shanghai-ing that overtook the Acadians of a former generation. Years after that tragic event, however, some of the survivors were allowed to return and rebuild their homes on such lands in that neighborhood as were not already occupied by the New England settlers. Many of the people here were well acquainted with my father, and often spoke of him to my brother and me. One venerable old Frenchman, named Benoni D'Entremont—he must have been about eighty years old and was evidently a person of great consideration among them—when he heard my name, said, "So you ze son of Nehemiah Doanes? I know him. I rassle with Nehemiah Doanes many a time."

One day a lot of Frenchmen came aboard the vessel with their families—wives, sons and daughters, big and little. Towards noon I began to get ready for dinner—corned beef and dumplings; and the girls pitched in and helped me. They could not speak English, and I knew no French, but that made no hitch in the conversation, and a lot of conversation went into the cooking of that dinner.

We lay in Pubnico ten days and got about half a load of fish; the remainder of the cargo we picked up in Barrington, Shag Harbor, Cape Island and Seal Island. After discharging the fish in Halifax, we went to Annapolis Royal for a load of fruit. Arrived off Annapolis town, we anchored and lay there a day and then sailed up the Annapolis River about ten miles to Bridgetown. This occupied two days; we got aground several times and had to wait for the tide. Although aground in a narrow river, when the ebb tide began we had to anchor to keep from sliding backward over the slippery mud that lined either bank.

We had been at Bridgetown only a few days when another schooner arrived from Barrington, Captain Alfred Shepard, and Elisha Hopkins mate. Uncle 'Lisha—"Old Head," they called him—was a dry, jokey old fellow, always merry and keeping everyone around him brim full of fun. Captain Shepard had a lot of salt catfish aboard, and it was beautiful sport for Uncle 'Lisha to trade off that catfish as halibut in exchange for apples and cheese. Those poor countrymen knew nothing about fish anyway, and probably liked the catfish as well as they would have liked halibut.

One day aboard the *Favorite* we were to have guests to dinner, and in preparing for it Captain Crowell wanted some fresh meat. So he bought an old ram off a retired sea captain named Marshall, and had it killed, and I roasted some of it for dinner. It was so tough and strong that I had had a plenty just in cooking it. Captain Crowell carved it, and as he helped each one he gravely asked, "Will you have a piece of this ah . . . mutton?" and after they had struggled with it until they were tired he would say, "Won't you have another piece of this ah . . . mutton?" Captain Shepard was one of the company. When he returned to his vessel he told Uncle 'Lisha all about the ram dinner, and then all hands made a string of doggerel verses about it. The only fragment that sticks in my mind went something like this:

They threw him down upon the deck;—
Says Marshall, 'Here's your mutton, no mistake!'
Old Head stepped up and said, 'Oh, dam!
It isn't mutton, it's a ram!'

The Negroes in the neighborhood of Bridgetown were having a "Revival," and in the evening all hands would go ashore and attend the meetings. At one of them, to cap the climax of a gorgeous burst of eloquence, the preacher said, "It's just as onpossible for a rich man to get to heaven as for a dry shad to climb a sweet apple tree." Uncle 'Lisha, sitting beside me in the rear of the little meeting house, had had difficulties that evening with his nose, which he had hitherto quelled with his handkerchief; but when he heard this, as it were, a dart struck through his liver—not of conviction, however—the good soul had no great possessions that he should go away sorrowful. To prevent an explosion of mirth right out in the meeting, he made for the door and I followed him to share his reproach. Outside, Uncle 'Lisha lay down on the grass and rolled, choking and snorting with long-suppressed laughter.

Sundays were quiet days with us in port, especially away up here in the Annapolis River. The captain and my brother and Corning Crowell usually went to church. That left me alone to attend to my work and, when that was done, to find amusement for myself. Lying near us was a little schooner, the cook of which was a Brier Island boy about my own age, whom I found very good company. The orchards of church goers could be visited on Sunday mornings safely enough. On one occasion, however, by sad misfortune, we were discovered by an old Sabbath-breaker up in his apple trees, and the pious lesson that unregenerate sinner taught us with a hoe handle we were unable ever to forget.

The day we finished loading, the captain bought another ram from Captain Marshall and we started down the river. The wind was ahead, we got aground several times, and we were four days getting down to Annapolis Royal. I had not an opportunity of going ashore in this town, and was never there again. Parts of it seemed to be in ruins, while here and there was to be seen a red-coated soldier peeping out from behind an earthwork, for the British government still maintained a garrison there in the old fort.

It was the fourth of December, 1838 when we anchored again in Barrington on our way to Halifax, and the next few days we lay there selling fruit, cheese and cider. Men, women and children came aboard by dozens and stayed for hours. I got dinner for all hands, the principal dish being ram mutton. After the neighborhood was well supplied with "Up the Bay" produce, we sailed for Halifax, where we lay peddling fruit and vegetables at Market Wharf.

While lying here, the captain was at supper one evening, sitting so that I could not pass, and I needed something that was out of my reach beyond him. I asked him if he would hand it to me, and in doing so, as he brought back his arm, he upset the old tin lamp and spilt the oil over the tablecloth. He told me to be quick and give him something with which to wipe up the mess, and there being nothing handier than the dishcloth, I gave him that. He sopped up the oil with it, and said, "What for heaven's sake is this—the dishcloth?" With that, he dabbed it right in my eyes, mouth and all over my face, and ordered me to get him another cloth. I went up on deck and stayed there. The captain called me three or four times to come down, but nothing on earth could have made me go. I stayed on deck all evening until everybody went to bed and to sleep, and then I came below and turned in. That was many years ago. We are taught to forgive those who trespass against us, but only the Lord knows when I shall outgrow my resentment of that outrage.

On Christmas Day we sailed for Clyde to take in a house frame and lumber for the captain, and brought it to Barrington, and my voyage ended when we came to anchor on December 28th, in the Back-of-the-Island Channel. Captain Crowell's house was built there the following year.

Throughout the winter I enjoyed myself hauling wood, setting rabbit snares, hunting partridges and water fowl with Tommy Robertson. In the spring of 1839 I worked at home till the planting was done, and then shipped as cook and crew with Captain Jesse Smith, in the schooner *Two Sons*, owned by Mr. John Robertson. Mr. John A. Knowles (whom I did not then foresee as my future father-in-law) was mate and partner with the captain in the season's voyage, running between Barrington and Halifax. Whenever the vessel was in Barrington, I lived half the time with Captain Smith and the other half with Mr. Knowles, as they hired me between them.

Now there have been not a few venturesome skippers who hailed from our little port, but these navigators were not too bold. Their principle was that they could see better in the daytime where they were going than they could at night, so that sunset seldom found us outside of some harbor. For instance, we would get underway in Barrington at daylight, and along in the afternoon run in to Ragged Islands and anchor. If the wind was ahead next day, we stayed where we were. If it was fine and the wind fair, we would proceed on our voyage and perhaps go in to Port L'Hebert and stay all night; then fan out of the harbor in the morning, and that night anchor in La Have, and in the course of the next day or two fetch up in Halifax. So we crept back and forth, watching the weather, always keeping on the safe side, with no chance for anybody to display or use up much nerve.

The first time we came back from Halifax with the usual cargo of flour, molasses and other supplies which we discharged at Robertson's wharf, a lot of people were there from the South Side of Cape Island. At noon the captain and mate went home to dinner about a quarter of a mile away, and I was left on watch till they returned. Some half dozen South Side fellows thought this was their chance to go down in the hold and help themselves to sugar and molasses. I called to them to get away from there. They would not go, so I went down in the hold and shoved some of the boys away. They kept on meddling with the cargo, and I picked out one of the youngest of them, a lad named Nickerson, and knocked him down. His brother stepped up to interfere. The others, at the prospect of seeing a fight, lost interest in the sugar, and proposed that we go ashore and fight fair play.

Halifax Harbor in 1839

When the captain and Mr. Knowles came, I told them how I had held the field while they were away. Oh, they said, it was very wrong to fight, I ought to have gone and told them, and they would have come and driven the boys away. A likely thing, that seemed, to leave the vessel in charge of a parcel of boys bent on mischief. Anyway, that was not the sort of appreciation I had looked for, and besides, my eye was hurting me; so I started for home. Robert Robertson went up the road with me. On the way we met my father. He was quite concerned to see me in such a plight, and asked me what was the matter. "Oh, I've been having a little bit of boxing," I said, and on I went to the house, where mother's remedies and mother's consolation soon made me as good as new.

After hoeing potatoes for the captain took one week, and for Mr. Knowles the next, we made another trip to Halifax and back. On September 5th we were loaded with fish and lying in the Back-of-the Island Channel, ready to sail for Halifax. A tremendous gale came up and the schooner dragged but soon went aground in the mud, and with the flood tide the gale began to moderate. The next day we sailed. Every day while in Halifax we heard more and more of disasters caused by the late storm. Many fishermen were wrecked, and there was great loss of life. I saw a schooner towed in to Halifax, with the captain and one man drowned in the cabin. The vessel belonged to the eastward of Halifax; the captain's name was Watt.

In the latter part of October the vessel was laid up, I was paid off and was glad to be at home again for the winter. Around election time I took a slight interest in politics. "The man, not the measure," must have been the principle involved, for I remember the candidates but do not think I ever heard they stood for any measures. John Homer and Paul Brown, "the king of Cape Island," were seeking re-election to the Provincial Parliament; and Paul Crowell (called "Paul Labrador" for identification), who had been defeated when he ran before, was out for a vindication. There was a fourth candidate, but I cannot recall who he was. Only two could win.

The election was held in the Town House at the Head, and the polls were open for three successive days. This protracted period was a necessity because of the poor roads, which were then practically impassable for vehicles other than ox-carts. Carriages were rare sights, more curious than useful. The mail to and from Yarmouth and Shelburne went through Barrington once a week each way, on horseback. The doctor rode upon his errands mounted on his good gray mare, his medicines stowed in saddlebags. Much of the travel was by boat, subject to delay from wind and tide, and many would be unable to vote at all if the opportunity were shortened.

There were no ballots. Each voter appeared in the court room and stated orally his choice, and it was recorded in the presence of the crowd clustered there. It was before the Reform Laws had abolished the worst abuses of Election Day license, but in our highly moral community there was little disorder. One feature of the ceremony was really impressive. The voter when he entered the room removed his hat and stood as though observing a great solemnity—as indeed it was—until his vote was entered in the book. I was never at home at another election, and when in later years and in other places I saw the undignified attitude of those exercising this highest privilege of free men, my respect was increased for the people among whom I was reared, who approached the polling place as though it were an altar.

The contest was close, sometimes one side ahead, sometimes the other. On the last day, if a shallop which had grounded on the flats with a load of men from Cape Island—all prepared to vote for their fellow-islander, Brown—had floated in time, their candidate would have won. Homer and Crowell were elected. Both parties had half a victory, and the old cannon under the jail window, which had not known till the last minute which side it was on, boomed that night as much for one side as the other.

During the winter of 1840 Mr. John Robertson and Captain Jesse Smith bought a new schooner, the *Teaser*. In the spring of 1840 Mr. William Knowles went as mate, and I shipped again as cook, sailor and all hands. Between trips while the vessel was in Barrington I boarded at the captain's house, and during the season helped him work out his statute-labor on the highway and to dig a well on his place.

On one occasion while we were lying storm-bound at Cape Negro, a school of blackfish came into the harbor. The men went off in their boats, and by firing guns, splashing oars in the water and making a big noise generally, drove some twenty or thirty of them ashore and killed them. Their fat when tried out made about sixty barrels of oil.

Along in September, coming up the shore one day, there being a good deal of water in the vessel, Mr. Knowles called me to the pump. Without excuse, I refused, and he set out to give me a whipping. It was shockingly bad discipline on both sides. Mr. Knowles chased me but I easily kept out of his way, Captain Jesse did not interfere, and finally the affair blew over. The next time the vessel was ready to sail for Halifax I wanted to stay behind; so, as Mr. Robertson was going down, it was arranged that I should stay at his house and work while the vessel was gone.

A month of good times for me followed. Tommy Robertson and I worked and played in partnership during the day, and in the evening we played chess with his sisters. After Mr. Robertson came back, the captain's brother, Mr. Josiah Smith, took the vessel to Boston; but as I thought the mate would still remember me, I contrived to stay another month at Mr. Robertson's, and then went home. My brothers, Martin and Nehemiah, who had been together in the schooner *Victoria*, trading to the West Indies, came home about Christmas time.

— CHAPTER IV —

FIRST VOYAGE TO SEA

Spring 1841 to June 20th, 1842

WITH THE SPRING OF 1841 CAME THE NECESSITY FOR ME to find employment again. I was now seventeen years old. I had been three seasons coasting, and was anxious for a wider flight. My brother Nehemiah shipped as mate of the schooner *Eagle*, of Barrington, whose master was Captain Alfred Shepard. Mr. Thomas Chatwynd, of Woods Harbor, engaged to go as mate with my brother Martin in the *Victoria* and a couple of hands before the mast were needed. A young man from Woods Harbor named John Nickerson shipped as the starboard watch. I was the other half of the crew, and Nickerson and I took turns being cook.

We first went to Saint John, New Brunswick, and loaded with limestone for Halifax. After leaving Saint John, the wind being ahead, we were beating down the Bay shore between Digby Gut and Brier Island, and the flood tide making very strong, we could not gain anything, so we stood in to a place called Red Bay, just at dusk, and anchored. An anchor watch was set, and we were to get underway at three o'clock in the morning.

The mate had the first watch, and called me. After I had stood my watch, I went below and called John Nickerson. He answered, "All right," and I went back on deck. In a little while as he had not come to relieve me, I went down and found him still asleep. I shook him and said, "Come, rouse out; it's your watch on deck; this is the second time I've called you." "All right, Ben," he answered, "go to bed, and I'll get right up and go on deck." I went to my bunk and lay down. Being very sleepy, as soon as I struck the bunk, I went to sleep myself.

The first thing we knew, here it was five o'clock in the morning, the captain had waked up, gone on deck, and found no one on watch and the ebb tide half spent. All hands were called out in a jiffy, and we knew there would be the devil to pay, with no pitch hot. Inquiry was made why no watch had been kept. The mate said he had stood his watch; I said I had stood mine. The captain turned to John Nickerson and asked, "Have you had any watch?" "No sir; nobody ever called me." "I called him, sir," I said, "so I turned in and went to sleep."

That ended the inquisition for the time being, and we got under way. It was my turn to be cook, and I got breakfast. After breakfast, the mate came down the companionway and ordered me to bring him a reef-earing.

Unsuspectingly, I brought him one, and he said, "Now, take off your coat; I'm going to give you a thrashing." I asked him what for. "Because you lay down before you were relieved on watch." He had no doubt that I had

Opposite:
The shorter voyages of
Benjamin Doane

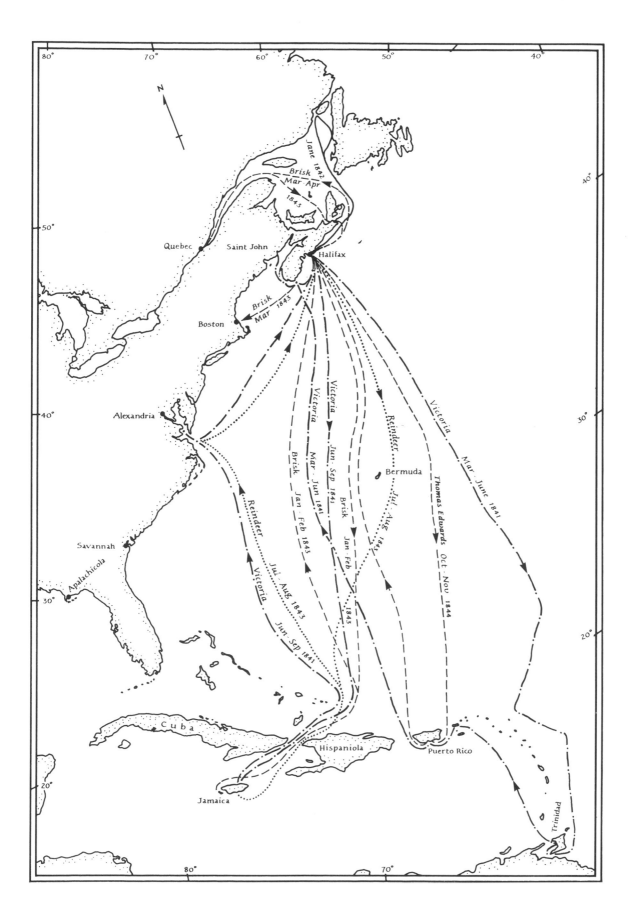

Jane 1842

Brisk
Mar Apr
1843

Quebec   Saint John   Halifax

Brisk
Mar 1843

Boston

Victoria

Victoria

Victoria
Jun Sep 1841

Reindeer

Victoria
Mar June 1841

Alexandria

Bermuda

Brisk
Mar - Jun 1841

Brisk
Jan - Feb 1843

Brisk
Jan - Feb
1843

Reindeer
Jul Aug 1843

Thomas Edwards
Oct - Nov 1844

Savannah

Apalachicola

Reindeer
Victoria
Jun - Sep 1841

Victoria
Jul Aug 1843

C u b a

Hispaniola

Puerto Rico

Jamaica

Trinidad

called the man, but he said I had no business to go to my bunk until the other man had taken my place on watch, and that he would give me something to make me remember it all my life. So he gave me a good rope's ending, and, as he said, I have never forgotten it, nor what it was for, nor that it was my brother who did it. No doubt I deserved it, but the memory of it was a cloud between us for the rest of our lives.

We sailed from Halifax on March 20th, 1841 with a fresh northwest breeze, bound for Trinidad, St. Thomas and Puerto Rico, in company with a topsail schooner belonging to Jeddore, Nova Scotia, Captain James Hopkins, also bound for the West Indies. Now I began to learn what going to sea meant in earnest. When night came there was no friendly harbor to dodge into, and as much sail was carried by night as by day. Reefs were put in only reluctantly, when whole sails could be carried no longer; with the first lull, out came the reefs again; no opportunity was lost to make a mile, if hull and rigging would stand the strain. Not that my brother Martin was reckless; he knew when it was time to take measures for safety, and took them, and in an emergency he was resourceful and ready to meet it; but he watched wind and weather, and took every advantage that as a sailor he knew how to take to put his vessel forward on her voyage.

In spite of driving when we had the chance, the passage was long and tedious. We had strong northerly gales on leaving Halifax, and for a few days made good progress; then the weather became warmer and the wind moderate. The captain and mate set to work carpentering, fixing up the cabin. After a while it fell stark calm, and continued so for nearly two weeks. At night we would clear up the decks where the carpenter work had been going on, and throw the shavings overboard, and the next morning the shavings would still be in sight. The ocean was covered with vast fields of brown gulf weed which, under the hot sun, seemed to form a solid crust, burnt and desolate, stretching away miles and miles in all directions. In reality, no region of the earth was fuller of life, and the appearance of desolation at any time was quickly dispelled by a glance overboard alongside. That immense area was the home and happy hunting ground and shelter of teeming tiny populations, of all shapes, graceful and grotesque, and of every hue of brilliancy by day, darting in and out of cover, and at night glimmering with a soft phosphorescent radiance.

On April 9th there came a light air from the southward, which gradually strengthened and became more easterly, and we worked along slowly for several days. On the 14th a man at the masthead reported land on the starboard beam. We were then about in the latitude of Barbuda, and the captain thinking we had got too far to leeward, we hauled up sharp by the wind, heading about south southeast, keeping a good lookout. But it proved to be "Cape Flyaway," for after finding that we did not come up with the land on that course, we kept off, and on the twentieth saw Tobago, and hauled across for Trinidad.

Three times we entered the second Bocas, but were becalmed and drifted back with the current. Finally we got through and beat up the Gulf of Paria to Port of Spain. Here the captain sold all but a small portion of his cargo, taking his pay in bills on St. Thomas, and we sailed for that island, where we had some cargo to land, consigned to Mr. Thomas James. At St. Thomas the

Cape Flyaway is not a real place, but a figure of speech for a vain hope. [1]

captain changed his bills for gold, and then we went to Guayama, Puerto Rico.

We left St. Thomas at 4 P.M. of May 4th, and the next morning at eight hauled in to a bay on the coast of Puerto Rico and came to anchor, thinking it must be our destination. A pilot came off and told us the port we were in was Patillas, and that Guayama was about ten or fifteen miles further west; and he offered to pilot us down there. Accordingly, we got under way again, and anchored in Guayama about eleven. At noon the Custom House boat came off to us. As we had no bill of health, we were informed that we must lie in quarantine for thirty days. The captain tried to explain that we were all in good health and had not been in any sickly port, but his explanations were only met by Spanish shrugs and grimaces. Seeing the pilot on board of us, the officer pitched into him and gave him rats for being there; told him he ought to have taken a line and towed alongside, and was going to make him ride out the quarantine with us, but the pilot parleyed and palmed it over with him some way, and he was at last allowed to go home in his boat.

In the outer roads at anchor near us, we saw the schooner *Eagle*, of which, as said, Captain Alfred Shepard was master, and my brother Nehemiah mate; and Joe Hopkins, a boy about my own age, an old playmate and a tiptop fellow, was one of her crew. It was against the law for vessels in quarantine to communicate with each other; but unbounded respect for the law was never characteristic of Nova Scotia sailors, so as soon as it was dark, we took our boat and went aboard the *Eagle* and passed the evening. The next morning the health officer came alongside with our consignee. They had a long talk with the captain, during which he took occasion to say that he had no bill of health, clean or foul, but that he had come there to buy a load of sugar, and had the gold down in his cabin to pay for it, but of course he could not afford to lie off there idle a whole month, and he supposed he would have to run down to Turk's Island and get a load of salt. As they were about to go ashore, the consignee found a chance to say to the captain privately that he thought probably we would be let out of quarantine the next day. And so it was, according to his word; the health officer's boat boarded us again and gave us pratique—leave to come in and discharge ballast, and later to load.

The *Eagle* got out of quarantine about the same time and as loading sugar was heavy work, we helped each other. Joe Hopkins and I had great times together. After loading sugar all day, we were dirty from head to foot, and as sticky as tar babies. We would jump overboard with our clothes on and have a good swim, and the action of the salt water and sugar drainings upon our clothes and skin was such that soap and hot water could not have taken the dirt out better. Then we would come aboard, strip to our waists, sit astride of a chest and box with each other openhanded. There we would have it until we were deaf and out of breath, each wishing the other would cry quit, but determined not to be the first to give in.

Having finished loading, the *Eagle* and *Victoria* sailed in company for Halifax. The voyage home was without incident, except for our fouling the *Eagle*. In luffing across her stern, our jibboom caught in her mainsail, tore it, and unshipped her mainboom. Our jibboom carried away, and we went clear. A day or two after we finished repairing damages, we took a heavy gale, and we saw no more of the *Eagle* the rest of the voyage. On June 10th we made Cape Sable, went through the West Passage, and home to Barrington. The next day the *Eagle* arrived.

After a day or two at home, we proceeded to Halifax and discharged. I had to work hard all day hoisting out sugar, then do the cooking in the evening, and stay aboard all night and keep ship. After the cargo was out, we took the vessel to Paine's wharf, where we hove her down and graved her bottom. The captain then chartered to go to Falmouth, Jamaica; Alexandria, Virginia, and back to Halifax.

On June 26th, 1841, we sailed for Falmouth, with a load of fish, hoop poles, staves, shingles and lumber, a real West India cargo. We arrived at Falmouth on July 26th, and discharged, went to Alexandria in ballast, where we loaded with flour, and on September 7th arrived in Halifax. On the seventeenth, we were back in Barrington again, and the vessel was laid up in Woods Harbor for the winter, so my voyaging for the season came to an end.

My brother Nehemiah left the *Eagle* and shipped as second mate on board the brig *Gem*, with Captain Benjamin Doane, bound to Leghorn and Malaga, in the Mediterranean, while for me the usual round of fall and winter work and play went on. On New Year's Day Nehemiah arrived home, and left again in March, mate of the *Gem*.

During the spring of 1842, Mr. Obediah Wilson, Jr., fitted out the old schooner *Jane*, and Captain Solomon Kendrick was to take her on a whaling voyage to Newfoundland and the Labrador. I shipped as after-oarsman in the mate's boat. We had to wait for the ice to break up in the Gulf of St. Lawrence before starting, and that left considerable time on our hands. While I was so engaged killing time, about the middle of May, Captain Joseph Robbins, with the schooner *Adrianna* came to Barrington from Yarmouth, bound on a trading voyage down the shore, and I engaged with him as mate. We went to Cape Negro, Shelburne and Liverpool, peddling cheese, hay and potatoes, three or four days in a place, and then moving on.

At Liverpool the captain began to talk of making a trip to Bermuda. That did not suit me, as it was now the last of May and the time was getting near to join the whaling schooner, so I told the captain he must get somebody else in my place. On the 31st of May, in the afternoon, he paid me off. I went up to a shop in Liverpool and bought a belt and sheath knife, strapped my bag on my back and started to walk to Barrington, a distance of about seventy miles. I had relatives named Swim living in Port Mouton. I reached there at sunset and stayed all night at their house. The next morning early I started for home. I tramped all that day with a load of fifty pounds or more on my back. It was warm and dusty, and I never was good at walking. When I came to the top of a hill and looked off to the next one, it seemed far away, and if I stopped for a moment I felt as if I was anchored and could never move again. But I kept on, and about four o'clock walked into Shelburne. I found out Joe Devine's house and put up there.

When a small boy I loved to spend evenings at their house, which was on what was called Lower Guinea, a hill back of the residence of my late nephew, Captain Hervey Doane. They would thrill my imagination with tales and songs of old Ireland, in which fairies and phantom knights and heroes did wonderful things, some bad and some good. My parents did not seem to mind how late I stayed at the Devines. Often I wished they had become alarmed and sent someone for me, as on my way home through the woods, near midnight, my head awhirl with the ancient ballads and legends, every rock and tree seemed to have behind it a goblin ready to carry me off to his secret cave, or a warrior in gleaming armor waiting—for me.

Joe and his wife Mary were an old Irish couple who had been tenants of my father and our neighbors for many years, and I received a cordial welcome from Mrs. Devine. When Joe came home from work, he said, "Good mercy, Ben, have you traveled all the way from Liverpool here carrying that bag? Well, I wouldn't see a dog that had bit me walk to Barrington with that load. You leave that here in the morning, and I'll send it to you by post." Accordingly, in the morning when I started, I was not so top-heavy as I had been, but my feet were weary and sore long before I reached home. Coming in sight of the house, about three hundred yards away, I looked up and wished I was there, for it seemed as hard to go that little ways as if it were so many miles.

For the next two weeks I was busy getting ready to go whaling, and on the 20th of June, sailed in the schooner *Jane* for Newfoundland and the Labrador.

— CHAPTER V —

A WHALING TRIP

June 21st to October 2nd, 1842

*C*APTAIN SOLOMON KENDRICK WAS AN OLD-FASHIONED gentleman of distinguished ancestry and commanding presence, standing six feet two inches, with a huge powerful frame, and as much above the ordinary man in intelligence as in physical proportions. He was a veteran sailor and whaleman, having three times, while following his adventurous calling, circumnavigated the globe.

His great uncle, Captain John Kendrick, born in Harwich, Cape Cod, at the end of the eighteenth century, left Boston with two ships, the *Columbia* and *Lady Washington*, on a voyage of discovery along the Pacific coast of America. He discovered a river, which he named for his ship, the *Columbia*; and leaving his second in command, Robert Gray, with one ship to explore the river, he sailed in the *Lady Washington* to the northward, along the shores of Vancouver Island. Gray returned to Boston before him and received all the credit of the discovery of the Columbia River, which history, with strange perversity, has insisted upon according to him.

Mr. Jethro Covil, of Cape Island, who had been down to Labrador fishing a great deal, was pilot and the captain's boat steerer. The mate was Mr. McNally from Saint John, New Brunswick. John O. Crowell, of Barrington (afterwards a Cunard pilot) was the mate's boat steerer. Among the crew were Knowles Hopkins and his brother Henry, from Barrington; Philip Crowell and Joshua Nickerson, whom we called "Slaughtery," from Shag Harbor; Joe Frost, from Argyle; an Irishman named Shea; and John Baker, who hailed from Gayo, Newfoundland. The remainder of the crew were from Saint John.

The cook we called Quaco, after the port from which he hailed. He was not a very good cook, and every Sunday Mr. Covil came into the cabin to take his Sunday dinner, because he thought I was a better cook than the cook; but to make sure that everything should be to his taste, Mr. Covil superintended matters himself. Quaco disliked this "synod of cooks" and when he could stand it no longer, he set out to give me a thrashing down in the between-decks. He would have done it too if Slaughtery had not been there and stood my friend. As it was, I received a black eye, but the neighborly help of Slaughtery turned the odds against poor Quaco and he fled from the field.

At noon of the fourth day after leaving home, we passed inside of the Island of Scatarie and into the Gulf of St. Lawrence. A week of rough weather ensued, during which we saw no whales, and then we went into the Bay of St. George, on the west coast of Newfoundland. There we found grampus

In whaling journals a stamp was often used in the margin to document encounters with whales. A whole whale indicated a successful capture and the flukes an unsuccessful chase

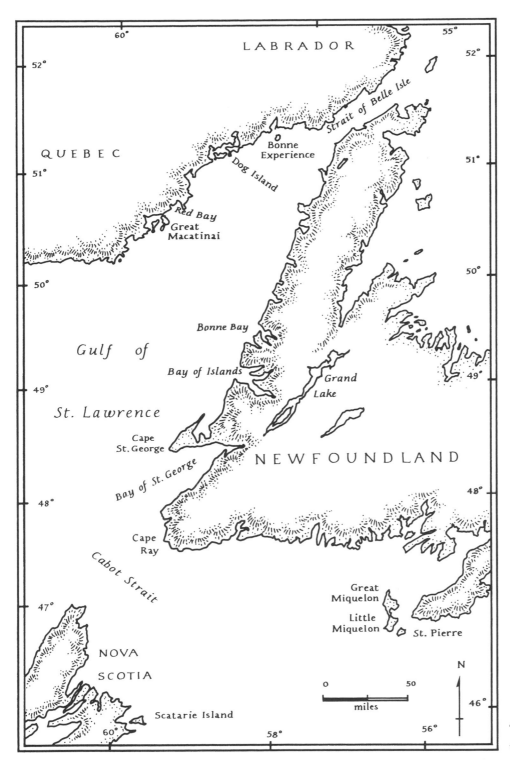

LABRADOR

QUEBEC

52°

60°

55°

52°

Strait of Belle Isle

51°

Bonne
Experience

Dog Island

Red Bay
Great
Macatinai

51°

50°

Gulf   of

Bonne Bay

Bay of Islands

50°

St. Lawrence

Grand
Lake

49°

49°

Cape
St. George

NEWFOUNDLAND

Bay of St. George

48°

48°

Cape
Ray

Cabot Strait

47°

Great
Miquelon

Little
Miquelon

St. Pierre

NOVA

SCOTIA

Scatarie Island

60°

58°

56°

N

0   50

miles

46°

The Newfoundland
whaling grounds

**Roche Harbor and
Bonne Bay**

whales in abundance, but the trouble was to get them. Every morning whales were seen and we lowered the boats and gave chase. For hour after hour we pulled at our oars with all our might, but to no purpose; none of the boats ever got near enough to strike. After seven days of constant but utterly unprofitable oar exercise from daylight to sunset, we shifted our ground and went further up the coast, and anchored in Rocky Harbor, at the mouth of Bonne Bay.

There on July 13th we went out as usual at four o'clock in the morning, looking for whales, and after manoeuvring all day long trying to get up with one, at four in the afternoon the chance came to our boat steerer, and he sent his iron, as the harpoon is called, well into a fine big humpback whale. Who can imagine Captain John O. Crowell—a man of exquisite formal dignity—harpooning a whale? Immediately we were off with a rush, and the line attached to the iron was whizzing out at a tremendous rate; but in a second or two, being new and kinky, it fouled and rose in coil out of the tub, the coils, as they flew out, catching upon and breaking two of our oars. The boat's head was pulled under, and she filled with water. The boat steerer cut the line, and off went the whale. We bailed out our boat and went back aboard the vessel, tired, wet, hungry, and oh, so disappointed.

Two days later the captain's boat had a little better luck, but even his experience was bitter-sweet. Humpback whales were plentiful but very wild, and we had been out since daylight which in that latitude in summer comes very early in the morning. The captain's boat was chasing a cow whale, which was accompanied by a young calf, and while the two were running side by side, the captain lanced the calf and killed it. Prompted by its mother instinct, which is specially strong in the humpback variety, the whale stopped suddenly and rolled on her side, as if to take her stricken infant to her breast. Then the boat steerer, Mr. Covil, struck her between the flippers and made her spout blood. He had killed her with the iron. But no sooner was the whale dead than she sank in the middle of the bay. After her dying flurry, when it was evident that the carcase would sink, our boat fastened to it, and then when it had sunk we ran out anchors in different directions to hold it in case it should rise, and buoyed the anchors. The calf, for which the mother had sacrificed her life in vain, was all we had left to tow on board.

After sundown a boat was sent out to the buoys to keep watch by the sunken whale all night. The next day there was a thick fog. We had one boat out watching for the dead whale to float; the rest of us were busy "cutting in"; that is, stripping the blubber from the young whale, and trying out the oil. Then came several days of rain and heavy gales. It was impossible to keep a boat watching for the sunken whale. A good lookout was maintained on one of the headlands, but nothing was seen of it. When the weather had moderated sufficiently, we went out to search, but neither the whale nor the buoys nor anchors could be found. It must have risen during the gale and gone to sea.

Trying out our little whale was not a big job, and when that was finished we went to look for more whales. Bonne Bay is about twelve miles deep from the mouth to its further inland extremity, and we chased whales in and out from the head of the bay to the headlands. Late one afternoon, the mate's boat got fast to a large humpback whale. Then the trouble began. We were near the upper end of the bay when we struck him, and he ran with us full spring clear to the head of the bay. The water was flying, the boat's bow ducked under, and she filled with water. Some of us stood by with buckets to bail, while the others hauled line, trying to get close enough so that when the whale stopped the mate could lance him. We hauled up on him as far as his flukes, and the mate, with the boat spade, tried in vain to heave him to by chopping the sinews of his tail.

After towing us to the mouth of the bay, the whale turned and ran in as far as the water would let him, then down the bay again, past the heads and out into the gulf, flying along, our boat just clear of his flukes, and the mate, as I say, prodding away at his tail in vain endeavors to slow him down. The other boat was following us, far behind, prepared to assist us if the chance offered, or to pick us up in case our boat got stove. At sunset the captain signalled us to cut the line and come aboard. But the mate held on until we were away out to sea and the long twilight had ended. One slash of the mate's knife set our unconquerable courser free, and we went back to the vessel, which we reached about midnight, damp and discouraged.

About three days afterwards, a vessel belonging to Gaspé, Quebec, fell in with our wounded whale. He was so gashed and cut about the tail that he was then very weak and was easily captured. Our irons were found in him marked with the vessel's name. The same Gaspé vessel also had the luck to pick up another of our lost prizes, the sunken whale that rose with its anchors and went to sea in the storm. It was what they called "blasted," that is, it had begun to decompose. They tried it out but it made very inferior black oil.

It was some consolation that the day after our failure the captain killed a big humpback whale, and both boats helped to tow him alongside with songs and cheers. After trying out his oil and stowing it down, we got wood and water and, leaving Bonne Bay, sailed over to the Labrador shore. We went into Great Macatinai Harbor for two days, but finding nothing in our line, sailed for Dog Islands.

There I saw for the first time an Esquimau in a kayak, with a double paddle. It made no difference how many times he upset, he could always turn right side up again as long as he held to his paddle. The only whaling experience we had here was that one day our boat got fast to a whale, but the iron drew out and we lost him.

From Dog Islands we cruised back to the Newfoundland shore, and across again to the Labrador, without being any better off. We lay some time in Red Bay, where we saw a few whales but they were so wild we could not get near them. After another cruise across the Straits we anchored in Bonne Experience, and then went to Dog Islands and down to Macatinai again. This cruising back and forth may seem monotonous enough as it is recorded here, but it was far from being so in fact. Though we did little at whaling, which was business, we had plenty of first rate sport.

The Labrador coast is fringed with small islands, which are the breeding ground of many species of ducks and gulls. On foggy days and at other times, as it often happened, when there were no whales, Mr. Covil and I would take our guns and go in a boat among the outer islands to shoot ducks as they flew in between the ledges. In the course of a morning we would shoot perhaps a dozen or so. Then we would take our birds aboard the vessel, and all hands would pluck them, but I followed the order of exercises even further, for I often cooked them and, of course, never missed any meals.

On our next cruise over to the Labrador shore, we reached Great Macatinai Harbor late in the afternoon and anchored. The captain then took one boat and the mate another, and we started for the bird rocks to get eggs. We got, perhaps, ten or fifteen dozen, and went home.

We made several trips to those bird islands after eggs and young birds. The latter when about a month old were very fine eating. The eggs of the eider duck and gull were all that we bothered with. The other varieties were apt to be strong and fishy. The sea duck and black duck do not breed on the islands. They build their nests away in the interior beyond the first range of mountains; but the noddy, gull and the other waterfowl, lay their eggs right on the rocks, and if let alone for three or four days, the whole island will be covered with eggs. During the summer vessels go to the islands and gather the eggs for market. We saw a shallop of thirty-five tons loaded with eggs in bulk. That is, when they got five or six tiers in, planks were laid across, the ends resting against the ceiling of the vessels, to prevent pressure upon the eggs underneath, and to sustain the next tier; and so on until loaded full. Such business must, of course, in time, as I am told has been the case, diminish the source of supply; but during the summer the old *Jane* cruised over that ground there was no lack. It was wonderful to see the innumerable hosts of birds, millions upon millions of them, that covered the sky. They were like a big thick cloud, shutting out the sun and literally darkening the air.

On October 2nd we were back in Barrington again. I had shipped for six dollars a month and the hundredth lay—that is, one drop of oil in every hundred should be mine. That would have been very good if we had done well; but we had only caught about seventy-five barrels of oil altogether, humpback, blackfish and porpoise. I received twenty dollars and forty cents wages, and a small quantity of three different kinds of oil, half a barrel full in all; and that was what I had to show for three and a half months of work.

— CHAPTER VI —

THE *BRISK* AND THE *REINDEER*

October 3rd, 1842 to August 1843

$\mathcal{A}$FEW DAYS LATER MY RETURN FROM THE LABRA-
dor on October 2nd, Nehemiah arrived home from the Mediterranean to spend the winter, and he and I helped our brother Martin
rig the brig *Brisk*, which had just been launched at Mr. William Muir's yard
in Shelburne, and of which Martin was to be master in the West Indies trade.
After she was rigged, I went in her to Halifax, where she was chartered to go
to Savannah la Mar, Jamaica. While loading, I was taken with the mumps,
and as the captain had never had them, he did not want me on board. So, my
brother-in-law, Captain Seth Kendrick, being in Halifax and ready to sail for
Barrington, I took passage home with him.

Martin arrived in Shelburne from the West Indies on December 23rd,
and the next day came home. On Christmas Day he and I went to Shelburne
in a blustering snowstorm, and the next day we sailed for Halifax in a heavy
northwest gale. On New Year's Day, 1843, we anchored in Halifax Harbor.
It was a still morning, intensely cold, and while we were aloft furling the
sails, we noticed that one of the crew, a Shelburne Negro, was not helping
much and seemed barely able to stay on the yard. After we came down on
deck, the mate, Mr. Pelham, seeing him standing shivering, asked him what
was the matter. "I don't know, Sir; I'm turning all white, Sir." "Turning
white, hell," said the mate; "you've frozen your fingers"; and going to the
harness cask, he drew a bucket of brine and plunged the man's hands into it.
Oh! how he did sing out, *mortbleu*. But his hands were held in the brine
until they hurt him no more.

On January 13th we sailed for Savannah la Mar, Jamaica, where we
arrived on the 30th. One Sunday morning while lying there at anchor, in
about three and a half fathoms of water, the crew all went in swimming. It
was calm, the chain was slack and the vessel close up to her anchor, which
we could see on the bottom as plain as day. One of the men made an
unsuccessful attempt to dive down to the anchor and when he came up he bet
me a dollar that I could not do any better. Overboard I went and down to the
anchor, took hold of it and turned around, gave a kick and came up, and it
was my dollar. That put me in the humor to try something more difficult.

We had a little grappling, a four-clawed anchor without any stock,
weighing about forty pounds. That was thrown overboard, and I dove and
caught hold of it, hooked one claw over my shoulder and started to swim to
the surface. But it was a different matter this time. When one dives
unencumbered, as every swimmer knows, coming to the surface is not

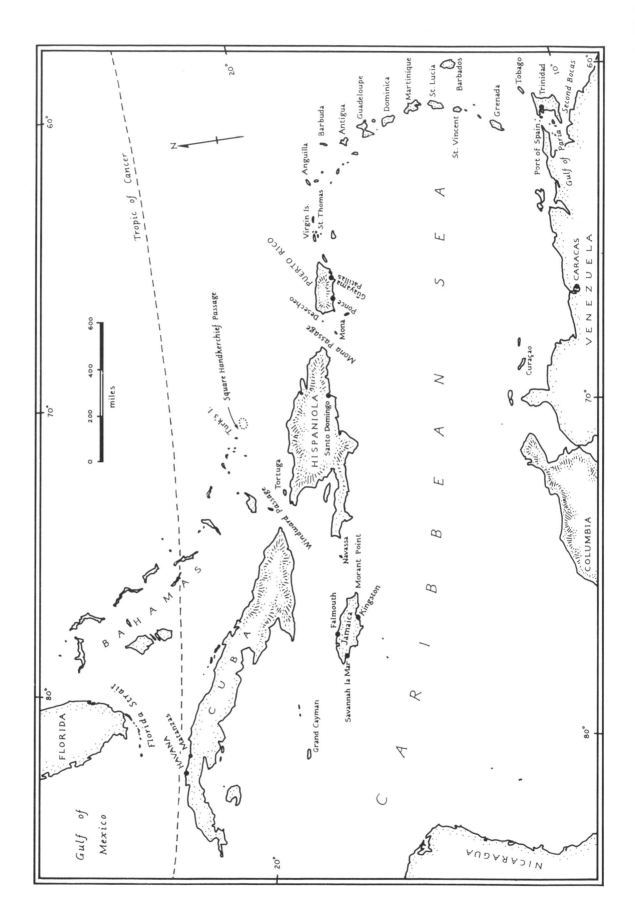

attended by any effort, the natural buoyancy of the body bringing one up. Now, with the 40-pound anchor to carry, I turned and looked upward. The bottom of the boat was almost directly above me, with the men's heads over the side looking down, and the water around it strewn with bits of floating seaweed, wood, cocoanut husks and such like drift stuff, while a little farther off hovered the dark shadow of the brig, like some great impending monster ready to settle and keep me down. I can see it now as the sight impressed me then, the magnifying power of the water making the distance to the surface appear to be hundreds of feet, whereas in reality it was only about twenty-one. So I struck out with all my might for top water and the sweet air, and after a hard struggle, during which I was constantly tempted to tilt the old anchor clear of me and let it go, I came up alongside the boat and caught hold of the gunwale, pretty well exhausted and quite content, as one of the men took the grappling off my shoulder, to pass the remainder of that Sabbath Day more in accordance with the quiet manner in which we are taught it should be observed.

With a light load of pimento, logwood and rum and a few dry hides, we sailed for Halifax. A few days after passing Cape Antonio we took a violent northwest gale. We shortened sail to close-reefed fore-topsail, reefed foresail and three-reefed mainsail; as the gale increased, we furled the topsail; an hour later we took in the foresail, and hove to under balanced mainsail. The gale still increasing, with a tremendous sea, and the brig being very light, she was lying down on her broadside and driving very fast. There was then great danger of the cargo shifting, which, of course, would mean our capsizing, and it was necessary to get the top hamper off her as much as possible.

The captain asked Mr. Pelham if he thought he could send down the topgallant and royal yards and the topgallant mast. "If you think you can't do it," he said, "I will cut the backstays, clap a tackle on the foreto' gallant stay, and pull the mast over the bows." "No, no," said the mate, "try the other thing first; give me that boy, and I will send the spars down all right." He was a little man, Mr. Pelham, but full of energy. He came along to me and sung out in a big voice, "Take the end of that rope in your hand and come up after me." He took a block and I, a rope, and up we marveled aloft. The brig was lying almost on her beam ends, and the wind was so strong at times that it blew the mate up against the rigging and he had to wait for the flaw to pass before going further.

We sent the royal yard down by the royal halliards. Then we put a strap around the topgallant mast-head, hooked a block into it, rove a yard rope through the block, swayed up and cockbilled the topgallant yard, knocked off the lifts and braces, took a turn of the gasket around the backstay, and sent the yard down. The royal and topgallant masts were in one piece, and the next thing was to send that down. We put a block on the cap of the topmast, rove our mast-rope, and cast off the seizing of the rigging; then on deck they slacked up the backstays and hove away on the mast-rope, we knocked out the fid, and in short order down came the topgallant mast on deck. We got the rigging all stopped and made fast, but the ship was still laboring heavily.

The captain said, "Well, one thing more we can do for her, and that is send down the foreyard, and when that is done it is either float or sink, for we can't do anything more." So up went the mate, taking me with him

Opposite:
The West Indies

THE BRISK AND THE REINDEER 29

again. We got tackles up to the foremast head, and swayed up the yard, put guys on it to keep it from rolling one way and the other, unshackled the slings and truss, got a tackle out to the bowsprit, pulled on our head tackle to keep the yard off the mast, and lowered away on the masthead tackle, keeping guys and lifts taut all the time; till we landed the yard on the rail, and then made all things fast and snug. The brig lay then quite comfortably, and so we weathered the gale. That afternoon we got up the foreyard again, and the next day we sent up the other spars. By daylight of the following day we had studding sails set alow and aloft.

When we arrived in Halifax, we found my brother Nehemiah in the schooner *Victoria* ready to sail for Bermuda and waiting for a fair wind. With him were my old friend, Wilson Crowell, as mate, and my two nephews, Thomas Knowles and William Doane. The evening before they sailed, March 5th, I went aboard the *Victoria* and stayed all night. We passed a happy evening, and Nehemiah and I slept together for the last time in our lives. On their return voyage, Nehemiah was taken with typhus fever. Out on the broad sea, without medicine or medical skill, loving friends did what they could, while the fever consumed his life away. He died just as the vessel made the Sealing Islands, which lie off the southern end of Nova Scotia and about thirty miles from his mother's door. The next day the vessel came into Barrington Harbor with her flag at halfmast and anchored in the Passage. The boat pulled ashore and was met at the wharf by my mother and youngest sister. No need to tell them for whom the colors were flying. All were alive and well before their eyes, but the son—the brother.

Such a cloud, however, was unforeseen and unfelt on the morning when he and I bade each other light-hearted sailor's farewells and went on our different roads of duty.

After the cargo was all out of the *Brisk*, the sailors were discharged, and only the captain, the mate and I remained by the ship. One night when the mate had gone ashore, a heavy southeast gale with snow came on. The brig being light, she hove down on the wharf. The captain and I got a hawser up to the masthead and took it around to the opposite wharf to windward and hauled it taut, which kept her from capsizing altogether. She stove in all her bulwarks, ground up all the fenders and chafed her bends very much, beating against the wharf. We hunted around in the storm and found a lot of bundles of hoop poles, which we used for fenders. When one bundle wore out we dropped another in its place. It kept us up all night, but we saved the vessel from destruction, which was more than some others escaped in Halifax Harbor that night.

The brig being repaired, she was chartered for a voyage to Boston with coal, and thence to take freight to Quebec. Mr. Pelham left, and Thomas Chatwynd shipped as mate. Levi Crowell, of Woods Harbor, one of the smartest sailors I ever met, was one of the crew. On March 27th we arrived in Boston and moored at Market Wharf. My first walk ashore in Boston did not inform me very much. All I remember is that my companion and I got lost among the crooked streets and had to ask a policeman to show us the way back to the ship.

When I got back to the dock it was low tide, and the brig was so much below the wharf that I could not reach her. It was as much as eight feet in a horizontal line from the edge of the pier to the forerigging. I knew better than to wake the captain up at that hour by calling to anybody to come and help me aboard. So I made a jump in the dark, off the stringpiece of the wharf, and fortunately landed in the rigging, got down on deck, tip-toed to my bunk and turned in.

On our way to Quebec, we called in at Barrington to take on board the captain's wife. Shortly before passing Cape Gaspé in the Gulf of St. Lawrence, I remember being much impressed with the appearance of a huge rock which projected high out of the water, with a big archway through it. It is called on the chart Percé Rock. Odd rock formations seemed to be rather a feature of that locality, another instance being the headland quite appropriately called the "Ship's Stern."

From Quebec we sailed for Halifax with a load of salt and ten Irish passengers, two young men and eight young women, all possessed of the usual amount of vivacity with which their race is endowed. They brought with them their own provisions, and as we had no steerage, the forecastle was given to them and we sailors all lived and slept in the forward cabin. At the Strait of Canso we were fog-bound for several days, which time the captain and his wife employed in visiting relatives ashore.

The night after we got through the Strait of Canso it blew up a heavy southeast gale and the passengers were dreadfully frightened. If spirits summoned from the vasty deep come when they are called, then we were well surrounded that night, for every saint in the calendar was specially requested in the most persuasive brogue to stand by us. To add to the terror in the forecastle, one of the sailors made a rope fast to a big piece of wood and hung it over the bow. With every pitch of the ship, the stick would strike ker-bang against the bow, and with every thump came a chorus of howls from the terrified passengers. We endeavored to pacify them, telling them the storm was nothing more than usual and that there was no danger. But it had no effect, they knew too well why this misery had befallen them. Being unprepared for the delay on account of fog, they had run out of provisions the day we resumed our voyage, which was a Friday. That morning the captain had sent them some pork, and being by hunger made bold, they had eaten heartily of it, thereby breaking the Christian canon; and they were convinced that the storm had in consequence been sent as a punishment upon them.

The bad weather continuing, our watches below were constantly broken into and all hands had but very little sleep for several days. Levi Crowell and I were in the mate's watch. Levi and the mate were cousins. The night before we reached Halifax I became so drowsy while steering that I asked the mate to take the wheel a few minutes, which he did, and I went and washed my face in salt water to drive the sleep away. In a little while I was winking again; I could not hold my eyes open. So the mate took the wheel again and I climbed up to the topmast-head. The change and exertion revived me, and I could then keep awake.

The next morning we arrived at Halifax. After the cargo was discharged, we unbent the sails and put them away, and painted the ship's yards. The topsail sheet was left hooked into the ring of the slings of the foreyard, and the other end, being too short to belay, was made fast to the pin below by a rope yarn. While painting the foreyard on the inshore side, I was sitting on the footrope and, in order to paint underneath the yard, took hold of the topsail sheet with one hand, reaching out with my paint brush in the other as far as I could. As I did so, the rope yarn parted. That allowed the sheet to unreeve, and I pitched head foremost off the footrope. My clutch, however, on the sheet turned me as I fell and I struck on my feet on the capstan of the wharf, just grazing the shoulder of a ship carpenter named Mr. Mackie, who was doing some repairing to the brig. Of course, it made me see stars. I sprained my ankle, and every joint in me was sore. The brig *Gem* of Barrington was lying on the other side of the wharf, and her captain, Benjamin Doane, saw me fall. He ran and helped to carry me into the *Brisk's* cabin, where he bathed me, gave me a dose of something from the medicine chest, and put me in my bunk.

The *Brisk* did not get a charter right away and we went off to an anchorage in the stream. All hands were discharged but Levi Crowell and me and we kept ship, the captain boarding ashore with his wife and only occasionally visiting us.

Tired of waiting for the *Brisk*, I shipped for the first time as able seaman in the brig *Reindeer*, built and owned in Barrington and chartered by a Mr. Hamilton, for a voyage to Kingston, Jamaica; Alexandria, Virginia, and back to Halifax. I vowed many times before the voyage was over that I would never forget the captain, but I cannot now recall his name. The mate was a Mr. Bell, of Cape Negro. The captain was drunk when we went to sea, as were most of the crew, and the mate, contrary to all sea etiquette, had to take the ship out of port. After getting out clear of Sambro, we began to sway up the sails and tauten the sheets. I was at the wheel. The mate said to me, "Luff her up and shake her while we haul the sheets." I luffed and kept the sails shivered till he sang out, "Keep her afull." It was the first time I had been shipmates with a travelling wheel on a tiller abaft the rudder head, and becoming confused, I hove the wheel the wrong way. Up she came into the wind and caught aback. We had to wear around—lower the mainsail and brace the yards, causing a lot of trouble The mate came aft to me and said, "What the devil do you mean, catching the ship aback that way? Do you want to take the spars out of her, *or are you drunk too?*" I was very much mortified at the mishap, and explained that I was unused to that kind of steering gear.

During the course of the voyage, we had to shorten the main-topmast backstays. They had been set up on their ends before, and the mate wanted a Flemish eye made in the ends and to have them set up in the lanyards. The captain was about half-sawed on this occasion, as he was all the time when not dead drunk, and he said he would superintend the job. He asked one and another of the men if they could make a Flemish eye. Bill Dunkerson, an English ex-man-of-warsman, said he had never heard of one; and I believe the captain knew as little about it as he did. However, Billy got a round cursing for his candor, and the captain then asked me if I could do it. "I have made them," I said, "but I don't know now whether I can or not." "You're another of these eel-grass sailors, ain't fit to be aboard a vessel. You go forward and slush down the to'gallan'mast," was the send-off I received, and I obediently went aloft with my bucket of grease.

There was another sailor aboard, a Nova Scotian, who was a good second to the captain in all his accomplishments. The captain was taken with his assurance, thought him a great fellow, and told him to go ahead and make a Flemish eye; but first he had the mate cut the backstays and mark them where the eyes were to be made, and then the captain went below. When I had come down on deck again, the mate was cursing away at the man,—rip-rip-rip—"You've spoilt this backstay." The captain came on deck to see what was up. "What's the matter," he said, "ain't that a Flemish eye?" The mate stuttered. "N-n-no, b-by—! nor no other kind of eye. Here, D-doane, come and s-s-sit here and make a Flemish eye in this other backstay; and if you don't, I'll lil-lil-lick you till you can't stand." So I went at it. When it was made and served, Mr. Bell held up the two pieces of work and said, "There, that's a Flemish eye; but that other d-damn thing looks like a snake with a hop-op-optoad in his belly."

Mr. Bell was a fine man and a thorough seaman, and I remember his friendship with gratitude. After this incident, knowing that my stock stood well with the mate, the only decent man (barring the Negro cook) aboard the ship, I could listen to the captain's maudlin curses without any other feeling but hearty contempt.

We went through the Square Handkerchief Passage in the Bahamas, made Mole St. Nicholas, and proceeded down the Windward Passage between Cuba and Hispaniola, until we saw Cape Dame Maria bearing east fifteen miles, and shaped our course at noon of July 27th for Morant Point, Jamaica. We had only light airs throughout the day and night, and did not make much progress. At five o'clock next morning the captain came thundering at the forecastle door, bawling to us to turn out. We all turned out of our bunks and came on deck. He began to swear at us for steering the ship out of her course during the night. "Look there," he said, pointing towards the island of Navassa, which was in sight astern of us. "You have run the ship three points off her course, and we are down to the Grand Cayman. See the ship ready for stays!" So we 'bout ship.

The captain then sent me aloft to shift the main gaff topsail sheets, and hailed me at the masthead with, "What land is that to windward?" pointing towards Santo Domingo. As I had made several voyages up and down that shore, I recognized the high broken land that I saw, and answered him, "That land on the weather beam is San Domingo, Sir." "Then what island is that?" pointing to Navassa. "I don't know, Sir, but I have seen it before." "You be damned!" he bellowed; "that's the Grand Cayman"; and he stabbed his dividers into his chart, and stamped them both under his feet.

Coast of Jamaica near Morant Point

When I came down, old Abe Halliard (Abe King, of Barrington), the colored cook, said to me, "Why, why, Doane, don't you know that island? Why, why, I knows that island; that's Nawassa. Grand Cayman 'way off there about nor'west. I knows where we is, if the cap'n don't." Soon we saw a sail under Navassa. We wore ship and ran down and spoke to her; and then the captain, as well as the cook, knew where we were.

Discharging cargo in Kingston was hot, hard work. Even under slavery, which had then been abolished in Jamaica for about ten years, a day's work was limited by law to ten hours. But the law which protected the slave was not made for the sailor. We had to work from five in the morning until dark. The second day, the captain being ashore, drunk and reeling around the town in his shirt sleeves (a disgrace to us all), three of the men hired Negroes to work in their stead, and they lay down on the forecastle. At four in the afternoon, the hired men's day's work of ten hours was up, and they went ashore. The captain came aboard just as they left, and he made the men who had paid to have their day's work done for them turn out, and we all worked till dark.

One afternoon about two o'clock, a heavy thunder squall came up. We were lying at the end of a dock, with our anchor out in the stream and hawsers fast to the piles of the wharf. The force of the wind was such that a pile pulled out, and we broke away and went down afoul of another brig, named the *Lottery*. Her cathead caught in our netting, ripping it up, stanchions and all, and we went clear, carrying away the other vessel's cathead. Our anchor at last brought us up, and just as it did, another ship that had struck adrift came across our bows and carried away our jibboom. Our longboat was in the slip, tied to the dock, and there was such a sea on, the captain was afraid it would be smashed. He hailed a boat that was pulling ashore from another ship, and sent Billy and me in her to look out for our boat. When we got on the dock we found the boat all stoved to pieces, so that we could do nothing with her.

The mate meantime, aboard the vessel, was trying to get in the jibboom, which lay under the bows with the sail and rigging all on it. The captain hollered to Billy and me to come back. The only way to do that, as we had no boat, was to swim, so I jumped off the end of the dock and swam to the vessel. The captain was watching me, and when I came alongside, I asked him to give me a rope. The old rascal took no notice of me, though I asked him three or four times, so I swam to the bow and got on the jibboom. The mate handed me a strap, and I put it around the jibboom; they lowered down a tackle and I hooked it on, and then climbed up the tackle and helped heave the jibboom aboard.

Now, Kingston Harbor has a reputation for sharks; but though it was nearly an hour from the time I jumped off the wharf until I got on board the vessel, if any sharks saw me, I never saw them. I have heard that fish won't bite during a thunder storm, and as there was muttering thunder in the distance, even after the squall passed, that may be the reason I was unmolested. Billy waited on the wharf until everything was all over when, some boats putting off to other vessels, he got into one and was set aboard.

The day we were all ready for sea, the cook told us that we were almost out of provisions, only half a barrel each of rusty pork and beef, a scant supply of horribly weevilly hardtack, and no tea, coffee or molasses. We refused to go to sea until the captain procured more provisions. This he promised to do, and after dark a lot of stuff came aboard, among other things, some hams and what was said to be a ten-gallon keg of molasses. The captain asked us if we were satisfied now, and as we had no further objections to make, off we started, bound for Alexandria, Virginia.

Off Cape Antonio, we were chased all one afternoon by a suspicious looking craft which came out from the land, and which we took to be a pirate. She was a brigantine, that is, a square-rigged forward, with square main-topsail and topgallant sail, and fore-and-aft mainsail. If we changed our course, she changed hers, and she was evidently trying to come up with us, which we did not want her by any means to do. It had not been a great while since a Barrington vessel had been boarded right off Cape Antonio by pirates and the captain and most of the crew murdered. Just before dark a squall came down upon us, and night set in, and we got clear of her.

The voyage to Alexandria was the worst experience I ever had in the way of bad food, and that is saying much. The ten-gallon keg which was supposed to contain molasses turned out to be brandy, and the captain kept his skin full of it all the time. The cook opened a barrel of beef the morning after we sailed, but it was so rotten we could not stand the smell of it, and he headed it up again. He boiled a piece of the beef for dinner, however, but, hungry as we were, we threw it overboard untasted. The pork was a little better, although it was rancid and rusty. The only bread we had was hardtack which had been in the bread-locker two voyages, and it was black and hard and full of great fat weevils nearly as big as centipedes. The peas and beans were so hard that they would not make soup after being boiled all day long. Every other day we had a pound and a half of boiled pork divided among four of us, and a little bread and water, and on alternate days bread and water only. The cook parched and ground beans and gave us bean coffee without sweetening, and if we did not like that mess we could let it alone. In the cabin they had ham, tea and coffee with sugar, and other decent food.

After nineteen days we made Cape Henry, and stood up Chesapeake Bay. We were two days getting up to Point Lookout, and had gone but a few miles up the Potomac when, the breeze being light and ahead and the ebb tide running, we came to anchor to wait for the flood tide. When the tide slacked, the captain ordered us to heave up the anchor. We hove her short, and then we were so weak from starvation that we could not break the anchor out of the ground.

We slacked away the chain again, hoisted out the boat, and the captain took three of us ashore with him to get some provisions. He went off somewhere, and we knew that he did not mean to buy anything for us, so we determined to help ourselves. We raided a cornfield, pulled off our shirts, tied the sleeves around the collar, filled the shirts with ears of corn and brought them down to the boat. We met the captain waiting for us and went aboard the ship. The three shirts full of corn made two barrelsful. An oysterman came alongside, and we bought a barrel of oysters in the shell. The cook put the remaining piece of pork in the biggest kettle he had and as many ears of corn as it would hold. Then we gathered around the galley—eight all told— and as the corn got tender enough we fished it out and ate it with the raw oysters and slivers of boiled rusty pork. So we kept it going until the corn and oysters were entirely consumed. Oh, that was one grand revel of a feast. When it was over we tried the anchor again, got it in and proceeded up the river. Strange to say—or perhaps it is not strange—starved as we had been for weeks before, eating all that green corn and oysters had no ill effects upon any of us. It gave us all strength at the time, and did us no harm whatever.

In Alexandria we obtained new provisions and were better fed, and that particular grievance was a thing of the past. When we were ready for sea again, the captain came forward and made us quite a nice little speech. "Now men," he said, "I want you to come with me and finish bringing down the ship's stores, for we are not going to be short of anything this trip. And as it will be cold going to the northward—great change of climate between here and Nova Scotia—I will buy each of you three gallons of brandy and keep it in the cabin, and every time you reef topsails or shorten sail on the passage I'll give you a drink. No doubt we shall have a lot of reefing to do, and you know how cold it will be making the Nova Scotia coast."

He asked each of us in turn if we would agree to that. All the others said, yes, they were agreed. When he asked me, I said, "No sir; I never drink liquor for the good it does me."

"Then I'll see," said the captain, "that you don't have any."

"All right, Sir," I replied, "and I'll see that I don't pay for any."

He was hopping mad about it, but to no use. We brought the stores aboard, including the three gallons of brandy apiece for all hands but myself, and started down the river.

We had succeeded so well on the trip up the Potomac in our venture ashore, that we thought the trick worth trying on the way down. So one night the mate took two of us ashore and we went into a peach orchard. We had no more than set to work gathering peaches, when a charge of shot came *bang* right in amongst us—some one was there with a gun shooting at us. It scared us all so that we dropped everything and ran as hard as we could for the boat. Luckily, whoever it was did not chase us or set any dogs on us, and we got safely aboard again without either the fruit we went for or the bags we took to put it in.

After passing Cape Henry, we had strong northerly gales for several days, so the chance was presented for the men to call on the captain for their drink of brandy as per agreement. Six times they sent the steward for it, and as often they had a glass all round. The morning of the third day at sea, at four o'clock, in a stiff northeast gale, we two-reefed the sails, and when we came down we were cold and wet with rain and salt water. The other men tried to rally me for not being on the same lay with them in respect to the grog but they got very little fun out of it, and the laugh was soon on them. They sent old Abe, the cook, as usual, to bring them their nip, but he came back with the report, "The cap'n say they ain't no more; he say you done drinked it all up." The men were struck aback for a moment, and before they had thoroughly taken the bearings of old Abe's remarks, the captain, thinking probably they would not be satisfied with the cook's explanation, came on deck himself to see how they took it. They told him there must certainly be more than six drinks in three gallons of brandy; but he pitched into them—at that early hour he was comparatively sober himself—

threatening, cursing and declaring that they had drunk it all and would get no more.

We all hands left the ship as soon as she was made fast to the wharf in Halifax. When the other men went to Mr. Hamilton's office to be paid off, they told him about the brandy and molasses business. I met them afterwards, and they wanted me to tell the same story, but I made no promises. The next day I went to the owner's office for my wages, and found that the captain had me charged with three gallons of brandy. That was more than I could allow to stand to my account, and I told Mr. Hamilton that I had neither bought nor received any brandy during the voyage. We had no dispute about the matter at all; he paid me in full, and I gave him a receipt.

He seemed to want to enter into a conversation with me, and started it by asking what kind of a crew we had. I evaded a direct answer, as I did not like them and did not want to tell him so. He then asked me what kind of a man the captain was. I told him I did not like the captain, but that was no reason why he was not a good man. Next he tried to pump me about the brandy and molasses, and about the squall in Jamaica when we carried away the jibboom; but I told him that Mr. Bell, the mate, would give him full particulars about the whole voyage, that we had worked hard and lived hard, and now that I had my wages I was done with any concern about ship, captain or crew. During the talk Mr. Hamilton said he was going to make the captain pay for the brandy he had bought for the men in Alexandria and turn him out of the ship. I made no comment, though both suggestions met my approval, the one as an act of justice towards the men who had been so barefacedly taken in, and the other as decidedly for the owner's interest.

That evening I fell in with the captain on the street. He was in a great rage over what the crew had told Mr. Hamilton about him, and asked me what I had said. I told him that since I could say nothing in his favor I had said no harm, but for all that, as far as I could judge, his reputation with the owner tallied very well with what I knew of his principles; that I was very glad to be rid of him, and hoped I should never see him again.

— CHAPTER VII —

THE *THOMAS EDWARDS*

August 1843 to December 1844

O N ARRIVING IN HALIFAX I HEARD OF NEHEMIAH'S DEATH. About a week later the *Brisk* came in from the West Indies, and it was my hard duty to go aboard and tell my brother Martin of our loss. He advised me, as father and mother were all alone, to go home and stay with them until the following spring; which accordingly I did, for that purpose taking passage with Captain Jesse Smith, in the old *Teazer*, for Barrington. After a voyage of four days, prudently seeking a harbor every night, we reached home safely on August 31st.

I need not dwell upon the scenes attending my first days at home. My parents' grief over their great loss was keen and fresh, and wherever I turned I met with something to remind me of former happy associations that could never be renewed. How glad my dog Sailor was to see me! But old Jack, Nehemiah's dog, that had been to sea with him and loved him with a dog's devotion, was without a master, and his sense of bereavement was most pathetic. Poor old Sailor soon came to a tragic end. He was unjustly suspected of sheep killing, and the owner of the sheep, a man who had never been a boy, shot him. Jack's character was above suspicion, and he lived for many years, the family being much attached to him.

After the fall's work was done about the place, I made several visits around among the scattered members of the family, at Wood's Harbor, Shag Harbor and Cape Island. During leisure intervals at home, I fitted up for my young friend William Robertson a toy boat, about two feet long, which a sea captain had made and rigged for him, but which, like most other boy's possessions, had become dismantled. I rigged her as a brig, with fore and main royals, and everything complete, tops, caps, deadeyes, wheel and steering gear, chains and sails.

On November 20th, the brig *Thomas Edwards*, Captain Keith, arrived in Barrington from the West Indies. She was a pretty hard-looking craft. She had been cast away some time before, and the Robertsons had bought her as a wreck and fitted her up for sea; and after every voyage she needed as much overhauling as though she had been wrecked all over again. This trip was no exception, and operations were commenced.

Early in January, 1844, I went to Little River, in Yarmouth County, and spent about a month among relatives living there. While in Little River, I contracted a warm attachment for a handsome young girl, a daughter of one of my cousins. We never came to any hard and fast understanding and agreement, but I was certainly very much interested. A few weeks after returning home, therefore, I found myself thinking that another journey in that direction would be agreeable.

In company with my nephew, William Doane, who had left the *Thomas Edwards* when she was laid up, I walked to Yarmouth, via Wood's Harbor, to look for a berth. Little River was not much out of our course, and I found good anchorage there for a night at my uncle's house, where the interesting person before referred to was staying. Our errand to Yarmouth proving fruitless, we came back as far as Chebogue, where we stopped over night, setting out for home at six o'clock next morning. At Salmon River we were overtaken by Tommy Robertson, on horseback, bound for Barrington. In addition to his horse, he was furnished forth with a paper bag full of lozenges, for a lady friend, in one pocket, and a bottle full of "cure for all care", for himself and any old friend, in the other. We kept company, on the ride and tie principle, all day, during the course of which, in some way, the bag became torn and the lozenges strewn along the road for a mile or more. The bottle we set on top of a rock in Oak Park, and threw stones at it. Was it full then? Well, it was a good many years ago, and the whole truth about it need not now be told.

Two days after getting back from Yarmouth, I went to work on the old *Thomas Edwards*, helping to fit her ready for sea, and on March 20th, 1844 sailed in her for Halifax. Captain John Kendrick was master, and Bartlett

England, Ireland and Wales

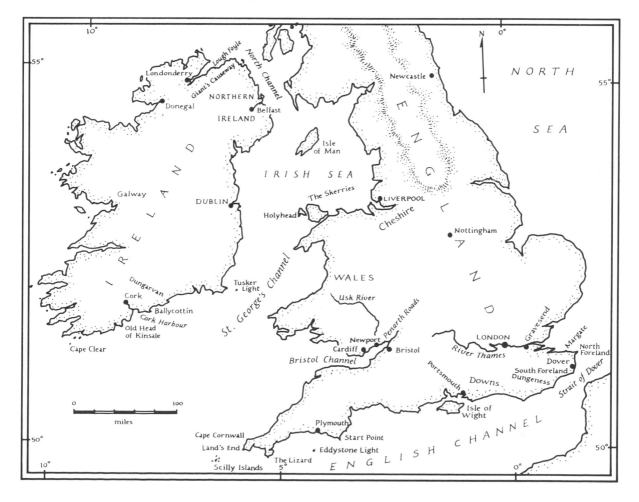

Covil, mate. John Cunningham, Gamaliel Banks, William Doane and I were before the mast. The cook was a son of Barzillai Hopkins. In Halifax, the captain obtained a charter to go to Cork, Ireland, for orders with a load of deals. As the brig had no charter when we left home, we had not signed articles, and were free to leave her if we wished. John Cunningham obtained a berth in Captain Darby's government cutter at three dollars more a month than he would get staying by the brig. William Doane had had enough of the *Thomas Edwards* anyway, so he took passage on a vessel to Boston and shipped out of that port. Seth Crowell, another Barrington boy, son of Ansel Crowell—or "Anty," as he was called, to distinguish him from another Ansel Crowell who was known as "Tack"—shipped for the voyage, but before we were ready for sea he ran away. Gamaliel Banks and I stayed with the brig, and two English apprentice boys, whose ship had been sunk in the ice going to Quebec, worked their passage with us.

We took in our cargo at Richmond up the harbor above Halifax. When the captain considered the vessel loaded, we came down and anchored off the town, ready to sail when cleared at the Customs House. In taking the charter, however, the captain had represented that the ship would carry a certain quantity more than we had on board, and the owner of the cargo insisted upon putting the whole of it on her. There seemed to be no getting out of it, so we rafted down a lot of timber and took on an enormous deckload, piled as high as the upper deadeyes and from windlass to taffrail.

On April 4th, we got under way and proceeded to sea, the wind fair and fresh to the westward. A few days out on our passage we encountered great numbers of icebergs. One evening at sunset we saw five at once ahead of us. Soon after it shut down thick fog with a fresh breeze and we took in light sails. At ten o'clock that night we passed within fifteen yards of a small iceberg, and the captain then thought it was time to lay to. We hauled aback and kept a man on lookout until the middle of the next forenoon, when the weather cleared and we kept off on our course. But bad weather was not absent from us long at a time, and, the decks being almost constantly full of water, we hove overboard about half the deckload to ease the ship.

On the passage I suffered intensely from toothache, and on the suggestion of someone that smoking would cure it, I borrowed a shipmate's pipe and tobacco, and began the habit which, except for a slight interval, I have devotedly followed ever since.

Twenty-five days after leaving Halifax we made Cape Clear and took on board a man from a fishing smack for a pilot. The next morning we saw Cork lighthouse; a pilot came aboard, bringing a letter for the captain, and we ran in and anchored in Cork harbor. I need give no description of Cork. Those anxious to know something about the place should apply to the numerous natives of that city who are to be found in every country.

The captain having received orders to go to Londonderry to discharge cargo, we filled our water casks and, late in the afternoon of May 4th, the pilot came aboard and we proceeded down the harbor, making sail as we went. The pilot's crew were drunk and looking for trouble, but they found that Nova Scotia sailors sober were just as fond of a fight as so many drunken Corkonians. After we got outside, the captain gave the pilot an order on his agent in Cork for the pilotage fee, and we hauled aback for him to leave. He

and his men, however, wanted the captain to make them a present, not only of money, but of provisions, which the captain refused to do, and they started to make a row. It was about eight o'clock in the evening and almost dark when the fuss began. The mate had sent me aloft to loose the gaff topsail, and while I was about it, words and gestures between the captain and the pilots waxed steadily higher and more expressive. At last I heard them threaten that they would take the ship back into Cork, and the pilot gave the order to brace the yards around. The captain immediately shouted, "Hold on those braces."

The foretopsail and topgallant braces led down through two blocks under the head of the mainmast. As soon as I heard the contrary orders on deck, I took the gaff-topsail gasket, jumped down, unseen in the darkness, on the crosstrees, and racked the topsail and topgallant braces, and then came down on deck. Our crew obeyed the captain's orders, and the pilot's men undertook to execute the orders given by him, and there was a lively scrimmage. The Irish at last obtained a temporary advantage; one of their men let go the weather braces, and those on the other side began to haul. They pulled and hauled and tugged away, but there was no budge to the braces. There the brig lay, drifting right off, and what was the matter nobody knew. Finding they could not brace the yards around, they changed their tune. "Let the old hooker go," they said, "and may she sink before she gets to Derry!" They got into their boat and pulled ashore, pouring out upon us as long as they were within hearing a choice assortment of the most lurid left-handed blessings.

As soon as they were over the side, the captain gave the order to brace forward the yards and fill away. The men went to the lee braces and began to haul, but of course could not move them until I had gone aloft again and taken the racking off. The old brig filled away then in short order; I loosed the gaff-topsail and came down on deck; we set the royals, boarded the fore tack, and let her go up St. George's Channel.

A two days' sail brought us around the north end of Ireland, past the bluish columns of the Giants' Causeway, and up Lough Foyle to Londonderry, the city of the great siege. I enjoyed many long walks upon its famous walls, which are wide enough for two coaches to pass, and out into country among the farms. At one farm house which I visited I saw a hog that was bigger than I had believed a hog could ever be. A gentleman who had a

Londonderry, Ireland, about 1835

large estate near the city—whether he was a duke or an earl, I did not know—bought a pair of moose antlers from me that I had brought from home, and put them over the gate at the entrance to his grounds.

From Londonderry we took a cargo of potatoes to Liverpool, England, where we arrived on May 24th, anchoring in the Mersey off the Salthouse Dock, and towards night hauled in to Canning Dock. Here everything looked to me wonderful and strange. The size of things impressed me. Instead of being at a little narrow wharf, rising and falling with the tide, we were enclosed by granite walls, and the water was always the same height. We were not allowed to have fires or keep a light burning on board in the dock, so the captain found us a boardinghouse where we took our meals. After discharging cargo all day, we had to stand watch at night; and if the dock police caught anyone asleep on his watch, he was fined five pounds sterling—an expense, however, to which none of us was put.

Daylight lasted until half-past nine, and in the evenings when off duty I sometimes went over to Cheshire and walked about the beautiful country, which hundreds of years ago was the home of my forefathers, and where the name Doane is still to be met with. One Sunday afternoon I went to look at Albert Dock, which was then just commenced. The next day we were busy aboard ship as usual, but all Liverpool had a holiday. Bells were ringing and chiming all day long, and I learned in the evening that the King of Belgium and Prince Albert had been in Liverpool at the laying of the first stone of Albert Dock, and the peal of bells had been in their honor and to celebrate the event.

On June 14th we sailed for Halifax, heavily loaded with salt, and as the wind was southerly, we went "north about," that is, around the north end of Ireland. After getting clear of the land, we took a strong west northwest gale with a heavy sea, which lasted for six days, during which time we remained on the starboard tack to the southward. We had a flush deck, no topgallant forecastle; we were deep loaded, and the sea made a clean breach over us, so that the man at the wheel was as wet as the man on lookout. We were soaking wet all the time, though, standing to the southward so long, the water gradually became warmer. The entrance to the forecastle was forward of the windlass, and the companionway was constantly closed to keep out the green sea. The forecastle leaked badly anyway, and everything in it became wet and mouldy, even our pillows became coated with a clammy blue mould, except where our heads—what chance we had—kept it worn off. Our bedclothes, besides, were wringing wet, and we went to bed wet and got up steaming. The decks and lee bulwarks, being submerged so long, became covered with slime, like a plank that had been drifting about in the ocean, and it was almost impossible to stand on the slippery deck.

We tacked ship to the northward on June 27th, 1844, with a fine breeze from the southwest. The sea went down very fast, and we set to work drying our clothes, and with scrapers, squeegees and brooms, cleaning the slime off the decks. But good weather of any duration was not to be had. All the bad winds were out of the bag at once and the good ones securely tied up in it, and we had nothing but a succession of gales all the way to Halifax. While we were hove to in a gale of wind, a heavy sea boarded us and stove in the forecastle, smashing the companionway and hatch utterly, like stepping on an old hat, and the whole forecastle was filled with water. We nailed it up and battened a studding sail over it, and then we had nowhere to sleep but on the cabin floor. Now a sailor's bunk would never be called a flowery bed of ease, but such as it is, he prefers it to none at all. The forecastle is the sailor's home, out of sight and hearing of the afterguard; and in the cabin we felt out of place, apart from the discomfort of sleeping on the deck and having no clothes to change off wet for dry. Our bulwarks were all gone long before we made port, and when, on July 21st, we came in to Halifax, we looked like a wreck.

I stayed by the brig a few days after arrival, shoveling salt down in the hold; but the mate seeming to enjoy the joke of dropping the tub, as it came down empty, on my head, we had a little exchange of repartee one morning before breakfast, which it took the captain's interference to put a stop to, and I left on the spot. In the evening I came back for my wages and clothes, and the captain asked me to go in the vessel again. I declined his offer, however,

Prince Albert's steam tender *Fairy* entering Canning Dock, Liverpool, in 1846

out of respect to the mate, and began to look for another ship. But Halifax just then seemed to be the only place in the world that was finished and needed nothing more done. One day I fell in with my nephew, Thomas Knowles, who had just come from Barrington, looking for employment; and together we made the rounds, up and down the whole length of the city, into all the shipowners' offices and on board most of the vessels at the wharves. They all told the same story, that they would need men as soon as they had something for their vessels to do.

A month of such monotony had passed when I met Captain Kendrick again. He informed me that he had a new mate, Mr. Richard Knowles, and asked me to go with him again in the brig. I told him that if he had a better ship I would sail with him all over the world, but the old *Tom Ed* would be my last choice, and if I could get any other vessel I would not go in her. Meantime the *Brisk* arrived in Halifax, and my brother persuaded me to go again with Captain Kendrick. Accordingly, I signed articles with him for a voyage on the *Tom Ed* to Antigua, St. Thomas, Ponce, Puerto Rico, and back to Halifax. Being in for it myself, I then coaxed Tommy Knowles to go with us, on the principle that misery likes company.

Our passage south was uneventful. In St. Thomas, the captain bought on speculation fifteen demijohns of gin. It came aboard in the last boat, and it then developed that we had *sixteen* demijohns. The captain said, "Well, men, since we have one over, you can have that to drink on the way home"— little thinking we should soon stand so much in need of it.

Cargo was very scarce in Ponce, and after waiting a long time for sugar droghers from down the coast, we only got about sixty hogsheads of sugar and a few puncheons of molasses, and this with ten tons of logwood was substantially all the cargo we could procure.

We left Ponce homeward bound on November 7th, 1844, going through Mona Passage. Nothing of note occurred until the 17th, when, with a big sea heaving from the west, the ship took a heavy roll, the mainsail slatted, and the head of the mainmast carried away in the hounds. Repairing this damage, which involved the sending down of the main-topmast, was a very difficult job, on account of the rolling of the ship. When everything was to rights again, the captain gave us all a drink of gin, which made us feel much better.

We were now somewhat lame in our spars, and obliged to carry sail carefully; but the old brig was still to take us through a worse experience than any we had yet seen. The morning of the November 22nd commenced with violent northeast gales and dark thick weather. We hove to under balanced mainsail. That split, and we unbent the fore spencer and set it for a storm mainsail. The mate and I then went aloft and sent down the foreroyal and topgallant yards and topgallant mast. While we were sending down the topgallant yard, the ship took a very heavy roll, so that her foreyard dipped into the water. As she rolled down, something jarred and the ship trembled. My thought was that the foremast was unstepped, but no immediate consequence was apparent, and we finished sending down the spars.

The captain was at the wheel all the time, and as we were lashing the spars on deck he sang out to us suddenly to get a hold of something. I grabbed the weather main rigging and hung on. Tom Knowles was to leeward of me, clearing up the decks, and had no chance to catch hold of anything. The sea boarded us, and he was washed overboard. As he was going, instinctively, of course, he threw out his hands. The peak halliards had swung away out to leeward, and he felt them touch him as he was borne along in the water. He clutched them with all his might, and as the wave receded he swung inboard by the halliards and landed safely back again on deck! The ship was hove on her beam ends, the forecastle was smashed down flat and filled with water, the galley was washed overboard and the stove knocked to pieces. At the same time there was a big rumble and shaking up sound in the hold, and we knew that the cargo had shifted.

The way of it had been this: the jar that I had felt when aloft was the breaking away of some molasses barrels in the wing, which rolled across on top of the other cargo and knocked down the toms or stanchions that held in position the big casks and puncheons. The very next heavy roll that the ship made, when we were on deck lashing the spars, the sugar shifted and pitched into the lee wing. One cask happened to go between the cabin bulkhead and the pump, and as there was not room for it to pass, it burst in the bulkhead. So that while Tom was picking himself up after his trip overboard, the cook came to the companionway and reported to the captain, "There's a hogshead of sugar, sir, come into the cabin."

The captain tried by wearing around and coming on the other tack to right the ship, but the attempt was not a success. The cargo being shifted all into one wing still held us on our beam ends, only instead of being heeled over to leeward, the sea now came tumbling in on deck, and to keep from foundering, we had to wear around again.

As soon as possible, we battened the forecastle down solid with boards and an old sail, and then went into the cabin, where we found that the hogshead of sugar had made a bigger doorway into the hold than was wanted. The captain and cook remained on deck to look after things there, and the rest of us took lanterns into the hold to see what we could do to right the ship up. Some of the casks were stoved in and the sugar scattered all around. Others had their heads knocked out and were empty, and with every roll of the ship they dashed from side to side. There by the dim light of the lanterns, it was difficult enough to dodge the flying casks; but sometimes the lights went out, and there were many narrow escapes.

We first pitched all the logwood that we could get hold of into the weather wing and down in the bottom of the ship. On that we spread an old topsail and shovelled the loose sugar upon it. Then we tried to roll to windward such of the hogsheads as we could move at all. It was slow, hard and dangerous work, but we worked with a will for our lives depended on it. Many times, just as we had succeeded in getting a cask in position, before we could secure it a heavy sea would heel us over, and away the cask would go dancing smash bang to leeward. Then it was tackle it and get it up again, one man standing by with a tom to try to keep it in its place and stanchion it down. The empty casks we put securely in position, shovelled the sugar back into them and headed them up.

So we worked all the afternoon and through the night, and for the next two days. Not until November 25th did the wind or sea show any signs of abating. Every once in a while we would hear the sea board us, "souze,

souze," and wonder whether the captain and cook had been washed overboard. We would listen anxiously, and presently the captain would put his head down the scuttle and shout, "All right on deck." How good his voice sounded! When we were too sleepy to work any longer, we crawled out of the way of any loose casks and took a nap, and then turned to again. The galley being gone and the stove with it, no cooking could be done. While in Londonderry, the captain had bought a couple of barrels of clear sheer Irish pork, about eight inches thick with no lean on it; and as under ordinary conditions the sailors would not eat it, it was still in the storeroom. When we wanted anything to eat, we cut a slice or two of this raw fat pork and ate it with hard bread, sugar and a pannikin of gin. So that not only the extra demijohn, but several of the fifteen others of the captain's gin came in first rate play. At first, with the rolling and tossing of the ship, after drinking half a pint of gin, it was pretty hard to keep our feet, but in two or three days we could drink a whole pannikin full without it fetching us the least bit down by the head.

After making everything secure in the hold, our trouble was not over. As we were going northward, the weather was rapidly growing colder, changing in a few days from warm enough to go without coat or jacket to such cold that the water froze as fast as it flew on board. The forecastle being battened down, we could not get any change of clothes, and we had either to sleep on the cabin floor or in the storeroom across the heads of the barrels. It was about even-steven which we chose. The storeroom was the warmer of the two, and we spread what bedclothes the captain and mate could spare us on the ends of the barrels and lay down. In a very little while we could feel every chine in our ribs, and when we fell asleep from exhaustion, if we turned over we would waken with a cry of pain. When our sides were too sore to stand the barrel heads, we tried the cabin floor for a change. Lying down there between the chests, with our wet clothes on, we became so numb with cold that, when we got up, we hardly knew our own feet from anybody else's.

Imagine, under those circumstances, being roused up in a hurry to go on the topsail yard and reef in a gale of wind, when the ropes were as big as a man's leg with ice, or to take a trick at the helm and stand still for two hours in a regular built northeast snowstorm. The choice was mighty little between watch on deck and watch below. The cook's occupation being gone for lack of a stove, I think we must all have perished with cold had it not been for the quantities of fat pork and gin which we consumed.

Long before reaching Halifax, I had been certain that it was my last voyage in the *Tom Ed*, the only grave doubt being whether the end of it for all of us would not come before we could make port. We were, therefore, fit to receive anybody's congratulations on our safe arrival when, on December 17th, we came to anchor off Commercial Wharf. I did not leave the ship immediately, but stayed and helped discharge the cargo and strip the vessel for another overhauling. Then, learning that a schooner belonging to Yarmouth was about to leave for that port, I told Captain Kendrick that I must go home. We parted with regret; I was sorry to leave him, for I liked him immensely. As I was about to go ashore he said, "Well, Ben, if you won't go with me any longer, you certainly won't refuse to come down tonight and help me take what is left of that gin ashore?" That I readily agreed to, and ten demijohns safely crossed the Rubicon that evening—and no questions asked. The other six had been consumed by the crew on the voyage, which naturally knocked all profit out of the captain's venture in gin. But Captain Kendrick was gentleman enough to stand the loss without attempting to charge it up against his sailors; in that respect appearing in striking contrast to the captain of the *Reindeer*, who would have had his men pay for the brandy which he drank himself. That, however, is but one point, and by no means the measure of difference between the two.

— CHAPTER VIII —

PREPARATORY TO A LONG VOYAGE

January 6th to July 12th, 1845

Whaling barque
Margaret Rait of Saint
John, New Brunswick

*T*HE VESSEL IN WHICH I LEFT HALIFAX PUT INTO SHELBURNE for a harbor on January 6th and at my request, I was set ashore on the western side of the harbor, and took my land tacks for home, leaving chest and clothes to come by the vessel when the weather would permit. The remainder of the winter I spent after the usual fashion, gunning for birds in the woods and on the shore, and enjoying the social life of the place. In Little River, where I passed considerable time, "sleighing the dears," and fox hunting with the young men were the principal amusements.

In February a vessel was cast away on Cape Sable, and the materials saved from her were sold at auction on March 15th. Among those who attended the auction was Captain James D. Coffin, to whom I was introduced that day. He had lately arrived home from a four years' whaling voyage in the bark *Margaret Rait*, and was having a new ship, the *Athol*, built in Saint John, in which he would make another long cruise to the South Seas. Captain Coffin talked whaling to me, being thereto assisted by Captain Solomon Kendrick, with whom I had already made an eventful though profitless whaling trip to the Labrador. So far, in my West Indies voyages, the lines had not altogether fallen in pleasant places; the great change of climate, especially in the winter, was so sudden that it made men old in a few years, and anything seemed better than continuing in that trade. The adventurous element appealed strongly to me also; and being easily persuaded myself, I prevailed upon my father and mother to consent to my going whaling with Captain Coffin.

The *Athol* was to be ready about the middle of April and the intervening time I spent paying last visits to friends around the shores, not forgetting to stop and obtain the consent of one young lady in Little River, or rather, to tell her that I was going, as my mind was already made up. Without doing a great deal to earn it, I had the reputation among the girls at home of being something of a tease, and consequently was not very much in their favor; but when they heard I was going away on a four years' cruise to the other side of the world, they seemed to look on me with more feeling than usual, and as the time to leave home drew near, when I met them around at their little parties, they would smile and wish me good fortune, and some of them, under their breaths, perhaps, "God Speed Away," but they always ended with "safe return home," whether they meant it or not. However, I took it all as it was said and gave smile for smile.

At home, mother sat knitting and though she said little, I knew that her chief thoughts and all her hopes and fears were for me. Three of her sons had gone away to sea, never to return in life. Now I, her youngest, was about to go on such a long and dangerous voyage, and she was old, and feared she would never see me again. Dear, sweet mother! What prayers she has mingled with her tears for me! The religion which sustained and comforted her is now to the satisfaction of many largely explained away; but not the most learned and pious explanation can ever make me doubt that a mother's prayers are really heard and answered by the Ruler of the Universe.

At five o'clock in the morning of April 20th, I was called by my mother saying that two men and a boat were waiting at the marsh bank to take me on board the schooner *Bride*, Captain Coleman Crowell, which lay in the Back-of-the-Island Channel with her sails all hoisted, ready to leave for Saint

John, and in which I had engaged a passage. I did not wait for breakfast at home, but left the house as soon as I was dressed. I bade my father and sister good-bye without any show of feeling; but when I kissed my mother, my heart was full, and I could say nothing.

Before I got to the road, I heard my sister calling, saying that I had forgotten something. It was a package of carpenter tools, a present from Robert Robertson, and some writing material, the gift of his brother Tommy. I kept right along; I could not look back. Soon I heard her running after me, and as she came nearer I could hear that she was crying. I put my hand behind me and took the package from her without turning round or stopping and went on to the boat and aboard the vessel. There I met Captain Coffin, who was also on his way to Saint John to join the whale ship. He shook hands with me, but my feelings were such that I could not talk with him. I had never felt so about leaving home and going away to sea before.

Captain James Doane Coffin (1814-1885)

As the day wore on and the familiar marks of my native shores were left behind, I became more cheerful. After passing Cape Fourchu at noon of the next day, the weather began to look stormy. About eight o'clock in the evening, as we were going into Grand Passage, a shortcut into the Bay of Fundy, between Brier and Long Islands, on the north side of St Mary's Bay, there came on a thick snowstorm, and we ran into a schooner at anchor and carried away our headstays. We let go the anchor, but dragged ashore; so we let her lie for the night. At four o'clock in the morning the schooner was afloat, and the mate and I went ashore for a pilot. The snow was still coming down thick, but we got underway and made one tack. The second time she miss-stayed and fetched up high and dry on Brier Island at high water. There she lay for three days. We tried to dig her out, but all efforts to get her off proved vain.

On April 25th, a little shallop belonging in the vicinity where we were stranded being about to sail for Saint John, Captain Coffin and I took passage in her. The day was clear, but in the loud rote of the surf there was a warning that the weather was not yet settled. When we had gone about seven miles up the coast, we saw a large ship ashore. They made signals to us, and we ran in and anchored abreast the wreck. She proved to be a ship belonging to and bound for Saint John, from Liverpool, Great Britain, and had on board the copper and other fittings for the *Athol*. She had gone ashore in the same snowstorm that piled us up on Brier Island, and was now a complete wreck, lying broadside on and rolling with every sea. Her decks would go under on one side, and then the sea would strike her and roll her over inshore on her bilge, the rocks grinding her up like a mill. There was a great surf on the shore, which is lined with high cliffs in that locality, and it was a ticklish matter to land at such a time in a small boat. However, we put out and ran our boat into a little nook that made into the cliff, where we bore her off with boat hooks, and took off four men—the captain and three others belonging to the wreck—who wanted to go to Saint John.

After getting under way again, we had not proceeded far when the wind hauled to the north northeast, and it looked so stormy that our skipper thought best to put back for Grand Passage. So we bore up and ran back, and came to anchor about eight o'clock, right where we had started from in the morning, a couple of hundred yards from the old *Bride*, which was still

Saint John Harbor about 1827

ashore. They got the *Bride* off, however, that night without damage; and in the morning we sailed in company for Saint John, were we arrived that afternoon without further accident.

The *Athol* had been launched and was lying at a dock, with only her lower masts in, and no rigging on her at all, when we arrived. Noble Reddock, ship joiner, was putting in her woodwork, and the firm of Dickson & Pitman were engaged on the rigging. I went to board at first in Portland village, with a Mrs. Crawford, close by Portland Church. I had not been in Saint John many days when I met two cousins, sea captains, who were living there—Simeon and Joseph Kenney. The latter had been mate with Captain Coffin in the *Margaret Rait*, and was now awaiting the arrival of the whaleship *James Stewart*, of which he was to be master on her next voyage. Captain Simeon's wife, Olive Doane, was also a relative and an old friend from Little River, Nova Scotia. I was very glad, therefore, about a month later, to change my boarding place to their house, which continued to be my home during my stay in Saint John. Captain Simeon soon after sailed for London in the bark *Charlotte*, taking his son Thomas with him.

Not to be idle while waiting for the *Athol* to get ready for sea, I obtained employment for a time with Mr. Reddock on the *Athol's* carpenter work. About the time that job was finished, the *James Stewart*, on June 3rd, announced her arrival by the firing of cannon off the mouth of the harbor; and I was employed by a Captain Quick (at two dollars and a half a tide) to go in a tugboat with him and others, including five riggermen, down below Partridge Island and tow the whaleship up to town. I then worked on the *James Stewart* about three weeks, unloading and stripping her, and hauling her on the ways to be repaired. Having finished with her, I was employed for a month or more by Dickson & Pitman on board the *Athol* and in the rigging aloft.

It was an unlucky move for me that I ever set foot in Portland. In those days, the only way to town from there was over the bridge and through York Point, unless one went away around by Chipman's Hill, which was miles farther. The York Point population was largely Irish, mostly of two classes, Orangemen and Ribbon Men. Every St. Patrick's Day and July 12th, these two opposing societies had their respective parades, which always ended in a big fight; and on any holiday there was sure to be more or less disturbance between them. Of course, I, being a stranger in Saint John, knew nothing about the affairs of either faction.

Soon after going to board in Portland, a man whose acquaintance I had made presented me with an old sword cane, which had evidently seen very hard usage. The blade and handle were in good condition, but the cane itself, or sheath, was so badly split as to be useless. I tied it up securely, intending after getting to sea to make a new cane for it.

On Friday evening, May 23rd, I left the house after supper, to go on board the *Athol*, taking the cane with me for the purpose of leaving it there for safekeeping. It was a rainy evening and almost dark when I crossed Portland Bridge, with the cane under my arm, and passed on the other side several young men sitting down. As I walked by, one of them said, "Hello, where did you get that cane?" Another said, "Say, where are you going with that cane?" And a third said, "Hey, come back here with that cane." I walked on, not saying a word, with the cane still under my arm. Presently I heard someone coming up quickly behind me, and then whoever it was grabbed the end of the cane.

I caught it by the handle and, wheeling round, tried to pull it away from him. The blade came partly out, seeing which, my opponent gave it a twist to prevent his having the stick and me the blade. We had a little tussle at arm's length, one trying to take the cane away from the other. At last I thought, "Well, I'm enough for you at a clinch; I don't know whether I shall be at a stand-off or not." So I grabbed him, and we began to wrestle. In a minute or two, I had him in a good position, with my knee behind him, and gave him a throw backwards. But we were so near to the front of a building that as he went he struck against the side of the house and was able to recover himself. He came at me again, and as he did so, he yelled for help. In response, out came a big Irishman from a cellar close by, and without a word to either of us, he struck me full with his right hand under the jaw, and the first thing I knew I was getting up in the middle of the street, both knees of my trousers torn across from seam to seam, and two men were standing over me, beating me with their fists.

Where the cane was then I do not know and made no effort to find out, for being outclassed in size and numbers, I thought it was time to show them my sailing qualities. They chased me a little ways, but I do not, therefore, take any credit for making them run. I ran, however, a good while longer than there was any call for, not stopping till I was aboard the *Athol* where I stayed for a while, talking the matter over with the shipkeeper.

My jaw kept swelling and paining me more and more, and about ten o'clock I started back for my boarding house. I walked along through York Point and down the hill to within a hundred yards of where I had been assaulted, when I saw a number of people standing about in the street ahead of me, and two men came out from them as if to meet me. I crossed the street; they passed by on the opposite side and then crossed and followed up behind me. I crossed over again and walked back to where a brick building had been torn down, and filled my pockets with broken bricks, thinking they would be useful in helping me across the bridge, once over which I should have no difficulty in getting the rest of the way home. When I came again, however, to the spot where I had turned back, the street was full of people talking excitely. This startled me so that I got out of the neighborhood as quietly as possible, though not so quickly as on the previous occasion. I went down aboard the *Athol* again, and lay on the bare bunk boards all night.

The next day, May 24th, the Queen's Birthday, was a holiday which Mr. Reddock, for whom I had been working, duly observed. I went home in the morning, but my jaw was so sore that I could not eat any breakfast, and for nearly a month afterwards I had to live on soups and other "spoon victuals."

I never found out who it was that hit me; but of the one that first attacked me and grabbed the sword cane, we shall hear again. I was told after this thing happened that the cane had belonged to an Orangeman and had been captured by one party from the other perhaps half a dozen times, and that many a bloody row had taken place to recover its possession. Be that as it may, the mere sight of it that night was enough to start the York Pointers up to make trouble; and the whole colony of them seemed to be stirring

Partridge Island about 1840

about it all night. It will be remembered that this was the year of the Potato Famine in Ireland; that the Irish feeling against England was at the time very bitter; that there were constant rumors of midnight drilling of Ribbon Men; and that three years later, the trouble culminated in the Rebellion of '48. It is, therefore, quite supposable that on this 23rd of May, the eve of a national holiday, when I wandered through York Point, I either disturbed some gathering of Irish Revolutionists, or aroused their suspicions, which were not allayed when they found I had a swordcane in my possession; and that my second appearance later in the night called them out in force to resist any invasion which they may have suspected was intended upon their preserves.

On July 10th we finished rigging the *Athol* and took her down to Partridge Island, where she remained at anchor until the 12th. The intervening day I spent very happily with my cousin Mrs. Kenney, her eldest daughter, and another young lady, on a picnic to Indian Town, reaching home again about eight o'clock. In the evening I went with the young ladies over to Reed's Point, where in the bright moonlight we could see the Athol off at anchor, as beautiful a ship as lay in the harbor. She was to be my floating home for years to come. What strange lands she would bear me to; what dangers I should meet. With perils and hardships of the sea I was familiar enough; but now must endure them, perhaps should be overcome by them, at the ends of the earth. Such gloomy thoughts I could not drive away, and undoubtedly they made me a very dull escort.

— CHAPTER IX —

THE CRUISE OF THE *ATHOL*

THE WESTERN ISLANDS

July 12th to September 7th, 1845

The ship *Athol*
engraved on a sperm
whale's tooth

ARLY IN THE MORNING OF SATURDAY, JULY 12TH I SENT MY CHEST
and clothes on board the *Athol*, returning to Mrs. Kenney's for dinner, and then went down to the wharf to see if we were to sail that day,
half hoping that the ship had gone and left me. I met the captain who said
we would sail at four o'clock; so I went back to the house and bade my friends
good-bye. Mrs. Kenney had been to sea on many voyages with her husband,
and as a sailor's wife, she understood my feelings on setting out on such a
voyage. Handing me a glass of wine, she took up another and said: "Cousin
Ben, before we say good-bye, I am sailor enough to take a parting glass with
you. May you have good health and fortune, and may we meet again."

Those few words, so sincerely spoken and showing such real interest and
friendship, cheered me wonderfully, and I went down to the ship as light-
hearted as I had ever been in my life. Late in the afternoon the captain came
on board with his wife and little daughter Esther, who were to go with us,
and at seven we were under way, a thick fog closing down upon us and
lasting until we were out of the Bay of Fundy.

The morning of the third day out, the fog lifted and we saw Seal Island
bearing east northeast, distant eight miles. The captain had left his case of
charts at home in Barrington, and being anxious to get them, he asked me if
I could pilot the ship down inside the islands and through Barrington West
Passage. I did not like to take the risk, so we kept on our course, bound for

the Western Islands or Azores, where we were to ship two more boat-steerers and part of our crew.

The officers of the ship were:

Captain, James Doane Coffin; mate, Joseph Taylor; second mate, Thomas Thomas; third mate Amzi Dauton; fourth mate, John Shields.

A young Scotchman named MacDonald, who had been studying medicine in Barrington under Dr. Geddes, was down on the articles as "Doctor." James Craft and I were boat-steerers, and had our quarters in the steerage. The carpenter and cooper also lived in the steerage with us. The carpenter was a Prince Edward Island Scotchman. The cooper was Patrick Shields, uncle to the fourth mate.

The crew were the usual nondescript lot always found on whaleships, composed of everything but sailors. Some of them had never been to sea before. One was an ex-college professor; another had been clerk in a bank. They had been ruined by drink. A third had been educated for the ministry, and owed his downfall to an affair such as Joseph was fortunate enough to escape from with Mrs. Potiphar. Those who had had previous experience on salt water were a riffraff of all nationalities and colors, most of whom had been whaling before.

Samuel Pinkham, of Barrington, was cabin boy. The cook was an old Negro, from New York, whom we called St. Jean d'Acre, because he claimed to have been with Admiral Sir Sidney Smith at that station in the operations of the British squadron against Bonaparte in 1799. He described with great circumstantiality a sortie at night made by the British sailors, in which he had participated, when they destroyed a mine which the French had dug under the walls of Acre. His yarns, if they did not always bear the earmarks of truth, at least showed a lively imagination—which latter faculty, I know, seafaring men are often accused of having highly developed. But in my experience I cannot say that I have been able to trust the word of landsmen in general any further than that of the run of sailormen.

From the captain down, none of us received any wages. We were all on shares, or lays, a loose-jointed sort of partnership. The owners paid for the victualling and disbursements of the ship. The oil that we should get was common stock, in which each had an interest according to the lay on which he was shipped and the quantity taken while he was on board. The captain had the twentieth lay. As he would be paid off last, if there was anything over, he would receive a share of that; thus he stood a chance on the settlement of the voyage, to get even as high as the twelfth. The mate had the thirtieth lay; the second mate, the fiftieth; the cooper and carpenter, each the seventy-fifth, and the men the one hundred and twenty-fifth. From each one's share deductions are made for the expense of loading and unloading, and a small percentage is also taken out for cooperage and gauging.

After getting clear of the coast, the regular routine duties on a whaleship were laid out and kept up. In the morning, as soon as it was "light enough to see a gray horse a mile off," lookouts were sent to the fore and mainmast heads; at eight o'clock, a third lookout went up the mizzenmast; and a constant watch was maintained till sunset. Being fitted out exclusively for sperm whaling, we had no crowsnests. The lookout went to the topgallant masthead and leaned over the royal yard, without shelter of any kind. Crowsnests were used only in the far north seas or high latitudes, where the men at the masthead needed shelter. The only ships that I ever saw fitted with crowsnests were several that had been right whaling away to the north of Kamschatka, in the Bering Sea. Boats were lowered every day and the lads exercised at the oars and trained in getting away and coming alongside. Irons, lances and spades were ground and fitted with poles and lines. Boat sails, masts and sprits were got ready; and the cooper was busy making piggins, tubs and kegs.

Besides the work of fitting out the boats to lower for whales, the *Athol* being a new ship, there was a great deal of other work, such as setting up the rigging, hitching and seizing off lanyards, squaring ratlines and innumerable other things. This class of work only a sailor can do, and there was not an "able seaman" in the forecastle. The officers themselves (other than the captain) knew next to nothing about seamanship or "sailorizing"; they were simply whalemen. The fourth mate could make a short splice and an eye splice, but a long splice was beyond him; and none of them knew how to put on a seizing or how the rigging should be turned. Consequently, as I had been doing this sort of work for the past six years, I now had all I could do superintending and teaching others; and what I did not know how to do, the captain himself had to come and show us.

While things were going on so, on Monday, July 28th, we saw a shoal of blackfish, a species of small whale. Look in the dictionary and you will find that the scientific people, who consider it indispensable for their purposes to give even the commonest creature a name composed of two long words in some dead language, call this harmless animal Globiocephalus svineval. We lowered three boats and gave chase. I steered the mate's or larboard boat; Craft, the second mate's or waist boat; and one of the sailors steered the third mate's or low boat. When we got up to them I put one iron into a big fellow, intending for safety to throw the second into the same one; but instead, another blackfish having popped up in the way, I struck him, and there we were bridled, fast to two at once. The mate and I changed places, he going forward to lance the blackfish, while I took the steering-oar. He had not been forward long when one of our team started to go one way and the other the other. That brought one of them abaft the boat, just clear of my steering-oar, doing his best to tow us stern first, while the other was towing ahead. We hauled line first on the one ahead, and the mate killed him with the lance; then we hauled in on the other and killed him.

Just as that operation was finished, another blackfish started up alongside the boat, and the mate darted his lance and killed him, without the formality of having him harpooned first. That made three for our boat, although we had been fast to only two. The other two boats got one apiece. The five blackfish made fifteen barrels of oil.

This is as good a place as any to explain that although all hands are entitled to share in the blackfish oil the same as in any other, as a general thing, none of it, except indirectly, ever benefits the crew. In the ports which the ship makes for the purpose of refitting, the blackfish oil is usually sold, as far as it will go, to pay the port charges and victualling bills; and as in that way better food is apt to be provided than if the owners were paying for it

Globiocephalus svineval *was the scientific name published by Gray in 1846 for the pilot whale in the western North Atlantic. It was changed to* Globicephala melaena *in 1898.*

themselves, there is no disposition on the part of the men to complain of this custom.

On Sunday, August 10th, we made Flores, one of the Western Islands, a mountain top rising out of the sea. On Monday we ran in close to the land, and the captain went ashore to buy potatoes and other vegetables. Not finding all he wanted, we went around into the bay on the north side of the island, where we anchored.

While ashore here, Craft and I took a long walk out, or rather up, into the country. Becoming thirsty, we stopped at a house and asked for water. We were handed cups of the native wine, which is the universal beverage of the people themselves, and which they offer as freely as water to the passing stranger. The wine of the island, of course, is of different grades, some more expensive than others; but a bottle of passably good sweet wine could be bought for two cents, and ten cents would buy a very fine quality indeed— pure grape juice, all of it.

In the doorways of the houses, women were spinning flax by hand. They had no wheel or other artificial contrivance but a spindle-shaped piece of hard polished wood, about nine or ten inches long, perhaps an inch and a half in diameter at one end and going to a point at the other. Holding the point of this spindle, with a little tuft of flax, between the thumb and finger of one hand, they gave the spindle a twirl, which, instead of falling, as one would expect, right to the floor, twisted the flax and by its weight drew out the thread. When it had spun out so long as to reach the ground they wound the thread up on the stick, took a hitch around the little end and twirled the spindle again; and so on, with lock after lock of flax. The thread produced by this simple means was very fine and even, and the white and blue linen homespun made from it and worn by the islanders was a well woven fabric.

Having shipped a boat-steerer named Francisco, Francis in original, and taken on board about forty barrels of potatoes, we next went to Ponta Delgada, on the south side of Flores. This was a beautiful town, built on a high hill, a sort of capital, the residence of the governor, the commander of the garrison and other officials. The better class of houses are generally stone and brick. In the suburbs, for the houses were simply wattled huts, they were coated with plaster. I saw no horses or carriages, which indeed would not be well adapted to the steep, narrow, stony streets. All the transportation that is required, whether passenger or freight, is on the backs of mules and donkeys.

Here we took in a good stock of potatoes and live hogs, sheep and poultry, and also shipped a boat-steerer named José and two men, Antonio and Manual.

San Jorge, Fayal and Pico Islands, Azores

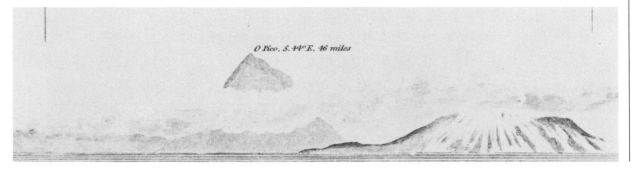

O Pico, S. 44° E. 46 miles

The Western Island Portuguese, though rather poor sailors, made excellent whalesmen, and nearly every whaling vessel afloat had several of them among the crew. José had been with Captain Coffin on his last voyage in the *Margaret Rait*; and as he may stand as a representative of his class, the following anecdote which I have heard the captain relate will serve to illustrate one prominent characteristic of all of them, their intense superstition.

While the *Margaret Rait* was in the vicinity of the Galapagos Islands the steward, in a fit of temporary derangement, committed suicide by jumping overboard through the cabin window. His effects were administered upon by the captain and sold at auction to the crew. José bought the steward's jacket. Nearly a year afterwards, while on the Off Shore Grounds of Peru, José was at the wheel, about an hour past midnight, when he suddenly left his post and ran forward. He got as far as the mainmast before the officer of the watch noticed him and hove him to. He was shaking like one in an ague fit, his jaws chattering and his eyes rolling out of his head with horror. It was some time before a connected enough statement could be got from him to explain such unusual conduct. At last, when his tongue and teeth had become sufficiently harmonized again to speak in English, he said that while he was standing at the wheel, looking at the compass, a little man dressed in a pair of duck trousers and a cotton shirt—(a very good description in a few words of the late steward)—came and stood close to him and looked him hard in the face;—"and he no belong de ship! Me no know what he want of me. Don't cause I got his jacket. I paid de mauney for de jacket. Hand de jacket, anyhow! I heave him overboard!"

On leaving Flores, we shaped our course for the Cape Verde Islands, running all day and shortening sail at night, and keeping a sharp lookout for whales, as we were going over good whaling ground. The captain put up a bounty of five dollars and a suit of clothes for the man who should raise the first whale. Nothing to excite a whaleman's curiosity, however, was met with on the passage. For two days the Peak of Teneriffe, in the Canaries, was in sight. As we sailed on hour after hour, and still that one white mountain peak, far above the clouds, shone in the sun, it seemed that it must be following us and made me think of the Rock which, in an old book that was read a good deal when I was young, is said to have followed the Children of Israel when they were in the wilderness.

We took the northeast trades in 24° N, and on Sunday, September 7th (my birthday), we made the island of St. Jago, one of the Cape Verdes. In the afternoon, we beat into port in company with the U.S. sloop of war *Yorktown*, Commander Charles H. Bell.

The Cape Verde Islands have come into prominent notice since the writing of these memoirs was commenced as the rendezvous of the Spanish fleet under Admiral Cervera in the Spring of 1898, prior to his sailing for the West Indies. Previous to that their claim to notoriety, so far as I know, rested in the fact that a man named Baker, who had shot Bill Poole, a New York prize fighter, sought but did not find a refuge from justice in the islands. After the shooting, which occurred in New York, Baker ran away and got on board a ship, which sailed for the Cape Verdes. A day or two afterwards the manner of his disappearance and the destination of the ship were discovered, and a ship called the *Grapeshot*, reputed to be the fastest ship in the United States, with several policemen on board, started in pursuit. The *Grapeshot* arrived in St. Jago one day, and the other ship the next; the officers captured Baker, and without any extradition proceedings or international ceremony, took him aboard and brought him back to New York.

The islands were, and I suppose still are, frequently visited by whaleships upon the same errand as ours, to procure tropical fruits. We took on board two boatloads of oranges and bananas and other fruits, and sailed to cruise on the Abrolhos Banks, off the coast of Brazil, till late in the season—when it would be summer in the southern hemisphere—and then to go around the Horn.

At this point our real whaling voyage began; and before continuing the narrative, I shall endeavor to set forth some more or less technical information in regard to whaleships, the way they are fitted out, and the business conducted, having particular reference to methods employed on the *Athol*. Those of my readers who are not sailors, or who may be impatient of such details and do not wish to have the thread of events, such as it is, broken in upon, may very conveniently skip the following chapter.

— CHAPTER X —

THE WHALESHIP AND HER APPOINTMENTS

A whaling ship with her sails aback, trying out a whale

A FULL-RIGGED SHIP (SUCH AS THE *ATHOL* WAS) IS PREFERRED for whaling, on account of the square after sails. By throwing the main and mizzen topsails aback, sternway can be given to the ship; and she can be made to forge ahead a little by backing her main-topsail and having the fore and mizzen-topsails braced forward. Very often if the whales are plentiful, the mainsail is unbent so the smoke from the tryworks will not dirty the sails. Very few whaleships have any houses on deck; if any, I never saw one; a flush deck is more convenient. The cabin is below, aft, lighted and ventilated by windows in the stern, deadlights on the side and a skylight on deck. The steerage is between-decks, over the after hatch, just forward of the cabin, and is lighted from a booby hatch which covers the

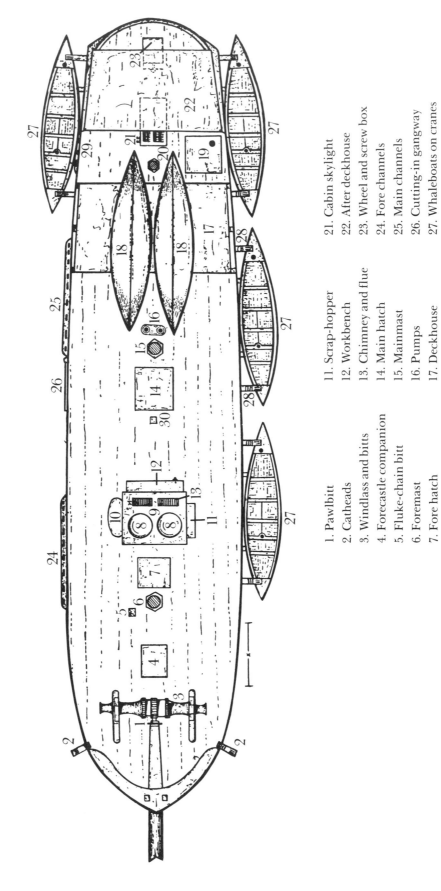

FIGURE 1: DECK PLAN OF THE WHALING BARK *ALICE KNOWLES*

1. Pawlbitt
2. Catheads
3. Windlass and bitts
4. Forecastle companion
5. Fluke-chain bitt
6. Foremast
7. Fore hatch
8. Trypots
9. Tryworks
10. Cooler
11. Scrap-hopper
12. Workbench
13. Chimney and flue
14. Main hatch
15. Mainmast
16. Pumps
17. Deckhouse
18. Spare boats
19. Galley
20. Mizzenmast
21. Cabin skylight
22. After deckhouse
23. Wheel and screw box
24. Fore channels
25. Main channels
26. Cutting-in gangway
27. Whaleboats on cranes
28. Boat davits
29. Mizzen channels
30. Bitt (for the belly-chain of the whale).

hatchway of the upper deck. There is usually a small topgallant forecastle extending as far as the pawl bitts. The forecastle is below the spar deck. The windlass is abaft the pawl-post, and the entrance to the forecastle is just abaft the windlass.

A whaleship generally carries two spare spars, suitable either for a topmast or a main or foreyard, blocked out eight inches square in the rough; also a spare topgallant-yard or two and jibboom, blocked out rough, and plenty of material in the rough for studding sail booms, boats' masts, etc. There are two large holes cut in the taffrail, about a foot above the deck, one on each side, say eighteen inches in diameter, and lined with lead. The large spars are run out through these holes about eight feet, the inboard ends being lashed to ringbolts in the deck and stanchions made for the purpose; while across the outboard ends are lashed the small spars. This manner of carrying the spars out over the stern is a very distinguishing feature of whaleships by which their character can be made out as far as the hull can be seen.

On each side, just forward of the foremast, are two large mooring pipes, through which the fluke chains are led to fasten the whale to the ship. The fluke chain is of three-quarter inch iron, with a large ring in one end. When the whale is brought alongside, he is laid tail pointing forward and head aft, usually on the starboard side. A bight of the fluke chain is rove through the ring and put around the whale's flukes; the other end leads in through the pipe and is made fast to heavy mooring bitts in front of the foremast, leaving slack enough for the whale and ship to roll freely.

The main hatch is immediately forward of the mainmast. There the cargo is put in and out, and the blubber lowered down. On the starboard side, abreast the main hatch, the rail is cut for a gangway, which can be removed and reshipped at pleasure, to facilitate taking cargo or cutting in a whale. The galley is abaft the foremast, abaft that is the forward hatch, and abaft the forehatch the tryworks are built. For that purpose, first, there are coamings about eight inches high bolted down on the deck, inside of which the deck is sheathed with paper and boards, and the boards are caulked. On top of the boards, bricks are laid, two bricks high, about the width of a brick apart, so as to leave spaces where water can run to protect the deck from fire. On these bricks the bottom of the tryworks is built of solid brick; two fire arches are made, facing forward, and a trypot is set over each arch and bricked around. The pots hold about nine barrels apiece. Two iron knees on each side of the tryworks hold them securely in place. The cooler is a large brass or copper pot, nicely fitted and lashed alongside the tryworks to starboard. Into it the hot oil is dipped out of the trypots, whence it is put into barrels.

Between the main and mizzenmasts are the overhead bearers. They are two upright posts on each side of the deck, with beams across, about six and a half feet high. On top of them are kept spare boats, lance and spade poles and light spars.

A four-boat ship will have on the port side a boat on the after quarter, called the larboard boat, a midship or waist boat, and a bow boat; and on the starboard side, one boat on the after quarter. The starboard boat is the captain's. If he does not go down, that is, leave the ship to chase whales, or command his boat,—it is the fourth mate's. The larboard boat is the mate's; the waist boat, the second mate's; and the bow boat, the third mate's.

FIGURE 2: SIDE AND INTERIOR PLAN OF THE WHALING BARK *ALICE KNOWLES*

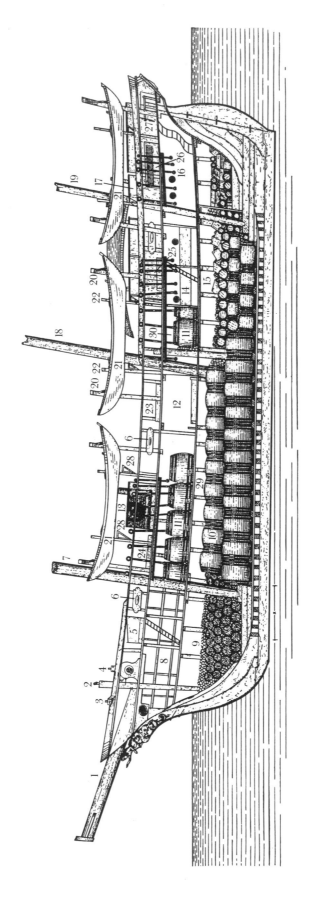

1. Bowsprit
2. Pawlbitt
3. Cathead
4. Windlass and bitts
5. Forecastle companion
6. Mooring pipes
7. Foremast
8. Forecastle
9. Fore hold
10. Casks for oil

11. Casks for oil (between decks)
12. Blubber room
13. Tryworks
14. Steerage
15. After hold
16. Captain's cabin
17. Galley
18. Mainmast
19. Mizzenmast
20. Boat davits

21. Whaleboats
22. Boat bearers
23. Main hatch
24. Fore hatch
25. Booby hatch
26. Cabin skylight
27. Wheel and screw box
28. Cranes for boats
29. Lower main hold
30. After 'tween decks

On board the *Athol* the boats hoisted up to iron davits. At that time most ships had wooden davits; but before the end of our voyage iron ones were frequently seen. Between each pair of davits, boat-bearers are constructed by setting two pieces of timber perpendicularly, each at one-third the distance between the davits, the timbers running down about two feet below the planksheer or covering board of the ship, spiked to her side, and bolted to the rail; the lower ends bevelled off flush to the side of the ship. On these timbers wooden cranes are hung with snipe-bill hinges, in either of two positions, higher or lower, depending on the weather. Between these bearers, on the ship's side, are two oak sliding-boards, reaching from the lower part of the lower wales to about two feet above the ship's main rail, kept off from the ship's side down by her waterways about four inches, and from her bulwarks seven or eight inches; thus making a springy, smooth slide for the boats so that they will not catch on the wales of the ship in hoisting or lowering.

At the head of each davit hangs a three-fold tackle, made by reeving a rope through a three-sheave upper block and a lower block with two sheaves. The lower blocks hook into eyebolts at the bow and stern of the boat, to hoist her by. When that is done, the cranes are swung out under her keel, and the boat, resting upon them, is thus kept from sagging while hanging in the davit tackles. To keep her from swinging with the rolling of the ship, a rope, called a gripe, is passed from the side of the ship, underneath and over the top of the boat, hauled taut and made fast. In a heavy seaway, when the ship is pitching, small tackles are hooked to the bow and stern of the boat, to prevent her swinging forward and aft; they are called jig tackles.

These boats are sharp at head and stern. They pull five oars—harpooneer, bow, midship, tub and after oar. About two feet from the stem of the boat a thick piece of plank, called a thighboard or clumsy cleat, extends from gunwale to gunwale, with a half-round place cut midway of it, for the harpooneer to put his thigh in to steady himself when standing up to harpoon the whale. Between the thighboard and the stem is the box—a platform set down about six inches below the gunwales—in which are coiled the stray line and the short warp. On top of each gunwale from the thighboard to the stem are fastened strips of two-inch oak. Their forward ends are left about two inches apart, forming the chock, through which the line runs out. The chock is lined with thick sheet lead, to keep the line from burning or wearing either the wood or itself. In each cheek or side of the chock, near the top, a small hole is made, and a piece of wood about the size of a lead pencil is put through, above the line, to keep it from being flicked out easily, and if it is necessary to jerk the line out quickly, the stick can be readily broken.

The sternpost of the whaleboat projects upward about eight inches. For about three feet forward of it, from gunwale to gunwale, the boat is covered over with cedar boards, excepting the after piece, which is of three-inch oak and extends out about six inches on the starboard side. On that the steering-oar rests. Two holes are bored in the sternpost, through which and over the steering cap a strap made of rope covered with leather is passed, one end having a knot in it. The other end is put through and clinched, to keep the steering-oar in its place. On top of the sternboards, running fore and aft, is an oak plank, tapering from six inches wide forward to three inches at the

Boat spade

FIGURE 3: DECK VIEW OF A WHALEBOAT READY FOR THE CHASE

Scale 3/8 inch to 1 foot

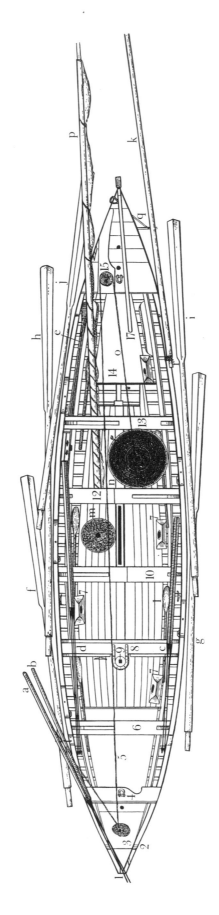

a. First iron
b. Second iron
c. Spare irons
d. Lances
e. Boat spade
f. Harpooner oar
g. Bow oar
h. Midship oar
i. Tub oar
j. Stroke oar

k. Steering oar
l. Paddle
m. Small tub
n. Large tub
o. Tow line
p. Mast and sail
q. Steering oar brace
r. Lashing or strap for
   steering oar

1. Bow-chocks
2. Top or false chocks nailed on gunwales
3. Box of boat
4. Clumsy cleat or thigh thwart
5. Bowsheets
6. Harpooner thwart
7. Peak cleats
8. Bowthwart
9. Mast-hinge and strap
10. Midship thwart

11. Gunwales
12. Tub-thwart
13. Afterthwart
14. Sternsheets
15. Loggerhead
16. Rudder
17. Tiller

after end. In this and in the boards on which it is laid, a hole three inches square is cut, through which runs a piece of oak, its lower end resting in a step at the bottom of the boat. The upper end, which is a round post about eight inches in diameter and fourteen in height, is the loggerhead.

About four inches from the bottom of the boat, a platform runs from the after thwart to the sternpost; and the same forward, from the stem to the harpooneer's thwart. The after platform is called the sternsheets; the other, the bowsheets. The boat is planked inside, or ceiled inside to within a few inches of the gunwale. On the ceiling, pretty well down on the bilge, opposite each rowlock, cleats are nailed, having holes in them in which the oarhandles are put to peak the oars. Besides oars, the boat is furnished with five nicely made paddles, one kept under each thwart, ready to paddle with in calm weather when the noise of rowing would alarm the whale. Between the after-thwart and the tub-thwart is a tub, in which is coiled from 100 to 150 fathoms of whale line. A smaller tub between the midship and the tub-thwarts holds about half as much line.

In sperm whaling, besides the two harpoons in use, each boat usually carries four spare harpoons (commonly called irons) in sheaths, which are made fast under the thwarts; also two spare lances and a boat-spade. The latter is a piece of fine steel, about as wide as a digging spade, but shaped more like the blade of an oar or a huge chisel, and ground very sharp on the sides and end. It is provided with a wooden pole about six feet long. It is sometimes, but very rarely in sperm whaling, used to chop the flukes of a running whale; its principal service being, after the whale is killed, to cut a hole in his head, through which to reeve a line for towing.

On top of the thwarts lie two lances for use in killing the whale. From the gunwale, abaft the harpooneer's thwart, is a piece of oak about two inches square and a foot and a half high, with three prongs at the top. It is called the crutch, and in it the poles of the first and second irons are laid ready for use; the points of the irons rest in little cleats on the bow. The crutch also serves as the forward pin of the harpooneer's rowlock. In the bow and sternsheets are cases containing a sheathknife and hatchet, to be used when necessary,—for instance, to cut the line if it should get fouled. There are also in the boat a keg of water and one containing a lantern with candles and matches and a quantity of hardtack.

The ordinary harpoon is of untempered wrought iron of the first quality, double-barbed. It measures from the end of the barbs to the point about five inches, and across from tip to tip of the barbs, about the same. The shank is of very soft and tough wrought iron, so that it will bend without breaking, about two and a half feet long, with a socket for the pole. When the pole is fitted into it, a piece of rope, called the iron-strap, is placed with a round turn on the shank close up to the socket and led up on the pole about two-thirds of its length, hauled very taut and seized to the pole. A sheath is kept on it when not in use.

The lance-head is a piece of finely tempered steel, elliptical in shape, about three-eighths of an inch thick, four inches long and three wide, welded to a half-inch steel rod six or seven feet long. It is ground to a razor edge from shank to point on both sides, so that it will cut its way out of a whale as easily as it will cut in, for the lance is thrown into a whale and jerked out again

Harpoon

Lance

repeatedly. The rule in cutting either an iron or lance pole is, for the one who is to use it, to rest one end on deck and cut off at a point as high as he can reach with his hands. That would make a lance, pole and shank, not less than twelve, and more often fifteen feet long.

One of the ship's officers is in charge of each boat. In chasing whales he takes the steering oar and directs manoeuvres until the whale is struck with the harpoon. Hence he is called the boat-header. From the fact that from the time the whale is struck until it is killed the harpooneer steers the boat, he is always called on American ships the boat-steerer. On getting into the boat the end of the line is passed to the boat-steerer, who reeves it out through the chock, coils about seven fathoms of stray line in the box, and bends on the end to the strap of the first iron. The bight of the line is taken from the tub and put over the loggerhead. Another piece of line, called the short warp, about five fathoms long, which is also coiled in the box, is bent to the second iron; and with the other end a running bowline is made, outside of the chock, around the main line, so that the latter will slip through the bowline. Then the order is given, "Line your oars," that is, to put the line on top of them. After the lines and irons are all ready for use, the boat-steerer takes to his oar, with the others.

A whale when feeding and unsuspicious of danger, after coming to the surface, will often move around in a circle, say a mile in circumference, and by the time he gets around to where he came up, he will peak his flukes and sound, or go down again. This circular motion of the whale is called milling. A large sperm whale will sometimes stay down for an hour and twenty minutes. I have known several do that—timed them, myself. When he has sounded so heavy as that, on first coming to the surface, he lies very still and spouts two or three times. His breath is hot, and he will blow a great deal of vapor. Then is a good opportunity, if the boat is nigh enough and in the right position, to go up and strike the whale.

The end of a sperm whale's head is as blunt as the end of a cask, whence his nickname of "squarehead." He can see directly in front of him and, by lifting his flukes, he can see right astern; but his eyes being a good ways from the end of his head, between the corner of his mouth and his fin, perhaps on that account he is not, when undisturbed, liable to be watching directly ahead or astern. In rough weather, a boat can approach within two hundred yards of him in any direction, whether on his beam or quarter, without his taking any notice. In a calm it is not prudent to approach nearer than half a mile when the boat is "on his eye," which would be about two points from right ahead or right astern. When so near and in a position to be seen, the boat must lie still and every one in it be very quiet until the whale either passes on or turns head to, so that the boat is off his eye again. In rough weather, the boat generally rows or sails right up to him; in a calm, before getting within hearing distance, the oars are peaked and the men take their paddles.

When within two or three boat's lengths of the whale, the boat-header motions to the boat-steerer to stand up. If it is rough, he tells him first to ship in his oar, which he does, blade forward, without rising from his thwart; and as he shifts it along between the men, he will say, "Light harpooneer," that is, for the men to take the end of his oar and light it along over the thwarts without making any noise. All orders and movements are given and executed as quietly as possible. The men are not allowed to speak or to look around. As soon as his oar is laid on the thwarts, the boat-steerer stands up, gets a brace with his thigh in the clumsy-cleat, and takes the first iron in his hand. If the boat is going on after the whale, the boat-header steers her just across the corner of his flukes, going up on his right side, if possible, so as to give the boat-steerer a right-handed dart, and by the time the bow of the boat is abreast of the whale's hump, the boat-steerer darts his first iron and instantly taking up the second, attempts to put that also into the whale; but whether he hits the whale with it or not, he darts it at him.

In the whale's circular motion, or milling, he will in some part of his circuit be heading right for the boat, and if near enough, the chance is then presented to take him head and head. In that method of attack, the boat is pointed right for him, and when he is a couple of fathoms off, the boat's head will be sheered to port, so as to let the whale pass without striking her. Now, the top of a sperm whale's head, though a great quaking mass of blubber, is so tough that an iron cannot penetrate it. The boat-steerer, therefore, waits until the bunch of the whale's neck, which is, say, ten feet from the end of its head, is past him before darting his iron. The whale on seeing the boat becomes alarmed, and rounds himself up ready to plunge under. His back is then taut, and the iron will go in clear to the hitches.

Fastening to a whale is the most dangerous part of the work. As soon as the iron touches him, he strikes with his tail towards the side in which he feels the sting, and if it reaches the boat at all it is pretty sure to stave a hole in her. But the instant the iron leaves the boat-steerer's hand and the necessity for silence is over, the boat-header shouts "Stern all!" and the men take to their oars and back the boat out of the way. The boat-steerer then unsheathes the lances and puts them up in the crutch; the boat-header comes forward, while the boat-steerer goes aft and takes the steering-oar, and from that time manoeuvres the boat to give the boat-header a chance to lance the whale. After backing clear of the whale, the men peak their oars and turn on their thwarts, facing forward, ready to haul line; if ordered to take their oars, they wheel around facing aft again and pull the oars out of the cleats, ready to back or pull, as they may be told.

After being struck the whale usually, not invariably, sounds, and as he goes down the line runs out at the chock, the boat-steerer holding it, with nippers on his hands to protect them from burning as it slips round the loggerhead, and keeping as hard a tension on the line as the boat will stand. The object is to tire the whale out as fast as possible. If the line were held too hard, he would pull the boat under; but the boat-steerer puts just enough tension on it to keep the water sipping in over the stem of the boat. The tub-oarsman, when the whale was struck, in obedience to the boat-header's order "Wet line," has thrown two or three bucketfuls of water into the line-tub, for if the line is not well soaked the intense friction soon sets the loggerhead smoking. In his downward course the whale takes out sometimes a hundred or a hundred and fifty or even two hundred fathoms of line before he turns to come up. As soon as the line slackens, the men lay hold and haul in. On coming to the surface again, the whale rushes off in one direction or another, the boat flying along after him; more line is hauled in, until the boat is nigh enough and sheered into position for the boat-header to lance him. When lanced in a vital spot, he spouts blood, or "Flies the red flag," as the crew poetically express it; and at last, old leviathan, after a terrible final struggle, rolls up fin out, and dies.

When practicable the ship sails up and takes the dead whale alongside. In case there is no wind he has to be towed to the ship. It sometimes happens that his jaw hangs open, and it is then easier to tow him by the flukes. Otherwise, as the action of the sea will cause him to drift ahead about a mile an hour, the line is made fast right by his blowhole and he is towed head foremost. When the fluke chains are on, the boat-steerers take charge of the preparations for cutting in. Quarter-watches are kept through the night, that is, the four boats' crews, each superintended by its boat-steerer, divide up the time till daylight. The fore, main and mizzen-topsails are double reefed, and the main-topsail braced aback, so that the ship just forges and drifts a little, keeping the mooring chains taut and the whale close alongside. Blocks are sent up and shackled to chain pennants around the masthead, and tackles rove off, the lower blocks being furnished with immense iron hooks. The cutting-in gangway is taken out, and stages hung over the site for the officers to stand upon while cutting in.

At daylight all hands are called. The first and second mates get over on their respective stages, one forward and one aft of the gangway, with their spades, ready for cutting in. A boat-steerer and one man, usually his bow-oarsman, are in the blubber-room to stow away the blubber as it is lowered to them. Another boat-steerer, barefoot and clad in not more, sometimes less, than shirt and trousers, and with a monkey-rope around him is prepared for overboard duty.

The first overboard falls to the boat-steerer of the starboard boat; and then those of the larboard, waist and bow boats, in the order named, take their turns. He whose overboard it is does nothing else while a whale is alongside, except to go over on the whale's back when required, to hook on tackles as the various parts of the whale are ready to hoist in. If another whale is taken alongside before the first is finished, the same man officiates for overboard duty for the second as for the first, a change being made only when there is an interval between cuts. In cold weather the old boat-steerer generally keeps his monkey-rope on, so that if he falls into the water he can get out again quickly; but if, as is usually the case in sperm whaling, the ship is in the tropics and the water is warm, he will go overboard without any monkey-rope.

The way a sperm whale is cut in:

1. **Fluke chain**
2. **Blanket piece**
3. **Crown piece**
4. **Jaw bone**
5. **Case**
6. **Junk**

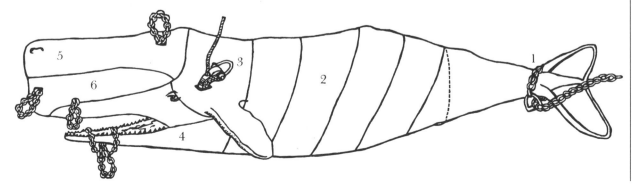

The water around a whaleship, as may be readily supposed, is swarming with sharks that are darting about as if raving distracted, crazed by the sight and taste of blood, now launching themselves full length out on the whale's back, and now running head on with stunning force into the ship's side, snapping at slivers or anything they can get hold of, and if it should happen to be a man's leg or both legs, the sharks do not consider beforehand whether they will relish it afterwards or not. Everybody knows how slippery a newly caught fish is, and a whale is just as slippery. When barefooted, a man gets on a whale's back, therefore, it is only a matter of a short time before he falls off. Now, he might get jammed if he slips down between the whale and the ship, but on the other side, there is always room enough, even if it is in a shark's mouth. It is the duty of the officers, however, who are cutting in the blubber, when a man slips into the water, to keep the sharks away from him by chopping at them with their spades. A shark's skin is tough and not calculated to improve the edge of a spade, which must be kept very sharp, so the poor boat-steerer, as he tries to scramble up on the whale's back again, sometimes thinks the officers have made him take too hard chances with the sharks, rather than hit out at them and risk dulling their spades.

The first operation in cutting in is to cut the crown piece, that is, to make a half-circle in the blubber just forward of the whale's eye. Through the crown piece a hole is cut, a tackle is lowered down, and the boat-steerer having the overboard detail gets on the whale and puts the hook into the hole. Oftentimes a chain strap is put around the flipper and a tackle hooked on to the strap, to keep the whale on its side and prevent it rolling. The falls are then taken to the windlass, the mates keep cutting around the body of the whale in a strip five or six feet wide; the men heave away on the tackle, which hoists the blubber, and the whale rolls gradually over and over as the blubber is peeled off. The strip of blubber thus raised is called the blanket piece. When it has been hoisted until the two blocks of the tackle come together, it will measure from the body of the whale to the hook in the block, say, thirty feet.

The boarding-knife, which has a blade about as long as a cavalry sabre, sharpened on both sides, and a handle with a cross-piece on the end like a spade, is then used to cut a hole in the blanket-piece. This is called "boarding the piece." Through this hole the strap of the block of the second tackle is passed and toggled on the opposite side; the tackle is hauled taut and taken to the windlass; the piece is then cut off about two feet above the toggle, and the upper piece is lowered away into the blubber-room. Then another piece is hoisted, boarded, cut and lowered in the same way, and so on. The fluke-chain, which has a swivel in it so that it will not twist up, is slacked away to keep the piece opposite the gangway, and one continuous spiral strip is cut round and round the whale's body from head to tail. When the tail is reached, it is unjointed and hoisted in, fluke-chain and all, on deck, and sent down to the blubber-room. The saying is that the flukes and fins will make as many gallons of oil as the body and head make barrels. Of course, the drippings from the blanket-piece as it hangs over the heads of the men, blood, water and oil, make them as greasy and dirty as if they were inside the whale; but in sperm whaling there is no strong smell about it, it is always sweet, and no one minds that.

Boarding knife

At the same time that the blanket-piece of the sperm whale is started, the unjointing of the jawbone begins, a process which is completed when the whale is rolled over so far that the opposite side comes up. The jaw is then hoisted in and left on deck. As the whale rolls, his head is gradually cut off; and this job is accomplished by the time he has made one and a half turns. In right whaling, the scalp with the bone, the lips and throat are cut off and hoisted in separately.

In the top of the sperm whale's head is the case; the part below the case is the junk. While the whale is fairly on his side, a hole is cut with a half-round spade through and through the junk, and the pieces shoved out, hooked with a gaff and brought aboard. A dipsy lead with a line attached is then let down through the hole, caught with a gaff underneath and pulled aboard, where the lead is taken off. A chain strap is tied in its place, lowered overboard and drawn up through the hole in the junk, and the two bights of the chain are tied together, ready to hook on when the head is to be hoisted in.

Upper jaw and baleen of a right whale being hoisted aboard

If the whale is very large the whole head cannot be hoisted in on deck, but the case must be first separated from the junk. The after part of the case, which is very tough and sinewy, is called "witchet." Before the head is cut off a large curved needle, threaded with a piece of ratline stuff, is worked through the witchet, and by its aid a small chain strap is pulled through, and the two bights of it are tied together. After the head is off, a tackle is hooked into the big chain strap that goes through the junk. It is hoisted up till the head stands up and down, and the officers with their spades carefully divide the junk from the case. These are left alongside till the remainder of the whale is cut in, and are then hoisted aboard separately.

The case of a large whale will make, say, twenty-five barrels of clear free oil, containing about seventy-five per cent of spermaceti. In the warm weather its contents are liquid; in cold weather they are of about the consistency of soft lard. The case oil is baled out and put through the tryworks to evaporate water, and is stored by itself and commands a very high price. The junk is apparently clear fat. Parts of it are put through the tryworks; other parts are cut into pieces about eight inches square and the oil is squeezed out by hand. The junk oil is nearly as rich in spermaceti as the case, and ranks next in price.

In the blubber-room, the lean is cut off the blubber, which is then cut into "horse-pieces," about nine inches wide by eighteen inches long and of its natural thickness. The horse-pieces are pitched up on deck into a tub alongside the tryworks, and are then put on the mincing horse and minced, that is, cut into thin slices like the leaves of a book. The mincing knife is something like a drawing knife, except that the handles are straight instead of turned down. The minced pieces are put into another tub, whence they are pitched as required into the tryworks. An expert mincer will seldom make a sliver, but will mince the horse-pieces into leaves of equal thickness or thinness, all held together by a small strip along one corner, which is left uncut. If they should not keep up to the standard of thinness the officer of the watch trying out will warn the mincers to be more careful by shouting, "Bible-leaves, there, boys—bible-leaves! Don't mince that blubber so thick."

For fuel for the first whale, all that is required is wood enough to try out the first kettle of blubber. After that the scraps are burnt and are sufficient to try out the whale, and more. Of what is left, enough is saved to start fires for the next whale. The rest is thrown overboard; or, if the ship is in the neighborhood of islands where such coin is current, the scrap is used in barter with the natives for fruit and vegetables. In some of the South Sea Islands whale scraps are a much-prized article of diet.

The blubber in the tryworks requires constant skilled attention. Great heat has to be applied to bring out the oil, but if it burns or a bit of scrap scorches on the bottom of the kettle, the oil darkens and will not bring full price. It would never do to dip the oil directly from the trypots into the casks, for the heat shrinks the wood so fast that the hoops would almost drop off

Mincing knife

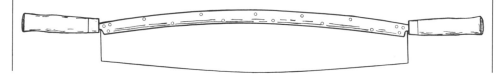

over the bilge before the cooper could do anything with them. So the oil is first dipped into the cooler, and from that, still hot, into the casks. No cask is considered fit to stow down until it has been three times to the tryworks, that is, until it has been filled with hot oil and set to cool three times. Any shrinkage after that will not allow of much leakage. As the casks are filled up they are strung alongside of the rail on their ends and made fast, and after the trying-out is completed and the oil perfectly cooled, they are stowed down permanently in the ship's hold.

The oil itself shrinks in cooling about one gallon in sixty or seventy. And since there is more or less expansion and contraction of oil due to climatic changes of temperature, a gimlet-hole is made and left open in the top of every cask, to give vent to the air; otherwise, in cold weather the contraction would draw in the heads of the casks, or in the tropics the expansion would burst them out.

While a whaleship is being fitted out for her voyage, the first hogsheads stowed, forming the ground tier, are large tun butts, holding about 280 gallons or nine barrels apiece. These are filled with water and salted, to prevent shrinking and rotting. They are bedded and coigned, so that no amount of motion of the ship will disturb them, and there they stay for years till the ship returns from her voyage and the cargo is discharged. Hence, to say of a man, "He is as restless as a ground-tier cask," would denote to a whaleman that the person referred to is of a somewhat torpid temperament.

When a considerable quantity of oil is accumulated and cooled, in barrels on deck or in the between-decks, the cargo will be broken out until the ground-tier casks are reached; the salt water is pumped out of such of them as it is intended to fill at the time, and they are swabbed out dry. A tub made by sawing one of these tun butts in half is placed on skids over the hatch, a hole bored in the bottom of it, and one end of a canvas hose 50 to 75 feet long is tacked over the hole and the other end let down into the hold. The barrels of cool oil are then rolled up on skids to the tub, and the oil is allowed to run into it, whence it is directed through the hose into the ground-tier casks. That is the operation of "hosing down."

In the between-decks, stowed on end, are pipes holding about 300 gallons each. They, as well as all other oil receptacles (except the ground-tier casks) go to the tryworks and are filled with hot oil three times, to shrink the wood, and coopered so that there is no danger of leakage, before they are finally struck down below. For small stowage, there are two kinds of casks of irregular sizes—"ryers," made of hogshead staves with 12-inch heads, holding a little more than a barrel; and another made of barrel staves with small heads, which hold about half a barrel. They are manufactured aboard the ship by the cooper and his mates.

Once every week, while the ship is in hot weather, a stream of water, by means of the tub and hose, is sent all over the cargo of oil to keep it cool and prevent its expanding and oozing out through the vent holes; and every step of the process, from cutting in, to hosing or stowing down, is attended with the greatest care to guard against waste or leakage.

— CHAPTER XI —

ABROLHOS

September 8th to December 4th, 1845

OR A WEEK AFTER LEAVING THE CAPE VERDES, WE SAILED along, everything in readiness, but seeing nothing and nobody but ourselves. Every night at sundown we double-reefed the sails so as not to go over the ground too fast in the dark, and at last vigilance had its reward.

On Sunday, September 14th, a flat calm prevailed when at daylight the mastheads were manned and all hands called to wash decks. Hardly, however, had the lookouts got aloft, before that startling, welcome sound was heard from the fore and mainmast heads at once, "There she blo-o-ws—ah blo-ows!" All work was dropped in an instant.

"Where away?" hailed the mate.

"Right on the port beam, not two miles off."

"Put your line in the boat," were my orders from the mate; and the other boat-steerers got the same word from their respective boat-headers. Before that was done the captain, wakened by the bustle and just turned out of bed, came on deck, one hand holding a spyglass, and the other temporarily fulfilling the duty of a pair of suspenders.

"What's up, Mr. Taylor?" he asked.

"Sperm whale, by thunder, Captain," said the mate, who had hopped into the main rigging and made out the low bushy spout of a "still" whale.

"Larboard and waist boats, lower away!" were the captain's orders, as he started up the fore rigging, bound for the topmast crosstrees, to watch manoeuvres.

The mate and I got into the larboard boat, hoisted, swung and lowered, and as she touched the water we unhooked the tackles, and the boat's crew followed down and took their places. Mr. Thomas with his boat-steerer and crew manned the waist-boat; and together we pushed off in pursuit of what proved to be a lone bull sperm whale. After we were clear of the ship we found that our bow oarsman was Dr. MacDonald.

It being calm, we could not use sails, so we rowed until we were within about half a mile of the whale and then peaked our oars and took to paddling. Now the boat that had the best chance would go on and get fast, but neither must interfere with the other's chances. For some reason the whale was suspicious and keeping a pretty good lookout, sounding for a few minutes and coming up perhaps head to us, but when we paddled for him, the first thing we knew he was broadside on, and then we had to lie still and wait until we were "off his eye."

After two hours or more of such manoeuvring, the whale went down tail toward us, about a quarter of a mile away, and as he did not say, of course nobody knew where he would come up; but we paddled along toward the spot where we had last seen him. Suddenly the mate, with excitement leaping into his eyes, told me to stand up. I did so, taking in my paddle; and as I turned round, the first thing I saw, perhaps a hundred yards ahead and about twenty feet below the smooth surface, was the whale coming up—rising—rising, not directly towards the boat, but to cross quartering the bows. The mate with the steering-oar laid the boat's head to intercept him, and the men kept paddling, while I stood ready, iron in hand.

Then up came that mighty bulk, not six feet away, the spray of his spouting flying almost into my face, his glistening black skin marked with the white scars of former wounds, while huge parasites upon his body, finding themselves lifted from water to air, wiggled for a moment and then settled down close and still. Let anyone inclined to scepticism in religious matters have that sight presented at close quarters for the first time, and I think he would gladly subscribe, heart and soul, to the whole Catechism, Shorter or Larger, for one moment's assurance that he would ever see another day. I know that in an instant I thought of all the wrong things I had ever done, and the good that I had left undone. But swift upon the back of bootless regrets came an overpowering feeling that past offences would be as nothing compared to the eternal disgrace of a "faux pas" now, and as the boat's stem touched him, with all my strength I let him have both irons—and away he went with them, full dash, the poles sticking up in his back like stray hairs on a bald head.

Oh, such a noise as all hands then set up! We clapped our hands and shouted and hurrahed like children, so that we could have been heard three miles away, if anybody had been there to hear. After putting the lance in the crutch, I went aft and took the steering-oar, and the mate went forward. Obeying the mate's orders, the men faced forward on their thwarts and hauled line, and as they pulled, one started a song—short verses which he sang alone, and all came in heavy on the long chorus.

As we got nearly up to the whale he sounded, and we had to give him the line again; but I "wrung" him down with a turn or two round the loggerhead, and the boat's bow dipped till the water came in over the stem. By and by a nip a little too hard on the line, as the boat was rising a swell, put her head under too far, and as the water poured in the mate sang out—with some grace notes added, which were excusable under the circumstances—"Slack line! Slack line! D'you want to sink the boat?"

About one hundred and twenty fathoms were run out before we felt the line slacken as the whale turned to come up, and the men tried once more to haul line. At first it came in only inch by inch, for in his upward course, as the whale dragged the bight of the line from that depth, the strain on it for a time was almost as great as while he was going down. Gradually, however, it came in faster, and at last the whale broke water a hundred yards ahead and, exhausted after his deep sound, he lay still and spouted.

"Now, boys, drop the line and take your oars—pull away!" whispered the mate. And I laid the boat's head toward the whale, about two fathoms off and just aft of his fin. The mate drew back to dart his lance, but hesitated, and I wondered why.

These are probably parasitic copepods, many species of which also occur on fishes. They are all highly modified and generally comprise a long stalk with a lump at its end, usually with no visible appendages. The head is buried in the skin of the host. Some species of these parasites can be five inches or more in length.

"I want to get a good set on him," he said, as if I had asked the question. So I sheered in a little closer. The mate let go his lance, and the instant the whale felt it he struck towards boat, the corner of his flukes reached our bows and knocked a hole through, big enough for a man to crawl out through.

The whale was off again like a flash. The mate jerked back his lance and darted when the whale was all of ten fathoms off, and struck him too, but at that distance made only a trifling wound. As the water rushed into the boat the crew ran aft, which trimmed us so by the stern that the hole was almost out of water. But we were going at such a rate that she still scooped it in entirely too fast. Two men grabbed piggins, another a bucket, and the doctor kicked in the head of the water keg, and all of them went to work bailing as hard as they could. But lively as they were, they could not keep her free, and the water, running aft and gathering all in one end, threatened to swamp us.

The mate sang out, "Pull off your shirts, boys, and hats too, and give them to me—quick." Every man climbed out of his shirt, rolled his hat in it and passed the bundle to the mate, who stuffed the whole wad into the hole and braced it in with his feet. That kept out some of the water, anyway.

The whale now showed the effects of the lance. His lungs filled with blood; he stopped in distress, and red jets rose from his spout-holes and colored the water around him. Now, if we were not a wreck ourselves, we could haul alongside and give him another lance; but before we could do so he spouted clear and started off. We should never be able to kill that whale alone—not even prevent him from going off with our irons and line. We held up a waif—a little flag on a short pole—a signal to those who might see it that we had a stoved boat. To keep from sinking we had to slack the line, but held on all we could, and before our line was out the waist boat, which had been left far behind but had kept pulling for us ever since we got fast, came alongside.

"Take our line, Mr. Thomas," said the mate, "and we'll have that scoundrel yet."

"Can you take care of yourselves if I leave you?" Mr. Thomas asked.

"Oh, yes—yes; quick—don't argue, for King's sake."

The men stopped bailing and gave the second mate our line, and away went the waist boat in tow of the whale. Our boat, now separated from its motive power, stopped, filled and sank, gunwales level with the water. We took our oars and put them athwartships, securing them with a turn of line around the thwarts, to keep the boat from turning over, and then sat still in her, a little more under water than out, four miles from the ship, with the tropical sun, now near noon beating down on our bare heads and shirtless backs. We were thick-skinned enough, however, to stand it—all but the poor doctor, and my! how his back blistered!

The ship's position at noon was 10° 11' N, 23° 00' W.

The captain was spying us from the ship's fore-topsail yard, and in about an hour the bow boat with four men came to us, and the mate and I got into her and put off to help Mr. Thomas kill the whale, leaving the crew of our boat still clinging to their oars. But the captain, seeing that all hands were not taken out of the water, sent the starboard boat after them, which picked them up, took the stoven boat in tow and returned to the ship, where the doctor and his boat-mates, though they had missed their breakfast, were in time for a late dinner.

When the mate and I got up to the whale again he was already near the end of his dying flurry, and we only had a chance to give him one more lance before he turned up dead. The second mate had given him a lance or two; but as the larboard boat's irons were in him, and the first lance of the mate's had brought him to spouting blood, there could be no disputing that it was the mate's whale.

As it was still calm, we had to tow the whale to the ship. The boat that picked up our crew came to help, and all three boats went at it. When within about fifteen hundred yards of the ship, we bent the three boats' lines one to the other and took the end aboard. One boat stayed by the whale, while the others went aboard, and there all hands clapping on to the line could pull at the same time the ship to the whale and the whale to the ship. It was eleven o'clock that night when the whale was taken alongside and moored; and Mr. Taylor and I, before getting anything to eat, went and put on new shirts.

Several weeks now elapsed before the humdrum routine was again interrupted by the work that we really came for. On October 1st, we saw finbacks in 11° 11′ S; and on the 4th, saw breaches which we thought were made by sperm whales, but were disappointed. On the 7th we lowered for whales at 5 P.M., in company with the boats of the ship *Christopher Mickel*; but her boats frightened them and we got none.

On Tuesday, October 14th, just one month after taking the first whale, the lookout at the masthead, at 2 P.M. reported a pod of sperm whales to leeward. All four boats lowered and put after them hurry-scurry—who will be first, with some, and who will be last, with others.

We set the foresail and mainsail of our boat and sailed down before a strong breeze towards the whales, which were coming leisurely to windward. We singled out a large cow whale, and manoeuvred to take her to head. We were on the port tack; that is, the sails were out on the starboard or right side of the boat. It was natural to suppose, therefore, that when we got close enough the mate would sheer to the right, so that the left or clear side of the boat would shoot up alongside of the whale and give me a chance for a right-handed dart. When the mate ordered me to stand up, however, I saw the whale coming past me on the starboard side, which made it left-handed and somewhat awkward for me to strike him. But worse than that, as I drew back the iron, the mate, losing his presence of mind, let go the foresheet, and the sail blew right away foreward between me and the whale, and the sheet took a turn around the shank of the iron. There were only a few seconds in which to strike or lose the chance of doing so. The mate cried out, "Why don't you dart? What are you waiting for?" But I had no time then to free my mind to him on that or any other subject. I had to take the turn of the sheet off the iron, and hand the sheet to one of the men for him to haul in, before I could even see the whale. When that was done, I set one iron well in, and pricked the whale with the other, and in less than half an hour it was turned up dead.

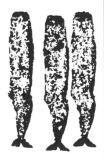

The other three boats all got fast, and all saved their whale but the bow boat—the third mate's. They parted their line and lost the whale. The ship sailed down and hauled aback just to windward of us, and we ran a line to the ship and hauled the whales alongside, which we completed doing about ten o'clock at night. The usual preliminaries were performed, and we commenced to cut in at daylight.

We got those whales in 18° 11′ S, 35° 52′ W. They made thirty barrels of oil apiece. Our first whale made eighty barrels.

Dull times came again once more. Weeks passed without a sound from the masthead. In 19° 2′ S; 37° 41′ W, we spoke the whaleship *Samuel Adams*, of Provincetown, ten months out, 250 barrels. Her record tended to confirm the impression which was growing upon us, that sperm whales were to be picked up about once in a blue moon. If breaches were reported, they would turn out to be made by killer whales or thrasher sharks, splashing around after their peculiar fashion. Or, if we got the word, "There she blows," and were sure we had at last raised a school of sperm whales, we would soon find they were nothing but humpbacks or blackfish.

The spout of a sperm whale when he is "still," that is, wandering around, feeding—not running or making a passage—cannot be seen very far, especially if his blowhole is out of water. He will then blow nothing but his breath, and the vapor of it curls forward, spreads out low and disappears in an instant. Hence the whalemen's rhyme,

"A low bushy spout—sperm whale, no doubt."

Blackfish make a little puff, and are sometimes mistaken for sperm whales. Most of the other species of whale blow up a long, or, in whaling phrase, a lance-pole spout, rising high in the air and drifting away with the wind. A sperm whale, when making a passage, travelling fast, may start to blow when a sea is washing over his head, or just before reaching the surface, and he then raises a considerable jet of water.

The right whale's spout goes up in a perfect fork and falls away on each side. The only whale that is often mistaken by his spouting for a sperm whale is the humpback. He has a forked spout, but it is not very high, and one side is lower than the other, and unless one is close he cannot see that it is forked.

Usually there is no difficulty in distinguishing a sperm whale from any other, for when he is not disturbed he spouts regularly, perhaps thirty or forty times, at shorter intervals than other whales, and the intervals between will not vary a second. If there is uncertainty from appearance the man at the masthead is ordered to sing out every time she blows, and the captain takes out his watch and counts the seconds between each hail. That is called "taking the tenor of the spout." In thick fog, or at night, when whales are heard near the ship, sperm whales can be told from any other, without seeing them, by the fact that after they spout they draw in their breath silently. When the drawback is heard, it is as if the whales had said, "We are finbacks—grampus—right whales—sulphur bottoms—anything but sperm whales." The drawback of an old right whale is like a tremendous roar— Owooo-ooop.

One foggy day near the middle of November, about four o'clock in the afternoon, the fog lifted and we saw three sperm whales quite near the ship, to leeward. All four boats went down after them. We did not set sail, but rowed down before the wind and in our manoeuvres a large whale came up so that we could take him head to head. We pulled for him, keeping his blowhole in line with his hump, until within about fifteen fathoms of him, when he either saw or heard us. He turned broadside to, and whirled off to his right. The mate immediately became uncontrollably excited—much more so than on any previous occasion—and instead of throwing the boat's head to port, to follow the direction in which the whale had turned, he kept right on the same course. I saw that we were going too far off, and waved to him to lay in towards the whale, as at that distance there was no chance at all of getting fast. He paid no attention to the gesture, however, but told me to "give it to him." I looked at him and shook my head, but the mate in a fairly frantic tone, sang out, "Why don't you give it to him? What are you scared of?"

I ought not to have let his words influence me, as the boat-steerer must use his own judgment when to dart and when not to, without anybody's orders. If he gets a good chance to strike and refuses to use it, or darts and misses, of course, on complaint being made, he will be tried and warned, and for a second offence, disrated. Even when near enough, it is better not to dart at all than to miss.

We were all of seven fathoms off, and as the mate would not head the boat in for the whale, we should get no nearer. I knew that if I darted, the iron would not hold, even if it reached the whale, and that I would be called a miss; but the ugly feeling that rose in me at the mate's last words gave me a little more strength than was natural, and I let go as hard as I could. As I did so, the mate sang out, "Hold water! Stern all!" and the boat had sternway by the time the second iron could follow the first. The first one just reached the whale but did not stick, and the whale went his way rejoicing at the humbug we had made of it.

The other boats were also unsuccessful, and we all returned to the ship empty handed, to talk over our failures, as down in the mouth as a French three-decker.

When we got aboard the mate told the captain that I was frightened and missed the whale. The captain sent for me and questioned me in the mate's presence. I denied being frightened and told him I had put all the power I could into the iron, and that I took out all the line there was in the box, which was seven fathoms, and that Mr. Taylor himself, who could dart farther than anybody else in the ship, could not have struck the whale at that distance and got fast. Fortunately, the waist boat was nigh enough for the second mate to see our manoeuvres, and the captain calling him aside, he must have confirmed my story, for the captain decided in my favor and said that, although I ought not to have darted, he would not find any fault and hoped we should all have better luck next time.

This was the beginning of a trouble which grew more and more serious as the voyage progressed. From that time on, Mr. Taylor was my enemy; but that was only incidental, because he knew that I knew he was liable to lose his self-control in going on to a whale. Apart from what passed in the conversation at which the captain, the mate and I were present, when I spoke in my own defence, his reputation never suffered from any word of mine. Notwithstanding, it was known all over the ship that the mate had acted strangely on two occasions in going on to whales. He felt the low estimation of him which was entertained by officers and men, and it made him supersensitive, morose and overbearing. With some on board, my own stock went down very low. I said nothing, although I felt unutterably ugly about it. The captain and second mate, however, retained confidence in me, in return for which they won my unbounded, undying devotion.

— CHAPTER XII —

RIVER PLATTE: TO CAPE HORN AND CHILOE

December 5th, 1845 to March 17th, 1846

*T*HE ABROLHOS HAVING PROVED TO BE BARREN GROUND, we went further south and cruised for a month or more off the mouth of the River Platte (Rio de la Plata), in 40° to 42° S, and about the 50th meridian. We saw sperm whales to windward on December 5th and set all sail to beat up for them. When night came half-watches were set, and we expected to be up with the whales by morning but never saw them again. Humpbacks and blackfish were all around us in abundance, but we did not try to take any, as they make a great deal of dirt. We caught a few porpoises and tried them out, and used the oil on our gear to keep it from rusting.

Black looks began to appear on the faces of the crew, and all hands were very much discouraged—all but myself; my worrying days had not then begun. Soon after leaving Saint John I had made a desk alongside of my berth, with a place to set a light upon in the evening, and had kept up the practice, commenced when I first started going to sea, of keeping a journal or diary for the purpose of improvement of handwriting. I made a little wooden stamp the shape of a whale, and when we captured one of those animals, besides writing the particulars of the occurrence, I illustrated it, as it were, by stamping the profile of a whale on the page, and noting the latitude and longitude where taken. When we saw whales without taking them, only the uplifted flukes were printed.

But dry times make a dry narrative, and for over three months about all there was to record was the weather. During this time I turned my attention to some long neglected studies. In Saint John I had bought a slate and a Thompson's Arithmetic, and I now commenced to brush up my ciphering. Beginning at the miscellaneous examples at the end of the first four rules, I worked through Reduction, Ascending and Descending, Proportion and Practice, and started on Fractions. I learned the rules by heart, new methods and short methods, the whole thing.

Having decided to give up cruising this side of the land and try our luck around the Horn, we sent down royal and topgallant yards and topgallant masts and made everything snug, in anticipation of the uproarious weather we should meet off that dread promontory. We worked slowly south, shortening sail every night, and making sail and manning the mastheads every morning at daylight, so as to have a good look all over the ground. So Christmas passed, which the crew celebrated on beef, duff and molasses, and the officers on roast pig and plum pudding. A week later a beautiful summer's day ushered in the New Year of 1846.

On January 10th, right whales were seen on the starboard beam, coming towards the ship. One of them came up close and ran into us about amidships, but he could not hurt us, for a right whale's head is too tender. The officers wanted to lower for them, but the captain said, "No, we are sperm whaling now, and we won't glue up with right whales just yet."

The weather becoming chilly as we increased our latitude, the captain brought up the slop-chest, and all who needed warmer clothing supplied themselves. I bought two blankets and a coat. The mastheads had to be relieved every hour on account of the cold, but a good lookout was constantly kept, as the whales are large in the vicinity of Cape Horn. On January 20th, we made Staten Land, Cape St. John, bearing south, distant fifteen miles, at 54° 40′ S, 63° 50′ W. We could not see the tops of the mountains because of the fog; and the breeze falling light, and a strong current setting to the northeast, we drifted off, to the regret of the Captain who, while in with the land, wanted to get an observation by which to compare his chronometer. At 2 P.M. the same day, we spoke the whaleship *Java*, of Fair Haven, three months out, sixty barrels of oil.

The captain went on board and returned with a few newspapers, from which we learned, among other things, that a wonderful steamer constructed of iron had visited New York, and that $6,000 exhibition money was taken from the crowds who came to see such a curiosity, that the Mormons and Antis were threatening a civil war; but best of all, that a world's convention was about to meet somewhere in the United States, having for its object the reformation of society and the banishment of sin and misery from the world! From observations subsequently made, I have reason to believe that that convention adjourned with its work still partly unfinished.

On the 21st, a fine afternoon with a light breeze and not much sea, we saw the bold cliffs of Cape Horn bearing west southwest, distant twenty miles. Four days later, land that we took for Cape Horn was again sighted. During the intervening time we had been baffling around, with light winds and for the most part but very little sea. Cape Horn certainly had been sleeping on its reputation. Now, however, it was time to rouse itself. In the morning when we made the land, it was perfectly calm and the sea as smooth as I ever saw it anywhere. An hour later, the long-footed Cape Horn swell, which, world without end, rolls on and on, had become very heavy, rising with astonishing quickness, though there was then little more than a light air stirring. By nightfall it was blowing a screaming gale, and the good ship *Athol*, with everything snug alow and aloft, was bousing into it on the offshore tack.

The ship constructed of iron was probably the **Great Britain,** *which visited New York City on its maiden voyage in 1845.*

The "Antis" were those hostile to Mormonism. The previous year the founder of Mormonism, Joseph Smith Jr., had been arrested and murdered by Illinois militiamen. The sect leadership eventually split and Brigham Young led the majority of members to Utah in 1846-47.

Cape Horn

While we were reefing the topsails that afternoon, William Mills, a Saint John's man, who pulled the after oar in our boat, was knocked off the main-topsail yard. The mainsail had been hauled up but not yet furled. The main-topsail flapped up over the yard, and as he put both hands to it to press it down, it suddenly collapsed and he pitched head foremost into the belly of the mainsail. As he was rolling out of it, he caught one of the buntlines and hung on for dear life. The second mate, Mr. Thomas, scurried up the main rigging to the man's assistance, piping out encouragingly in his high pitched voice, "Hold on—hold on my lad; I'll get you." "No fear for me," Mills replied, "I'll hold on, I warrant you." And hold on he did till Mr. Thomas had pulled him up to the quartering of the yard. It was a very narrow escape, but Mills was saved for future usefulness.

Every day we saw great numbers of albatross, cape pigeons, penguins, right whales, humpbacks, porpoises and seals, but no sperm whales, which were all we wanted. The cape pigeon is a species of petrel, speckled black and white. We dipped several of them up with a scoop net when they came alongside under the lee. The cook's experiments with them demonstrated that they are no use for food. Like the albatross, they cannot fly from the deck.

The albatross has several scientific names, more or less lengthy, but full of meaning to an ancient Greek or Roman, as required by the rules of the naturalists. The sailors' name for him is "gooney". How the notion arose that sailors in general entertain for this bird feelings of attachment or superstitious awe, I do not know. *The Rime of the Ancient Mariner* has no doubt tended to strengthen such an impression, and possibly has actually created the feeling. But if such a sentiment exists, I have never encountered it. On board the *Athol* were men who had not only read Coleridge, but could make pretty fair poetry for themselves, and others who could not read at all; but one and all, while off the Horn, on moderate days when the ship was making little headway, engaged in fishing for gooneys and caught numbers of them with hook and line.

Our mode of catching them was to bait the hook with pork, fasten it to a small piece of board, and allow it to drift astern, paying out the line for thirty or forty fathoms. The gooney would come sailing along, spy the bait floating on the board, and go down and grab it. When he had swallowed it, we gave the line a jerk and pulled him in. Sometimes he would fly almost the whole length of the line, and then dash down into the water and sprawl out his feet and wings. It usually took two men to haul one in over the rail. Landed on deck, the gooney was still full of fight, his powerful mandibles snapping at everything within reach. A man's finger would be nothing at all to him; he could snap it off like a pipe stem.

I do not dare say how many feet the largest gooney we caught measured from tip to tip of his wings. The books mention twelve or fourteen feet as the limit. If I were asked, I should say considerably more than that. I believe we caught them measuring fully eighteen feet from tip to tip.

Profiting perhaps by his failure with the cape pigeons, the cook was more successful in making gooney meat undergo "a sea change into something rich and strange," at least, if not a very palatable mess. First he skinned and cleaned the birds and parboiled them for about twelve hours in

There are 13 species of albatross known in the world, each with its own scientific name. The maximum wingspan of the largest species, the Wandering Albatross, is 11.5 to 12 feet.

Catching an albatross aboard HMS *Challenger* in the mid 1870s as was done aboard the *Athol*

sea water. Then he picked out all the bones and sinews, squeezed and wrung the flesh dry and, mixing it with potatoes and broken pieces of hard tack, minced it up fine and made it into balls, which we called gooney forcemeat. These were fried and eaten. There was scarcely a taste of anything at all to them, except a fresh something with a meaty fibre. After many months of salt diet, anything fresh was a welcome change, and albatross served the turn very well if nothing better could be obtained.

Not only for purposes of food, however, were gooneys killed, but often merely to gratify that savage instinct which sometimes possesses men to kill for the sake of killing and to gloat upon scenes of suffering. That tendency in me received one day a check, the influence of which has never left me. It was when the sharks were thick about the carcase of a whale which we had alongside, and I was chopping at them with the spade. A large gooney scaled down to pick up a sliver that lay drifting in the "sleek water." A sudden thoughtless impulse made me strike at him, and the keen edge of the spade gave him a glancing blow upon the neck. He trailed away, mortally wounded, his snowy breast reddening with his blood, his reproachful eyes upon me as they glazed in death. No "Hermit good" for me can "wash away the albatross's blood," and time cannot dull my remorseful memory of the pitiful scene.

In the afternoon of Thursday, January 29th, in 57° 58′ S, 74° W′, a dense fog which had prevailed suddenly lighted, and right near us we saw a French man-of-war. We spoke her and found she was bound home. Here was a chance to send letters. Every one who had friends to write to hastily scribbled a few lines, and we took the letters aboard in the mate's boat. We did not pay any postage, as there was no foreign postal system at that time established; so the forwarding of letters was entirely complimentary on the part of whoever undertook it; and yet, I have no doubt that most of them reached their destination.

The Cape being fairly doubled, we stood up along the coast of Patagonia, with four or five men constantly aloft, keeping vigilant watch for the squareheads and the low busky spout. On February 2nd, sperm whales were seen going to windward, eyes out that is, going so fast that when they came up to blow they thrust the whole length of their heads (twenty to thirty feet) into the air, showing their eyes—as one would say of a horse or dog running away, "There he goes, tail out of joint." Under those circumstances, we did not lower.

Right whales and finbacks were seen every day. On the morning of February 6th, we made an unnamed, uninhabited island about five miles from the main land, in 45° S, 74° 5′ W. It was bold water right up to the wooded shores, and we ran in close and hauled aback the yards within a mile of the land. There we saw right whales in great numbers, and the mate was fiercely in favor of lowering for them. In fact, all the officers favored it; but the captain steadily and stoutly refused to do so. He said, "No, we have come on a sperm whaling voyage, and we won't change our gear and go right whaling till we have used up two or three years anyway." At noon we braced forward and stood on our course for the island of Guafo on the coast of Chile.

The following Sunday morning (February 8th) we saw a ship, the *Chili*, of New Bedford, chasing a shoal of sperm whales. We followed them and lowered, and I was soon busily occupied trying to gain back my reputation. By fortune's kind favor I struck a 50-barrel whale, and made him spout blood with the iron. We soon had him turned up and brought alongside, the island of Guafo in sight, distant twenty-two miles; 44° 03′ S, 74° 42′ W. It was my turn overboard on this whale, and in addition to the water being cold, the sharks and gooneys were as thick as thieves in London. But the boat-steerers have a good billet trying out, though they have a bad one cutting in; and it

was soothing to the spirits of all to see the tryworks heated again after cooling for five months.

The *Chili* spoke us while we were boiling. She was seven months out, and so were we; but she had 380 barrels of sperm oil, which, though poor enough, was about 160 barrels better than our own fare.

We cruised off Guafo for about six weeks, but did not get another whale. One sperm whale that we chased proved to be a humpback. We gave him up and chased a right whale instead, but he is living yet for all that I can say.

Three other ships were on the same ground when we arrived: the *Chili*, just mentioned; the *Russell*, of New Bedford, Captain Morse; and the *Catawba*, of Nantucket, Captain Coleman. The Captain of the *Russell*, of whom we saw a considerable amount on board the *Athol*, for Captain Coffin enjoyed his company, was a fine example of the American gentleman afloat. On February 11th a fourth ship made its appearance and ran down to speak us. She was the *James Stewart*, of Saint John, Captain Joseph Kenney, five months from home. Captain Kenney was welcomed on board the *Athol* and stayed till eleven o'clock that evening. He brought Captain Coffin's charts that he had left at home, and also several letters.

The presence of the other whaleships lent a social aspect to affairs, for in the evening when two or more sail were in sight there was a good deal of "gamming," as visiting was called. The ceremony of "speaking" is much more formal among whalesmen than I have ever seen practised in merchant ships. There is a general realization among whaling captains that they are "no hold clavers" with their neighbors during working hours; but along about four o'clock in the afternoon, when two ships are in sight, the social instinct will often assert itself, and the ship to windward will hoist her colors as a sign that she is willing to accept an invitation to run down and speak. The leeward ship, being favorably disposed, hoists her colors, backs her main-topsail and heaves to; the windward one squares away, runs down before the wind and across the stern of the other ship. As she comes within hailing distance, the captain of the approaching ship hails:

"What ship is that, pray?"

"The A _____ of N ___ B _____ ," comes the response.

"Who commands the good ship A _____ ?"

"Captain C _____ ."

"Hope you are well, Captain C _____ ."

"Quite well, I thank you. What ship is that, pray?" and the same questions and compliments are exchanged; and one or the other accepts an invitation to come on board.

While the captain of one ship is calling upon the captain of the other, the mate of the other goes aboard the one. The visitors are thus on equal terms with their hosts, like to like; the visiting captain or mate being received by his equal in rank in the cabin, the boat-steerer finding his congeners in the steerage, and the boat's crew gravitating to the forecastle among their own kind.

One other custom connected with gamming I must mention, which in my experience is singular to whalemen: that is, for the entertainers to open their sea chests in the presence of their guests and entreat them, "If you see anything there that you would like, please help yourself. You are very welcome." This is not a mere meaningless formality, like the Spaniard's "My house, Senor, is yours," but a genuine privilege, which is never abused, though seldom utterly declined. By this means, in addition to the swapping of whaling yarns and general interchange of ideas with our neighbors, these visits give opportunities for novels, newspapers, articles of clothing, curios, "scrimshonting" (fancy articles made of whales' teeth or bone), etc., to find new and more appreciative owners.

As whalemen's hours are from daylight to sunset, "early to bed" was a rule which executed itself, visitors generally departing in good time for their own ship. One interchange of visits, however, was prolonged much further than was arranged for. Late one Saturday afternoon, Captain Kenney came on board the *Athol*, and Mr. Taylor went to spend the evening with the mate of the *James Stewart*. His boat-steerer (myself) and crew of course accompanied him. About sunset, the fog shut in and prevented the return of the boats to their respective ships. For four days the fog continued as thick as it ever was between Clam Point and West Head, and during that time the *Athol* had two captains, while the *James Stewart* had two mates. We shortened sail and stood back and forth, beating on the heads of empty casks during the day, and hoisting lights at night, so as to be heard or seen if we should pass near the other ship. At daylight of the fifth day the fog cleared off, and we saw the *Athol* standing for us, the island of Guafo in sight.

When we got aboard our own ship we found a tragic event had occurred in our absence. About wash-deck time one morning, an Englishman, named Hugh Mickens, started a row with a Portuguese boy, little José, and commenced to beat him. Mr. Thomas did not see what was going on, so the captain interfered and, after a little talk, sent Hugh aloft to slush down the topgallant mast. He was called down to breakfast, and after breakfast he refused to come on deck in his watch. The captain called all hands up and ordered Hugh to be brought. Mr. Thomas went down into the forecastle to fetch him out, and instantly hailed the deck:

"Pass a line down here quick, boys. The damn fool's cut his throat! Haul him out of here!"

They did so and carried him aft. He had given himself a pretty good slash with a razor; an inch lower, and "the subsequent proceedings" would have been all the same to him. The doctor sewed up his throat, and he was put in irons and laid in his bunk. Being let out of irons and permitted to go on deck, he tried to jump overboard, but was prevented. By some means he procured a knife and, putting the handle against the rail, was about to run against it when one of the sailors grabbed him and thwarted that manoeuvre. The "darbies" were then put back on him and he was placed in a room alone, where he could not injure himself, and kept there till we went into port, when he was discharged.

We now parted company with the *James Stewart*, expecting to meet in San Carlos, Island of Chiloe, the captains having agreed to go in there at the end of another week. Four days of the intervening time, a strong west southwest gale prevailed, right on shore. When it began, we found the ship was embayed between Guafo and a lot of islands to the southward. Tacking ship every two hours, we made the land on the weather bow on each tack. We had to carry sail to claw off shore as hard as we could, all hands on deck for over twenty-four hours. Besides the constant gale, there were frequent violent squalls during which we made a fearful leeway, losing all we had gained in several tacks, for when they struck we had to shorten sail. When the squalls had passed, we set sail again and staggered on. After banging away in that style for a day and a half, we at length made Guafo on the lee bow, three miles distant, and let her go till she was clear of the land and we had a good offing. Then we hove to. The gale could roar then, as it did, for two days longer, and nobody cared.

At sunrise on March 17th, 1846, we were off the north head of Chiloe, where we spoke the whaleship *Minerva Smith*, of New Bedford. At noon we were sailing up the harbor of San Carlos; and about three miles from town, in eight fathoms of water, our anchor found the mud, a substance to which it had been a stranger for over eight months.

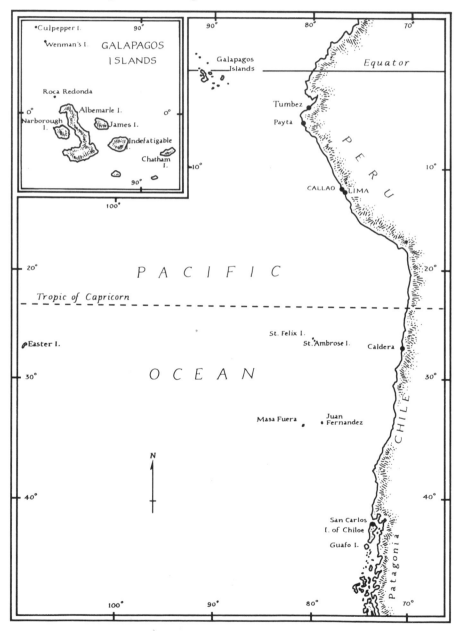

The west coast of South America

— CHAPTER XIII —

SAN CARLOS TO CALLAO

March 17th to mid-May, 1846

WE LAY IN SAN CARLOS FOR FOURTEEN DAYS, GETTING wood and water and recruiting for another cruise. Contrary to expectations, vegetables were scarce, though by the manner pursued in buying them, the prices were quite reasonable. It is the custom, as I have stated, to purchase ship's supplies, as far as possible, with blackfish oil. We had none, so the captain got up a lot of calicos, powder, tobacco, a little rum, and other prime necessaries of civilization, which he bartered with the market dealers for the produce of the country. On such articles in Chiloe there was a heavy duty; but, as is sometimes the case, even in Anglo-Saxon communities, in this little Chileno port, the government did not always receive its full dues of what was actually paid in at the custom house. Under such circumstances it seemed a perfect waste to pay legal duties. For the purpose, therefore, of preventing the custom house authorities from defrauding the treasury, we loaded a whaleboat with our merchandise and, at night, guided by the official pilot, rowed to one of the little islands in the harbor, and landed the stuff on the beach. Just at the head of the beach there was quite a spacious cave, to enter which we had to crawl on our hands and knees. In there we rolled our freight, from whence we removed it at convenient opportunities to town.

Plaza at San Carlos, Chiloe in 1835

A description of this out of the way corner of the earth, as it was at that time, may have some interest. I cannot do better than give it in the Captain's own words, copied from his private journal, which privilege has been recently extended to me by his son, my esteemed friend, Mr. J.F. Coffin, of Truro, Nova Scotia:

To judge of San Carlos merely from what I saw of it, I should pronounce it one of the most miserable of places I ever saw; but the winter being about setting in, caused the place to present a more doleful aspect than it would at a more favorable season. The winter is not cold here, though the place is in latitude 42°, ice never forming to the thickness of half an inch; but the rain—don't mention it. We arrived on the 17th of March and sailed on the 1st of April, and during our stay, I believe we had four fine days. The rest were rainy, and generally very rainy.

The town of San Carlos is small, containing probably about 2,500 inhabitants. Its buildings are of wood, and I was surprised to learn that they are generally quite proof against the rain, for to judge from their appearance, one would think them a sorry defense against the heavy rains which they have to withstand. After a frame is put up, the walls are merely boarded, and the roof is covered with boards about five feet in length, put on after the manner of shingles. I could not but wonder that these people could, by sticking up a frame and heaving a lot of boards at it, produce a dwelling almost proof against water; and our carpenters, after puzzling their brains and exhausting their ingenuity, as well as the timber, boards, shingles, nails, birch bark, sheet lead, putty, paint, and so on, cannot one time in ten build a house that will keep its floor dry.

Of the wealthier classes I had not an opportunity of knowing much; but of the peasantry I saw enough to enable me to form an opinion. Before I went to San Carlos, I thought from what I had heard that it abounded in all things which might be expected of an agricultural country; but I soon learned that all the potatoes which the farmers disposed of came from their own scanty sustenance. I went one day four or five miles up the harbor to a farming village for the purpose of procuring some fowls, pigs and so on; but to my surprise, they had none or very few indeed.

The surrounding country is very fertile and salubrious (notwithstanding its winter rains), and presents most beautiful scenery. The land near the sea is somewhat irregular, at the back of which is a range of very level land, which forms a beautiful middle ground to the picture which the Andes present as they rise above it. Now a perfect pyramid in shape takes the eye; then a chasm; and then a range of rocky precipices. These mountains are perpetually covered with snow far down from their summits, and when seen on a clear day present a most sublime landscape.

The captain and his family had a pleasant visit ashore at the houses of an Englishman and an American, who had lived here for some years. Three days' liberty was given to each boat's crew, and the boat-steerers were allowed every other night off.

Besides the *Athol*, there were several other whaleships in port, and a number of small coasters, and the combined forces of sailors on shore leave were able to keep the town wide open all the time. Four of our men, cordially supported by a number of convivial souls from other ships, made the peace officers work overtime to such an extent that they were one day honored with a position in the stocks and private apartments in the jail at night. The next morning, however, the prison was somewhat out of repair. A dozen or more of its tenants had gone out through the breach; but as they had left town, the local Dogberry could well afford to call the rest of the watch together and thank God they were rid of so many knaves. Eleven of our men deserted. Three Spaniards and a Frenchman were shipped to take their places as far as they would go round, and on April 2nd, with a good supply of fresh provisions and water, we sailed for Callao, expected to cruise for whales along the coast on our way.

We shaped our course for the island of Juan Fernandez, which everyone knows of as the home for several years of that Scotch sailing master who was the original Robinson Crusoe. On April 9th, at ten o'clock, we were within about sixty miles of the island. The weather was fine, with a gentle breeze from the northward. This was good whaling ground: the lookout aloft was never more vigilant, and the deck was anxiously waiting for news from the masthead, when a strange and far more startling cry than "There She Blows" reached our ears. All work was dropped, and the men gathered forward in little groups and talked in low quiet tones. The captain had not been on deck all the morning, neither had anything been seen of Dr. MacDonald. Mr. Thomas had been walking around with little Esther, the captain's two-year old daughter, in his arms, doing his best to interest her in watching porpoises under the bow, or anything else that would keep her amused on deck. At last the captain appeared and blushingly announced to Mr. Thomas but we all heard him, that it was a fine healthy boy, and that mother and child were doing well; and he took little Esther in to see her new brother.

At 10:30 we hoisted the ship's colors, and the boat-steerers set their flags at head and stern of their boats, in honor of our little stranger and to welcome him into this world of waters. The sailors at once christened him "Alexander Selkirk," but the parents named him James Fernandez Coffin. That afternoon we rose a shoal of blackfish, lowered and took seven of them. Not a bad day's work for the captain. Seven blackfish and a baby boy do not come to a whaleship every day. In the evening all hands gathered as usual in the "jocund twilight" on the forecastle; but this evening being an extraordinary occasion, all skylarking, single-stick duels and other boisterous fun were omitted, and we confined ourselves to singing songs in honor of our new shipmate.

Single-stick dueling was simply fencing with wooden swords or sword-length sticks.

During the next ten days we sighted the islands of Juan Fernandez, St. Ambrose, Masa Fuera, and St. Felix, but alas, no whales. The captain then concluded to stand in for the coast and run down to Callao, ship the rest of his men and then steer for the Off Shore of Peru whaling ground.

James Fernandez
Coffin, born aboard the
Athol, off Juan
Fernandez Island, and
his wife

On May 2nd, in 26° 40′ S, 75° 20′ W, we spoke the *Henry*, of Salem, ten months out, with 200 barrels of sperm oil, 300 barrels of right whale oil. She was as long from home as ourselves and quite as lean, from which fact, after the manner of mankind, we derived much consolation.

On May 6th, we made the coast of Chili, about Caldera, the mention of which to old whalesmen would suggest the story of "Caldera Dick." He was an enormous sperm whale, so named from the frequency with which he was encountered off Caldera; the ocean for a circuit of several hundred miles north, south and west of that point, being his dooryard. It was long before my time that he flourished and fell. His career covered the whole history of the American whale fisheries in the South Sea from early Colonial times, and succeeding generations of whalers tried in vain to capture him. The difficulty was not in striking him. He bore scores of harpoon wounds, but never had a lance touched his hide. When a boat approached him, he lay still and took the harpoon, and then began his game. If the thrash of his flukes did not

stove the boat, he sounded at once and then coming upon the boat from below, took it in his jaws and made matchwood of it. Such were his favorite tactics, but he was resourceful, and suited his play to the emergency of the occasion. Many a boat and many lives had been sacrificed to him. Harpoon guns and bomb lances were then far in the future; but such advances as had been made in science and the art for his destruction he overmatched with instinctive cunning. "Darts he counted as stubble; he laughed at the shaking of a spear."

But at last an evil day befell him. An old Nantucket captain—I regret that I do not remember his name—devised a scheme so novel that it was beyond all whale-philosophy. He made a large oval cask, strongly bound with iron hoops, and the heads braced from the inside, so that they could not be stove in, harnessed it securely with ropes, and attached a whale line to it. Falling in with "Caldera Dick," he placed the apparatus in a boat rowed up to the doomed brute, fastened to him with both irons, threw the cask overboard and hurried away. Old Dick tried the same whale-tricks with the cask that he had used on boats. When he grabbed it from below in his jaws, it slipped out uninjured. Struck with his tail, it rose lightly in the air and fell back with a bounce safe and sound. Surprised and puzzled, he tried to escape into the depths. But the buoyant cask acting as a powerful drag on him, he soon rose for breath. Like a dog with a tin kettle tied to his tail, he became panic stricken, until, utterly exhausted and gallied, he lay helpless and succumbed to the remorseless lance of his tormentor. I firmly believe it was this story, told and retold in the forecastle of every whaleship, which gave to Herman Melville, that over-imaginative sailor, his first conception of *Moby Dick.*

On the same day that we sighted Caldera we spoke the ship *Japan* of Nantucket. We made her out to windward in the morning. In the afternoon we hoisted our colors as an invitation to her to run down and speak us. When she was about a half a mile off we backed our main yard and let the ship come to. We had a good rap full when the main yard was backed and were under a good headway. The man at the wheel put his helm hard down, without the officer of the deck noticing it, and the ship luffed up suddenly. As she came to the wind our fore-topsail caught aback, which would have brought us around on the other tack, with great likelihood of running afoul of the *Japan*. To prevent this, we braced the fore-topsail around to box her off, and that gave us considerable sternboard; and as the *Japan* was crossing pretty close under our stern—too close for prudence—our spare spars that were run out astern raked her fore and aft, carried away her bulwarks and tore two of her boats all to pieces. Such a mishap necessarily detained the captain of the *Japan* on board his own ship. Captain Coffin went aboard of him, and the *Japan's* mate came aboard us; but the strain on the feelings of the two captains caused by the accident made only a short call advisable. We soon parted company and made all sail for Callao.

From 18° S, where the coast begins to trend to the westward, down to Callao, we kept in sight of land, from ten to seventy miles distant. Sometimes the peaks of the Andes appeared just above the horizon, and at others the whole slope from shore to summit was visible. In the bright sun, the yellow sands which covered the mountain sides shone like running rivers of gold, and it was easy to imagine how such a sight might have made visions of limitless riches float before the eyes of the early Spanish explorers and their cut-throat crews, and hurried them on with lickerish tongues to slake their thirst for plunder and to quench in blood a civilization gentler and far more humane than their own.

Very likely that thought did not present itself to all of us, though there were among our number some to whom Pizarro and Atahualpa were as familiar names as Hosea and Habakuk to the average person. To others, doubtless, the empire of the Incas appealed only as extraordinarily high land. One simple-minded Englishman, in particular, who had signed the article with an X, was unable to reconcile the evidence of his senses with a bit of rather reliable information which he had recently picked up on board the *Athol*. He had been prone to believe that, since the sea was level, the earth must be flat, but yielding to the familiar forecastle arguments, that ships appeared and disappeared on its surface as if they were sailing over a hill, and that whatever way we went, the horizon always presented at sea an unbroken circle, he had reluctantly assented to the dogma of the sphericity of the earth. But the Andes restored his original faith. One day when we were close to shore, he looked long and wonderingly at the towering mountains as they appeared through successive rifts in the clouds, and then remarked in his peculiar, unspelling, native accent: "Ram me into a 78-pounder, if I'll believe again that the world is around."

A day or two before we went into port, the masthead reported sharks— the ocean covered with them. In a few minutes we ran among them, and then we saw they were swordfish, dotted all over as far as the eye could reach. We lowered a boat, and when we got up to one I planted an iron clean through him. We hauled him up to the bow of the boat and made him fast there. Three or four more I struck, but the iron would come right out; and at last we found that unless we were close enough for the iron to go through and through their bodies, it would not hold. We caught three and brought them aboard, and had fresh swordfish for supper. But we salted down two barrelfuls. It made a very good change of diet.

On Saturday evening, May 9th, we saw St. Lorenzo Island, the south point of the harbor of Callao, and the next morning we came to anchor in the bay, in eight fathoms of water. Lying near us were the United States man-of-war *Congress*, commanded by Commodore Stockton; a French man-of-war, and the English ship *Fanny*, the latter loading for London, to sail in a few days. Thinking this a good opportunity to send letters home, many of us spent Sunday morning preparing our messages, which we took on board the *Fanny* and confided to her captain's care. I sent three letters: one to my father and mother, one to Thomas Robertson, and one to *somebody else*. The one to Tommy reached home, and I was told it was the only one received from me by any of my friends during my absence. All the others I wrote, whether before or afterwards, fetched short of their destination.

Having deposited our letters, those of us who had shore liberty spent the afternoon seeing the sights of Callao. As in all Spanish towns, its churches for size and solidity were out of all proportion to the houses. On our way back to the ship, which we reached at sunset, we rowed across to the south of the town, and to the right of the regular anchorage, where just one hundred years before old Callao had been sunk by an earthquake. The water there was not very deep, and on looking overboard some of the men pretended they could see the tops of the old houses. I saw the bottom, but nothing that I could say was the top of a house, or any part of a house. On the land, the ruins of the part not submerged were plain to be seen. That part of the harbour is buoyed out, and vessels are cautioned against anchoring there.

Callao, Peru, in the mid 1800s

My observations of Callao having extended throughout one whole Sunday afternoon, I might of course be entitled to speak authoritatively and at length upon the customs and institutions of the country. But I shall forego that privilege and, instead quote from Captain Coffin's journal, as I have been permitted to do, the note which he made on his previous visit to Callao in 1842:

Callao is the seaport of Lima, which is the capital of Peru. There is a very good road of nine miles length between them, and the surrounding country is fertile and level; but the state of the government, what with the indolence of the people, is very unfavorable to its cultivation. The houses of the city of Callao, like those of Lima, and indeed of any other part of Peru, are so constructed that one good rainstorm would bring them to the ground. They are simply built, being framed of very light timber, and the frame wattled with bamboo, something after the manner of a crockery crate. They are then plastered with mud both inside and out, and the outside is white-washed. The inside of the best are papered. The expense of living in this country is great. . . . Ten dollars will buy a pretty good pair of pantaloons, and fourteen dollars a fair pair of boots. Laborers' wages are a dollar and a half a day, and a custom house officer's bribe as much as he can get.

— CHAPTER XIV —

FIRST CRUISE OFFSHORE

Mid-May to September 5th, 1846

*C*ALLAO AND ITS FRAIL INHABITANTS WERE NOT LONG AN influence in our sphere, for the day following our arrival the captain went ashore and shipped four men—two Americans, a Hanoverian and a Spaniard, and thus reinforced, we resumed our cruise, working slowly towards the Galapagos Islands. On the fourth day out the frigate *Congress* overtook us. It was the time of the Mexican War, and she was then on her way to join the rest of the American squadron at Monterey.

All that the curious could desire to know about the Galapagos had already been published by the British government a few years before the *Athol* was among the islands. The matter consisted of the notes of a young and promising, but not yet famous, English naturalist, Mr. Charles R. Darwin, who had accompanied a surveying expedition to that part of the world. His book, however, was not in our library. Those to whom *The Voyage of the Beagle* is available need not learn from me that the Galapagos are of volcanic origin, lying under the equator, six hundred miles from the continent of South America. The water surrounding and separating them is very deep and kept cool by a current from the Antarctic Ocean. On only one of the islands is there any fresh water. It is one of the smallest of the group and is inhabited by convicts.

Albemarle, the largest of the group, is about seventy miles long, with a ridge of high mountains extending its length. At its northern end, nine miles north of the equator, rises the cone of a volcano. Fifteen miles west from the North Head, and overlooking Lee Bay, lies Roca Redonda (Round Rock)— ''Rock Dunder'' sailors call it—about three hundred feet high. It is only a few hundred yards in area, but half of it is in the northern and the other half in the southern hemisphere. The water for a mile or two around it is comparatively shoal.

On Saturday, May 23rd, at daylight, we were lying becalmed in the mouth of Lee Bay, when from the masthead we saw a ship chasing whales. We lowered all four boats and pulled after them. Before we got up to them one of the boats from the other ship got fast, which frightened the other whales and made them very cunning. It being calm and smooth, we had to paddle. They would allow us to come within fifty or a hundred yards of them, and then start off. There they kept fooling us till about two o'clock, when the waist and bow boats gave it up and returned to the ship. We kept at it in the larboard and starboard boats until sundown.

The *Athol* was then nowhere in sight, but shaping our course by the bearing of the North Head, we started to pull back into Lee Bay, expecting to meet her coming out in search of us. We rowed till midnight without seeing anything of the ship or her lights. We then took in our oars, hoisted a light, set a watch and went to sleep, tired, hungry and thirsty. The next morning at daylight we saw two ships to the northward, off Roca Redonda. We pulled for them, and at ten o'clock went on board the *President*, of Nantucket, where we took breakfast and filled up our water keg. They had not seen the *Athol* and could give us no news; but seeing four ships off Narborough and supposing one of them to be the *Athol*, we pulled for them. They proved to be the *George*, the *Balenor*, the *Nye* and the *George Porter*, of Nantucket. Captain Pease of the *Nye* and Captain Arthur of the *George Porter* were friends of Captain Coffin and we were soon made to feel at home, Mr. Shields and his crew on board of *Nye* and the rest of us on the *George Porter*. They told us the *Athol* had stood offshore to keep the run of her boats—so that with the wind moderate and the strong current, she could not get back to pick us up; and that we had better stay where we were till she came after us.

After partaking of Yankee hospitality for four days, on Friday morning we saw two ships off shore, standing in for us. One of them was the *Boy of Warren*, Captain Barton. The other we made out to be the *Athol*. Mr. Taylor and Mr. Shields started off for her, and Captain Arthur also took his boat and went on board the *Athol* to visit Captain Coffin. I was left on board the *George Porter* to steer her third mate's boat in case we should see whales during the day; but that opportunity not arising, I got back to my own ship early in the evening. The captain had been worried over our long absence and had sent the second mate ashore into Lee Bay with water and provisions, to look for us; but our boats had been on board about two hours before Mr. Thomas returned.

The day following we went fishing and sealing off Roca Redonda. With the help of lance, harpoon and musket, we caught three seals; and we loaded the boat with fish. The latter very much resembled codfish, but they had no beard under their chins. They did not taste as good as codfish, but while they and the seal flipper were fresh, the cook was a busy man.

While we were around the Galapagos, three of the boats went ashore after tortoises. They can be kept alive for a long time and are a useful article of fresh diet for men who are compelled to live year in and year out largely on salt provisions. To get the tortoises, we had to climb the lava cliffs two or three hundred feet above the sea. The cliffs had frequent fissures in them hundreds of feet deep. Yet up there on top of rocks often inaccessible to us, or to anything, one would think, but the birds, were these tortoises. We wondered how they could cross such chasms; and I do not suppose they did. Still, how did they get there in the first place? What they could feed on, I do not know, for there was not a sign of vegetation or a drop of water among those mountains—nothing but the naked rock. Just around the shore at Lee Bay were some few spears of grass and a little plant, something like a cabbage; but from fifty to five hundred feet above the sea, which, I guess, was as high as we climbed, there was not even a cactus.

We saw tortoises weighing perhaps 150 to 200 pounds, with initials and dates cut in their shells with a knife. Their safety lay in their great weight, for

we picked out the lighter ones, and loaded all three boats with all sizes from twenty to ninety pounds. The tortoise's feet and legs are about the shape of an elephant's and, I should judge, comparatively stronger. We amused ourselves riding them. A man would step on top of one weighing say sixty pounds. At first, of course, it hauled its head and legs into its shell; but by and by it would stretch them out and start off with the man on its back.

The waters around the Galapagos had proved for us more barren than their black desolate shores; so on May 30th, 1846, availing ourselves of a fine topgallant breeze from the southwest, we hauled by the wind and stood off shore. Early in the morning of June 11th, we saw the American ship *Iris* chasing whales. We lowered and soon were fast to a large whale. There was a fresh breeze and considerable sea, and as the whale tore off to windward, head to the sea, the boat leaped, bang, bang, from top to top of the waves, so that, sitting on our thwarts, the sensation was a good deal like riding a bucking bronco bareback.

We had no particular trouble until Mr. Taylor had given him his death wound with the lance, and then he went in to sell his life as dearly as possible. After receiving a lance which set him spouting blood, he ran for some distance with the boat in his wake, and then with two sweeps of his flukes turned stem for stern and made for us full speed. We lined him, that

"We amused ourselves riding them"

is kept the boat heading right for him, his blowhole in line with his hump, till he was within a few feet of us, when with a stroke of the steering-oar I sheered the boat to one side to let him pass, and as he rushed by, partly rolled on his side and snapping with his jaws, he received another lance which caused him additional trouble.

Down he went, but not far, for the line was soon slack; and we knew that his tactics were to come upon us from below. Every man had his head over the gunwale, on one side or the other, peering down into the water. Presently one of them sang out, "Here he comes—here he comes! Back water!" All hands sprang to their oars and backed a few strokes, but the whale turned in his upward course to intercept us. "Pull, boys, pull!" shouted the mate; and as the boat responded to the forward stroke, the head and jaws shot out of the water just clear of our sternpost and shut with a resounding snap. Off he went a few fathoms and lay still, spouting thick blood. We crawled cautiously towards him, to finish the work, when with great swiftness he began to roll over and over on top of the water towards us, winding the line round and round his body. We had to slack line and pull for our lives, and as he floundered past we were all but swamped in the boiling sea, while torrents of salt water raised by his labors fell upon us and half filled the boat.

By the time we were bailed out the fight was over and our victim lying fin-out, dead. At 2 P.M. we took him alongside and made him fast, in 6° 42′ S; 105° 14′ W. He made one hundred barrels of oil. I saved some of his teeth and a part of his jawbone, of which I made a cane.

On June 16th we spoke the ship *Sarah Francis*, of Fair Haven, twenty-nine months out, 1,100 barrels of sperm oil. On the 18th we saw a good number of whales, and all four boats lowered. Ours was lucky in getting fast. As soon as the whale was struck, the others took alarm and made off as fast as they could, and our captive after them. He shortly took us right into the midst of the herd of frightened whales. As we were running side by side with a large 70-barrel bull, Mr. Taylor darted at him with his lance, with such effect that he was soon in his dying flurry. One of the other boats came and fastened to him, but he was practically a dead whale before they reached him.

The one we were fast to gave us a long hard fight—and won. We hauled up on him and the mate gave him a lance, but before we could stern-all to get out of his way, he hit the boat a mighty blow with his flukes, which lifted her clear out of the water, smashing her beyond all repair, and he went off scot-free. We clung to the shattered fragments of the boat for about an hour and were then picked up.

Ever since we had been in the Pacific, whenever there was any gamming, we were sure to hear of stories told by our mate to the officers of other ships, reflecting on the courage and ability of his fellow officers and especially of his boat-steerer. These stories as they came back to us were to the effect that he had had to kill all the whales we had taken, because the other boat-headers were incompetent; but that we should have done a great deal better if his boat-steerer were not a coward and afraid to strike a whale. It was good, therefore, for all of us to get offshore, where the opportunities for visiting and spreading tales were fewer. Our tempers, however, did not improve towards the mate, and there were frequent discords.

Mr. Taylor was a native of Fredericton up the St. John River; and people from that way are sometimes called "yellow belly ponders." The phrase has reference to the yellow pond lily; but up-the-river folks do not like to hear it. On one occasion when we were in the sail-room, stowing sails, Taylor called me a "longshore cousin of the captain," and I called him a "yellow belly."

"I'll fix you for that," he said, and came at me. We had a scuffle and he went down on his back. He was a great deal stronger than I, but I was quicker and rather hard to hold. It commenced as if all in play, but it was really in earnest; I know it was with me, and I am very sure it was with him. After he was down, I would have pounded him if I had dared. I supposed, if I had, they would have put me in irons; and I did not like him well enough for that; so I got up laughing, and the affair passed off as a little fun.

Not long after that, there was some difficulty down in the steerage between José and Francisco, the two Portuguese boat-steerers, and Craft, a Saint John's man. Craft was in poor health. He and José clinched, and the third man interfered; so I pulled off my shirt and stepped up to see fair play. In crossing the steerage, I hit the lamp, which upset on my back and covered me with oil. I caught hold of José and was using him up pretty fast when Mr. Taylor came walking by on deck, and as the booby hatch was off he could see right down into the steerage. He came down the ladder and pretended to part us, but his real object was to vent some spite on me. He grabbed me from behind to give José a chance to punch me, but dripping as I was with oil, and mad now from head to foot, nothing could hold me long. Getting clear of Mr. Taylor, I squared round to stand off the two of them. The mate and José tried to catch me, but I was too slippery for them and we had a lively time of it. Francisco and Craft kept up their separate struggle, and the five of us together no doubt made noise enough to be heard all over the ship. At last the captain appeared and, stepping down the companionway, said, "Mr. Taylor, you ought to stop that work. Why haven't you stopped it?"

"Well," the mate replied, "I found them fighting and I thought I better let them go on and have it out. I knew very well who would get the worst of it."

"Who would get the worst of it, Mr. Taylor?" I asked.

"You would."

"Well, if you think so, come and try it."

"Stop-stop-stop!" the captain's voice broke in; "Mr. Taylor, instead of preventing a row, you are trying to stir up one."

Since getting our last whale we had been for some days fitting up our boat to use a gun, which, it was claimed, would shoot a harpoon fourteen fathoms and send it three feet deep into a whale. The barrel of the gun was about three feet long; the stock was a good deal like that of a pistol. It was mounted like a swivel, working on a pivot set on top of a post, which was placed in the bows of the boat and braced with iron. The stock was held with one hand and swung in any direction, elevating or depressing the muzzle to suit the object fired at. We had tried it several times at a barrel thrown overboard, sailing down as nigh as we wanted to and shooting. Once or twice we hit the barrel, and as often missed it. Our orders were, every time we lowered from the ship, to put the gun in the boat. All the rest of the gun-gear was kept in the boat, except the cartridge which was to be put behind the harpoon. I did not like the thing at all and felt much surer of getting fast under the old method of "wood and blackskin"—bringing the boat near enough to touch the whale—and setting the iron in by hand, than by this contrivance for flying darts at a distance.

While we were employed fitting up our boat to shoot whales, on June 28th, whales were seen and the waist boat got one that made about sixty barrels of oil.

A day or two afterwards it was my masthead lookout from two to four in the afternoon, and the captain came up to keep a lookout with me. He began to talk about home, etc., and at last the conversation got around to the way matters were going on board. In reply to his questions, I told him how the mate had begun to dislike me and of the tales I had heard of his accusing me of cowardice. "If you think, Sir," said I, "that I am afraid to strike a whale, I don't want you to let me steer a boat; but my mind is made up that if I hear again of Mr. Taylor's saying I'm frightened, the next time he puts me alongside of a whale, I'll dart my irons pole foremost, and you can break me for it." The captain assured me that he had never entertained anything but a good opinion of me, and told me to behave myself and he would stand by me.

"Well, sir," said I, "I will try to deserve a good reputation, but if Mr. Taylor ever puts me near enough to another whale, we'll ride him like a new main tack, or stove the boat."

The captain smiled at my vehemence, but it was not many days before my words were made good.

On Thursday, July 9th, during my masthead, at two o'clock, I sighted whales broad on the weather bow, going to windward. The yards were backed, all four boats lowered, and we pulled up to windward. They were large bull whales, going quite fast, apparently making a passage or fighting. We pulled for about an hour, each boat-header selecting his whale. The second mate's boat was the fastest, she got farthest to windward, and the bow and starboard boats followed her. We kept pulling along somewhat to the left of the course of the other boats, following a large whale until he sounded perhaps a half a mile ahead of us.

While the whale was down the mate asked me if the gun was in the boat. I said no, that I had forgotten it. At that he began to call me all sorts of things for leaving the gun behind. Well, as I had been to the masthead and raised the whales, and had been kept there reporting their movements till the boat was lowered, I had only had time to slip down the backstay and jump into the boat as she shoved off from the ship, without thinking of anything. So that was the reason I had forgotten the gun. I did not like his remarks, but did not offer any excuses and said very little to him, as we were not good friends and the less I said then the better. But I kept thinking, "Perhaps I'll satisfy you yet."

We pulled to windward for about three quarters of an hour, and then hove to, waiting for the whale to come up. We expected, from his size, that he would stay down about an hour. All hands kept a good lookout around until, the mate spying something to leeward and thinking it might be a whale, we kept off before the wind and put the sail up. There was a good strong breeze, with considerable sea, and we had a large foresail, so that to steer before the wind soon made a man's arms ache. The mate had only steered a little while after the sail was set when he told me in a very surly way to come aft and take the steering-oar. That really was not part of my duty, but I obeyed, and the mate went forward to look out for the whale. In about half an hour he came aft again and said, "Now go forward and look out for that whale."

"What whale?" I asked.

"There's a whale there, right ahead. Roll up the sail."

I went forward, rolled up the sail and took the mast out. I guess I used a little more energy in doing it then was necessary, for I was ripe for a row. He noticed my manner and let out on me a most insulting remark. I made some reply, the best I could think of at the moment, and he said, "Mind how you talk back to me, or I'll come forward and throw you overboard."

"Come on," I said, "we'll meet amidships and go over together."

"If you don't hold your tongue I'll heave a spade at you," was his next threat.

"Oh, Mr. Taylor," said I, "you better do nothing of the kind; I've as many tools in my end of the boat as you have, and if you miss me—."

"Shut up your— —head," he snapped, "and look out for that whale."

I kept a watch out ahead, and by and by he said, "Do you see him?"

"No," I replied, "I don't see a whale. That's a couple of blackfish."

The mate was right, however, and what I took for blackfish was no doubt the whale turned on his side, with his fin and the corner of his fluke out, which looked like the humps of two blackfish.

About that moment, one of the men, pointing to windward and off to the northward, exclaimed, "There's white water." We all noticed it, about three miles off, and supposed—and the fact turned out to be—that the waist boat had struck a whale. I kept a good lookout, but saw nothing more; and if what I had seen was a whale, he must have gone down and the boat passed over him, for in about fifteen minutes he broke water to windward.

I sang out, "There he is, right astern of us." And by the time the mate could look around, the whale had turned on his back and was coming directly for us, piling up the water with his great square head, and opening and shutting his jaws with a snap like the slamming of a door.

We were luffed to, lying in the trough of the sea, drifting. The mate kept right off before the wind, and shouted to the men to take their oars. Before they had time to do so, the whale caught up to us, turned on his side and made a grab for the sternpost. But the mate with a stroke of the steering-oar gave the boat a rank sheer, and the great jaws came together without any wood between them.

When the whale found he had missed his hold, he turned back up and went down under the boat until his blowhole was about abreast our forward thwart. Then he raised so that the boat grounded on him, gradually slipping, slipping, but still going along with him at a high speed. I caught up my iron and tried to get in shape to dart, but the boat jostled and I stumbled against the crutch and broke it, and the second iron fell overboard. I regained my feet with the first iron still in my hand, and by the time the bunch of his neck was past me, I drew back to strike.

The mate in a terrified voice called to me, "Don't you strike that whale! Don't you strike that whale, I tell you!"

He might as well have asked me to please see him safe home. Looking at him over my shoulder, I said, "Who's afraid now, Mr. Taylor? I'll strike him if he knocks us into ten thousand pieces." And the comforting thought went through my head, "The water's warm if we do drown, and it's no worse for me than for the mate." Then with all my venom against the mate giving me strength, I set the iron down into the top of the whale's back till it fetched up against the hitches. He gave a big rouse with his flukes, and as the boat capsized I jumped overboard.

I swam off a minute and then looked round. The boat was bottom up, and I saw the whale break water about two hundred yards from it, with the iron-pole sticking straight up in his back, and off he went. The men climbed up on the bottom of the boat, and as the line was running sizzling across it, the mate told one of them to cut it. I stayed out of the way till all the men were on the boat, so that nobody would get hold of me, as some of them were not good swimmers. Then I swam to the bow and pulled myself partly up, my legs hanging in the water each side of the stem.

"Is there any room here for me?" I asked. As I spoke, the jaw of the whale shot up on one side of the boat and his head on the other, not three feet from me. Throwing myself backward, I pushed off with my feet from the boat, and

"He gave a big rouse with his flukes, and as the boat capsized I jumped overboard"

heard the crash of splinters and the cries of the men as I swam clear. I looked round just in time to see the whale as he spouted after cutting off the head of the boat. He was slowly turning jaw-downward, and a little Spanish-Chilean was lying on the flat of his back, both feet and hands in the air, on the side of the whale's head. He instantly slid off, and I was afraid he had fallen into the whale's mouth, but the whale in turning had rolled him off the opposite side.

Then I swam away from the wreck as fast as possible, trying to keep ahead of the whale so that he would not see me. The after oarsman, William Mills, an excellent swimmer, followed me. When we had gone forty or fifty yards, we looked back and saw the whale lying in the fragments, biting and snapping at everything he could get hold of, and whenever he felt anything against his flukes he knocked it sky high. He had a good time there for what seemed to us about half an hour. He bit all the oars in two, smashed the stern of the boat to pieces, and even bit the lantern keg and boat kegs, masts and sails—everything that he could see or feel. At last the chips were so small and scattered about that there was no more sport in it, and he disappeared.

I said to Mills then, "I guess the whale's gone. Let's go down and see if anybody is left alive." So, being to windward of the boat, we swam down carefully, and as we were getting among the wreckage I saw the mate's hat on the water. I swam towards it and was about to pick it up when the mate popped up under it. He spurted out a mouthful of water and, staring around, said three or four times, "Oh, dear—oh, dear!" For fear he would catch hold of me, I swam away as hard as I could, and after a few strokes my hand came in contact with a piece of the steering-oar—about half of it. I gave that a shove towards the mate. He caught and held to it for support.

There was a Frenchman who had grabbed the mate and dragged him under, but he succeeded in kicking the Frenchman loose, and then both of them clung to the piece of oar. At that point I began to get frightened—not about myself; whether I would get out of it dead or alive never entered my head. But I was afraid the mate would drown. I felt no sympathy for anybody else, but all my hatred against him had soaked out and I felt sorry for him. I wished I had not acted so and brought him to such extremity. But there was nothing more that I could do for him, and I said to Mills, who kept at my side, "We had better get away from here; the whale has left and come back three times, and he may come again." So we struck out together.

Now, the other boats had all gone to the right of us, to windward, and the ship was about six miles off to leeward. It was no use to try to swim for the ship, we never could reach her. The sun was about three quarters of an hour high, so that with the short tropical twilight, in not more than an hour it would be dark. We decided that we must swim out to the right and try to intercept the boats, which were up to windward and before sunset would be running down towards the ship. Our only chance was to get between them and the ship so that they would come across us. In our judgment, they would pass about half or three quarters of a mile from where our boat was chewed up.

When we first started out, each of us had a piece of an oar to help keep us up, but they retarded us so much that we threw them away and trusted to "our own boat and oars." In a little while we came across the waifs, which must have been about the spot where the boat was capsized. They were little Union Jacks, fastened to a light ten-foot pole. To hoist one waif is a sign that we have struck a whale. Two waifs meant a stoved boat or a dead whale. We took both waifs, drew our sheathknives and cut the little stops around them, and every few minutes held them up, and then lowered them and swam on.

The sun was creeping perilously near the horizon when on top of a sea we spied the fourth mate's or starboard boat coming down before the wind with her sail set. We shouted and held up our waifs until they saw us and steered for us. When they got within hailing distance, we told them that the mate's boat was stoved all to pieces and all hands were drowning. They immediately trimmed in their sheet and came by the wind, and were going to run right past us in their haste to get up to where the rest of the crew were. But we made two or three desperate strokes, grabbed the gunwale and climbed into the boat. They told us the second mate's boat was also stoved by the whale which he had struck, and the bow boat had picked up her crew and was towing the stoven boat to the ship.

When we got up to where we had left the men, we found the mate and the Frenchman still on the steering-oar, and the Chileno and the midship oarsman, a Negro, were clinging to pieces of the wreck. We looked around for the whale but saw nothing of him, so we took the bow of the boat which the whale had bitten off, and which was the only part that remained together, and towed it down to the ship. All the rest was smashed into pieces that you could pick up with your thumb and finger. We hoisted in the bow of the boat on deck. It had been braced with iron for the gun, and it held together in spite of getting a rap from the whale's tail. If the gun had been in the boat, it would have gone to kingdom come with all the rest of the gear, and I should not have been the least bit sorry.

For some days afterwards the mate was a sick man. His struggle with the Frenchman had nearly worn him out, and he was almost ready to let go when rescued. While he was laid up, the captain asked him how it all came to happen. Of course, I did not hear the conversation, which took place in the cabin, but I was told that Mr. Taylor gave me great praise for the manner in which I followed his directions in striking the whale, and that he said I was not frightened at all.

I said nothing about the occurrence to anybody; but pretty soon it was whispered around among the officers that Taylor was shaking like an aspen leaf as he stood aft in the sternsheets, begging me not to strike. Some of the men must have told it, for I am sure it did not come from me.

That ended my experience with a harpoon gun, and I was determined not to go in the ship another voyage, but to leave as soon as we went into port, unless I could be transferred to another boat; and so I told the captain.

Following the accident, we were busy fitting out new boats, grinding new irons and lances, making boatsails, etc., to supply the place of the lost gear. The captain let me do nothing else, and stood my masthead for me, while this work was going on, so that by Saturday night we were ready to lower for whales, if any should be seen. Day after day, however, no good sounds were heard, though we continued to see good signs, such as squid, large flying fish, and streaks on the water.

On July 11th, one year from the day we left Saint John, we spoke the ship *Pacific*, of New Bedford, Captain Hoxey, twenty-one months out, 1500 barrels of sperm oil. Our catch for the twelve months had been 470 barrels. Priest and levite would certainly have passed us by on the other side, for we were entirely out of suits with fortune and too poor to pick.

On the 14th we spoke the ship *Robert Edwards*, of New Bedford, Captain Burgess. The *Robert Edwards* ran down to leeward of us and lowered a boat, and her captain with his wife and child came on board. It did our souls good to see the meeting between the women. They ran towards each other, shook hands, hugged and kissed, like sisters that had been long separated. As the two ships remained in the same vicinity for some time, several visits were interchanged, and we rigged a whip and chair with which to hoist the ladies out and in.

But one more whale was caught on this cruise, and that was by one of the other boats, on July 27th. He made forty barrels. On August 9th, we spoke the *Arnolda*, of New Bedford, Captain Coffin, twenty-five months out, 1,000 barrels. About two weeks later, the captain decided to bear up for port to recruit water and provisions. We were only three months out from Callao, but had not filled our water casks since leaving San Carlos, and the water supply was too low for us to linger.

It was essential that the daily consumption of water should be greatly reduced, and the officers proposed that the men be put on an allowance. The captain, however, was opposed to it. His theory was that if a man knows he can drink as often as he wants, he will only drink when thirsty; but that if he is limited to a certain amount, he imagines himself thirsty all the time, and after using up his allowance he is grumbling and discontented until the next issue. So that captain hit upon a plan by which all hands could drink whenever they wanted to, and still use but very little water.

The scuttle-butt was allowed to go empty, and a large cask of water with only a two-inch bunghole in it was lashed aft, abaft the mizzenmast. The dipper was a tin tube about fourteen inches long, and of a diameter just sufficient to go through the bunghole; a piece of lead was soldered on the side, so as to tip it down in the water, and to the wire bale a string was tied. But the dipper was not kept in the cask. The mizzentop was the place for it, so that when a man wanted a drink he had to go to the mizzentop and get the dipper, come down, draw the water from the cask and pour it into his drinking cup. Then he had to carry the dipper back to the mizzentop and make it fast there again. One man was not allowed to get a drink for another, but each one had to make these two journeys aloft for himself whenever he wanted to quench his thirst. Consequently, it was only when he really needed water that one would take so much trouble to get it; and by that means the supply was made to last until we reached port.

On the morning of August 25th we passed within eight miles of Wenman's Island, one of the Culpeppers. That evening as it grew dark we saw a bright light off to the southeast, which we supposed was from a ship trying out oil at night. Later in the night, however, we made it out to be the volcano on the North Head of Albemarle, which had been silent for many years, now in a state of eruption.

On Saturday, September 5th, at 6 P.M., we came to anchor in the port of Tumbez, Peru, in eight fathoms of water, a mile and a half from the shore.

— CHAPTER XV —

TUMBEZ AND PAYTA

September 5th to September 28th, 1846

Balsa Raft

TUMBEZ BAY IS AN OPEN ROADSTEAD IN WHICH A VES-
sel anchoring in eight fathoms of water, a mile and a half from
the shore, is sheltered from the wind around about twenty points of
the compass. Tumbez River empties into this bay. At the entrance of the river
is a bar on which the sea breaks heavily when there is a fresh breeze. Inside
the bar about a quarter of a mile, on Tumbez Point, are three or four shanties
where beef is slaughtered and jerked, and supplied to whaleships or loaded
on catamarans that do the lighterage and coasting trade of the country. The
catamarans are rafts made of balsa logs fastened together by treenails or
lashings to cross-logs laid on top of them. In the middle is a large cribwork
of logs eight or nine feet high, for living quarters and in which the cargo is
carried. The raft has sometimes one, but usually two, large lateen sails, and
between the logs two or three boards are shoved down, which answer as a keel

or centreboard, to keep the raft from drifting to leeward when on a wind.

The offal from the slaughtering attracts to that vicinity great numbers of sharks and crocodiles, and their presence is apt to make an upset on the bar a serious matter. I remember hearing Captain Solomon Kendrick, who it will be remembered was an old whaling captain, tell of having his boat capsized in the surf on Tumbez bar. It was after dark, their shouting failed to attract anybody's attention from land, and they were fast drifting out with the current, when one of his men took the risk of the sharks and crocodiles that he knew were all around him, and swam to the point, where he found a boat and came off to the rescue of his companions.

Besides the slaughtering establishment, a pulpourie is conveniently located on the point, so that the thirsty sailor is separated very handily from a liberal share of his spending money before he reaches town, nine miles up the river.

On the night following our arrival the wind blew heavy and a number of these catamarans drove ashore on Tumbez Point and broke up. In the morning the logs were scattered all along the beach, and men were engaged in picking them up and rebuilding the rafts. Balsa wood was then generally unfamiliar to North Americans. I had never heard of it, and it was marvel to me to see ordinary men handling those great logs so easily. We went ashore, and to test my strength I tried with all my might to lift one end of one of the logs. It came up so easily that I nearly fell over backwards.

We remained at anchor near Tumbez Point for ten days, getting wood, water and provisions. We filled the water-casks two miles above the point. For wood we took the mangrove on the side of the river. Its roots grow up above the mud from five to nine feet, sprawled out like gigantic spiders' legs, and we had to climb up on them to cut the tree down. The wood is very hard and heavy, and as the young trees are slender and straight we selected many of them for iron and lance poles. The river fairly swarmed with crocodiles. At every opening in the cane brake as we passed to and from the ship, three or four big saucy fellows would slide down the bank and go off slowly, as if deliberating whether it was worthwhile to get out of the way or not. We shot several of them, but they all sank in deep water.

I did not see the town of Tumbez because, at the captain's request, I went about five miles up the river to a plantation owned by a wealthy Spaniard and spent three days procuring potatoes and other vegetables for the ship. The old Spaniard and I had our meals together, and the rest of the family— his wife and four children—ate afterwards. He was a great talker and entertained me with tales of hunting and of political revolutions. In turn, I told whaling and sea stories. He could not speak English, and I knew but little Spanish. When we could not make ourselves understood by words, we eked out the conversation very well with gestures, at which he was expert, and I gradually improved. It was interesting to watch the farm laborers dig sweet potatoes. These were not planted in hills or rows, but broadcast like oats, and the men squatted or kneeled down and dug them with large knives. They called the potato "cammoty." In three days time we loaded a large scow with pumpkins, bananas, plantains, limes, and 100 barrels of sweet potatoes, and took them down to the ship.

From Tumbez we sailed on September 15th for Payta, a short distance to the south, where we anchored on the eighteenth. Here, Craft, who was now a very sick man, was put aboard a whaleship bound home. At my urgent insistence it was arranged that I should leave Mr. Taylor's boat and steer Mr. Thomas; and a young man named Aaron Kappe, whom we found here—a son of a well-known Jewish auctioneer in St. Thomas, West Indies—was shipped as the mate's boat-steerer. I had known Kappe before, and have met him several times since, in New York, as master of a brigantine.

The town of Payta, built on the open seacoast, has been repeatedly, in the various wars between England and Spain, sacked by British privateers, and when there were no wars, by the undiscriminating buccaneers. In 1586, Sir Thomas Candish, following close on the track of Admiral Drake, burned and plundered the town. In 1709, the *Duke* and *Duchess*, privateers of Bristol, having on board Alexander Selkirk, whom they had lately found at the Island of Juan Fernandez, cruised for some months off the Saddle of Payta, as the mountains back of the town are called, where they took several valuable Spanish prizes that were endeavoring to make that port. And in 1741, the famous Captain George Anson captured and burned Payta, took over £30,000 of silver and other precious metals, and destroyed property estimated by the Spaniards at more than a million and a half sterling.

On account of the good anchorage, Payta, at the time the *Athol* was there, was much frequented by whaleships as a place of refreshment. It was then a town of perhaps 8,000 inhabitants, mostly a mixture of Spanish and aborigines. The men were as a rule fine looking. Very few of the women, according to our northern standards, could be called beautiful. They ordinarily wore short dresses, satin shoes and no stockings, and all, as the captain expressed it, "appeared to wish to treat a stranger with all possible attention and complaisance." The houses, as in Callao and Tumbez, usually had the ground for the floor, were generally of the wattled "crockery crate" type, with thatched roofs and mud-plastered sides. The town is surrounded by sandy plains utterly bare of trees or grass, and every drop of water had to be brought in on mules' backs a distance of fifteen miles. Naturally, but little of it was wasted in washing.

As rain is very rare, Payta is a good place in which to paint a ship. The third day after our arrival we had finished painting the *Athol's* hull and were painting the spars, the square sails being unbent and hanging in the earings, and the fore-and-aft sails hoisted up on the stays. While Mills and I were painting the doublings of the foremast-head we saw a cloud rising over the land. Soon a light breeze struck, bringing off with it thousands of mosquitoes, and when the cloud came overhead it began to sprinkle rain— a thing that had not happened before in many days—and spotted all our paint. During the shower we heard the people ashore shouting with astonishment at such a wonderful phenomenon. There were children then half grown in Payta who had never seen rain before.

The only green spot within six miles was the Protestant burying ground, close to the beach, about three miles from town. A little nearer town was the Catholic burying ground. That was on the beach under a high and rather remarkable sand cliff. It was about half an acre, with a picket fence around it. On the land side, almost against the cliff, was a large shed open in front towards the sea. In the middle of the yard stood a huge cross, around

which was a pile of human bones, the accumulation of ages and ages, I suppose, for it was over fifteen feet high. The mode of burial was to wrap the bodies in cloth and cover them lightly with sand. The dogs and vultures and wild animals came and dug them out, devoured the flesh and left the bones to bake in the sun. When the bones were well dried out they were picked up and thrown around the cross. At any time in the graveyard human hands and legs could be seen sticking out of the sand, partly eaten by dogs. The wealthy people, I believe, were buried in under that shed; I never knew exactly, but that is what I think.

In the Protestant burying ground, which was about a third larger, there was no cross, and it was strewn all over promiscuously with bones. The bodies were buried about a foot under the sand, and where the dogs hauled them out and tore them to pieces they were left to lie. That probably accounts for the grass. If the bones had been picked up perhaps the grass would have perished. No wonder "God's Acre" was so tiny, when its occupants were dispossessed after so brief a tenancy.

Half of our crew were allowed ashore at a time. The port watch could not leave the ship till the starboard watch came aboard. As I was going ashore one morning to bring off the liberty men, I passed the government faluca with the *capitan del puerto* (port captain), the *aduanero* (customs officer), the *capitan de las guardas* (captain of the guard), and a number of soldiers on board. They were going off to an American whaleship which had just arrived, to take out of her a man who was supposed to be one of the mutineers of a brig that had sailed from Callao for England and had been taken by the crew and scuttled about the Galapagos Islands, the captain and officers murdered and a large amount of money landed and buried. An old Irishman named Patrick O'Dea, who kept a hardware store where I went to buy some rasps and files, told me the story of the mutiny. The prisoner was brought ashore handcuffed. I saw him on the wharf and talked to him. He was a native of Rhode Island and had in his chest a large knife and a caulking mallet and irons. The mallet and the handle of the knife were inlaid with silver, pearl and shells and different kinds of wood—his own handiwork. He pointed out the caulking tools, as they were searching his effects, and asked if they looked like the belongings of a pirate; but when the Peruvian officers saw the knife, they professed to regard it as an important clue to the crime, and passed it from one to the other with very significant shrugs and glances. Whatever became of the man I do not know. Unless he had the means of bribing the authorities, or obtained the protection of the American or English consul, I fear that his guilt or innocence made but little difference to his fate.

Mr. O'Dea had lived in Payta for thirty years, was married to a native woman and had a large family. His hardware store was a favorite meeting place for sailors, several of whom were usually sitting around the door. He spoke Spanish fluently, but his brother Dan, who lived with him, could speak only English and an occasional Spanish word—all with a strong Irish accent. The little boys playing in the street were the plague of Dan's life. They would fill a basket of stones and empty it in front of the store door. Dan would rush out after them, shouting, "Ye spalpeens, git out of here wid your damn paydros, or I'll scalp ye." Our Portuguese boat-steerer when they heard him remarked, "Oh, dat nice name he speak—Dom Pedro!"

The best hotel in Payta was kept by an Englishman named Smith. Dr. MacDonald was one evening playing billiards in Smith's hotel with a cigar-maker named Antonio Something-or-other when Kappe and I came in. In the room also was an old English resident of Payta who, it was said, had once been very wealthy, but drinking and carousing had broken him down. It only took about one drink to get him a little off, and this evening he had had several. This poor fellow was putting in his oar from time to time, making remarks about the game, till Antonio lost patience and told him to go home. Good natured hints had no effect on the drunken man, and Antonio attempted to put him out doors, but the Englishman caught hold of him and they began to wrestle. Dr. MacDonald, billiard cue in hand endeavored to part them, and with the peacemaker's usual bad luck, he stuck the end of the cue with great force into Antonio's eye. Antonio gave a howl of pain, which apparently did more than anything else to floor the Englishman, for down he went in a heap in one corner, while Antonio danced around the floor, holding both hands over his injured eye, yelling, *Carrajo! Carrajo! Oh! Oh! Carrajo!*"

The poor doctor stood amazed for a moment, and then he stepped up to Antonio to see what he had done and to offer his sympathy and help. He knew only a few Spanish words, but he tried to express his regrets in that language. *"Oh, Senor,"* he said, *"yo no entendi"*—which meant, as he thought, "I didn't mean to." It really meant "I did not understand." That did not seem to Antonio any apology at all for poking his eye out and had no soothing effect upon him whatever. He evidently thought Dr. MacDonald had taken sides against him in favor of the English. He stopped capering around, and putting one hand over his sound eye, he bent his head back and looked at the chandelier. What he saw there, or rather, what he did not see, caused him to break out again, this time in "English as she is spoke" and in a most doleful tone. "Me no look a bit," he moaned—"me no look a bit!"

The doctor succeeded in pacifying him after a while, or thought he had, and to cement his good will, invited Antonio into a little booth curtained off at one side of the room, to drink a bottle of wine with him. The waiter was a little slow in bringing the wine, and Dr. MacDonald, anxious to get Antonio to drinking, stepped out of the booth to hurry the waiter up. As he left the room, the Spaniard whipped out at another door, and was gone when the doctor and waiter returned.

That worried the doctor very much. He did not play any more, but sat watching Kappe and me play pool and billiards till a late hour, when he said he must go to his boarding house, which was five or six hundred yards from the hotel. He was afraid, as the cigar-maker had left him so abruptly, that he might be waylaying him or have some evil intentions towards him; so Kappe and I went home with him.

On our way back to the hotel, Kappe proposed that we stop at a little wine shop or *pulpourrie* which he knew about at the end of a narrow alleyway off the main street. We went in and called for a bottle of wine. While we were drinking, the landlady came to us and said, "*Quereis vosotros ir a su casa?*"—"Do you want to go home?" We answered, no, that we had not finished our wine. Then she began to talk, talk, talk, in Spanish, but as women are apt to do, she spoke so fast we could not understand her. Presently we heard low voices outside. The old woman rushed to the door and slammed it and put a bar across to prevent its being opened. A man on the outside shook the door and asked to be let in, but our sentry told him to go away. When all was quiet again, Kappe and I, having finished our wine, rose to go. The old woman took down the bar and, putting her head out, looked down the alley, then opening the door wide, remarked "*Esta claro*," and we went out, she keeping the door open to give as much light as possible, for it was very very dark.

We had gone about half way to the main street when we saw a few feet ahead of us two men standing against the wall, one on each side, wearing ponchos. A ray from the lamp in the doorway glinted on a knife which one of them had not quite concealed. We said "Good evening," but they made no reply and stepped in front of us. We jumped back, undecided what to do; but as just then the door behind us was shut, it was no use to retreat, and the only thing left was to rush them, if we could. Our eyes had now become accustomed to the darkness, so that we could see as well as they could anyway.

With a one, two, three, we made a spring forward. The man on my side was a little in advance of the other, and as I came up to him he went sprawling and I jumped over him. Kappe hit his man a blow which knocked him sidewise against the wall, and Kappe sprang clear, but the fellow brought his arm around with a backward swing, and I felt the sting of a dagger in my back as I darted past him. I cannot say whether they chased us or not. I do not think they did. When we reached the hotel, the blood was running down my back from a small stab wound. Fortunately the knife had struck a rib, and all I needed was a little sticking plaster. As the hotel was full, we could not get a bed. They gave us some blankets, and we lay down on the billiard tables and went to sleep.

I have no doubt our assailants were hired by Antonio for Dr. MacDonald's benefit, and Kappe and I having been seen in his company, they were not at all particular because he was not with us when they made their attack, but even preferred to assault two rather than three. The keeper of the *pulpourrie* evidently had wind that an attempt upon us would be made and was anxious to get us out of the house before it happened. But we did not set on foot any investigation into the matter. Murders were daily committed in the most public manner. Walking along the streets of Payta in the daytime, I have heard a sound of scuffling and of angry voices in a wine shop, when suddenly the door would fly open and a man or two pitch headlong into the street, crawl off a few yards and die in a wallow of blood. When such things are commonplace occurrences, little adventures like ours would be too insignificant to notice.

Everyone who has been much among the South Americans has observed with what enthusiasm they join in the celebration of saints' days, and what heartiness and zeal they exhibit in carrying out the details of a street pageantry. The festival of some very exalted saint occurred while we were in Payta, and as strangers are always cordially treated on those occasions, a number of us from the *Athol* attended. Over the street, for several days previously, arches had been erected, decorated with colored ribbons, and in a little niche in each arch was placed the image of a saint. On Sunday morning the whole town turned out to church. The ladies, gorgeous with silken mantuas and glittering and tinkling with ear and finger rings, occupied the body of the house, within a double row of pillars which supported the roof, and in the entire absence of pews, they squatted on the floor, from which they rose at different points of the service to a kneeling position. Being unused myself to such exercises, I appreciated the force of the captain's statement that "he thought he should need paunch mats on his knees before he could endure so much humility." Just inside the line of the pillars extended a single row of chairs, which were occupied by the gentlemen; and between them and the walls crouched the people of the lower classes. Each person as he entered the church was presented with a green lime stuck full of cloves, having a colored silken tassel on each end of it, and a loop or becket by which to suspend it to one's coat button. What its significance was I have never been able to learn.

I cannot attempt to describe the religious services. A large painting of the Virgin in a gilt frame was an object of much attention, being borne about the church by four priests, the kneeling worshippers moving out of their way as they approached. The incense was kept replenished by four Negro girls dressed in white, and the pungent smoke which pervaded the place kept everyone coughing. The ceremonies in the church being ended, a procession was led through the streets by a number of priests bearing an image of the Virgin, which was richly dressed in embroidered silk. Behind them walked the Negro girls with the incense. Next came four priests carrying a large white canopy, which they held aloft by staves at the four corners; and then followed the male members of the congregation in the order of their wealth and social position, each one holding a candle. The ladies had betaken themselves to the balconies and windows, whence they strewed flowers upon the heads of those in the procession. As each arch was reached, the parade halted and the priests kneeled to the saint whose image occupied the niche and repeated a prayer. So a tour of the town was made, terminating at the church door again, where a final prayer was offered and the crowd broke up.

All these performances had been as pompous and imposing as the participators could render them with the aid of music and external display; and while, probably because of the novelty, their solemnity did not impress me, everything was done with devout intent. It seemed, therefore, strangely inconsistent that the same people, excepting the clergy, should immediately afterwards join in pure buffoon mummery which was a satire and parody of the sacred rites in which they had just been engaged. The religious procession having disbanded, a most grotesque masquerade followed, making the same circuit of the city, in which the devil in effigy took the place of the Virgin and the saints, while fantastic costumes, painted faces and ribald songs and laughter were substituted for the vestments and liturgy of the church. Such travesties of sacred ceremonies are, however, of rather ancient origin. I would not attempt to say when they were first introduced. For all I know they may antedate Christianity itself. But readers of Scott's novels will remember that in The *Abbott*, which is a tale of the fifteenth century, a very similar burlesque following a solemn religious festival is described.

— CHAPTER XVI —

THE SECOND CRUISE OFFSHORE TO HONOLULU

September 28th, 1846 to early April, 1847

WITH EIGHT NEW MEN OF EIGHT DIFFERENT NATIONS, on September 28th, we sailed a second time for the Off Shore whaling ground. During the passage off the boat-steerers were busy painting and fixing up their boats. The waist boat, which was now my special charge, from its position in the davits—amidships to port—gets more of the smoke from the tryworks than the other boats, and on that account it seemed to need more painting. The brushes, paint and oil were under the mate's control. When I went to Mr. Taylor for paint he was very surly and would not give me any. "The damn old dung boat," he said, "she ain't worth painting." Mr. Thomas, by the captain's orders, helped himself to paint, and our boat was put in first class order. True, she was soon smutted up again, but it was not the smoke from trying out the *mate's* whales that did it.

In the first four weeks we had several unsuccessful chases, and one of the boats of the American ship *Herrold* picked up a whale right from under Mr. Taylor's nose. On Monday, October 26th, we rose a large sperm whale and lowered the boats. The bow boat got fast and hauled on to lance him. Mr. Dauton was the luckiest man in the ship for striking whales, but the most unfortunate in killing them. Before Dauton could get in a lance his boat was stoved. Mr. Taylor was close by, and instead of trying to get fast, he stopped and picked up the bow boat's crew. But before the whale could wave us good-bye the waist boat was on him, and we soon had him turned up and brought alongside. He made 106 barrels of oil.

After coming on board, the first and third mates had an angry dispute. Taylor said it was his chance to go on to the whale and that Dauton took it away. When asked why he had not gone on after the bow boat was stoved, "Oh," he said, "I didn't want to kill a dead whale." He meant a whale that another boat had struck, because it would count for the boat that first struck him. But that whale was worth a good many thousand dollars, and with the boat stoved, they would have lost him if some one had not come and killed him for them.

The bad blood between the first and third mates continued to foment. One morning at daylight as Dauton and his boat-steerer were stepping into the rigging to go aloft, Mr. Taylor snapped out, "Now keep a good lookout up there and see if you can't raise a whale."

"What the devil do you mean, talking like that to me?" Dauton retorted, jumping down on deck.

"I'll show you," said Mr. Taylor; and the two men rushed together.

Taylor was very tall, slab-sided and wiry. Dauton had as many inches in height and more than twice as much girth, and though a clumsy man ordinarily, yet when in a passion, he was very handy. The mate was promptly laid on his back on deck, with Dauton's big chubby hands at his throat choking him. The crew were washing deck, and several of them came running aft and hauled the third mate off, and a rascally English beachcomber cried out, "Let's raise a bloody mutiny and throw this fat— — — —overboard." Backing him up were the bad men of the forecastle, a little beady-eyed Peruvian, an Austrian who had deserted from the Peruvian army, a Frenchman ex-army and navy both—his face and arms all powder-burnt and terribly scarred—and a New York mulatto. Behind them came the whole crew to see which way the cat would jump. The captain was called, and he with the second and fourth mates and the boat-steerers, hastily armed with lances, spades, harpoons, etc., drove the men forward. The captain then in a quiet voice assigned the different gangs of men, each in charge of an officer, to their respective duties, and the affair was over for the day.

The next morning, after everybody had had twenty-four hours' time to think, all hands were called aft. The captain stood facing the crew, the officers and boat-steerers standing beside him. He asked who it was that raised the cry of mutiny. They one and all answered, "I didn't, Sir"—"Me no say dat"—"'Twan't me"—"Not I, Sir."

"Well, anyone of you that has any fault to find with my rule aboard this ship, speak right up now and let's hear it."

They all professed their perfect satisfaction with everything.

Then the captain lectured the men and told them that as long as they behaved themselves they would be well treated, but that the first sign of insubordination would be visited with such punishment that the one guilty of it would wish he had never been born. That was the end of any appearance of disorder on this cruise. We had a pretty hard set of men, however, especially those obtained in Payta, who were only shipped for the cruise and could not be trusted to sing out for whales even if they saw them.

Mr. Thomas having a great name as a whalesman, I was most anxious to do well as his boat-steerer. On November 7th, we saw a shoal of sperm whales. They were wary, and we chased them all day. At five in the afternoon, Mr. Thomas put me close on to a large whale—100 barrels under his hide if there was a drop. No need of any flying darts with Mr. Thomas for boat-header. "Wood and blackskin" was his steady rule. This was no exception, and I set the irons in with all my might. It was disheartening then, not ten minutes afterwards, for them to draw out and the whale go free. If it had happened in Mr. Taylor's boat, a terrible matter would have been made of it. But Mr. Thomas's reputation was so secure that he did not need to blame a boat-steerer for anything that was not his fault. When the captain asked how the irons came to draw, Mr. Thomas said, "Oh, I don't know. I have seen irons draw a dozen times when they were well drove in, and there's no accounting for it."

"Well," said the captain, "if you are satisfied, I am."

A week or two later we had a long chase after a lone whale. Towards sunset the starboard boat had the chance to go on, and José, the Portuguese boat-steerer, darted. As he did so he jumped overboard to escape being hit by the whale's flukes. It was said by the men, and I believe myself, that José struck the whale and the irons came out. At all events, we never saw the whale again. An inquiry was held that evening by the captain and officers. José insisted that he struck the whale; Mr. Shields declared that he missed him. Mr. Shields was a very conceited man with no great amount of judgment; but being from Saint John, Mr. Thomas, his fellow-townsman, was always in his favor. Mr. Thomas said that from his point of observation—we were about a mile away—it seemed to him that the irons went into the whale, but as Mr. Shields was right there and could tell better about it, he was satisfied that Mr. Shields told the truth. Mr. Taylor when asked for his opinion evaded an answer. So they broke poor José as boat-steerer, but let him live in the steerage and keep masthead, for he was a capital lookout.

On January 8, 1847, we spoke the American whaleship *Formosa*, bound home. Her captain's boat-steerer was a Kanaka or Sandwich Islander. He did not wish to go to the United States, and José who had been disrated, was anxious to return; so as our next recruiting port was Oahu, an exchange of José for the Kanaka was satisfactorily arranged.

During the cruise we also spoke the American whaleship *Joseph Maxwell*; the *Garland*, *Henry*, and *Spartan* of Nantucket; and the *Pacific*, *John Adams*, *James Allen*, *Menker*, and our old friend, the *Robert Edwards*, of New Bedford. Captain and Mrs. Burgess of the *Robert Edwards* came on board the *Athol*—a pleasant reunion for the ladies after a separation of six months.

That Fortune is a fickle jade, and as hard to woo afloat as she is reputed to be ashore, is well illustrated by comparing the records of some of these ships. The *John Adams*, eight months out, had 900 barrels of sperm oil. The *Garland*, thirteen months out, had 130 barrels. The *Pacific* in twenty-four months had 1,800 barrels; and the *Spartan*, thirty-five months out, had 1,500 barrels. While the *Robert Edwards* on January 17th had done nothing since we spoke her last on July 29th.

In this connection, I am reminded of an old New Bedford captain, whose identity need not be disclosed. I dare say his memory survives and this anecdote may still be remembered about the wharves of his native town. He was recognized as a very capable whalesman, but in addition he bore the reputation of being a hard old rip. A long time having passed without his seeing whales, it is said, he once cut a big hole in the bunt of his main-topsail, in order that the Great Author of Nature might look down without obstruction, observe that his blubber room was empty, and send him a whale.

On January 14th, the U.S.S. *Erie* spoke us in 4° 59′ S, 101° 47′ W.

On February 2nd, in 3° 15′ S, 101° 48′ W, we spoke the U.S. transport ship *Thomas Perkins*, of Boston, Captain James P. Arthur, with troops from New York bound to California, to fight Indians and Spaniards—and incidentally to acquire the territory of California for the United States.

Mr. Thomas having been for some time seriously troubled with a swelling of his knee for which Dr. MacDonald had no cure, an army surgeon from the *Thomas Perkins*, at the captain's invitation, came and cupped it and prescribed a remedy which soon brought the patient around. Captain Arthur and some of the army officers also came on board to look at our whaling gear and to pay their respects to Mrs. Coffin. Captain Arthur was a gentleman of fine appearance, and the dashing army officers in full dress uniform, which they wore in honor of Mrs. Coffin, presented a unique sight on board a whaleship. But their elegant bearing and glittering attire were not enough to cast in the shade our own dignified captain, dressed in his best blue broadcloth, as he and his self-possessed lady dispensed the hospitality of the ship.

The two ships lay aback all the afternoon and the boats passed several times between them, exchanging little delicacies, such as hams, butter and cheese, while the sailors bartered "scrimshonting" articles, that is whales' teeth, canes, ditty boxes, etc., for tobacco. We also did a brisk business trading off our well-thumbed books for new novels and newspapers. Though the *Thomas Perkins* was bound for San Francisco, as there was then no Pony Express across the Rockies and the western plains, it was no use to mail any letters by her.

The *Thomas Perkins* had on board a quantity of mill material and machinery. I wonder if it was the erection of this in California that led to the discovery of gold.

Our whaling operations were not eminently successful on this cruise. I have already recorded one capture and two failures. The next chance we had was spoiled by the starboard boat frightening the whales. On January 25th, the waist boat got a large whale under untoward circumstances, and another on February 13th. On February 26th, Mr. Shields killed a small whale. Poor Kappe by that time had his opinion to express, softly, about Mr. Taylor. Kappe had his racial characteristics of energy and enterprise in competition with others, and he declared that Taylor would not give him a chance but gave way to other boats. Taylor could not now, however, say that he threw up his chance because he could not trust his boat-steerer, for Kappe's reputation was unassailable.

The *Menker*, when we fell in with her on February 28th, 1847, was boiling with the blubber of a 100-barrel whale in her blubber room. They told us that on the 25th the captain's boat had got fast to a whale and the line caught around the boat-steerer's leg and took him overboard. They cut the line, but could not save him. The poor fellow was drowned, as has been the fate of many other good man. The story as I heard it in all its details greatly impressed me, and though I was neither in the land of the living nor on praying ground, but on shipboard numbered among the rough sons of Neptune, I thanked the kind Providence which had spared me hitherto.

But a few days afterwards, March 4th, I witnessed a similar though not so speedily fatal accident. I have said that Dauton was a lucky man. When he went down for whales, he seemed to pay no attention to where he was going, but to steer at random anywhere; a whale would rise close by, and his boat-steerer would slam an iron into him. Then there would be work for all hands. Somebody had to kill Dauton's whale. This time was no exception. Taylor and Shields had gone off in one direction, and Dauton and Mr. Thomas kept together. Mr. Thomas pulled for the whales, but Dauton did not know where he was going. The whale was down, and the captain up on the fore-topgallant yard was pointing, Dauton did not look to see where. Away he went, splash, splash.

The first thing he knew, the whale was right under his bow. Francisco, the Portuguese boat-steerer, plunged the irons into him and jumped overboard on the opposite side. In an instant up went the boat into the air, with a big hole in her, made by the whale's flukes. Francisco swam to our boat; the others gathered around the bow boat and tried to right her. The whale sounded, and one of the men became entangled in the line and was taken down. He drew his sheathknife and cut the line between him and the whale, and came to the surface. Ordinarily we should have left the men by their stoved boat to take care of themselves while we went after the whale; but with a half-drowned man to look out for, it was different and we picked them up and pulled for the ship. When the whale came up, he was going to windward, eyes out, with two irons sticking in his back.

The condition of the man who had been towed under by the whale being past Dr. MacDonald's slender skill, and his chance for life most desperate, the captain decided to make all sail for port and put in hospital in Oahu, whither we were bound.

In the afternoon of March 18th, during my masthead, we made the island of Hawaii, bearing north northeast. It was very high land, and the first I saw of it was above the clouds, thirty miles distant. This is the largest of the Sandwich Islands, as they were named by Captain Cook and were then generally called. The name Hawaii is a native word, and the phonetic spelling, "O-why-hee," given by Captain Cook quite fairly represents the sound on a native tongue. But for some unknown reason that form was not considered satisfactory and the change was made to "Ha-waii," the French spelling of La Perouse, which to an English ear does not at all suggest the pronunciation. In consequence, the word is now generally pronounced "How Are Ye."

On Saturday, the twentieth, we made Oahu (Captain Cook's Wahoo). The pilot took us into a snug little harbour protected from the sea by coral reefs, and we came to anchor in five fathoms of water, off the town of Honolulu, a cable's length from the shore. The captain asked the pilot where he could find comfortable lodgings for himself and family, and was rather astonished to learn that there was neither hotel nor boarding house in the town but that he would probably soon become acquainted and find plenty of places at which to stay. The captain went ashore to market, and while he was gone we had a call from a missionary, the Rev. Samuel C. Damond, pastor of the Seamen's Bethel, with whom and his family Captain and Mrs. Coffin later became acquainted and with whom they boarded while we were in this port.

Honolulu in 1847 was a busy little place. Ships were arriving and leaving every day, from ten to twenty being generally in port, principally "spouters" like ourselves. There was but one wharf, and that did not extend out to deep water. Only a vessel of very light draft could lie to it, and it served chiefly as a landing place for boats. From the head of the wharf, the principal street led up through the town, at the farther end of which were the well-built houses of the missionaries, with broad verandahs, almost concealed by the luxuriant trees and foliage, their grounds surrounded by hedges with arched gateways covered with flowers. On this main thoroughfare were a number of wooden dwelling houses and shops and a few built of stone or coral. The

houses on the side streets were almost entirely in the native style, constructed of bamboo with thatched roofs, some of them quite high in the walls.

Not far to the right of the main street was situated the palace of King Kamehameha, while farther in the same direction, were the Greenwich Hospital and the Catholic Church. A long walk out back of the town took one to Punchbowl Hill, the crater of an extinct volcano, or in another direction to the Peri, a perpendicular cliff several hundred feet high, at the base of which broke the waves of the Pacific. To the right or east side of the town, the road led out to Wyateetee Plains, a grazing ground for cattle, about two miles broad between the mountains and the sea. The owner of the cattle was an English runaway sailor who had married a native wife and whom the King had appointed head pilot. With the pilotage business he combined the supplying of beef to the town and to the ships that resorted to Oahu Harbor for refreshments. He and his sons were fine horsemen, and it was one of the sights of the town to see them ride out on the plains and lasso the cattle. The pilot's daughters were extremely beautiful. A few years before I retired from the sea, a Honolulu lady who was my passenger told me they all died at about thirty years of age.

Beyond the plains is Diamond Head, where the mountain comes down to the sea, and near its base was the country residence of the pilot, surrounded by cocoanut groves and the most luxuriant fruit trees that I ever saw. All sailors think they can ride horseback. Parties of them (which I joined as often as I could) rode out daily from town to Diamond Head. There they put up at public gardens where they could play bowls, billiards, etc., or sit in the shade and drink anisette, papilon and other cordials and strong waters.

Immediately on arrival, our sick shipmate was sent to the hospital. We visited him several times, and he was still living when we left port, but we heard that he died soon after. Our best amusement was to ride out on the plains towards Diamond Head and play billiards at the gardens with the men from other whaleships. On these excursions, the boat-steerers of the Nantucket ship *Phinney* were my usual companions.

The peculiar liquor law of Honolulu was strictly enforced. Not less than a bottle was allowed to be sold at a time, and the liquor could not be drunk on the premises where it was bought. Brandy, rum, gin and whisky cost four dollars a bottle. Yet, with the crews of a dozen whaleships ashore at once, a great deal of drunkenness was seen. In fact, all the drunkenness there was visible, for the liquor had to be drunk in the street—not from glasses, with water on the side, but the bottle passed from mouth to mouth and the stuff was swallowed neat, till a docile, simple-hearted knot of men were transformed into a set of howling savages such as the "King of the Cannibal Islands," in his best days, never dreamed of.

On Sundays many of us went to church, usually to the Seamen's Bethel, where the Protestant service in English brought over us a home feeling which time and distance made doubly strong. Some of the congregation were darker than we were accustomed to seeing at church. King Kamehameha and his family frequently came to hear Mr. Damond preach. They and many other natives dressed in the American or European style. Many more, however, had on go-to-meeting clothes of a mode never made in Paris. Where the women wore only a grass skirt and a pair of shoes, or a nightshirt and a bonnet, and the men stalked into church late full-dressed in a gee-string and a beaver hat, it was no sign that the sermon was not eloquent if our attention sometimes wandered from the timely truths which it presented.

It was laughable to see our Kanaka boat-steerer dressed in his shore clothes. He was an athletic fellow, and on shipboard, barefooted and scantily clad, he was agile and handy. But his self-respect demanded that he should not appear in town among the brethren of his youth unless arrayed in conventional sailor costume—blouse with broad collar and silk neckcloth, and wide bottomed trousers belted in taut at the waist and "furled in a cloth" across his bulbous breech. His feet, which from infancy had never known restraint, were crowded into tight-fitting coarse shoes that made him waddle as awkwardly as a duck on a hot plate.

The art of swimming, as in all the islands of the Pacific that I know about, was developed here to an extraordinary degree. While babies were learning to walk, they also learned to swim, sometimes acquiring one accomplishment first, sometimes the other. Boys swam off to the ships at anchor and played around them all day long. Two little fellows once jumped overboard off our main-topgallant yard, passed under the keel of the ship and came up on the other side. Men, women and even children swam off and returned to land again through the heaviest surf. The strongest white swimmer I ever saw would consider it no choice at all between drowning and trying to swim out or in through such breakers as the Kanakas, young and old, sported in like so many seals.

Those who have heard the native language of the Sandwich Islands and pronounce it musical must have a most ultra-classical ear. The words themselves reduced to writing and then spoken by a foreigner are agreeable enough; but a conversation between two Kanakas sounds as if they were trying to talk while occupied with the throes of seasickness. Repeatedly I have had to walk away out of hearing of them to prevent a heaving in my own midriff caused by their guttural, not to say ventral, tones. What is apparently the same word conveys different meanings, according to the emphasis and accent with which it is uttered. *My-ty* expresses not three, but a dozen, stages of goodness; and *ah-oorhee-my-ty* stands for all shades of badness; the inflection denoting the different degrees of intention.

The staple food of the people was a substance called *poi*, made from the root of the taro plant. It somewhat resembles white flour paste. Every morning men brought it to market in great calabashes hanging to a pole which they carried between them on their shoulders. If kept a few days, the *poi* turns sour and ferments, but it was as much eaten in the sour state as before fermentation. It is of a clinging ropy nature, and the manner of eating it was to thrust the fingers into the dish, pull out with a knackful twist and convey to the mouth as much as can be taken in that way, and when the fingers were sucked clean, the operation was repeated. The thinner the *poi* is made with water, the more difficult it is to handle, and it is appropriately classified, according to density, as one-finger, two-finger and three-finger *poi.*

A Kanaka, to illustrate his appreciation of the different grades of his national dish, would plunge first one, then two, then three fingers into an imaginary bowl, hold up his hand a moment as if poising the *poi* upon it, and say as he finished sucking, "One-finger *poi my-ty, my-ty!* Two-finger *poi my-ty.* Three-finger *poi ah-oorhee-my-ty!*" The first opinion he passed with beaming face and enthusiastic expression; the second, with a little longer countenance, regretful shrug and grimace, and plaintive equivocal tone; while at the final verdict, every movement, look and utterance carried with it the idea of slim diet and hard times.

— CHAPTER XVII —

JAPAN SEA

Early April to early July, 1847

*Y*AMS AND OTHER VEGETABLES WERE SCARCE AND VERY dear in Honolulu, and though we were in port longer than usual, we were able to stock up only meagrely for another cruise. During our stay we caulked and payed the *Athol's* decks and topsides, and scraped and painted her down to the copper sheathing. Two of the eight men who joined us in Payta left, and four able seamen were shipped to make up a full crew. They were as good men as ever walked a deck, but we just escaped having two most undesirable shipmates. The trypots were always kept covered with tarpaulin when not in use; but a day or two before we left, the second mate noticed that the covering of one of them was somewhat disarranged, and on investigating, he found two men, a white man and a Kanaka, stowed away in it. They were runaway convicts who had swum on board and hoped in that way to find liberty; but the captain sent them ashore and turned them over to the police.

On April 9th we were ready for sea and sailed for the Bonin Islands. Such music, I believe, was never heard in Wahoo Harbor before as was made while the men of the *Athol* were heaving in the anchor. The best singers on board carried the song, and all joined in the chorus, which echoed far back among the mountains and was reverberated again to the sea, while the shores and reefs were lined with women and children, shouting and waving us Aloha, Aloha,—farewell, farewell.

A sail of ten days took us past the islands of Hessian, Decerta, Halcyon and Lamira. "Their idle names occupy spaces on the charts, where no land ever was, and thus deceive navigators, who will one day or other meet with them several degrees to the northward or southward," was the querulous complaint of La Perouse in 1787 when, having shaped his course to pass between Lamira and Decerta, as laid down on Anson's Spanish chart, he saw nothing of them. Lack of accuracy of position was, indeed, the common failing of all ancient charts, the early navigators being unable often to determine within several degrees of the correct longitude; with respect to latitude they were much more exact, though occasionally an error of thirty miles or so would crop up. Improved apparatus, especially the chronometer, had by this time reduced navigation to a practically exact science; but even then, the utter absence of reliable charts under which Captain Coffin labored was a serious drawback, and anxiously would he pore for information over the pages of the navigators in these seas of the previous century. And when, perhaps at nightfall, an uncharted low-lurking coral reef would be described, or our ascertained position should place us within sight of some island marked upon the chart, while all around us was the great unbroken circle of the sea and sky, with what unbounded respect were we moved to regard those hardy spirits of long ago whose adventurous errant prows were:

"The first that ever burst into that silent sea."

On May 1st we made Coffin's Island, one of the Bonins, and had a hard unsuccessful chase to windward all day after a sperm whale. On the 4th we saw Parry's Group. The weather was dark and threatening, and a strong gale sprang up. We were running west for Harbor Island, shortening sail gradually as the gale east northeast increased, the wind east northeast, and a huge swell running *in the opposite direction.* While scudding under double-reefed main-topsail, foresail and fore-topmast staysail, driving and smothering in the long heavy head sea, we ran amongst a large shoal of sperm whales. We luffed the ship to the wind and hove to. There for two days we lay, before the gale abated, with whales all around us, taunting us with our inability to lower and get at them. On the 7th when the gale was over the whales had disappeared.

We cruised around for a week, making all sail and manning the mastheads every morning, standing by the wind during the day, and when anything was seen to leeward, running down to make out what it was; at night shortening sail and keeping to the wind, tacking ship at midnight.

On Saturday, May 15th, at 1 P.M., we made Harbor Island, distant northwest, 35 miles. This island lies in 28° 20′ N, 130° E, and belongs to Japan. At six o'clock next morning, the island bearing north, 15 miles distant, we saw whales and lowered. Our boat was soon up with a small one, hardly more than a calf. It was three months since we had been alongside of a whale, and the smallest favor was welcome. It was, therefore, a very anxious moment. "Now for a good chance," I whispered, as we were getting pretty close. "Wait till I tell you to stand up, and you'll have chance enough," Mr. Thomas answered, in the same low tone. At the word from him, I stood up and planted the irons so well that the whale had his death wound from them and in a few minutes was turned up dead. The larboard boat had a chance at more than one large whale, and did strike one, but the irons did not hold.

When we got aboard with our sprat, Mr. Taylor was telling how he happened to let a 100-barrel whale escape; but the captain's sceptical attitude towards his explanations, and the ill-suppressed sneers of others soon put the mate into a most sullen mood. In the steerage, Kappe told us plainly, what the captain and other officers more than half guessed, that Mr. Taylor trifled with the whales till he frightened them, and that the one they struck was so far off that the first iron merely pricked him and dropped out.

Two other ships on the same day got whales in sight of us—the *John A. Robb*, Captain Winslow, and the *Triton*, Captain Spencer, of New Bedford. The latter was ten months from home, 1,000 barrels of sperm oil—an excellent record.

One fine morning as we were standing in pretty close to Harbor Island, the masthead reported shoal water ahead. We tacked ship and sent a boat to sound it. It was an uncharted coral reef about a mile long, with two fathoms of water in the shoalest part, bearing west southwest, six miles distant from the native village at the head of the bay. Daylight and fine weather and a

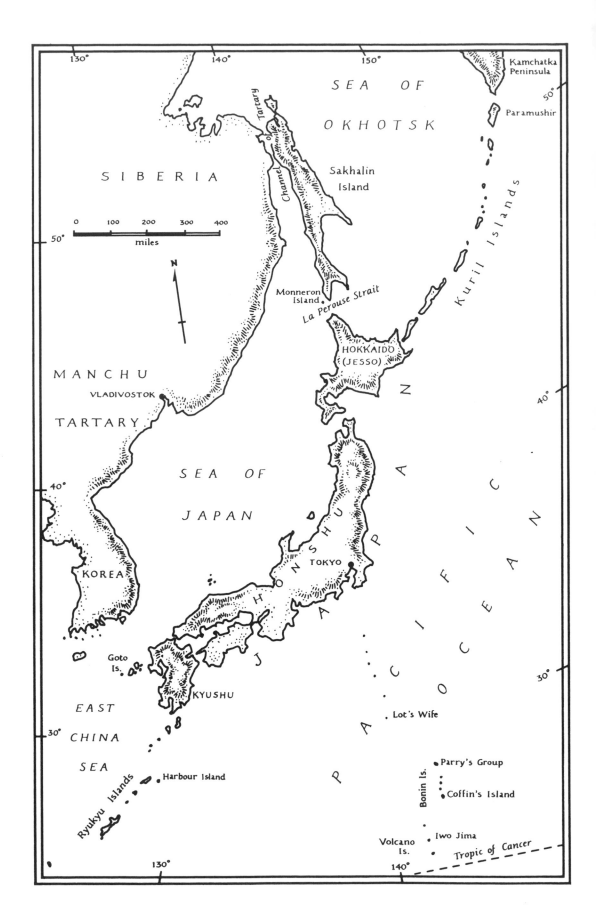

sharp lookout saved us from littering that coral strand with the *Athol's* ribs and trucks and our little stock of oil. Fortunately sailors are not given to dwelling upon what might have been if tempest and darkness had prevented any warning of the lurking danger.

Nor were thick clouds and darkness even at noonday long withheld from us, for two days after discovering the reef, we took a heavy gale which, at its height, blew about as hard as I think it ever does. It was my morning watch below when all hands were called to shorten sail and make ready for a typhoon, which all appearances indicated. It began from the southwest, Harbor Island bearing northeast, distant fifteen miles. The clouds hung low, just over the mastheads, shutting out all but a little gray daylight, and the driving spume thickened with the increasing gale. We first took in the mizzen and fore-topsails, close-reefed the main-topsail and foresail, and carried on to her to get clear of the land. While we were aloft furling the fore-topsail, a sea jumped over the bowsprit and burst the fore-topmast staysail all to pieces. The ship lying constantly on her beam-ends, to ease her we next sent down the fore and mizzen-topgallant yards. That was no more than done when the weather boats broke their gripes and blew up over the davits into the rigging. By the time we had them lashed securely again, the ship pitched her jibboom under and broke it off at the cap; and it was a difficult dangerous job to clear away and get the jibboom and rigging in over the bow.

The wind was all the time backing till it came from the northeast; but the swell continued from the westward, so that, as is a remarkable fact about the sea in this part of the world, we had the sea one way and the wind blowing either across or against it. With the shifting of the wind, there was no more danger of a lee shore, so we hove to, and as the sea would take the ship under the stern and send her ahead against the wind, it made things fairly shriek. We then sent down the fore and main-topgallant masts, and goose-winged the mizzen-topsail without much difficulty, but we had a great struggle to do the same with the main-topsail.

We had to secure the weather clew of the sail so that it would not beat all to pieces, but though fifteen men went aloft to do it, we could not get the sail fast, for it was slatting over and under the yard at such a rate that it would kill anybody who went out on the footrope. Two of us went up to the main-topmasthead, and I went down the weather lift to the yardarm; the other man with a whaleline made a bowline around the lift and slacked it away by littles till I got hold of it. The flapping and jerking of the sail in the wind shook everything so furiously that my teeth would not stay clinched, and I became almost numbed with the violent shaking and wrenching, but as quickly as I could, I took seven or eight loose turns of the line around the yard, made the end fast, then throwing the turns in as much as possible, while the others got hold of the line in the bunt of the yard and hauled it taut, and by that means we smothered the sail. Then we put a strap around the sail in the slings of the yard, put a toggle in it and twisted it up tight, and there we had a regular goose-winged main-topsail. So we lay under the lee clew of the mizzen and main-topsails till the gale began to moderate, which was about midnight.

Off Harbor Island being good whaling ground, we continued to cruise in that vicinity. On the morning of Thursday, May 27th, the island bearing east northeast, 20 miles distant, we raised a school of sperm whales, and

Opposite:
The Sea of Japan

again our dingy old waist boat had the good fortune to get one—another small one. He came up suddenly right in our way, when we were not looking for him. The starboard boat (Mr. Dauton) got fast, but their iron drew out and they lost the whale. Late in the afternoon we saw whales again, but a fog shut in which ended the game in their favor. The next day the whales were still there, going to windward. We pulled for them in company with Mr. Dauton, but did not have a chance to strike. The *Triton's* boats were also after the same whales, but had no better success.

On May 31st we spoke the bark *Canmore*, Captain Cudlip, of Saint John, New Brunswick, nineteen months from home, 800 barrels sperm oil, 500 right whale oil, and our boat went aboard to hear the news; but from the one spot of earth dear to me, old granite-bound Barrington, they had no news to tell.

Harbor Island, at that time, as now, was under the domination of Japan, and as in the Japan Islands proper, all intercourse with foreigners was strictly forbidden; but Harbor Island possessing neither fortifications nor military force, there was nothing to prevent any ship from at least entering the harbor. Communication with the shore, however, was seldom had by whaleships. Their only purpose in attempting it would be to obtain water and provisions. But it takes two to make a bargain, and the inhabitants were understood to refuse all negotiations for trade, never coming alongside in their boats, as at all the other Pacific Islands, though we often saw them fishing close inshore. Watering involved sending casks ashore and men to fill them, and the danger of having their crews taken prisoner while out of reach of their boats and either killed or held for ransom, made such attempts

Whaling barque
***Canmore* of Saint John,**
New Brunswick

unfeasible. It was, therefore, a novel adventure that Captain Cudlip proposed on June 1st, the morning after he arrived, that his mate and Captain Coffin go ashore and try to open a trade with the natives. We had, as intimated at the beginning of this chapter, been unable to supply all our wants at the Sandwich Islands, and the effort seemed to our captain worth making, to get what we could here.

Accordingly, the captain brought out a lot of ribbons and trinkets and a number of pieces of cotton prints, that he had for trading purposes, which were put into the boat, and I was among the number that went ashore with the captain. For a case of emergency, we took with us four muskets and a cutlass apiece. The *Canmore's* boat was furnished in about the same way. The highly cultivated broad fields and gardens on each side of the harbor, with the quaintest little thatched houses scattered here and there, presented a landscape very beautiful and cheering to eyes accustomed to scan month after month only the weary wastes of the sea. A year later, as I sailed up from Margate Roads to the City of London, I was repeatedly reminded of the captain's comparison of the scenery of Harbor Island to that along the banks of the Thames. That, however, was still in the "Pre-Machine Age." I doubt if, through the factory smoke which shrouds the approach to London by sea, the resemblance would be observed today. Lament we must that Progress is constantly offering up Beauty as a sacrifice.

As we came near to the village at the head of the harbor, we observed the natives leaving their houses and running into the woods. A number of men dressed in long white robes remained to watch us until we landed on the point adjacent to the village, and then they too disappeared among the trees. Leaving our arms with four men to guard the boats, we went up to the village and walked around among the houses. They were all deserted, neither man, woman nor child to be seen, and everything lying just as it had been thrown down when the inhabitants fled; but the captain gave strict orders that not a thing should be disturbed or touched. Occasionally a white robe appeared and disappeared in the edge of the wood. Our every movement was evidently being very anxiously watched. Seeing that they made no offer to come near us, we went back to the boats, took two or three pieces of prints and a few other things and laid them on a rock, and then getting into our boats, pulled off about a quarter mile from shore. In a little while two or three natives ran down out of the woods, grabbed the things off the rock, and ran back as hard as they could.

After waiting a sufficient time for the articles to be inspected and produce their proper effect, we went ashore again and called. First, two of the white robes came down to us, then another, and another, till thirty or forty men stood before us, their inscrutable dark heavy faces displaying neither curiosity nor fear nor any other human emotion. There were seven of the white robed gentlemen, armed with magnificent Japanese swords in carved ivory scabbards; they carried themselves with great dignity and appeared to be the head men. The others were dressed, after the Japanese fashion, in white and blue cotton cloth; all had guns, and some both guns and swords. The swords, though they looked as if they would be quite formidable in the event of a collision, were not of as fine appearance as those worn by the gentlemen of the white robes. The guns were not calculated to impress us with much respect except as relics of antiquity; venerable legacies from the owners' fathers' great-grandsires, who had doubtless received them in barter from the earliest explorers in these seas. They were huge matchlocks, like our old Plymouth Rock muskets, the matches hanging about the breech in half a dozen loops. How such musketeers could have lit their matches if they had had occasion to shoot, we had no means of knowing and no desire to test.

Captain Coffin made signs, pointing to their fields of crops, that he wished to purchase some fresh vegetables; but they answered by signs that they had none to part with. Then he put his hands to his head to represent horns, and bending over lowed so like a cow as to bring smiles to all those blank stolid faces. The senior white robe bowed and indicated by signs that we should have a "moo-moo." Turning, he spoke to several natives near him, who ran into the woods and in a few minutes drove out a heifer about three years old. This we slaughtered and dressed, dividing with the *Canmore*, and returned on board.

The whales, though still frequently seen in this neighborhood, were now extremely shy. On June 4th we saw sperm whales going fast to windward, and lowered the boats in company with the *Canmore*. Our boat got ahead of the whales, but they were so wary we could not get near enough to strike. That evening Captain Cudlip spent on board the *Athol*. He told the captain he had recently spoken the English ship *George Holmes*, which had come from the Sea of Japan and reported finding plenty of right whales, but that they had not taken any on account of not having good right-whalemen.

The next day, Captain Coffin consulted with his officers as to the advisability of going into the Japan Sea, filling up with right whale oil and ending the voyage. Mr. Thomas was an experienced right-whaleman, and favored doing so. Mr. Shields always agreed with Mr. Thomas. Mr. Dauton had no opinion to give. Mr. Taylor who had reserved any expression till the others had spoken, proposed returning to the Offshore of Peru, though a year before when we first came into the Pacific, he had suggested abandoning sperm whaling and fitting up for a right whaling voyage. The captain decided with the majority, and we parted company at noon with the *Canmore*, bound for the Japan Sea, which lies between the coast of Tartary and the Japan Islands. Since the beginning of the voyage the *Athol* had taken 14 whales, yielding 781 barrels, as follows:

Sept. 14, 1845	80 barrels	1
Oct. 4, 1845	90 barrels	3
Feb. 8, 1846	50 barrels	1
Jun. 11, 1846	100 barrels	1
Jun. 18, 1846	70 barrels	1
Jul. 27, 1846	40 barrels	1
Oct. 26, 1846	106 barrels	1
Jan. 25, 1847	80 barrels	1
Feb. 13, 1847	100 barrels	1
Feb. 26, 1847	30 barrels	1
May 15, 1847	15 barrels	1
May 27, 1847	20 barrels	1
	781 barrels	14

On June 7th, we saw two tall peaked rocks, which are well named the Ass's Ears rising inquiringly out of the water, as if to learn what brought us within their lonely exclusive horizon. But more inquisitive ears than those of stone, and eyes sullenly curious, if not malicious, were directed toward us that morning. Besides a number of fishing boats from the small islands that lie off the great island of Kyushu, which generally scurried out of our way as we approached, two large shampans or Chinese boats of about 150 tons, with huge mat sails, and each having an enormous rudder and two steering oars, met us and then kept off and followed us, apparently taking our measure before deciding whether or not to make closer acquaintance. At that time the Chinese pirates were very bold, and their recent depredations upon merchant ships induced the English government the following year to send a man-of-war into those waters, which, after coming to broadsides with some of the marauders, swept that peril from the sea.

The suspicious movements of these two vessels made Captain Coffin resolve to see what they meant. We hauled up and ran right for one of them, all hands standing by with guns, pistols, lances, harpoons and cutlasses. As they luffed to avoid a collision and we ran alongside, everyone of us, from the captain to old Jean d'Acre, sprang up on the rail and shouted, brandishing our weapons and firing a pistol or two to help along the noise. The poor Celestials, squealing with surprise and fright, hauled by the wind in a hurry and went their way, while we continued ours. In the afternoon we passed the island of Goto. The next morning we made the coast of Korea, and ran the strait of that name through. We sailed along about sixty miles of the east coast of Korea, the undulating forest-clad mountains which form the sea wall of that hermit kingdom presenting very pleasant scenery.

We were now fairly entered upon our new cruising grounds and could not help but entertain hopes of retrieving our fortunes among the right whales, which seemed to be plentiful. We had been busy during the passage in changing from sperm to right whaling gear, and were anxious to be at work. Right whales being much larger than sperm, the lances used in right whaling have larger heads and longer shanks. The shank of a sperm whale lance is only four or five feet long; that of a right whale lance from seven to nine. The irons also are longer and heavier; and generally not so much line is needed as for sperm whales. In right whaling we always kept the tackles up, made fast, stopped to the rigging so they wouldn't dangle about; but in sperm whaling we always took the tackles down after cutting in, and when we got a whale put them up again.

On June 10th we saw several whales going very fast to the northward, and we steered after them. The farther north we went, however, the atmosphere became more dense, until the fog closed down on us for days at a time, preventing all whaling operations. On the 15th, in 41° 50′ N, 137° 50′ E, in a temporary lightening of a thick fog, we saw a large right whale passing so close across our bows that the ship frightened him and we had to luff to avoid ramming him. Later in the day three or four more were seen, the boats lowered, and ours was almost up to one when the fog began to shut down, and the captain signalled us to come aboard. Mr. Thomas held out against the signals till we were in a boat's length of the whale. The fog had then hid the ship from our sight, and that with the approaching night compelled us to give up the chase lest we should lose our bearings and not be able to regain the ship.

The next day the fog cleared at an early hour, whales were seen, and at nine o'clock we were alongside the first right whale I ever struck. He was a monster, three times as big as any sperm whale. Just as I was about to dart, he spouted, and the noise of the drawback so startled me that I think my hair stood on end; but in spite of my little panic, both irons struck him solid. Such a pity then that he had not run but a little ways before our line parted and he got away. At two in the afternoon, we were down again after whales. Mr. Taylor's boat got fast. His line caught in the tub, and they threw it overboard to prevent its catching anybody, holding to it, however, in the hope that it would clear in the water. But when they hauled it in it was still foul, and as we were close by, we fastened to the whale and killed him. Three minutes after he was dead he sank.

The frequency with which right whales sank after they were killed was a calamity for which there was in those days no remedy. In the modern steam whale ships which fire harpoons and bomb lances from a little cannon on deck, a contrivance is used, I am told, for pumping air into a stricken whale that obviates all risk of loss from sinking. Many of the right whales which the *Athol's* boats captured sank beyond recall before they could be brought alongside. If we had had a means of inflating them to make them float, the ship's people and owners collectively would have been many thousands of dollars better off. Fortunately, the sperm whale does not have the bad habit of sinking after turning up fin out, or the profits of a whaling voyage would have been much more speculative in the days to which this narrative relates.

The improvements in gear, however, have banished from the whaling industry much of the spirit of adventure and of emulation in daring which, in the days of "wood and blackskin," were essential to the success of a voyage. A letting down of this element had been for some time apparent in some quarters on board the *Athol*, and the mechanical substitutes for it had not yet been invented. The consequences were sad enough and might have been worse but for the captain's strong dominating will and the loyalty of those not caught in this ebb tide.

A day of fog intervened, during which three or four whales were in sight or hearing of the ship most of the time. On the 19th in a clear interval, we lowered for whales, and the waist boat again fastened to one, and again our line parted. The larboard boat chased him for a considerable time but without success, while we returned on board. Though Mr. Thomas still insisted that his line was a good one, nevertheless, to please the captain, who was all patience in the matter, he condemned the old line, and we coiled a new one.

When the mate came on board again, the captain and Mr. Thomas were leaning against the capstan, discussing the merits of hemp and manila lines, Mr. Thomas preferring hemp. The hatch was off, and I was down in the steerage in sight below them; they could not help seeing me there. Mr. Taylor stepped up and said, "How was it, Mr. Thomas, that Doane missed that whale?"

"I don't know, I guess he hit him."

"Hit him, no; he never touched him. I saw the irons go over his back."

Though Doane calls them right whales, all the evidence in his own narrative indicates otherwise. Right whales were so-called because they were relatively slow swimmers, had proportionately thicker blubber and floated when killed (they were the "right" ones to hunt). The whales Doane describes sank when killed, were very large and had to be one of the larger species of rorquals, probably fin whales, which were very common in those seas in the 1840s.

"Well, now, I thought they went into him."

"No, no, they didn't, for I was close up to him afterwards, and there wasn't the mark of an iron about him."

"Now, that's queer, too; for I saw both irons go into his back, and he took them off with him along with thirty fathoms of my line."

"Oh," said the mate, "I thought Doane must have missed him."

I remember how the captain looked during this conversation. I was looking right up into his face. He had a most expressive countenance, which reflected his sentiments as plainly as words. He stepped back and, speaking slowly, said, "Well, Mr. Taylor, you see, that time you thought a lie."

For several days following we saw whales frequently, and as often lowered but could not come nigh them. They were feeding on and near the surface of the water, and for some reason they are more shy at such times than any other. The "brit," which the right whale feeds on, is a minute species of mollusk, occuring in immense swarms. Each individual is about the size of a pin head. It begins its existence at a considerable depth, gradually coming nearer to the surface, where it dies. These swarms are so dense that they can be seen at a depth of several fathoms, turning red as they rise, the water often being colored with them far and wide. Then the whales are seen with open jaws, scooping their food, swimming on their sides through these schools of brit, righting themselves occasionally to blow, and then resuming the accumulation of more millions, which they absorb by suction, and which are prevented from escaping out of the whale's mouth by the fine filaments into which the baleen or "whalebone" divides.

On June 23rd at four in the afternoon, we saw whales scooping, lowered, and our boat paddled square on and off to a big one and fastened to him with both irons. As he went down, Mr. Thomas said, "Ah, Doane, you've done it for him now." And when he came up, which he did in a few minutes, he spouted thick blood. The harpoon had given him his death blow. A sperm whale wounded in that way would be more ferocious than at any other time, for he then goes in to sell his life as dearly as possible, fighting viciously till the vital spark expires. But a right or north whale, as far as my experience goes, is tame compared with his fiery-tempered southern cousin. As soon as he shows the red flag he sogs around in helpless agony and with a short last struggle succumbs. So it was with this one; he soon turned up, and we towed him alongside the ship alone, with much hurrahing and shouting.

Now we all had occupation, and everyone was in good spirits, or ought to have been, cutting in the first right whale; but the satisfaction felt by the others was as nothing to my joy, after repeated failures, at this success. The larboard boat had had as good a chance as we that afternoon and, while our whale was spouting blood, did make a vain show of going to strike another; but their actions showed plainly that it was all a sham. The mate's plea was that it was too near night; and the captain admitted it. But while that was reason enough for not striking at all, it was not a good excuse for pretending to start with no intention of striking. The fact is, Mr. Taylor was no longer master in his own boat; his growing timidity had given his crew a hold upon him, so that they would not pull or haul up to a whale unless they saw fit, that is, when they had a quiet one.

The day we finished boiling we were down again after whales. There

Brit is an old Cornish word for swarms of small, planktonic animals, including molluscs called pteropods (sea butterflies). Usually less than a centimetre long, they are extremely abundant in temperate seas and form a major source of food for right whales.

were four of them together, and Mr. Taylor's was the nearest boat. He kept his sail up till he was too near, and then the flapping of the sail and noise made in taking it in frightened them off. The waist boat struck a splendid whale as solid as ever, and as we flew along in his wake, hauling up on him, our hopes were high, when our new line, that we had used only once, parted, and we lost the whale. But the very next day, Sunday, June 27th, we retrieved the luck. At 6 A.M. we lowered, and this time, without mishap, the waist boat killed and towed a whale alongside. We finished cutting in and began boiling out the blubber that night. Monday morning was clear, and while half the crew kept up the work of boiling, two boats went down after whales, but in ten minutes were driven aboard again by the fog.

Tuesday, June 29th, 1847, completed the disgrace of our mate. We had the accumulated oil of two whales on deck, between two and three hundred barrels, and all hands were busy stowing down the cool oil, when at 10 A.M. whales were seen, and only the waist boat lowered. The weather was foggy, with strong breezes and a rough sea, but Mr. Thomas with his usual skill soon put me alongside a whale, which I struck. After he had run with us a much longer time than we were willing he should, constantly fearing—the wild pace we were going in that wind and sea—that our line would break again, the second mate's lance settled matters our way, and we brought the whale alongside. That made the third large whale our boat had taken in less than a week, to all the others' ne'er a one; and it was only human that some jealousy should be felt at our luck. But such feelings, born of proper rivalry, are no part of the account of this day's doings, which were but the culmination of a long series of events—the emptying of a cup that had long been filling.

While we were towing the whale, we saw the larboard boat, in charge of Kappe, pulling toward us, and wondered what was the matter. When he came up to us, he merely asked Mr. Thomas if he wanted any assistance and, being told no, went back to the ship. When we got aboard things were happening fast.

The captain had a day or two before charged the mate with his cowardice and inefficiency, and told him that another exhibition of such conduct would result in his being discontinued as mate. Seeing us having a hard run with our whale, and being as fearful as we were that our line would part any minute, the captain had ordered Mr. Taylor, who was unexcelled in his use of a lance, to go and help us kill the whale. But all spirit of co-operation in that quarter was extinct, and a grumbling objection about being sent to kill dead whales was the only response. The captain did not insist, but saying, "I don't know as it *is* any use for *you* to go," he sent Kappe down after us, and went aloft with his spyglass to watch our manoeuvres and to con the ship up towards us, so as to give us as little towing as possible in such weather. Kappe, it seems, was chasing us for an hour or more, unable to get anywhere anigh us till the whale was dead.

As we were nearing the ship, the captain came down on deck. As he passed Mr. Taylor, the latter made an insolent remark. A warning to be careful of his words threw the mate into an outburst of passion and he fell to cursing the captain, the ship, the voyage, and the universe in general. After a moment of amazement, the captain's anger was aroused, and he raised his spyglass as if to strike. As the waist boat's crew reached the deck, the mate seized a lance off the spars and made a lunge at the captain, who parried the thrust with his spyglass and hit the mate over the head. What would have been the outcome, I dread to think, had not one of the boat-steerers rushed between them and tried to wrench the lance out of the mate's hands. At the same instant, Mrs. Coffin, who had heard the high tones and come on deck, ran up with a most womanly scream and, placing herself in front of Mr. Taylor, begged him not to kill her husband. Her distress brought the mate to his senses. He dropped the lance and walked away. The captain called after him, "Go to your room, Sir; you are relieved from any further duty on board this ship."

Then calling all hands, the captain informed them that they were to obey the orders of Mr. Thomas as mate of the ship *Athol,* and installed him

**Mary Doane Coffin
(1817-1853)**

as acting mate. Mr. Taylor remained off duty for some time, how long I do not remember; idleness giving him an opportunity, which nobody need envy him, of thinking over the progress of events since getting our first whale. He was not a bad man; on former voyages he had earned an excellent reputation as a whaleman for zeal, energy and skill; and why he should have gone to pieces as he had in the past two years is a mystery known only to Him who knoweth our frame. The period of reflection while off duty restored him to saner views of what was owing from him in conduct towards the captain, and upon his expressing penitence for the past, he was reinstated as mate of the ship.

It will be remembered that Mr. Dauton, the third mate, had a remarkable record for striking whales—and as remarkable for losing them after striking. Especially had this been so of late. As soon almost as the bow boat was clear of the ship, it would be on a whale, and then in a few minutes the irons would draw and the whale go free. In the hope of breaking up this kind of thing the captain had given orders, when one of the boats was fast, for the others to assist in killing the whale. The result was that the rest of us were kept chasing Dauton's boat a good deal of the time, usually to no purpose.

At 9 A.M. of July 1st we went down in chase of whales, and about half a mile from the ship one came up right in front of the bow boat, which at once fastened to him, and away they sped to windward against a fresh breeze. "Well, boys, here's another hard pull for us," said Mr. Thomas, rather wearily; "give way, lads, let's see if we can save that fellow." So we pulled and pulled for about three hours, when Dauton's irons drew, and the incident closed.

At one o'clock whales were seen again going to windward. All four boats lowered, keeping together, and just the same thing happened. In five minutes Dauton's boat-steerer had struck a whale. As the irons entered him, the whale raised his flukes and brought them down with a tremendous crash on the head of another whale which at that moment happened to come up alongside of him. Away went Dauton in tow of his whale, past the other two boats, which had got a little ahead of the rest of us. They followed Dauton. Mr. Thomas was disgusted. "Nothing but another pull to windward for you, men," he was saying, when the midship-oarsman cried out, "Look, look, Mr. Thomas. Here's that whale close to us."

A glance in the direction indicated showed us the whale that Dauton's had hit, lying gallied, rolled and blowing, too scared to run. We headed for him at once, and after half a dozen strokes, Mr. Thomas told me to stand up. There was the whale right in front of us, standing plumb up and down, his head projecting ten or twelve feet out of the water. Mr. Thomas warned me, "Don't strike that whale in the head. Wait till he straightens out before you dart."

A right whale's head is very hard, and there are but one or two places in it where an iron will hold. One of those is in the bunch of flesh and blubber around the eyes. Headway being kept on the boat, we were within a second or two of running up against the whale, which was all the time settling down tail foremost. I darted and set the iron into the bunch of the eye, piercing it to the bone, as we discovered afterwards. He quivered all over as if he had the palsy. Then he straightened out and ran so fast that the water flew around us in blinding sprays. There was quite a sea on, and running head to it, the boat cut right through the waves, and Mr. Thomas's sharp orders to me, "*Slack that line,*" often terminated in a snort as the top of a sea slapped him in the face and half filled the boat. When the whale changed his course and ran in the trough of the sea, the water alongside aft would pile up three feet above the gunwales. Only constant bailing by all hands kept us from being swamped. We were getting pretty tired of it when the whale sounded suddenly, taking out 150 fathoms of line, but when he came up he was much exhausted.

Now we observed the third mate's boat pulling for us. His irons had drawn, and he was coming down to help Mr. Thomas, who was by no means hankering for his assistance. We all silently wished him half way to Halifax, and in a few minutes Dauton himself would have been glad to have doubled the distance. For in characteristic fashion, he pulled right on top of the whale, and as the monster felt Dauton's lance, he gave the bow boat a crack with his tail which stove it all to pieces, and then he started to run. We held on to the line and ran right through the fragments of the boat and the half dozen men in the water.

"Ain't you going to pick us up?" shouted Mr. Dauton, as we rushed by, making a wave that washed him out of harm's way. "Go to hell, go to hell!" screamed Mr. Thomas, sympathetically—"Get out of my way." And so we left them to look out for themselves, while we were very busy for the next half hour. One of the other boats came and saved the crew of the bow boat. By that time our whale was turned up dead, and we towed him alongside about sunset with the usual accompaniment of songs and cheers. This day's work was Dauton's last bungle as a boat-steerer. He kept his grade as third mate, but was not allowed again to take a boat down after whales, and as he was no sailor, he simply lagged superfluous on board till an opportunity presented for him to leave the ship.

When the whale was moored, quarter-watches were set—that is, the four boats' crews, each in charge of a boat-steerer, divided the time till daylight, preparing for cutting in, and a good lookout was also kept to see that the whale did not part her moorings, as a strong breeze and rough sea prevailed throughout the night. At five o'clock in the morning all hands were called and we began to cut in, but I will explain in as few words as possible why we did not continue at it long.

The first operation in cutting in a right whale is to put a chain strap around the fin, into which the tackle is hooked. The crown piece is then cut around the fin, and as that is hoisted, it raises the blanket piece, and rolls the whale over as the strip of blubber is peeled off. As soon as the whale is rolled on his back, the lower jaw is unjointed and hoisted in on deck, tongue and all (the tongue of a right whale is solid fat). This being a very large whale, it was necessary to cut the throat-blubber and hoist it in separate from the jawbone. As the whale rolls, the upper jaw is unjointed and, with the baleen attached, is hoisted in.

This description of the tongue of a right whale is further confirmation that the species was probably a fin whale which, like other rorquals, has a very soft and flaccid tongue. True right whales have a very large and muscular tongue.

This could not be done on account of the heavy sea. We hooked on to his fin and started to heave, but the ship rolled so that the fin-chain parted. We made another attempt, but parted the chain again, and a gale springing up from the northeast, we were compelled to wait for more moderate weather.

There was a serious objection to this delay. The work of cutting in must be pushed with all possible speed. The blubber being a non-conductor of heat, the temperature of the carcase, after it is brought alongside, never grows less, and decomposition or "blasting," as it is termed, soon commences and proceeds with great rapidity, thereby rendering the oil dark and injuring its quality. To remedy this to some extent, we scored the whale—cut gashes from the water's edge on one side to the water's edge on the other side, from head to tail, so that the sea would wash in and keep the blubber cool, all that was out of the water. Then we slacked away several fathoms of the fluke-chain and let her lie under close-reefed fore and mizzen-topsail, and double-reefed main-topsail, spanker and fore-topmast staysail, which would make her reach ahead a little and keep the chain taut. But the wind and sea increasing, the fluke-chain parted and the whale went adrift. We had to lower a boat, put an iron into him and haul him alongside again. Then, for fear he would again strike adrift, the captain ordered that he be made fast by the ship's hawser. Accordingly, an eye was spliced in the end of the hawswer, a noose put around the whale's fluke, and about forty fathoms of hawser were paid out.

The fore and mizzen-topsails and spanker were then taken in, and we lay to under double-reefed main-topsail, fore-topmast staysail and a dead whale. A watch was also kept from the tops, not only to have an eye on the whale, but to look out for breakers. Owing to bad weather, our observations for several days had not been reliable, and the charts were known to be inaccurate and incomplete; but we knew that with a northeast gale the coast of Manchu Tartary was somewhere under our lee.

At 4 A.M. of Saturday, July 3rd, all hands were called to cut in. The weather was more moderate, though there was a very heavy sea running. The whale, which was a good deal blasted, was hauled alongside and the fluke-chain was put on him. When about three pieces had been boarded and the head hoisted in, the blanket piece no longer quite followed the scores before referred to as having been cut. A long sliver on the side of the blanket piece flapped about as it was hoisted to the masthead, striking the falls of the second tackle, and making it very difficult to hook on in order to cut and lower the piece into the blubber room.

After a number of unsuccessful attempts to hook on had been made, two men caught hold of the block, one on each side, and put the strap through the hole made for that purpose in the blanket piece. The captain, bracing his foot against the hatch coaming, took hold of my shoulders to steady me, while I put one foot against the block to keep it in position long enough for another man to put the toggle in the strap on the other side. But before that could be accomplished, the ship fetched a heavy roll down. As she came back, both the captain and I would have been pitched down the hold if he had not released me. So, warning me to look out for myself, he let go his hold. The same instant, this flap of blubber above mentioned, dangling from the blanket piece, struck the fall, causing the block to fly out of the men's hands. Away it swung clear across the deck, as the ship rolled the other way, while I, slipping on the oily deck, to avoid going head foremost backwards down the hatchway, flung out my hands to catch anything that might be within reach. The fourth mate, who had boarded the piece, instead of putting the boarding knife into the sheath, as he should have done, was holding it point downwards on the deck, leaning against the handle. My left hand caught the naked blade and slipped down its keen edge clear to the deck. Somebody grabbed me and prevented my falling into the hold. As I regained my feet and saw the condition of my fingers, I am afraid I did not feel very grateful to him for saving me a broken neck.

The fore finger had only a flesh wound, but the other three were hanging by mere shreds of flesh. "Poor miserable devil, wedded to misfortune!" were my first words, as the captain took my hand, and his expressive eyes kindled with sympathy. He took me into the cabin, and he and Dr. MacDonald did what they could for me. My hands, of course, like every other part of me, were covered with train oil and the "blackskin" of a blasted whale. The doctor hastily prepared some bluestone water, and my hand was put into it, to clear the wounds of foreign substances. Then the cuts were stitched up, my hand was bandaged, and I went to my room. For three days the bandages were to remain undisturbed. That time I spent in enforced self-contemplation, suffering great pain but forgetting it frequently as my mind dwelt on new and gloomy prospects.

Recent events on the whaleship had opened an opportunity for advancement. The first and third mates were practically broken and would leave in the next port we made. In the natural order, Mr. Thomas and Mr. Shields being promoted, I had looked forward to being made third mate. Now, I would probably lose my hand, and with it all chance of promotion; indeed, I should be unfit to continue as boat-steerer. To leave the ship at her next port, with nothing but the sea to look to for a livelihood, was about equivalent to being marooned on a half-tide ledge. I thought my working days were done, and I remember comparing my situation with that of Napoleon and repeating to myself, with a personal application, the lines of the old song:

> Oh, Bony, he's away from his warring and all fighting;
> He has gone to a place he can never take delight in;
> So he sits there and thinks of the scenes that he's been over,
> While forlorn he doth mourn on the Isle of St. Helena.

At the expiration of three days I went to the doctor again. On the bandages being removed, it was noticed that the third finger was black on the end, as if mortification had set in. The fore finger had begun to heal, and the other two were doing as well as could be expected. They all had their bluestone bath and were tied up again. The next day, the discoloration of the third finger had extended to the first joint, and I asked the doctor to amputate it there. "No, no," he said in his broad Doric, "leave it to me, and I'll save it." Calling the captain, he pointed out the limit of the black part and explained to him in many words that the "line of demarcation" had begun to form there. The captain listened attentively to the highly technical language. So did I, but comprehended nothing.

During the next four and twenty hours there was no pain in the third finger, and on the following morning, when the doctor made his examination, the black line had almost reached the second joint. Then I did

Bluestone water is a solution of copper sulphate, widely used as a disinfectant in that period. The name refers to the brilliant blue of the crystals. The solution was also called blue vitriol or blue copperas.

beg him to cut that finger off. He objected strongly, and we argued the matter. "Don't you see, man, that line of de-mar-r-cation?" he asked impatiently. "Yes, I see where it is now, but that line will be rotten tomorrow, like the one of yesterday is today."

He ceased discussing the subject with one so unamenable to reason, and went to his room, telling me to hold my hand in the basin of water till he returned. His box of instruments was on a chair beside me. As soon as his back was turned, I reached for that box and got one of his lances. It may have the best or the worst or the only one he had; it was a rusty looking affair, but I was determined to make good use of it.

I laid my hand on my left knee, putting the end of the third finger against the right knee, to steady it, and began to cut into the middle joint. I made a fine slash, and it hurt so that I cringed all up with pain; but I was doing this, not for amusement, but to try to save my hand, and time was precious. So I kept at it, working my finger, trying to find the joint, and there was only a little shred left to cut when I heard the doctor coming. With one last hack, I plunged my hand into the basin of water, as the finger dropped to the floor, and I looked up into the doctor's face as innocently as the Indian's dog after eating the moccasin.

The doctor sat down, and while arranging the bandages he talked about how necessary it was for me to follow his directions and have faith in him. In a minute he was ready and raised up my hand. He gave one look and jumped out of his chair—mad.

"I've a great mind to do nothing more for you," he said.

"I don't care whether you do or not."

"I could have saved that finger—I was going to save it."

"Well, you're too late to save it now."

Going to the captain's room, he called, "Captain Coffin, will you come here and see what this man has done?"

The captain appeared and asked what was the matter.

"See here, Sir," said the doctor, pulling my hand up to view; "he's cut his own finger off, and I could have saved it for him."

Stooping over, I picked up the cause of offence from the floor. "Look, Captain," I said, "at what he wants to save. It stinks. I don't want that thing on my hand, *saved or unsaved.*"

The captain burst out laughing, and with a few soothing words to two angry men, he left us to come to terms. The doctor, soon cooling off, resumed charge of the case and dressed my hand, and I went to my room much better pleased than at any time since the accident.

The process of healing progressed gradually, but the second and fourth fingers were stiff except at the knuckle joints.

— CHAPTER XVIII —

SEA OF OKHOTSK AND OFFSHORE OF JAPAN

Early July to October 3rd, 1847

WHILE MY FINGERS WERE HEALING, THE WHALING OPERAtions were a matter in which I had only a "thinking part." But thoughts nursed in enforced idleness, especially when accompanied by pain, are not always pleasant companions. To drive away morbid feelings, I turned to reading and rereading, through the captain's kind privilege, everything in poetry or prose that the ship contained, and copying and learning by heart the poems that pleased me most. During this time I copied into my journal the whole of Bishop Percy's *Hermit of Warkworth*, a poem of some eight hundred verses. I also committed it to memory from beginning to end.

Falconer's *Shipwreck* I pored over days at a time, with a sailor's delight at the accurate use of technical language in sublime descriptions of the tragedy of the sea. Byron, imbued through and through with a perception of the grandeur of solitary impersonal nature, in relation to which man with his sins and follies seemed so insignificant; and Scott, with saner eyes, beholding nature as equally beautiful but nothing worth except as it worked in and upon the hearts and minds of men—these wizards of our English tongue held me in their spell till *Marmion* and *Childe Harold, Lay of the Last Minstrel, The Corsair,* and the rest came so into my mental possession that now, sixty years after, I can follow them, page after enchanted page, with my eyes shut.

The only duty I was able to perform was, when the boats were down for whales, to manoeuvre the ship, under the captain's direction from his station on the royal yard, in keeping track of the boats. Dull as the work was, with none of the excitement attendant upon chasing whales, it was a welcome break in the monotonous days, and the practice so obtained in the quick handling of a ship under sail was in future years of great benefit to me.

On July 11th the mate, for the first time since being restored to duty, got fast to a whale. His line fouled, and Mr. Thomas had to kill the whale for him, which charitable act made Mr. Taylor very vexed and snappish. On the 22nd Mr. Thomas killed and brought alongside two whales between three in the afternoon and sunset.

Before we had finished trying out we came in sight of the western shore of Manchu Tartary, distant twenty-five miles, and stood close in with it in 42° 58′ N. It was the northeast headland of a deep bay, at the head of which is situated the town which the Russians now call Vladivostok. While the writing of the narrative has been dragging along, it has become a Russian

seaport. Whatever it was called when we looked into it, our chart did not state. Some places (like some people) have fame thrust upon them. Well, the Russians are not to be blamed for desiring a more practicable outlet upon the sea than can be found thereabouts. During the rigorous long winter, the bays are sealed with ice. The coast is set with dreary ledges of rocks, between which rip eternally swift currents that would imperil the navigation of any steamer. No sailing vessel could reckon with them even in clear weather; and clear weather for any extended time is almost unheard of. With us, dense fog prevailed every day till noon or ten o'clock, when it usually cleared up, to shut down thick again about four in the afternoon. It certainly required the exigencies of war to draw such a place into notice.

By the last week of July the whale feed was on top of the water, and the whales had left; so we stood to the northward—the direction they seemed to have taken. On the 28th we spoke the ship *Minerva Smith*, of New Bedford, twenty-two months out, 2,300 barrels of whale oil. On August 1st, off the entrance of La Perouse Strait, in 46° 10′ N, 140° 50′ E, the waist boat got a whale. The same day we spoke the ship *Sarah*, of New Bedford, and again saw the *Minerva Smith*. They had taken nothing since the middle of July, but had seen whales heading towards the strait, and were themselves bound through. The captain and his officers held a consultation about going farther north. They all agreed to his proposal of going into the Sea of Okhotsk, which lies between the Island of Sakhalin, the Kurile Islands, Kamchatka and the east coast of Russia, first taking a look into the Channel of Tartary, between Sakhalin Island and the Tartary Coast, as the whales seemed to be going that way.

On August 4th we were well up into the narrows of the Channel; the land was visible on either side, the water was shoaling rapidly, and we had seen no whales, so we put about ship and stood out with a fair wind.

On Sunday the 8th the Island of Monneron (so named by La Perouse for his chief of engineers), 46° 8′ N, 141° 11′ E, bearing northeast, distant ten miles, we made a raft of casks, and the larboard, waist and starboard boats under the command of the first, second and fourth mates were sent with them to the island for water. My hand was still very troublesome, but a walk ashore would be such a treat that I asked leave to go with the second mate. The captain consented, and in addition, lent me his fowling piece, as there were thousands of seals on the ledges that lay about the island.

As we drew in towards the ledges, the seals began to jump for the water, which they would reach before we were within shot of them. On a large ledge which had been crowded with them, one immense fellow was too slow in getting off. He was on a rock at the water's edge when the second mate darted his lance and drove it clear through him. As the seal plunged into the water, the protruding end of the lance caught on a rock and bent so that it could not be withdrawn. He was mortally wounded and died after running a short distance whereupon he sank. With the lance line we hauled him to the surface, and were trying to get a line around his flipper when the shank of the lance straightened out and he slipped off and went down beyond recovery.

The Island of Monneron is high and rough. Small streams of water flow down the sides of the mountains, and at the mouth of one of these we landed. Along the streams, wherever there is any shelter, grew a few stunted firs and willows. Elsewhere, the soil was covered thick with low shrubs and vines. Around the shores the soil was washed away for a width of about one hundred yards, leaving huge bare rocks, over and between and around which progress was very difficult. Upon these rocks, from the water's edge to the top of the beach, the seals loved to lie and sleep. If awake, they kept the air vibrant with their discordant howls. Many of them were fur seals, though the season for them was now over. The greater number were of the variety known as sea lion, and they appeared to be well named; for as they were now shedding their coats, their bodies were bare and smooth, while forward they were covered with long tawny fur; so that, perched on a high rock, with head and neck erect, they looked every inch the part.

While the men were filling the water, of which we took ninety barrels, I went off along the beach in quest of seals. The only percussion caps that the captain could provide were musket caps, much too large for the shotgun; so I had either to keep my hand constantly on the nipple while jumping from rock to rock, or leave the hammer down. In the one case the cap would frequently jolt off; in the other, there was danger that the gun would be discharged if I slipped or fell.

Seeing two immense sea lions up almost to the edge of the vegetation, I endeavored to get between them and the water. They saw and understood my movement immediately and made all haste, clambering clumsily down for the element where they could appear (and disappear) with more grace and to better advantage. I had much farther to go, but being better fitted by nature with means of progress over the rough ground, I intercepted the forward one of the pair by a few feet and with hasty aim drew the trigger. Click, fell the hammer upon bare steel—the cap had fallen off. I was down between two big rocks. Behind me a yard or two was the water, and ahead came this huge beast right into the gap, his bristly muzzle high in air, and his wide open pink throat emitting most rasping sounds of some great emotion, which might have been terror; but I did not so interpret it, and as his teeth really looked very serviceable, I side-stepped all I could, and tried to make myself as small as possible against the side of the rock, as he brushed past me and plunged into the sea. Once he was out of the question, I ran up out of the narrow pass to a roomier berth, recapped the gun and poured a charge of shot into the next one, which was ten or fifteen yards behind the first. A musket ball would no doubt have stopped him, but the shot did not reach a vital part, and he too, gained the water and was beyond pursuit.

I then returned to the boats and paddled one of them off to the ledges nearby and continued hunting seals. My plan of campaign was to intercept them, the same as before; but in addition to the gun, I carried with me this time the boathook and hatchet. First I would shoot the seal, then hook on to him with the boathook, and then brain him with the hatchet. By this thorough system I secured three seals.

My hand being still in bandages, I had in firing rested the gun over my wrist until the jar became too painful. The last shot was with the gun across my elbow. But holding her no matter how, the pain at last was too great, and I went back to the island, where the casks had now been filled and made fast. It being too late to return to the ship that night, we hauled up the boats and prepared to camp out, and then started to explore the island.

On a hillside we came upon a house abandoned for the season, in which were stored all the apparatus necessary for sealing. Near by was a large *parao* or *bateau* hauled up and covered over with grass and bushes to protect it from the weather; and on a higher elevation not far away stood what looked like a large dollhouse, with curved projecting eaves and elaborately carved folding doors. It was about four feet high, and two men could have picked it up and carried it to the boat; but we had our captain's orders not to disturb any property that we might find. We were probably correct in supposing it was used in the practice of their religion by those who frequented the island during the season of the seal fishery. Inside were several paintings in colors, and a number of carved figures, also variously colored. The paintings and figures were of men and animals, of the squatty type characteristic of Japanese art; but a person of even rudimentary taste could admire the exquisite skill with which the carving was executed in every minute detail.

Our curiosity after a time was satisfied, and the boat-steerers and crews returned to the boats. The second and fourth mates went off together towards the interior, and the mate took a tour along the beach by himself. A fire was started at our camping place and I was sitting down near it with the gun in my lap nursing my left hand and arm, which continued to ache clear to the shoulder. The men were standing about and fell to talking of the troubles of the mate, each one trying to exceed the other in their expressions of animosity, when he came in sight, occasionally turning or stooping as he strolled along. Suddenly, as the mate's back was turned, an Austrian whom we called Jack, belonging to the mate's boat, grabbed up my gun and, levelling it at Mr. Taylor, said with an oath, "I'll shoot him dead!" A man sprang forward instantly and after a struggle twisted the weapon from the ruffian's hand. Jack made a poor pretence that he was only joking and tried hard to laugh; but we all shrank from him, feeling that a murder had been only narrowly averted.

At daylight next morning we started with our raft of casks for the ship, and at noon, after the water was hoisted in, the three boats returned to the ledges and small islands to shoot seals. We had killed twenty-five when, at 4:30, we saw the colors flying, a signal for us to come on board. It being calm, a strong current had set the ship close in to a ledge, and we arrived none too soon to save her. In a few minutes she would have struck and no doubt been wrecked. All four boats clapped on, and after six hours of hard towing against the current, she was out of danger.

Tuesday, August 10th, brought fine weather and smooth sea, with the wind southwest. At 1 P.M., we passed through La Perouse Strait, between Jesso and Sakalin Islands into the Sea of Okhotsk; saw two junks and several smaller craft, which we supposed to be Japanese coasters and fishermen.

Today, the steward, a New York Negro, was asked to wash some dishes in the cabin, which he refused to do and chased the captain on deck with the carving knife. The reason the captain ran was that his wife and two little children were in the cabin, and to have the man follow him on deck was to provide for their safety. But as the man dodged back again, the captain returned and Mr. Thomas with him. They soon quieted the steward, put him in irons and shut him down in the ship's run, where he was kept in the shade, fed on bread and water till he was a better man.

For a number of days we hung in the straits with head winds and currents, during which we saw numbers of junks and *paraos*. When we displayed our colors, the larger craft usually hoisted the Japanese flag.

On the 11th the waist boat got a whale and towed him alongside with joyful shouts and songs. But the scene had no charm for me. I had to work the ship while the boats were away, and my fingers being cold and stiff and useless, I longed to be homeward bound. Part of the time it was foggy, and we could hear plenty of whales blowing but could not see them. On Saturday, the 14th, 45° 36′ N, 145° 27′ E—about 100 miles east of the strait— the waist boat began the day with the good deed of taking another whale. On the 17th, we spoke the ship *Hoquáw*, of New Bedford, eleven months out, 600 barrels. On the 18th, in half a gale and a heavy sea, the boats lowered in chase of whales and the waist boat got fast, but the whale stove the boat. The captain got a boat down off the bearers and took her to the second mate, put a sail around the stoven boat and brought her on board. The second mate killed the whale and brought him alongside.

Contrasted with this was the next day's work. The larboard and starboard boats got fast, and the fourth mate set his whale spouting blood; the mate's irons drew, and he went to help Mr. Shields, but soon they were both loose from the whale and lost him at 46° 38′ N, 146° 17′ E.

Sunday, August 22nd, began with strong breezes and fog hanging about the horizon. At 8 A.M. a school of large whales was seen, and the boats lowered. It seemed ordained that we should get most of our whales on Sunday. The waist boat struck one that was so large a seven-foot lance was not long enough to reach his life. Running within hail of the fourth mate, Mr. Thomas sent him on board for a nine-foot lance shank, which when put to use soon did the business. But the whale had run the boat about ten miles from the ship before he turned up, and the fog shut down thick. After waiting an hour, and the fog still continuing, the second and fourth mates started to find the ship leaving the first mate by the whale.

On board the ship we got up the big gun, a 14-pounder, and fired her at intervals, and the cooper kept drumming on the heads of casks to continue the noise. About noon the fog lighted, and the boats found the ship. From the masthead, the captain with his glass could see the whale, dead to windward. Mr. Thomas put some water and provisions in his boat and set out again for the whale, the fog shutting down again a few minutes after he left.

We kept plying to windward on short boards, occasionally hauling aback to listen, and firing the gun at frequent intervals. At dark we built a fire on the tryworks and kept a boat out on each side of the ship, within hail, with their lanterns up. The captain was very uneasy for the safety of his officers and men, as the wind was steadily freshening. At midnight we heard them hail off the lee beam. We wore ship, and lost them again—ran past them unawares. We came by the wind again, and on the second tack, half an hour after first hearing them, the windward boat saw their light. We lay the ship aback and ran a line to them and hauled the whale alongside. He was as long as the ship. The men no doubt were tired after their sixteen hours of hard work; but such a large whale paid for their trouble. He was secured at 46° 25′ N, 146° 30′ E. This was the largest and fattest whale I ever saw. His blubber was in some places three feet thick.

A succession of northeast gales now came on, which seriously hindered the process of trying out. We had to cool down the works and put out the fires for fear of setting the ship on fire by the oil slopping over. Whales were plentiful, but we did not lower, having as much as we could take care of on board. We had a heavy deckload—150 barrels of oil and a great quantity of bone and other lumber—which it was necessary to lash securely as we could not get it below; and we were obliged to carry sail to keep from drifting too fast toward the coast in the thick weather.

At midnight of the 24th, while the ship was laboring heavily in a cross sea, we shipped a sea which started several of the empty casks on deck and some of the oil lashings parted. We double-lashed the oil, cleared up the decks and took in the boats, the gale still increasing. At 2 P.M. of Wednesday, the 25th, it began to moderate and the sea to go down; and the next day we finished boiling, the east coast of Sakhalin Island bearing southwest, distant 20 miles, 46° 50′ N—about Cape Tonin. The whale made 206 barrels of oil, besides about ten barrels that were lost by cooling down the fires and leakage during the gale.

On the 29th, the waist boat took another whale in 46° 30′ N, 146° 30′ E. On August 31st, we spoke the ship *Josephine*, of Sag Harbor, ten months from home, 1500 barrels whale oil at 46° 29′ N, 146° 54′ E.

September 7th was my birthday. 50° 29′ N, 149° 15′ E we spoke the ship *Sheffield*, of Cold Spring, New York, thirty months out. Her captain bought three casks of bread and some beef from us.

Whales continued in great numbers and several varieties, finbacks, California grays, and some right whales, but they were too wild and shy to be taken; the boats would chase right whales day after day, all day long, and not get nigh enough to strike. On the 10th the waist boat killed a whale; and the next day, got fast again, but their line parted. Nobody but Mr. Thomas could get a whale, so the captain would not complain of his losing one, though he did wish Mr. Thomas would give up hemp lines and use manila.

On Wednesday, September 13th, we spoke the ship *Nassau*, of Sag Harbor, twenty-one months out, 700 barrels of whale oil—a leaner record than ours.

The weather being blowy and cold and the men but poorly prepared with clothing, the captain determined to leave this ground and start for the offshore of Japan, try for sperm whales again, and then proceed to Sydney, New South Wales. He was influenced toward this course, in addition to the other reasons, by the fact which we had learned from a ship that had recently spoken us, that since January "oil or blubber of foreign fishing" was being admitted free of duty in England. This would make oil cheaper in London; so, the American market being reserved for American ships, it were well to get our oil shipped from Sydney as soon as possible before the price was further affected by this change in tariff. At Sydney, he intended to fill up again the casks, make another cruise, and go home.

We made Paramushiro, one of the Kurile Islands, passed out into the Pacific to a good offing and worked southwest to 47° N, and then southeast by south, seeing nothing but finbacks; the officers and boat-steerers were employed fitting sperm whaling gear. During the passage, the mate had another scene with the captain, the particulars of which I do not know, but it made the captain all the more anxious to terminate the cruise.

On September 21st, in 39° 21′ N, 153° 8′ E, a gale began which ripened into a typhoon, lasting four days. It commenced at west southwest, with a heavy sea from the southwest—a little more than right angles to the wind. We hove to under close-reefed main-topsail and fore-topmast staysail, on the starboard tack, which brought the sea just on our lee bow. The wind increasing, we clewed up the main-topsail and lay aloft to furl it. While doing so, the boats blew up over the davits into the weather rigging until their tackles fetched them up. All hands lay down to secure the boats, but a sea from leeward took the bow boat right off the cranes and smashed the waist boat. We took the rest of them in and secured them. That done, we put a lashing round the bunt of the mizzen-topsail, loosed the lee clew and set it goose-winged, with a tarpaulin in the mizzen rigging. We had a deckload of oil from our last two whales—some 200 barrels—well lashed, but with the ship almost on her beam ends, laboring in the cross sea under the strain of the deckload on her upper works, she leaked badly, and the pumps had to be constantly attended to.

Whether there was any rain or not we could not tell—I hardly think it rained; but the sea drove like a snow-drift, the air so full of it we could scarce open our eyes. It was so dark that successive dawns, noons or sunsets were left to the imagination, as day after day the *Athol* with its freight of lives wallowed on, twisting and wringing like a person in pain, lifting on mountain seas and falling into their depths. Awful as was the situation and the anxiety of our minds, I remember how the groaning and working of the ship under the buffeting and strain reminded me of an old ox-sled creaking along a rough road on a frosty morning. I have noticed that homely scenes are apt to be suggested by circumstances of peril. It seemed incredible that anything of human construction could withstand the onslaught and shock of the warring elements. But "He that made darkness pavillions round about him, dark waters and thick clouds of the sky," preserved us. Beyond the loss of the boats mentioned, and two or three seas boarding us on the lee bow, staving bulwarks and starting a number of empty casks that were lashed on deck, we suffered no further damage until the wind had considerably abated, when we set the double-reefed main-topsail. A violent gust carried away the parrel of the yard; but we clewed up, lashed the yard, and set the sail again.

The gale gradually moderated on the fourth day. The clouds, as they began to open and the light from the blue above shone through, looked like mountains rolling on top of mountains from just over the masthead to thousands of feet above—a most remarkable sight, new to me, which I have seen only once since, and that a few days later, when another typhoon, longer and worse than the first, overtook us.

We were now down to 31° N. Unfortunately, we were not yet rid of our deckload. In addition to two hundred barrels of oil, we also had on deck some fifty casks of water, put there in making permanent stowage of the oil that had been struck below. At 1 P.M. of Wednesday, September 29th, we began to shorten sail, lash the deckload and secure things about the deck. By nine that night we were under bare poles, hove to with only a tarpaulin in the mizzen rigging. The gale began from the south, with a heavy sea running from west southwest. When the wind hauled three points, the swell still kept at the same angle to it. So that, hove to on the starboard tack again, this time the sea came from two points off our port or lee quarter. The lee deadeyes were constantly under water, and the great swells that took us under the quarter drove us ahead through the seething mixture of sea and air. At midnight of the second day, a sea from over the weather quarter carried away the lee quarter (larboard) boat. All the studding sail booms, oars and junk lashed to the spars over the stern had previously gone, as well as a coil of new three-inch rope. The men had to lash themselves on deck, to the wheel and to the pumps, which were constantly kept going. The violence of the wind after a time blew the top of the sea off, so that it was quite smooth, but it was one continual sparkle of fire night and day—the most marvelous phosphorescent display I ever saw, and the roar of the storm was so great that one could not hear another speak right alongside of him.

At one o'clock Sunday morning, October 3rd, it began to moderate, and as the wind abated the sea rose and the ship labored more and more. As soon as we could set a little sail, that steadied her and we made better weather, though the sea seemed as if it would swallow up the ship. The observation on Monday showed the latitude to be 29° 47′ N. With the sea driving us against the wind, instead of making leeway, we had in four days made over seventy miles of southing, hove to without a sail set, in a gale from south to south southwest!

— CHAPTER XIX —

"EVERY PROSPECT PLEASES AND ONLY MAN IS VILE"

October 4th to December 8th, 1847

*L*OOKOUTS WERE KEPT AT THE MASTHEADS BY THE dozen, but no whales were seen, and we continued making our way toward Sydney, via the Magellan Archipelago, the Ladrones and the Caroline Islands, the hands employed drying and bundling bone and stowing down bone and oil.

The island of Ponape, or Ascension, as it is better known to whalesmen, one of the Caroline Groups, was sighted on Wednesday, October 20th, at 11 A.M., bearing southeast, distant forty miles. As the natives were said to be friendly, the captain determined to stop and recruit water and vegetables. The wind was light and the strong current set us off so that we could not fetch the island that day. But if it had been invisible, we should have known it was there by the sweet odors of flowers that were borne out to us ten leagues and more away. It is about thirty miles long by fifteen in width, and is mountainous but not very broken. It is surrounded by a coral reef, just awash, on which the sea breaks, about three miles from the shore, with water deep enough for any ship inside. There are three channels through the reef on the north side.

Getting close in with the island on Thursday evening, we were carried fifteen miles during the night by the current, but in the middle of the forenoon of Friday, the 22nd, five canoes with about one hundred natives and two white men boarded us. With them were the King or Chief of the island and his two sons. They brought nothing except a few cocoanuts, which was a disappointment to us, for we had been so long without vegetables that scurvy had been making its appearance.

The white men were renegades of their race, injurious both to the natives and to those visiting the islands for an honest purpose. They were under the protection of the Chief, who permitted them to act as middlemen in all the trade between ships and the natives, in return for which they paid him a certain toll. Consequently, prices were high. The first white man to come on board engaged with the captain to supply us with yams at the rate of five pounds of tobacco, or five pounds of powder, or five fathoms of cloth, per hundred. They received about a quarter of the price in advance, with which to purchase from the natives. When the articles were delivered on board they took the remaining three quarters for themselves, out of which they paid the King's revenue.

Early in the afternoon, the white men and all the natives except the King and his staff who remained with us all night, set out for the island, somewhat reluctantly, owing to the distance, the strong current and the brisk headwind. The King and his sons were tall, noble-looking men, with long straight hair, smooth complexions and very good features; they were supple and active, and no doubt in battle were fierce and brave. The young men were eighteen to twenty years old. The father perhaps upwards of forty years of age, and our subsequent intercourse with him and his people showed him to be a sensible man, loved and feared by all his subjects. The island had formerly been divided among a number of chiefs, who were continually at war among themselves, but he had subdued the others, and was now, "from the centre all round to the sea," monarch of the whole island.

The King was the only one who was admitted on board armed. He carried an adze, the handle of which was the limb of a tree, cut out from the trunk so as to form a projection on the end about four inches long and two in width. Upon this was lashed the blade of a two-inch steel chisel. The handle was ornamented with scroll and fine criss-cross carving. It was a beautiful and formidable weapon and his inseparable companion. The King and his sons took their meals with the captain. While he was seated at the table, the King's adze hung over his shoulder, handle in front, ready to grasp. Their escort fared well among the men, and danced for us, boxed and wrestled, and sang the native songs. They were much interested in our single-stick exercise, at which some of the crew were very skilful; but they were generally superior to us in boxing and wrestling.

The Caroline and Solomon Islands

The next morning about twenty canoes visited us, and their occupants all came on board to see their Chief. This time there were women and

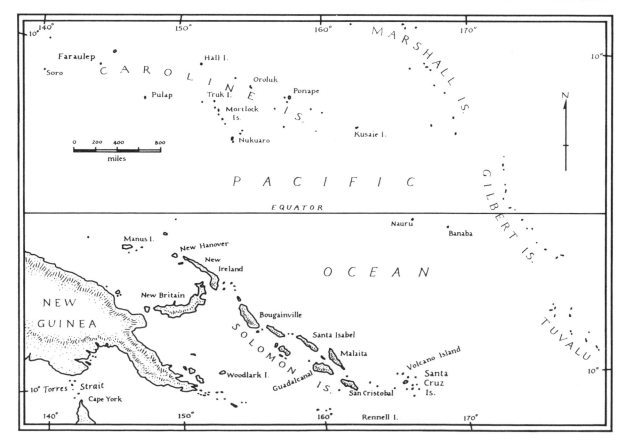

children as well as men. The day before there had been only men. They brought him sugar cane and the South Sea tipple—khava. This is a drink which, from its manner of preparation, can never become popular with white men. It is made by chewing the root of a species of pepper-plant and ejecting the chewed mass into a calabash or bowl, in which is laid a large plantain leaf or piece of tapa cloth (cloth made of the inner bark of the bread-fruit tree). Water is added, the contents are stirred around and left to stand a short time, and then the masticated khava is folded up in the plantain leaf or cloth and wrung out. The liquid ferments if kept long enough, but it is generally drunk unfermented and produces a drowsiness or mild fuddle of intoxication. Each family has its own khava chewer—usually an old woman.

Besides a quantity of yams contracted for by the white factor, the canoes brought a few cocoanuts, fowls and bananas, which the owners were permitted to trade for tobacco with the crew. The fowls run wild in the bush and have to be shot or caught when wanted. The islanders eat very few of them, and when short of tobacco will give a good fowl for a pipeful.

The natives were all over the ship in crowds, and as metal in any shape was immensely valuable to them, longing eyes were cast upon lances, hatches and things of that nature, and a close watch was kept to prevent small articles so tempting to our visitors from turning up missing. Such primitive people, still in the Stone Age, could hardly be considered morally censurable for appropriating objects of iron that came in their way, any more than we were guilty of cruelty to animals in killing whales when the price of oil made it so remunerative. Among themselves theft may have been a crime; but respect for the rights of other races, either in their lands or chattels are not held so sacred by the white man that he can afford to mark the boundaries of the Sixth Commandment for any one but himself. Our complete immunity, however, from such depredation was due to the strict commands of the Chief to his people, under penalty of death. A whaleship that had recently touched at the island had suffered seriously from thefts by the natives, and the King was anxious to efface the bad reputation thus created.

While the islanders were roaming about the decks, one of them in some way cast off the tackles and gripes of one of our boats, which, as the ship rolled, swung off the crane and fell down on top of a canoe alongside, parting her warp or painter and sinking her. The people in there, by a special mercy, were unhurt. But what a hubbub the accident caused. A dozen men or so jumped overboard to save the canoe, her occupants and freight, and there was a great deal of shouting and confusion. The captain even bustled around to show his concern for the mishap, and wished to lower a boat to assist in the rescue, but before that was done the other canoes had picked up everything and everybody, and the damaged canoe was towed ashore. The old Chief, throughout the commotion, looked on as calm and undisturbed as a statue; he minded the excitement of the others no more than if they had been a swarm of flies.

The canoes of this island are worthy of mention. They are by far the most ingenious examples of naval architecture that the South Seas produce. They are made of the trunk of the breadfruit tree, of an average length of forty feet, shaped and hollowed out by fire, stone implements, or such iron tools as of late years they had obtained from whalers. Projecting from bow and stern and three feet or more in height, is a single piece of wood, running off gracefully along each gunwale toward amidships, held to the main body by elaborate lashings. The hull of the canoe is thus composed of only three separate pieces, and no nails either of wood or metal are used in the whole structure. Extending over one side about seven feet are two thwartship beams, ten feet apart, lashed to the gunwales. From the outboard ends a log is suspended, thirty feet long and eight inches in diameter. Each end of this log or outrigger curves upward like a sleigh runner and presents a sharp edge to the water. In carrying sail, it is kept to windward, and its weight prevents the canoe from upsetting. If the breeze is fresh, a man crawls out on it to increase balancing power. A single mast is stepped amidships, upon which is hoisted a large mat squaresail. When working to windward, instead of tacking and carrying the outrigger to leeward, the sheet is taken forward, and the canoe comes by the wind other end foremost. The paddles are beautifully carved and polished. The bow and stern, sides and gunwales, thwarts and even the outriggers are also carved in checks, scrolls and grotesque figures, which are further ornamented by staining in blue, red and yellow. In modelling, construction and ornamentation, the canoes are almost entirely the work of the women.

On Sunday, October 24th, we stood in toward the island until we saw the surf on the reef, and then hauled aback, made a raft of water casks, and with two boats towed them ashore through an opening in the reef on the northwest side, attended by the Chief and about thirty canoes. Mr. Shields went in the starboard boat; Mr. Thomas in the waist boat, and I with him.

Inside the reef are several small islands, on one of which lived the white man who was our supply agent, with three native wives. After landing the raft, we rowed out to his house and had supper, consisting of breadfruit, yams, roast fowl and cocoanut milk. Though he was under the Chief's protection, he apparently depended somewhat upon himself to keep his own home secure, for he had two cannons mounted—a four- and eight-pounder— and a good supply of muskets and ammunition. In his house were a considerable store of English prints, beads and knives, the property of a company of Hong Kong merchants, whose agent he was. These he used in his trade with the natives for sandalwood, tortoise shell and *beche de mer*. The latter is a repulsive looking sea worm found on the coral reefs, which the natives gather, cure by boiling and drying, and furnish to the white traders, who sell it to the Chinese, by whom it is esteemed a great table delicacy.

The most interesting thing that I saw at the white man's house was a still, the coil of which he had made of two musket barrels. The Chief, though he enjoyed his daily draught of Kava, would not allow alcoholic spirits on the island, and it was all the white man's life was worth to be discovered importing them. But for his own use he had devised this rude method of making alcohol from cocoanut sap, and his appearance indicated that he probably consumed the bulk of his product.

This man's marital experiences were peculiar, as they certainly were extensive. As mentioned, at this time he had three wives. But they had a number of predecessors who when about to become mothers would disappear, despite his most careful watching, never to be seen or heard of by him again. As explained by him, the clan system under which the native society was organized is, compared with our simple rules of relationship, extremely complicated. Everyone, high and low, male and female, belongs to some particular tribe and is bound by the regulations which control that particular tribe. Whole tribes are regarded as brothers and sisters, and intermarriage among them is strictly prohibited on pain of death; and even intermarriage between one tribe and another is subject to minute regulation. On the other hand, all the men of certain tribes are regarded as the husbands indiscriminately of all the women of certain other tribes. But thorough as their system was, it made no provision for the classification of a half-breed race; and it was to this that the white man attributed the fact that he had no children and that his wives should disappear at the most interesting junctures.

Mr. Shields with his crew remained all night on the white man's island. Mr. Thomas and his men accompanied the King ashore to his house, where we were entertained with singing and dances till a late hour. Then mats and tapa blankets were furnished us for sleeping. The next morning, Monday, October 25th, the ship was twenty-eight miles off shore, becalmed. We filled our water casks in a few hours, and spent the rest of the day seeing the sights of the island. The King gave each of us a guide and a token which served as a protection or pass wherever we went. In the evening, the ship being still offshore, both boat's crews were made welcome at the Chief's house and entertained in the same way as on the night previous, only the program was vastly more elaborate than the first. Readers of Captain Cook's Voyages will find in substance a good description of the manner of our entertainment in Mr. Anderson's account of the festivities held in his commander's honor at Tonga Island.

The men of Ascension Island are tall and stalwart, generally over six feet in height. The women are diminutive, none exceeding five feet. Both men and women have smooth olive complexions and regular features. The men seemed quite indifferent to trading. Not so the women, who used many arts and some blandishments to induce Jack to give up good plug tobacco for more cocoanuts and bananas than he could possibly keep from spoiling on his hands. Judged by our standards, the women of the middle and lower class would be called utterly immoral; but their freedom of conduct and absence of marital fidelity is regarded by them as a matter of course and an injury to no one. The upper class is chaste and virtuous, in that respect an example worth following in lands many degrees of longitude away.

The dress of these people is graceful and well adapted to their tropical climate and aquatic habits. The men wear a grass kilt which reaches to the knees, topped by a broad belt woven in beautiful designs of many colors. The women wind about six yards of tapa cloth around their waists, the ends hanging down gracefully in front and behind. Both men and women wear a grass tippet over their shoulders, and a broad yellow band around their heads to keep the hair smooth. All these articles of dress are made by the women. The belts, as well as the tapa cloth, are woven with little sticks similar, except as to size, to those used by sailors for weaving sword mats.

As curios, I bought a number of full native costumes, in exchange for tobacco. The kilts and tippets were cheap and easily obtainable; but the belts, genuine works of art both in color and design, were more valued by the owners, as they deserved to be. Two I acquired after sharp negotiations from different sources, for five square plugs of tobacco apiece. But my especial admiration was for the belt worn by the King himself, which being made known to him, he took it off and handed it to me, and in return graciously accepted the same quantity of the circulating medium as I had given for each of the others.

The houses generally have an underpinning of stone, and a framework of quite heavy timber ingeniously lashed together. The roofs are neatly thatched with flags or palm leaves, projecting at the gables and eaves about ten feet, to furnish shade for the sides which are left open in fine weather. Curtains of small reeds are hung outside the framework, which in rainy weather are let down, making the interior perfectly tight and comfortable. The floors are of small poles—the King's houses had boards dubbed smooth with the adze—covered with mats. Some houses had but one room. Others were divided into rooms by reed curtains about seven feet high, the space above to the ridgepole being open. The people have some taste for cultivation of the soil, as evidenced by their extensive plantations of yams, bananas, taro and cocoanuts. The breadfruit is ripe on the island the year around.

On Tuesday morning, the 26th, the ship being within eight miles of the island, we tried to raft our water casks, but when we reached the mouth of the channel, the heavy sea stove several of them, and we were compelled to give it up and spend another day and night on shore. I employed the time gathering marine shells and other curios. Tortoises abounded, several of which I killed, weighing between 40 and 50 pounds, and added their shells to my collection.

Mr. Shields's boat went aboard the ship, and returned with astonishing news. Amzi Dauton, the third mate, who had been broken as boat-header, and the carpenter, an Englishman whom we had picked up at Callao, had formed such warm attachments for two olive-hued ladies that, with the captain's consent, they had resolved to leave the ship and live as Kanakas on this island, away from society, friends and the world. When the news got around among the natives the success of the two favored belles caused many other women to deck themselves in all their finest tackling, with the hope of enticing others of our company to remain with them. They flocked around in great numbers, decorated with fancy headbands and sashes, necklaces of shell beads, sharks' and porpoise teeth, armlets of tortoiseshell, etc., but they made no further permanent conquests. It might be the life of the free, but it had some ugly drawbacks. While walking around with some natives, I had seen an Englishman, dressed native-fashion, who had been living there about three years and who was a running sore from head to foot with a kind of leprosy. It is said that the native diet renders white men specially liable to this disease, its effects being increased by excessive kava drinking.

About 3 P.M. Wednesday, October 27th, we got alongside the *Athol* with our water. We also brought off three boatloads of yams, breadfruit and bananas, and twenty-five dozen jungle fowl. In the last boat ashore went Mr. Dauton and the carpenter to become family men among the Ponapeans. The captain gave them their discharge papers and a statement of their account-a paper showing that up to date the ship had taken so much oil, of which their

What Doane calls leprosy was probably yaws, a disease which causes extensive open sores on the skin and was widespread in that part of the world. It is much more unsightly than most cases of leprosy.

share was so much, and that they had drawn a certain amount; so that in case of their ever returning home they could obtain the balance. Before sunset we had our water all in and stowed, made sail and stood out to sea, waved adieu to the islanders and left them and their new citizens to take care of themselves. Light breezes continued through the night, and next morning this beautiful island was still in sight, bearing west by south, distant forty miles, but its wise and potent King, his lusty heathen subjects and Christian renegades had passed out of our lives, and the island while we gazed was gone from our horizon for ever.

Five days of cruising for whales ensued but to no purpose. The only strange object raised from the masthead was, on October 29th, an uncharted ledge of rocks, about a quarter of a mile long by two hundred yards in width, a dozen or more of the rocks out of water. We passed within three miles of it. The ship's position at noon of that day was 6° 2′ N, 161° 40′ E.

On Sunday, October 31st, we saw Strong's Island, bearing north northeast, distant thirty miles. During the day we spoke the ship *Volga* of Fair Haven. Being short of water, with the prospect of a long passage to Sydney, the captain, after sending a boat aboard the *Volga* for information, determined to try the island for water. At one o'clock canoes with about forty natives came off to us. Among them was the King's son with a white man for interpreter. When within six miles of the island we started a raft of casks for the shore, with two boats, accompanied by the natives. We entered as fine a harbor as I was ever in in my life, and at 9 P.M. landed, made the raft fast, and by invitation went up to the King's house to pass the night.

Kusaie, or Ualan, or Strong's Island, is the principal island of the outer or easternmost group of the Carolines. The harbor where we landed is on the southwestern part, at 5° 12′ N, 162° 58′ E. The island is mountainous and had the most pleasing appearance of fertility and habitableness of any I have ever seen in the South Seas. There was, however, very little cultivation of the soil; the natives had no bent for agriculture. Yams were not planted at all; breadfruit, bananas and cocoanuts grew spontaneously. The houses were large, well built and comfortable, the villages neat, with well kept grounds and walks. Indeed, "Every prospect pleases, and only man is vile."

The people were a savage suspicious-looking set of copper-colored rogues. The men and children went entirely naked; the women wore a sleeveless shirt or sack reaching to the knees. The expression of treachery and cruelty seen on so many faces was not rendered more attractive by the sight in the harbor of the charred remains of two whaleships, which about two years before had called here for wood and water, were taken by the natives and burned and their crews massacred.

The King of the island was upwards of fifty years of age with an only son. His house was in a large circular enclosure, with broad walks 150 yards in length and covered with mats leading up to it. When the canoes went out fishing in the morning the first fish caught was always brought ashore for the King's breakfast. The man who carried it, as soon as he came within the circle of the royal grounds, dropped to his knees and crawled into the presence of the King; and in retiring he crawled backwards the length of the matted walk till he was outside the enclosure. On all occasions his subjects never approached him except on all fours. The old King spoke English very well. Speaking of the fate of the two whaleships referred to, he expressed great penitence and regret for the event, said that his people should not commit any more such deeds, and that he wanted ships to come without fear and supply their wants at his island.

Besides the white interpreter before mentioned, we found an Englishman on the island who had been left by an English whaleship in the previous year. It was evident that they were not missionaries, but the King had heard—perhaps from them—of missionaries, and was very desirous of having the gospel preached to his people, "for," said he, "they are bad men, very bad." The King of Ascension also had besought Captain Coffin to have a missionary sent to instruct his people. The same requests were probably made of every whaleship that touched at these islands; and they were not made in vain. A few years afterwards, I think about 1850, a missionary from Massachusetts, named Doane, began his devoted service among the Carolines, which he continued in spite of arrest and imprisonment by the Spaniards, up to the time of the transfer of the islands in 1899 to Germany. Under the benign sovereignty of that nation, the gentle Ponapean and fierce Kusaian alike will doubtless soon be beyond all need of pious instruction.

We set about filling our water casks the first thing in the morning. The stream from which the water was obtained was perhaps a mile from where we landed with the raft, and to bring the water we employed about twenty women, each carrying a dozen or more cocoanut shells hung over her shoulders. These the women filled at the stream and emptied into the casks, marching back and forth till the work was completed. The boat crews remained at the landing to watch the rafts and boats, as it was deemed prudent, especially as the ship was nowhere in sight, to keep together and offer no temptation to the natives to attack us.

By noon all the casks were full; but there being a strong breeze with considerable sea, and the weather looking squally, the *Athol* had gone out for sea room. The watering party, therefore, spent the afternoon looking about the island in company with the two white men and two or three natives whom the King detailed for our bodyguard. We visited a number of villages, and saw the women weaving their belts and making mats. As at Ponape, except for the assistance which the men render in canoe building and fishing, the women do all the work.

On Wednesday morning, November 3rd, the weather was rainy with fresh breezes, and the prospect was presented of another day on shore, but about eleven o'clock, the ship made her appearance and we started with the water. The Englishman desiring to go to Sydney with us, we took him as a passenger. About a mile outside the reef we met the ship, considerably to the captain's surprise, as he thought we were weather-bound ashore. We were off none too soon however, for by the time the water was hoisted on board, the wind had fallen very light, and with a heavy sea heaving on, it was no place for us to linger. The weather continued so moderate that for the next two days we remained in sight of the island, which in a clear atmosphere is visible at a distance of more than forty miles. When on the fourth day after leaving the island a strong breeze sprang up, the sea was so remarkably smooth that there were absolutely no waves or swell to give the ship motion, she moved only ahead as if sailing on a pond. It was such an experience met with by the early navigators that gained the Pacific Ocean its name.

The lookout for whales was resumed with vigilance, as we were on good whaling ground and the signs of their proximity were abundant. My hand had now healed so well that, though the fingers were stiff and tender, I was anxious for another chance to strike a whale; and Mr. Shields had promised to let me steer him the first time the boats were lowered. Every day we saw finbacks in great numbers, and on Wednesday, November 10th, a week after leaving Strong's Island, sperm whales were seen at 00°, 15' N. The order to lower was given, and I was making for the starboard boat when the captain saw me and told me to remain on board and work ship, while he went to the masthead to watch the chase. So I had to stay behind and tack and half-tack in humdrum monotony until a whale was brought alongside by the starboard boat and made fast.

The work occasioned by this "cut," and the prospect which prevailed of more, required service from everyone, and the black steward who, ever since August had been kept confined and in irons, was set at liberty. It was not thought prudent, however, to permit him to work in the cabin, where he might find opportunity for revenge against the captain for his imprisonment, so he was sent to duty as a foremast hand. He looked pretty thin at first, but soon picked up to his usual condition, all the better for having been so long on a diet.

Whale signs continued plentiful, and lookouts were kept at the mastheads by the dozen, but though finbacks and porpoises in great quantities were seen daily, it was another week before the boats were again lowered for sperm whales. It was rather late in the afternoon when they were raised, and Mr. Thomas and Mr. Shields gave chase to windward. They were gone but a short time when the captain from the royal yard sighted whales not far to leeward. He came down and ordered the larboard boat manned and lowered, and took command himself, with me to steer him. The whales were very shy, but we contrived to paddle within seven or eight fathoms of one, when he either heard or spied us and shook his hump—a sign of fear or suspicion and that he intended in another instant to run. The captain told us to take our oars, and we pulled like good fellows. For a short time we gained slightly on him, and at the word from the captain I peaked my oar and stood up with the iron, ready to dart. But the speed of the whale was too great. The men did not need urging to do their best at the oars, but urged they were, vigorously, by the captain. It was all useless, however; we never were nearer than two boat's lengths from his tail—too long a dart to make any attempt— and he increased his distance every second.

While still making this hopeless chase, we saw another whale lying gallied, head up and tail down, rolling like a big can buoy in a tideway. We made for him and were almost within striking distance when he went down. By this time it was sunset, and having lost the run of the first whale, we returned to the ship. The other boats had been equally unsuccessful.

On Saturday, November 20th, we made Volcano Island, one of the Solomon Group, bearing south southeast, distant 45 miles at 8° 54' S, 164° 10' E. The next day we kept as Sunday, as we had not altered the day on crossing the 180th Meridian when bound from the Sandwich Islands to the Japan Sea, and we wanted our calendar of days to agree with that of Sydney.

Some of the men were a good deal mystified by this bit of routine. It seemed to them like a high-handed taking of a day out of their lives, and they were not disposed to accept with any comfort the statement that they would gain it back again when they got home.

We were now down in a part of the Pacific that is crowded with islands and shoals and coral reefs, so that the navigation required careful attention. Several days of bad weather, when no observations could be had, caused considerable anxiety, as the chronometer was nearly ten minutes slow and losing about four seconds a day, and the charts were known to be incomplete and inaccurate. Six men constantly aloft, with a bounty up for the first man who raised a whale, were enough to give warning to danger during the day. At dark we went about and until midnight sailed over the course made during the afternoon, and then stood back again, so that by morning we were in about the same position as at sunset the day before.

Smoky weather indicated our near approach to the Australian shore, and we began to think we should be in port without getting another whale. But early in the morning of Saturday, December 4th, all the mastheads at once informed us in effect that with proper management we should have good cutting and carving once more. The boats were lowered, and this time I shipped off in the starboard boat, as she was the last one down and the captain was at the masthead. The other boats chased a shoal of whales to windward; but not far from the ship we picked up one and soon had him turned up and moored alongside. Another shoal of whales hove to close by the ship. We hoisted the colors to recall the other boats, and then lowered again, and in half an hour we had killed our second whale. That made two whales for me in three hours, and they were the last. They made ninety barrels of oil.

I had recently crushed the little finger of my left hand—the one that had been cut—while planing a piece of whalebone. To keep the doctor out of practice, I had said nothing about it, but it had not done very well, and the work of throwing the irons, holding the line and steering-oar was extremely painful. My suffering nearly betrayed me. This disability I wished to conceal as much as possible, as I was convinced from the experience of the day that, once my fingers were well, I could do as well as ever in a whaleboat; and I did not want them to count against me when promotions came to be made at Sydney.

On December 8th we finished trying out, and commenced to clean ship and get ready to go into port. At noon of December 9th, we saw the coast of New Holland (as Australia was still commonly called), twenty miles distant. At 1 P.M., we saw the lighthouse which stands on a high headland, on the larboard hand, going into Sydney. At 4 P.M., we took on board a Sydney pilot and at five thirty, came to with both anchors in Pinch Gut, in six fathoms of water, abreast the Governor's house, Sydney Harbor, about two cables lengths from the shore.

During the past two years and a half, we had pursued our adventurous calling in all zones and half around the globe. The whaleman is subject to all the perils that other sailors encounter at sea or in port. He deliberately seeks a thousand others in the line of his peculiar duties, and casualties are accepted as matters of course. We had been singularly fortunate in escaping with but one serious accident—the fatal injury to the man who was towed under by a whale and who died in hospital at Honolulu. Delivered from every peril, we were now once more in port where life was secure and, protected on every hand, the people dwelt in safety.

Such were our natural reflections on approaching Sydney, until the pilot boarded us and told us of a shocking accident in town that morning. As we entered the harbor we saw the colors of all the shipping and on many staffs ashore at half-mast for the victims. The Governor, Sir Charles Augustus Fitzroy, and his wife, Lady Mary, were returning from a drive when the horses ran away and the coach was upset. The Governor escaped with a broken arm, but Lady Fitzroy, an ensign, and the coachman were killed. Our flag was set at half-mast with the others, out of respect for the dead. It seemed that death was as near by land as by sea. This lady's funeral on the Monday following our arrival was a solemn public occasion. She was beloved by all the people of Sydney, rich and poor. All business was suspended, the bells in all the churches tolled, and crowds lined the streets with bowed heads as the cortege passed.

— CHAPTER XX —

ATHOL, FAREWELL

December 10th, 1847 to March 20th, 1848

Sydney, Australia, about 1814

SYDNEY, AT THE END OF 1847, WAS STILL UNAWARE OF the golden treasure hidden in the earth nearby, which should soon cause it to spring into fame. It was even then a considerable port with a large export trade in wool. It is built on a point of land, nine miles from the mouth of the harbor, with Darling Harbor on one side and Sydney Cove on the other. Sailing up the bay, its sloping green shores dotted with villas and every breeze laden with the odors of a thousand flowers, we seemed to be entering an enchanted realm.

Acquaintance with the town strengthened first favorable impressions. In our walks ashore, it was fairly startling to hear English spoken on all sides; it seemed as if everyone must be talking to me, and that I should have to stop or turn and attend to what was said. A party of us coming to the gates of the Governor's Domain, the question arose whether we should be allowed in. "Good gracious," was the mild expletive of someone in reply, "they speak English here. If they don't want us in here they can tell us so." The Governor's Domain, however, was open to visitors, and worth seeing for its fine collection of mammals and birds and beautiful flowers. Our first dinner ashore we had at Toogood's Hotel.

The captain and his family found lodgings in the city, while cargo was being discharged and the ship refitted. For two weeks I continued to live on board the ship, working by day and in the evening finding such amusement as I could. Mr. Thomas had injured his leg while chasing whales shortly before we reached Sydney and was now living ashore at the American Hotel, kept by a Mr. Levy, while he was being treated by a Dr. MacCullough.

As I must have my fingers attended to before I could go to sea again, on Tuesday morning, December 21st, I called with the captain on Dr. MacCullough, for advice. The doctor said the joints had congealed, and he advised amputation. An appointment for the operation was made for the following morning, and I then went to the American Hotel to live till the *Athol* was ready for sea.

That afternoon Mr. Thomas hired a carriage and took me to call on a family of his acquaintance in Castlereagh Street. They were pleasant people, and through them we met a number of others, all free and sociable, much like our own Nova Scotians. In the evening Mr. Thomas and I went to the theatre and saw *The Bohemian Girl* and *Faint Heart Never Won Fair Lady*. During the next two weeks we saw *The Bohemian Girl* six times. We then knew by heart and by ear some of the songs. Mr. Thomas had a good tenor voice, and as for years I had been leader of the chanty singing on board ship, I thought I was a singer too. No one at any rate disputed that we both could sing, and in the social gatherings at the hotel and the houses of friends, we enjoyed ourselves singing *The Bohemian Girl* without protest from anyone and with some praise from our listeners.

At nine o'clock on December 22nd, Dr. MacCullough amputated my fingers, the captain and Dr. MacDonald being present. With my hand laid on my knee, the surgeon went to work, carving, unjointing and sewing, while I looked on, my well hand gripping the rungs of the chair and my teeth shut as hard as I could grit them. The middle finger was soon disposed of, and the little finger next received attention. The doctor tried in vain to strike the joint, and suspending operations, he said: "Why this finger has been crushed."

"No," said the captain, and turning to me, he asked, "Has it?"

"Yes," I said, "but you didn't know it." And I explained how, planing a piece of bone one day at the vice bench, the plane had slipped, and caught my finger between it and the vise at the end of the bench. "I didn't tell you about it," I said, "for fear you would think the doctor ought to attend to it; so I got a rag from the cook and wound it up in tar. I left it so for four weeks, and then it was well."

"Well," said the captain, "I guess MacDonald couldn't have done better than that himself."

MacDonald said nothing, but he looked as if such remarks in appreciation of his skill were quite too candid for him.

For lack of a joint in the finger, the flesh had to be turned back, and the bone sawed, and that was very painful. While we had been talking, I had let go the chair, and when the surgeon went to work again I took another hold, but instead of getting the bottom of the chair, I caught the captain's leg and gave him such a grip that he sang out *mortbleu*.

Those who have followed this narrative will remember that while up in the Japan Sea I had myself cut off the third finger, but as it was crudely done, the surgeon wanted to make a handsome job of it. I thought, however, by this time that I had had enough for one day, so well bandaged up, I went back to the hotel to dinner.

The two doctors, MacCullough and MacDonald, native Scotsmen met in this far country, left to themselves, had much to discuss of their native land, including its most celebrated product, about which they were very well agreed; but happening to get around again to the subject of the operation just performed, after the manner of their kind, they disagreed, and by this time being considerably by the head, the dispute waxed vigorous. To settle it, they came to the hotel while I was at dinner and called me into the parlor. There they took off all the bandages, talking excitedly in thick Glenlivet accents. I had gone through the original operations and watched the whole thing, without any worse break than pinching the captain's leg when they sawed a bone, but now when my fingers were laid bare, I fainted dead away.

When I came to my senses, they had satisfied themselves on the point in dispute and had gone, and the landlord's daughter, Brina Levy, was sitting on the sofa by me, bathing my head, while old man Levy was storming around, calling the doctors everything that he ought not to and declaring that if they came again he would not let them into the house. With the help of Brina and the housekeeper, Miss Josephine Day, I got to my room; and for the next three weeks I was very much indebted to those two good young ladies for their kindness and attention to me. Captain Coffin came daily to see me until I was able to go out, and invited me to call on him and his family, which I promised and fully intended, but too long neglected, to do.

By Christmas my hand was healing. In our austere, Puritan Barrington, Christmas in my young days was not much attended to. Coming in the dead of winter, about the only celebration it received was a "goose-shooting," as we called it—a gathering of the young men with their muskets to shoot at a mark for a prize. Here in Sydney, "Down Under," Christmas was a bright summer day, and it was faithfully observed as a day of merry-making. The parlor of the American Hotel—as doubtless was so in every home in Sydney—was gaily decorated with trees and boughs and flowers, and though there was no mistletoe under which the ladies might accidentally stray, yet the same privilege was exacted from them that would have been expected in old England under the mistletoe on Christmas morning. I am sure that Brina Levy and Josephine Day never told whether anybody kissed them that day, and as they did not tell, neither will I.

The holiday season was well filled with sporting events. As in all other countries under the Union Jack, tea and sport make up the half of life. If they interfere with business, so much the worse for business. On New Year's Day, 1848, the male guests of the American Hotel invited the ladies to the Home Bush races. We hired a fleet of cabs to transport us and obtained good grandstand seats. Between the races we all had dinner together in a tent. There was no trotting; it was all running races. The horse that won three out of five would be the winner. One of the horses was named "Sam Slick." So to the Antipodes—whether round the Horn or by the Cape of Good Hope, or both—had the fame of the great "Bluenose" writer, Judge Haliburton, borne the name of his homely hero. Of course, there was no other horse for my money but him. He won the two first races very handily. There were pedlars of various articles hawking their wares, one of whom was a boy with a dog and cart. During the third race, this dog ran away from this owner, and the rattling of his cart frightened "Sam Slick." He left the track and darted across the middle of the course, which was full of tree stumps. The young jockey could not control him, he tripped and fell, and a sliver from a stump pierced him between the neck and shoulder. His injury was such that his owner had him shot on the spot.

Such was the sad end, not only of my chance to win my expenses for the day, but of a noble animal whose magic name called up lively memories on this warm summer New Year's Day of scenes and people on the other side of the world in rock-ribbed, frost-bound Barrington. The commotion caused by the runaway racehorse compelled the mounted police, who were constantly on guard, to press the crowd back. While they were doing so, one of the police horses became unruly and with both feet kicked a man who could not get out of the way, full in the face. He was frightfully injured, but he was only a sailor, far from home and without any friends and there was no one but himself to care.

This accident to poor Jack, ashore and alone, made me think more intensely of home. There were some I knew who would remember and love me always. Perhaps by others I was already forgotten. But I recalled that Tom Moore, whose *Irish Melodies* I had read on board the *Athol*, had sung that "The heart that has truly loved never forgets." So, if I did not dream that night of any fickle fair one far away, perhaps I did of one as fondly fair with whom I had spent that happy day.

The races continued through the first week of January and I saw all of them. The features of the last day were a steeplechase and a donkey race. The latter, which was new to me, was a serio-comic affair—serious on the part of the participants, and wildly laughable to the spectators. There were eight or ten contesting owners, each of whom rode his neighbor's donkey, and the one that came in last won the *prise de grande*.

Thursday, January 20th, was an anniversary in Sydney, celebrated by a regatta in the harbor. Mr. Thomas and I hired a sailboat and took the ladies of the hotel to see the races, sailing and rowing. A line of buoys between the English warships *Rattlesnake* and *Bramble* was the starting point, the finish for the oarsmen being at a stakeboat further up the harbor, while the sailing race was round a triangular course down the bay. We took the ladies to dinner on an island in Sydney Harbor, and to the opera *Martha* in the evening.

Soon after the *Athol* arrived in Sydney, the Saint John, New Brunswick, whaling barque *Canmore* came in. As previously noted, we had been in company with her off Harbor Island, near Japan, nine months earlier, and with her boats had visited the shore and obtained fresh provisions. Seeing her come to anchor—a sailor can recognize a New Brunswick or Nova Scotia ship as far as it is visible—with Mr. Thomas I went to the boat landing to welcome her crew. To my surprise I saw among them the man with whom I had had the tussle over the sword cane in Saint John, nearly three years ago. The sight of him roused in me a desire for vengeance, but my fingers had just been amputated and I was then in no condition to fight. Some weeks later the *Canmore* was about ready to sail. By that time my hand was healed and, though it was still tender, I could not allow the opportunity to slip for squaring accounts with my old enemy. I sought him out in a waterfront resort which was none too respectable, and as he did not remember me I introduced myself and challenged him on the spot.

All whalemen become experts at boxing from daily practice in the second dogwatch, and my opponent had at least an equal match for me in the art. We sparred scientifically for a time until, in warding off my attack, he struck up my left hand, which made my fingers feel as if they were on fire. With a howl of pain and rage, I threw science and discretion to the winds and leaped at him over the top of his guard with my right into the middle of his face. The fray was over. He could not continue it because he was on the floor unconscious; and I could not strike another blow because my wrist was broken.

I walked back directly to the hotel, where good Brina Levy improvised a splint and bandaged my wrist—which, as she understood, I had injured by falling in getting out of the way of a team. Mr. Thomas learned the truth from one of the officers of the *Canmore*, which sailed two days later. I think Captain Coffin also was made acquainted with the facts. This I regretted, for I was ashamed of myself and knew any gentleman would condemn me for deliberately seeking such an encounter. Well, ruling one's own spirit is a life job, which is best managed by those who have little of it to control, or else are of a calculating nature, and I take little pleasure in those who fit either category. So hard it is for the many who pay the high price of their mistakes for everything they gain, to see the prudent and foresighted few take the prizes of life without contest except among their own kind.

As soon as my wrist was out of a sling, I went into a sail loft repairing the *Athol's* old sails, which at first was pretty hard work after almost two months of idleness. Mr. Taylor had been discharged and sailed for England in a wool ship before the mast. Mr. Thomas had been promoted to first mate, Mr. Shields second, and Kappe third, and the captain asked me to ship as fourth mate. In this I was disappointed because I had hoped for the third mate's berth. I could not blame the captain, however, for putting Kappe, a newcomer, one ahead of me, for whatever opinion I might have of my ability as a whaleman, it was plain to everyone that I had lost three fingers and was still obliged to be careful of my broken wrist; so I bowed to the situation with such grace as I could muster.

A day or two after resuming work, I made my long delayed call on Captain and Mrs. Coffin. They were in great trouble. Their little daughter Esther, now about four years old, was dangerously ill. Both parents were exhausted with care and anxiety, and the trade of nurse was unknown at that time in Sydney. This dear child and I had been great friends on board the *Athol* and for the next several days, the remainder of her short life, I helped all I could, by day and by night, in caring for her. She passed out of this world on Thursday, February 3rd, 1848. All the men of the *Athol* attended the funeral as real mourners, to bid farewell to our little friend. A shipmate who had recently died in the hospital was buried in the same cemetery. We visited his grave and on the spot subscribed a pound sterling apiece for a stone to mark the place of his long watch below. The stone was set before I left Sydney, inscribed with his name, the name of the ship and her captain, and a statement that it was erected by his shipmates.

As noticed at the beginning of the voyage, the officers and crew of a whaleship are not always sailors; and in preparing the *Athol* for sea, that state of affairs was at once apparent. Mr. Thomas, thorough gentleman that he was, made no pretence of seamanship. He kept occupied checking and stowing stores and various other jobs. Mr. Shields knew he was superfluous and was given a leave of absence. I was put in charge of sending down topmasts and yards, and lashing the heaving-down blocks preparatory to heaving the ship down for recoppering. Kappe, who was intelligent though no sailor, together with four men who had some sea experience, helped me. In a few days the ship was all ready for a good heave on the crab capstans. We hove her down and stripped off the old copper, which Kappe watched to see that it was not stolen, while I saw that the new was dressed down smooth and well nailed. It took two days to finish her and right her up, and the *Athol* was again home for officers and crew, her captain and his family. The sending up of topmasts and yards, the bending of sails and setting up the rigging, would be another week's work, and the *Athol* would then be ready for sea.

I am glad I did not sail on another whaling voyage, but the reason I did not was too trivial to relate. Mr. Shields (now second mate) and I had an angry dispute, which gave me a sudden resolve to leave the ship. I remembered the quarrels with Mr. Taylor during the past two years, and determined to wipe the slate clean and start a new log. On February 11th I told the captain of my decision. He tried to dissuade me, but soon gave it up, and handed me my discharge, a necessary document to entitle me legally to accept other employment ashore or afloat. This I at once deposited in the office of the Water Police for safekeeping until I had signed articles again for another voyage.

The same day Captain Coffin set about finding for me an officer's berth among the merchant ships in port. On the 15th he took me on board the ship *Hudson* of Liverpool, Great Britain, and introduced me to her master, Captain Pines, his wife and four daughters. There were also three of the captain's sons on board. One was mate, another a boy before the mast, and the third a child eight years old. The whole family had come out to Sydney with the intention of making it their home. But Mrs. Pines could not be long suited with any place on earth, and they were returning to England where she could live discontented forever after.

Captain Pines was so pleasant that I immediately suspected there was more to his manner than met the eye. However, the interview passed smoothly. He offered me the berth of second mate and I agreed to come on board the next day and commence duty. I returned to the *Athol* with Captain Coffin, bade Mrs. Coffin goodbye, and with a pat on the hand to her son, little "Nandy"—dubbing him "mizzentopman"—I left and went to the hotel with a heavy heart. I was as far from home as the shape of the earth would permit and I had parted with my last friends.

In such a state of mind it is best not to sit down in one's room alone. I walked out on the street again, and had not gone far when I was stopped by a shipping master who offered me a third mate's berth in a whaleship. I replied, with more heat than was called for, "No, not if you give me the fortieth lay!" I had no more than said so when Captain Coffin came up and recognizing the shipping master, said "Well, Benjamin, are you shipping on another spouter?" I assured him that was the last thing I would do, if I had to live and die in Sydney. He walked back with me to the hotel, cheering me with his kind and friendly words.

My blue mood was gone, and I spent a happy evening with Brina at the theatre. This sudden change in my feelings made me remember the words of Milton, which, of all things, he puts in the mouth of the devil himself: "The mind is its own place, and makes a heaven of hell, a hell of heaven." Repeating the words to myself with my head on the pillow, they brought back winter evening scenes in the old house at home, of my father reading *Paradise Lost* aloud. The world became for me not an outward vastness taking months or years to traverse, but a home for the minds of men, in which they can instantly be where their thoughts lead them. And then I woke up to a new day and new conditions, and to solid facts which test all theories.

On board the *Hudson* things had happened overnight. The mate, who was the captain's son, had run away after a violent quarrel with his father, who had threatened to turn him for'ard. The captain was naturally a good deal upset. He strove to be civil to me, invited me to breakfast with him and his family, and told me I must take charge of the cargo and act as mate. We were loading wool for London. For three or four weeks, as the carts came in from the country, I had to take account of the wool they brought and stow it, with the aid of two boys, and between times, with their help, I overhauled the rigging, sent down the topgallantmasts and topsail yards, and refitted all the rigging. In addition to the wool, we had 300 barrels of the *Athol's* oil. In that I had a personal interest to see that it was well stowed and to take the gauges of the casks, an account of which I sent to Captain Coffin. Meantime, the sailmaker sewed and roped new sails and repaired old ones, and the carpenter built a topgallant forecastle, fitted on the starboard side for the crew, the port side taking the place of the old galley.

The runaway son's absence continued. His eldest sister was outspoken in blaming her father for driving him away by his ill treatment. The captain angrily replied that if the boy came back he would put him in jail. On Saturday morning the mother and her daughters were going ashore, and as I helped them over the side, this eldest girl slipped a note into my hand and whispered, "For my brother, if you happen to see him on Sunday." But I was unable to be of service in that way. I never saw him. The poor father became more disagreeable and fault-finding toward me every day, alternated with occasions when he would assure me that he never had a mate that suited him so well. I would reply that he never had one who tried harder, whereupon he would complain to me about his children; and I daresay there was a good deal to his side of the story. The truth is, he was not only henpecked, but very much chickenpecked as well. He repeatedly pressed me to sign the articles as mate, and this I refused with the excuse that we were not yet ready for sea, that my discharge papers were at the police office and he and I both would be subject to fine if I signed without delivering them to him, and if he did not in turn deposit them with the police, properly endorsed. It would, of course, have been easy enough to get my papers any day within half an hour, but the real reason of my refusal was that my sympathy for him was changing to contempt, and resentment of his grumbling would make trouble. I could foresee that it would never do for me to sail with him.

By March 16th I had got the topgallantmasts up, the rigging set up and the yards crossed and everything ready for bending sails. The cargo was in, and as soon as a crew was shipped, the *Hudson* would be ready for sea. I discovered that the mate of a ship lying astern of us wanted to leave. I told him I was leaving the *Hudson*, and he asked Captain Pines for the berth. The captain took me into the cabin and made a last request that I go with him as mate. But I had borne with him as long as I could stand it and the wisest thing I could do was to refuse. I told him, however, I would stay by the ship until he had a crew and officers to go to sea with. He then hired the new mate and that same day shipped a castaway crew from a Bremen whaleship. The next morning they came aboard. Only two of them could speak English. Before starting to bend sails, I set them to washing decks. The captain came on the poop, and immediately he and the mate had a row, which the mate diplomatically ended by walking away. The captain then spied his younger son washing deck. He called him to him and abused him like a slave for doing such work *with his shoes on*! That spite being vented, he sent for the cook and berated him for giving the carpenter and sailmaker sugar for their tea when their allowance for the week had been used up. The cook offered a mild explanation and the captain kicked him off the poop. The cook kept on walking and went ashore declaring he was leaving the ship. The captain shouted at the mate to stop him, but the mate replied, "If you want him for your cook stop him yourself."

My turn came last. The captain made a tour of the ship with me to see what fault he could find. When we came to the sailroom, he asked if there was room on top of the new sails I had stowed there, for some old sails he had bought. I said no. "Then tear them down, damn it, and stow them so the old sails can go on top." I was not even fussed at this petty grumbling. I told him if he wanted that done somebody else must do it for I was leaving the ship at once. He came back with some high words, but I said, "Captain, I cannot talk with you for I might say something I would be sorry for."

I went to my room, made out my bill and presented it to him. He refused to pay it. I walked ashore and put my account in the hands of the Captain of the Water Police to collect for me. That official exclaimed as he took charge of the paper, "What sort of a fellow is this Captain Pines? He gives me more trouble than all the captains in Sydney!" The next day I went to the police office and got my money, then shipped as able seaman on board the bark *Bermondsey*, Captain Samuel Banes, loaded for London. I went to work getting her ready for sea, bending sails, taking down awnings and lashing the spars, all hands on board and expecting to sail the next afternoon. That night I spent at my hotel, and on Saturday morning, March 18th, bade Mr. Levy and the girls good-bye and took my chest on board. After washing down decks, the captain told me the ship would not sail until Monday and if I wished I could spend the meantime ashore. I was glad of this opportunity and went back to the hotel. That evening I took Brina and Miss Day to the theatre for the last time. Sunday afternoon I invited Brina out for a walk in the Governor's Domain and Gardens. Her father suggested that her kid brother go with us. We accepted the condition for there was no sentiment between the lady and myself except sincerest friendship and respect. We made our last farewells in the evening, and I was away and on board the *Bermondsey* in the morning by daylight.

My stay at the American Hotel was pleasant throughout its three months' duration, made so by the good will and kindness of the proprietor and his family. I look back upon it with happiest memories of those good people who made a stranger feel at home, though they were well aware it was no angel whom they entertained.

Before putting to sea again, I will relate briefly the fortunes of the *Athol* (as I learned her story years later) on her last cruise for whales. She sailed soon after I joined the *Hudson*, bound for the right whaling grounds in the Japan and Sakhalin Seas and the Sea of Okhotsk. Late in the afternoon of August 21st, 1848, all the boats were down chasing whales to windward. Mr. Thomas's boat was seen far to windward (the wind being westerly), fast to a whale. Near sunset the whale towed him into the sun's glare so that the boat's movements could not be seen from the ship. The ship beat up to windward, picking up the other boats, and as the long twilight was ending, the starboard boat brought a dead whale alongside. But Mr. Thomas was not there. In lancing the whale he was thrown overboard, sank and was seen no more.

The cause of his sinking so quickly is a mystery. The boat's crew told different versions of the accident. They agreed in saying that the whale, at the end of his last flurry, lifted his flukes over the head of the boat and sent him overboard. He caught the gunwale of the boat, but let go before anyone could reach him. Either he was stunned by the blow or the line fouled him and took him down. It is not easy to say how either could have occurred under the circumstances, and the secret will never be revealed until, as some believe, the sea shall give up its dead. As a fitting sequel to such a tragedy, while they were cutting in the whale the wind freshened, making a rough sea; the cutting pendant parted and the tackles came down, nearly bringing death to the second mate, Mr. Shields; then the fluke-chain parted, and this disastrous whale sank in the depths to which, in its death, it had sent my true friend, Mr. Thomas.

Apart from the sorrow over the loss of his brave and loyal officer, Captain Coffin felt that in consequence the whaling voyage could not be profitably continued. He determined to make a port and sell the ship, which would bring a good price in any Pacific port. He sailed for Honolulu where he sold the oil they had taken since leaving Sydney; and then what considerations led him to Goa, one of the most out of the way places in the world, I never learned, but in that tiny Portuguese colony, far up the Arabian Sea, on the Malabar coast, he sold the *Athol* to the Portuguese Governor. That lonely gentleman, surrounded with every oriental luxury but without family ties, wanted also to adopt little three-year-old Nandy, the Captain's son, holding out visions of the splendor which the gorgeous East showered on her barbaric sons and the wealth that might come to the boy from a career in that favored land. The parents, however, selfishly clung to their offspring, probably deeming better one year of Bluenose sailor life than a cycle of Cathay.

With the purchase price of the *Athol* in gold, Captain Coffin with his wife and son took such transportation as they could find up to Bombay. There they sailed in an East Indiaman for England and thence by Cunard steamer to Halifax. It is of interest to relate that Captain Coffin's uncle, Captain Peter Coffin, of Barrington, was pilot of this early Cunarder. He was a friend of Sir Samuel Cunard, who was a native of Halifax and who would have given him the command but for an English law which required that only an officer of the Royal Navy—I do not know what rank was necessary—could sail as master of a ship carrying Her Majesty's Mail. Sir Samuel must have held the skill of Barrington navigators in high esteem for within a few years three other captains from my native town were Cunard pilots, and at the time there were not many more ships in the line. Doubtless they would all have been in command but for the law which reserved such positions for naval officers.

Ship *Athol* engraved on a sperm whale's tooth

— CHAPTER XXI —

A VOYAGE ON A "LIMEY"

March 21st to July 24th, 1848

*T*UESDAY, MARCH 21ST, 1848 WAS A DAY OF FRESH breezes and clear weather. At 6 A.M. we cast off moorings from the wharf. At 10 A.M. a side-wheel steamer (it was before the screw propeller was in general use) made fast to us to tow us out to sea. At 4 P.M. the steamer cast off from us and we made sail, "homeward bound," steering southeast to pass to the southward of New Zealand. I cannot do better to show what life at sea is on such a voyage than to quote from my diary the daily routine for the first two weeks. It was kept in sea-time, the day commencing at 12 meridian.

Wed. 22nd. Fine breezes.... At 6 A.M. (that is, Wednesday morning, civil time) sent up the main royal yard. Steering southeast by east.

Thur. 23rd. Fine weather and gentle breezes from Northwest. Set fore-topmast and lower studding sails. Steering south by east.

Fri. 24th. First part fresh breezes and baffling. At 4 A.M. took in studding sails. Wind from south southwest. At 2 P.M. breeze freshens. At 3 P.M. two-reefed the topsails. Latter part breeze still freshening.

Sat. 25th. Strong gales. At 10 A.M. hove to under two-reefed main topsails and balanced reefed spanker. Head to southeast.

Sun. 26th. Gale continues with heavy sea. At 3 P.M. set close reefed fore-topsail, fore-topmast staysail and two-reefed mizzen; fore and main spencer single reefed.

Mon. 27th. Strong gales from south southwest. At 3 P.M. set double-reefed fore-topsail and reefed foresail and mainsail and stood by the wind to the southeast.

Tues. 28th. Strong gales from south southwest with a rough sea. Carrying all prudent sail. The passengers were seasick. Hands variously employed.

Wed. 29th. Strong gales and rough sea. Wind West. Steering east by south one-half south. Hands employed putting on chafing gear. They cannot remember my name, so they call me Yankee.

Thurs. 30th. Strong gales and rough sea. Hands employed securing the rubbish about the decks. At 5 A.M. two-reefed the topsails and took in jibs.

Fri. 31st. Commences with strong breezes from the northwest. Scudding under two-reefed fore and main-topsails. Middle part gale increases, the ship rolling very heavy. By the captain's calculation we are to the southward and eastward of the south cape of New Zealand Steering east southeast.

Sat. April 1, 1848. Strong gales; scudding under double-reefed sails southeast by east. At 4 P.M. close-reefed the main-topsail. Heavy sea running. Took in fore-topsail and fore course and fore-topmast staysail, and hove to under close-reefed main-topsail; blowing a violent gale from northwest.

Sun. 2nd. Strong gales and heavy sea. At 3 P.M. more moderate. Two-reefed fore-topsail, reefed fore-sail and fore-topmast staysail, and kept off before the wind scudding east north. Middle and latter part heavy squalls.

Mon. 3rd. Breeze moderate. At 2 P.M. set main, shook out one reef from the topsails and set the main-topgallant sail over reefed topsail. At 4 P.M. set fore-topgallant sail. Middle and latter part heavy squalls.

Tues. 4th. Strong breezes from northwest. Steering east northeast. Middle part more moderate with rain. At 7 A.M. saw the two small islands, the Antipodes of Greenwich, bearing Southeast five miles distant. . . . .

The above extract may be tiresome reading; at least any more of it would be, but there was nothing monotonous about living through it—not even to the passengers; they were too miserable to be bored, and the officers and crew were too busy.

This was my first experience in an English ship. It is an old saying that different ships have different fashions, and the only thing on board that was anything like what I was familiar with was the English language. Even that, to me, was spoken with a foreign accent. I had been shipmates with English sailors before, but when there are only one or two in a whole crew, their different way of speaking is laughed at along with their other oddities. Here, everyone, officers and crew and passengers, it seemed to me, must have learned English as a foreign language, so apparently artificial was their pronunciation. Doubtless my speech sounded as alien to them, for as mentioned above in my log, they called me "Yankee."

The captain was a dignified, entirely competent navigator, but a very easy-going shipmaster. He stood for conduct on the part of the crew which any captain I had ever before sailed with would have suppressed with an iron hand. What he could not control, he ignored. Consequently, Jack sometimes had his own way because he was better than his master. An instance of this occurred late in the voyage, when we were busy making the ship presentable for going into port—scraping the masts, painting yards, deck houses and bulwarks.

The port watch had been on deck in the morning scrubbing paint, with one man scrubbing the outside paint. This involved rigging a stage over the side and going on it with a scrubbing brush and a bucket of sand and water, and scouring the rust from the chain plates and other stains which had accumulated. It was the mate's or starboard watch on deck in the afternoon. The men had a council beforehand, to which I, being regarded as a "Yankee," was not invited, and they agreed that they would not go over the side and scrub paint. The weather was squally, and we scrubbed the inside paint up to 3 P.M., when orders were given to scrub the outside paintwork. They all refused to do it, saying it was not a proper place to send any man in that kind of weather. Now an absolute refusal to do duty is a serious matter, incurring forfeiture of clothes and wages. So the British way of shirking is to express willingness to obey but inability or fear as an excuse for refusing to do so. The mate asked each man in turn if he would obey the order. Some said they would if he would lower a boat alongside which they could fall into, if they should fall. That was absurd, because a boat alongside would smash itself banging against the side of the ship. Others said they would if they could have a lifebuoy to wear. That was nonsense also, for a man dressed up in a lifebuoy would be too clumsy to work. Others refused on the ground that though they were willing, they were afraid. The mate turned to me and said, "Yankee, are you scared too?" I said, "No sir, nor is anybody else, we are all refusing just because we don't want to do it. But," I added, "if this were a Yankee ship everyone of use would be made to do it. The rule there is, growl you may but go you must, and 'I can't' is no better excuse than 'I won't'." The mate reported the matter to the captain, who merely said, "Well, it's pretty near eight bells, let it go, it may be smoother tomorrow." The mate set us to taking in the stages, and nothing more was said about scrubbing outside paint, and we came into port looking very rusty outside, but about deck and aloft as slick as could be.

The mate, Mr. James Neatby, was a huge Welshman, queer all the time, and sometimes crazy. I was in his, the starboard, watch, and so had to get used to him. As recorded in the log, we had had a great deal of bad weather after leaving Sydney, and it continued with slight interruption all the way to Cape Horn, as was to be expected at that beginning of winter season in high southern latitude. On Friday, April 28th, the afternoon was calm with thick fog. At 6 P.M. the wind sprang up from northeast by east with squalls of rain, gradually freshening, and at midnight we took in the topgallant sails. Obviously we were in for another gale. The mate was full of native superstitions, which perhaps were as old as the magician Glendower, or even may have reached back to the time of Jonah, for the Welsh believe they were navigators long before any ships sailed to Tarshish. Anyway, he had great reliance on spells that could make the sea smooth or lull the wildest winds to gentle breezes. He expressed this faith at 4 A.M. by throwing the ship's cat overboard.

Every man in the watch, and later all on board, were indignant and aghast at his outrageous cruelty. The sailors were scared as well, and muttered for weeks afterwards that we needn't expect any luck on the voyage following such an ill-omened deed. And certainly, if there was any evil spirit in the poor cat, it must have joined with at least seven others as bad as itself in trying to revenge itself on its destroyer. From that day we had a succession of gales, with snow and hail and intense cold, which kept all hands busy taking in and reefing sails, unbending the remnants of sails that had split and blown away, and setting new ones. Fortunately, the winds were mostly well aft, and I would have cared little about the handling of frozen sails on icy yards in the long dark nights (for after all we were homeward bound) but for the effect on my poor amputated fingers. They would turn purple with cold and ache fearfully and I would have to rub them constantly to restore feeling to them.

So the cat's revenge, instead of landing where it belonged on Mr. Neatby's guilty head, was wreaked chiefly on the fingers of the lone Yankee sailor. And that is about as much justice, I think, as there generally is in such magic.

But the mate was more than queer. Often he was plain crazy, as was evinced in many irrational actions, generally harmless enough and not interfering with his efficiency in charge of a watch. Occasionally he had spells which incapacitated him from duty. A few days after the refusal-to-scrub-paint incident, the mate and I were over the side painting the bulwarks white, working on the same strake. He had finished his length and while waiting for me to finish, in order to shift the stage, he sat and painted his shoes white. I wanted to shout with laughter but dared not for fear he would send me after the cat.

The passengers were few and I remember them all, though I made no mention of them in my journal, except to say they were seasick. One was a man named Braithwaite, who had been a missionary in one of the South Sea Islands. His health had given way and he had been sent to Sydney, and was now on his way home. Because of his illness we saw little of him. Another was a nobleman on his travels, who had joined the ship at Manila. Very aristocratic—the world was made principally on his account—he condemned himself to the lonely ministrations of his valet, associating with no one. Then there was the Fat Boy. He was a great hulking, good natured overgrown kid, barely under age, a rich man's son, who had been sent on a sea voyage for his moral health. From his reports the prescription was an expensive one and had not made a complete cure, for he told us he had spent £500 in Sydney in five days. I asked him if he lost it in betting on "Sam Slick," but he said no, it was worse than that. He was a sociable youngster and would often come forward and join in the evening skylarking. He could box very well.

The favorite with us all among the passengers was a young English authoress. I am sorry I have forgotten her name. Like the Fat Boy, she had sailed in the ship from London and had seen Hong Kong, Manila and

Sydney. She kept a journal, and seeing me take the sun at noon she would ask me each day for the latitude. She had read a great deal and told me about a lot of writers whom I had not at that time heard of, among them Ruskin and Macaulay (the latter's history had not then been written), and about Dickens who was already famous, but whom I had not read. It was before Reade and Trollope were known, so we could not talk about them, but we discussed Dr. Syntax, which I had read on board the *Athol*. His doggerel led to a discussion of English ballads (she loved Percy's *Ballads* as well as I did), and then to English poets, particularly my favorites, Scott and Byron. She endeavored to impress me with Wordsworth, but I suppose he was over my head, at least he was too parsonish for a sailor. I tried to show her the thrill of steel to steel in *Marmion* and the fire in *The Corsair*, which she politely did not deny. I had the pleasure, however, of introducing her to Falconer's *Shipwreck*, and explained the sea terms to her, some of them even then obsolete. When she understood what it meant, she admitted it was poetry of a high order, but insisted that the unfamiliarity of people with the language of the sea would cause it to be forgotten—a fate, alas, which has long befallen it.

The ship itself, English built and representing in a general way the ships then doing the British foreign carrying trade, was a survival of the old era before the competition between sail and steam had compelled sailing ship builders to improve their lines. She was about 800 tons burden, and deeper and narrower in proportion to her length than our American ships. These features were due to an Act of Parliament then in force, which taxed ships according to their length and breadth. Her bows were as bluff and square as a sperm whale's head. She had little more bearings than a barrel, which gave her a rolling gait before the wind and a cranky tendency at all times. Her speed in a full-sail breeze, with studding sails alow and aloft, was about eight knots. At that time American ships in the China and London trade were capable of more than double that speed. British commerce would surely have suffered during the transition from sail to steam if English owners had not purchased the products of American and our provincial shipyards to meet the new competition of the Yankee clippers.

I have alluded to the fact that it was Samuel Cunard, a Nova Scotian, who founded the first trans-Atlantic line of steamers. And certainly with proper pride I may recall that it was my countryman, Donald Mackay, who made famous the new era of shipbuilding in East Boston, Massachusetts, gathering there shipwrights from his native province until the district came to be nicknamed "Little Nova Scotia." The ships launched from his yards were celebrated the world over for quick voyages to China, Australia and California. In self-protection, broad-minded British shipping firms, notably the Australian Black Ball Line, in spite of national jealousy and criticism, availed of his genius in the construction at Boston of ships to compete, when transferred to British registry, with the Yankee clippers. Anyone born in the Maritime provinces may be proud of the fact that the ship which first brought fame to the Black Ball Line was the *Marco Polo*, built in Saint John, New Brunswick.

But the contest of sail against steam was a losing struggle. Gradually, inevitably, sadly to the eyes of mariners of the old school, steam triumphed over sail. The forests of masts in every port have given place to iron funnels;

at sea their black smoke has dispelled the clouds of white canvas; the old-time sailor has either made snug harbor or eternal watch below.

On board the *Bermondsey*, however, we had neither foresight nor hindsight of such developments and were obliged to make up with such seamanship as we possessed for clumsy model and any defects in tackle, apparel and furniture. We carried studding sails whenever and as long as prudent. One cold day in a gale of wind, we worked under the lee of the longboat making nettles for studding sail covers, so that they would be ready to set at a moment's notice and could be secured snugly again when taken in. But with all the flogging we gave her, our average speed from Sydney to Cape Horn was less than five knots.

Wednesday, May 3rd, commenced with strong gales and heavy squalls of snow and hail from the south and very cold—steering east northeast. At midnight we hove to, the wind south by east. The mate had one of his spells and the captain was standing his watch. I was at the wheel. I had only one mitten, and in changing it from one cold hand to the other, I put one leg over one of the spokes of the wheel to hold it down. While I was doing so, the ship made a big pitch and roll, and my weight could not hold the wheel. It sent me over the top of it and I would have gone overboard without touching anything if it had not been for the spanker boom. The spanker was furled and the boom was on the starboard side to leeward. I landed right on top of the spanker gaff, which was lashed to the boom. I sprang to the deck and grabbed the wheel and hove it hard down before any damage was done. The captain certainly must have been asleep or he would have heard the wheel spinning around and noticed the change in motion of the ship. But his easy-going nature spared him many an anxiety.

Two days later it was still blowing a gale but the wind had hauled to the southwest, and we were scudding under two-reefed topsails and foresail, course east northeast. At 12 noon the captain judged the ship to be right off the tip of Cape Horn. The captain and mate were aloft as long as they could stand it, looking for the land, but they were driven down by the thick snow and hail and intense cold without seeing it. The captain's calculation must have been correct, for the next day, Saturday, May 6th, the southwest gale and the snow and hail squalls still continuing, we shook one reef out of the topsails and kept off northeast by east, a course which would have put us ashore if we had been the wrong side of the Cape.

We were once more in the Atlantic, which gave all a feeling of nearness to home, although for me, when we reached England, there was still the same ocean to cross before my native shores would rise upon my sight. While in the Pacific we had not sighted a single sail. It was cheerful, therefore, on Sunday, May 7th, to see a ship off the port bow, steering northeast, the same course as our own. She was too distant to speak or identify her nationality, but she was probably American for she outsailed us rapidly and was soon out of sight, going home. We all wished the old *Bermondsey* would log more knots but we were gradually working north, and by the end of the month the wintry aspect had yielded to our northern ideas of May weather. On the 11th at 48° 57′ S, 48° 6′ W we spoke the barque *Cartecheria* of Glasgow, from Liverpool bound to Valparaiso.

In the eagerness of being homeward bound, we carried all the sail the ship could stand day and night. Owing to her poor bearings, she was tender in a strong breeze, requiring the royals and topgallant sails to be furled, and reefs in the topsails. The main and fore courses, in the hollow of a sea, would be out of the wind, and as the ship rose to the crests the wind would strike them with sudden force, which would shake everything and everybody. On Tuesday, May 16th, the sea was rough and the wind increased rapidly to a screaming gale. By midnight we had shortened sail to foresail and double-reefed topsails, when we carried away the foretack bumpkin. That compelled us to clew up and furl the foresail, and we lay hove to until daylight. Then there was a gentle breeze from west by south, and we steered north northeast with all sail set, hands cheerfully employed fitting a new fore-bumpkin.

One thing specially irritating to all the crew—to me perhaps more than the others—was the British custom of keeping us on a weekly allowance of food. In the vessels I had sailed in the rule had been, work all you can and eat all you can. Here, it was work until you said you were afraid to do any more, and eat what was whacked out to you—bread, meat, sugar, tea, coffee and flour, lime juice and vinegar—and then go without until the next issue. The food was good enough, the salt horse and pantiles were of good quality. The bread, however, was a great trial to us. The heads of the flour barrels in the store room had been knocked in, and heather brooms were piled on top of them. Hence the flour, and the bread made from it, were chock full of leaves and twigs of the heather that the brooms were made of. This seriously interfered with the freedom with which it could be eaten. It made even the Scotch carpenter grumble; and if he could not stand it, what could be expected from some of the rest of us who had never seen heather before? I made out better than the others after running short. I did not like the lime juice. We did not have enough sugar anyway, and I did not want anything sour. It was only given to keep off scurvy, and the Lord knows we did not have salt beef enough to get scurvy. So I traded my allowance of lime juice for meat and bread (heather and all), or for whatever article of food I was out of toward the end of the week.

The weather gradually becoming warmer as we lowered our latitude, the evening skylarking became less interrupted. It is like a sailor to call singing "skylarking," for in the twilight, when the work of the day is done,

Up in heaven or near it,
He pours forth his full heart

in song. We did a great deal of singing and all enjoyed it, including the passengers. In the other amusements—boxing, single-stick and wrestling—that go by the general name of skylarking, I did not join, out of regard to my recently amputated fingers and broken wrist. Consequently, the "Yankee" did not stand high in our sports. On one evening, however, I did something to bring sporting credit to that name.

It was fine weather but there was quite a head of sea on. The ship was jumping into it lively when we started a jumping contest. The carpenter, a Scotchman, after looking at us for a while, bet two plugs of tobacco he could jump farther than any man there. A sailor named Wells urged me to take the bet. I knew the carpenter had a lot of tobacco and the rest of us were pretty short of it. I had only two plugs and did not want to bet both of them but Wells gave me one to bet with on the understanding that we would go halves if I won. A mark was made on the deck for us to toe and we were to jump aft as far as we could. One jump was to decide the bet. The stakes were put up, we tossed up for first jump and it fell to the carpenter. He made a leap, and where his heels struck a mark was made. I toed the mark, jumped and went over his mark about three inches. I took in the four plugs of tobacco and gave Wells two.

The carpenter looked the ground over again and said he believed he could beat that last jump. So the marks were rubbed out and a bet made of three plugs of tobacco. Again I went beyond his mark and collected the bet, which I divided with Wells. At this they began to chaff the carpenter for letting the Yankee beat him. That got his Scotch up. He declared he could jump farther than anyone on board and he was not afraid to make the same bet again. "But," he said, "we'll jump forward instead of aft." He jumped first, I followed and landed right in his tracks. He jumped a second time, doing a little better. I jumped and again landed with my heels on his mark. It looked as if we were going to tie. The carpenter jumped a third time, two or three inches over the second jump. They all cheered him and said the Yankee would have to go some to beat that.

I toed the mark again and stood a moment, swinging my arms until the ship mounted a high sea, and as she went down I sprang, the deck falling from under me. It was like jumping down hill, and I went about two feet beyond the carpenter's best mark. Then the cheering was for me, and the Fat Boy and all hands declared that Scotland was defeated, but none of them realized that it was only a worsting of Old Scotia by Nova Scotia. The poor carpenter felt pretty sore at losing eight plugs of tobacco over his enthusiasm about himself, and it did not soothe him when I remarked that there was a Yankee trick which he had not seen in my last turn. This seemed to give him an idea for he appeared to be plunged in deep thought, out of which he came up smiling with a new proposition. He had a scheme that would win back all he had lost.

"Now, Yankee," he said, "I'll bet you eight plugs of tobacco that you can't jump six feet off a board that I will lay on the deck." "All right," I said, unsuspectingly, "I'll take that bet."

"Look out! Look out Yankee!" cried the others, "the carpenter can play a trick too!"

"Let him play it," I said, "all I want is to know exactly what the bet is."

"It is just what I said it is," said the carpenter, "that if I lay a board on deck and you stand on it, you can't jump six feet from it."

That settled it, and I agreed to it. The carpenter got a board about two feet long, laid two belaying pins on deck and placed the board on them. I saw at once what his trick was. "Now," he said, "stand on that and jump six feet from it."

I knew that if I stood on the board and leaped forward the belaying pins would roll and throw me on my face. I stood up on the board, jumped straight up and gave a backward kick, which sent the board sliding half way to the mainmast, and my feet came down in the place where the board had been. I bent over and looked through my legs at the board where it had

"What do you think? Is
that six feet?"

brought up, some twenty feet away, and said, "What do you think? Is that six
feet?"

All hands roared, "Yankee wins! Yankee wins!" The carpenter
demurred, claiming that I had not jumped six feet from the board, but the
board had skidded twenty feet from me. I was prepared, on the other hand,
to say that the board had not been on the deck, according to the terms of the
bet, but on the belaying pins. But there was no occasion for argument. Right
or wrong, the verdict was against the carpenter. Everybody said that, trick for
trick, it was fair enough, and he quit the game sixteen figs of tobacco lighter
than he had begun, while I had enough, after sharing with Wells, to last me
home. I was not much of a smoker in those days.

Nearing the tropics occasioned us a lot of work. The unwelcome order
was given, "All hands turn to, sway up the sails and get a new suit ready for
bending." We broke out the sailroom and hauled a lot of old torn sails on
deck and set to repairing them. That done, we unbent the suit of new sails
that had stood the icy gales to the westward and south of the Horn and bent
the old patched ones to take us through the fine "flying fish" weather, up to
the northern "roaring forties." Then the change would be made again to the
best canvas we had. Sad to say, it was a Saturday when we finished this hard
work and there was nothing left of our weekly allowance to eat; so until
Monday morning we were on a water diet, and as the water was getting short,
we had to spread awnings to catch rain water in order to wash, if we wanted
to, as some did not. "God save the Queen," I could sing as heartily as anyone,
but I longed for the fleshpots of our provincial ships, whose sailors never go
hungry as long as there is a biscuit left in the bread locker.

We were beginning to see other ships with increasing frequency as we made slow progress toward home. On May 26th we saw a sail standing to the southwest. On the 29th we saw two more sailing south. What excited me even more that day was the sight of a shoal of sperm whales. On the 30th, as we were at the dull task of repairing sails, we saw two large sperm whales within biscuit-toss of the ship. They turned up and looked at us and then started off to leeward. Oh, to have changed the prosaic palm and needle for harpoon and lance and six lads in a whale boat, what a frolic we could have had. But if we had captured a whale it would have been no use without cutting-in gear and trypot or anything to contain the oil. So the old squareheads left to another fate. It was complication enough when on June 5th a school of porpoises came under the bow. We caught one, and with the cook's largest pot I tried out the oil for the ship.

On Sunday, June 11th, all hands were employed unlashing water casks from the side and lashing them amidships to the spars alongside the boats. The mate brought some spare pieces of hawser for lashings, and his orders were to splice them together and make a strap, pass the bights underneath the casks and spars, the two bights as they nearly met to be set up with lanyards. The rope was pretty large, and a Cockney sailor remarked, "We'll 'ave to 'ave a marling spike or a fid to splice this with; we can't splice it with our fingers." "Then tie a knot in it—tie a shroud knot," said the mate. "All right, sir," said the man. He fumbled and unravelled and tied and worked away, until the mate came back and asked him what he was doing. "Trying to make a shroud knot, sir," he replied, and it was well he said "trying," for he really was.

The mate lost patience, took the rope away from him and told another man to make a shroud knot. He tied a big bungling knot that is called the English or double shroud knot. This did not suit the mate and he turned to me. "Yankee," he said, "can you make a better shroud knot than that?" "Well, sir, I'll try," I said. I took the pieces of hawser, unlaid them and tied a knot that Mr. Pelham, the mate of the *Brisk*, had taught me to make, called a Spanish shroud knot. The mate looked approvingly at it and asked, "What kind of a knot do you call that?" I named it, and he said, "Well, I never saw a knot like that before." And doubtless he never had.

More and more ships were in sight every day, often half a dozen at once. I quote from my journal:

> Friday, June 9th. At 12 noon saw a sail two points off the starboard bow running down to speak us. Spoke her at 2 P.M. She proved to be barque *Union* of London, Captain Russan, 44 days from London, bound for Port Phillip, Australia. Lowered the boat and went on board for fresh provisions. Heard of the Revolution in France. The *Union* had lost a man overboard named William Brown. At 4 P.M. parted company and each took his course from 2° 0′ S, 20° 0′ W.

Two weeks later we telegraphed for an hour with a ship in company with us and then lowered a boat and boarded her. She was the barque *Tomitan* of Glasgow, Captain Turner, 114 days from Calcutta for London.

We got some fresh provisions from her—two hogs and three dozen cans of soup-and-bully. This was at 9° 50′ N, 22° 50′ W. On June 19th, at 20° N, near sunset I gazed wistfully at a brig which passed us bound south. From her spars and rig, I was sure she was a Nova Scotian, probably from Halifax for a South American port, and on board of her almost certainly were those who knew people that I knew. On the 20th a Dutch East Indiaman—I have forgotten her name—passed to leeward of us, bound home. We boarded her and bought some bread for sailor's use. On the 30th we spoke the barque *Expedition*, bound home, forty-seven days out from Rio Grande de San Pedro del Norte, South America, in 29° 30′ N, 40° 7′ W. On July 1st we spoke a British East Indiaman, bound home.

On Wednesday, July 5th, at 7 P.M., we saw the island of Flores, one of the Western Islands, or Azores, where the *Athol* had called in 1845 at the beginning of the whaling voyage, and where I had spent several days ashore. In those days, both "Flores" and "Azores" were pronounced to rhyme with "Tories." Nowadays I hear "Azores" pronounced in syllable to rhyme with "floors." I do not know whether "Flores" is pronounced "floors" now or not.

On July 6th we spoke the ship *Euphrates* of London, bound home, 100 days out from Calcutta and thirty-nine days from St. Helena. She reported the revolution in France, of which we had heard from the barque *Union*, and great fears of one in England. Upon hearing that I thought that when we arrived I should want to join the rebels, in the hope of some reform, so that British sailors need not go hungry at sea. The revolution in France referred to was the substitution of the Second Republic with Louis Napoleon as President for the monarchy of Louis Philippe, and the thing turned up was little, if any, better than the thing turned down—as sometimes happens in revolutions. In England the threatened Chartist Revolution of that year was averted because the misery and evils that created Chartism had been materially ameliorated by the Factory Acts and other reforms which reduced Chartism to an empty shell.

On the morning of July 15th, we spoke the ship *Spermaceti*, twenty days from Quebec, bound for Plymouth, Great Britain, at 45° 36′ N, 11° 50′ W. Later the same day we spoke the brig *George* of London, three days out from Torbay, England, bound for St. John's, Newfoundland. The next day we saw a great number of American ships. On the 19th we spoke a Dutch East Indiaman bound for Rotterdam. Her captain came on board the *Bermondsey* and exchanged some provisions with us. At noon of that day the Scilly Isles were distant 80 miles. On the 20th at 1 P.M., we spoke the ship *Pearl* of London, from Quebec for London. Her mate and two passengers came on board of us. They stayed until 4 P.M., and then we parted company.

This custom of ships exchanging visits when they met at sea was a pleasant relief on a four-month's voyage such as we were making, to the monotony of seeing no one but our own shipmates. Needless to say, since the coming of steam, which has made the longest voyages short ones, it is not done.

On Thursday, July 20th, four months from the time we left Sydney, at 4 A.M., we saw Longships Light—a ledge of rocks off Lands End; a little later we saw the Lizard Light, and at 9 A.M., the Eddystone Lighthouse. At 11 A.M., we were boarded by a boat from Plymouth to take our mailbags. Two of the

Eddystone Light

passengers, the nobleman and the Fat Boy, went on shore in her. Parting with one of them gave us no sensation. Throughout the voyage he had been merely so much human freight. But the Fat Boy's four months of clean, wholesome, merry life with us had made everyone on board his friend, and we waved farewell to the boat and him in it until she bobbed out of sight. We all hoped that the voyage had made a man of him.

By 2 P.M. we were off Start Point, and with all sail set all the afternoon, we sailed past the bold shores of England, specked with small towers and villages. At 4 P.M. of Friday, we passed the Isle of Wight, then Beechy Head and Dungeness, next the chalk cliffs of Dover and the South Foreland, took a pilot in the Downs, where a great number of ships were at anchor, and at 9 P.M., we came to anchor in Margate Roads. The captain went up to London by steamer. At 3 A.M. Saturday morning the flood tide made and we sailed up to Gravesend. Here the Channel pilot left us and the River pilot took charge.

Before taking leave of the Channel pilot, I must relate one last incident. The weather was thick and rainy and the wind southwest when we left Margate Roads, so we had to beat, and the pilot called for a man to heave the lead. One of the men was sent to the rigging and he had made a few casts when the pilot asked the mate, "Haven't you got a better man than this to heave the lead?" "Yes," the mate said, and he called another man. We were all at work, catting the anchor and fishing it and clearing up decks. The new leadsman made a cast or two, and after each cast the pilot would ask, "What water did you say?" Whatever answer he received, the pilot was evidently dissatisfied, for he called out to the mate, "Here, this man doesn't know how to heave the lead!" "He does too," said the mate, "for I heard him give you every cast he made." "Yes," said the pilot, "but he doesn't *sing* it!"

The mate came forward and asked, "Is there a man here who can heave the lead and give the long song?" After a silent moment, I answered, "Yes, sir, I can." "Then go and heave the lead." I went into the mizzen chains and hove the lead, giving the pilot the old-fashioned long song with every cast. After about two hours of that work, the pilot asked me if I was tired. I told him I was and should like to be relieved. So the pilot asked the mate for another man. The men forward, however, either from unwillingness or ignorance, all professed that they could not use the lead—all but Wells. He hove the lead, giving the long song for a few casts, and then only the depth. The old pilot would shout at him, "I can't understand that kind of talk; give me the long song!" Wells knew the words and the tune, but he had not much voice and soon asked to be relieved. So, as there was no one else, the mate said to me, "Yankee, you'll have to go and sing for that old fool again." And that made me a fixture in the chains until we anchored at Gravesend.

In these modern times the depth of the water at sea is ascertained by electrical apparatus, and heaving the lead is becoming a lost art. It may, therefore, be of interest to say something of the practice as employed in the days of sailing ships. For taking the depth beyond the 20-fathom limit, a deep-sea ("dipsy") lead was used. This was a billet of lead weighing thirty pounds, which was taken forward on the weather side, the line attached being led aft along the outside of the ship. The weather side was chosen so that, the ship's way being slacked, her leeway would prevent the line when cast from straying under her. The whole watch took part in the operation. A

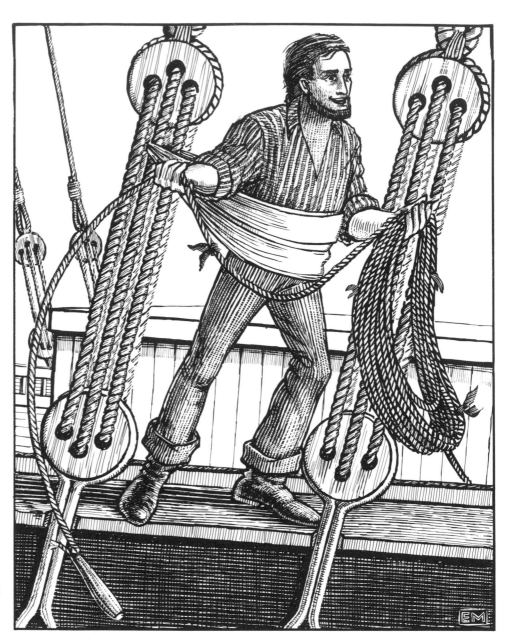

"I went into the mizzen chains and hove the lead . . ."

man on the forecastle head held the lead, and all the way aft to the poop, men were stationed in the fore, main and mizzen chains, each holding the line as it led aft; and the rest of the watch in convenient places along the rail. The officer of the watch stood by the rail of the poop, just abaft the mizzen backstay, with a bight of the line in his hands, ready to note the depth at the proper moment. All being ready, the man forward threw the lead overboard, shouting, "Watch, Oh Watch!" and ran aft. As the line came taut in the hands of the men in the chains, each in turn let go and gave the same cry, "Watch, Oh Watch!," leaped on deck and, with the others, ran aft to the poop. The officer let the line run through his hands to bottom (if there was any), whereupon a man at his side caught the line in a snatch block on the mizzen backstay, and all hands tailed on to haul in the lead. In this way any depth of water that need be sounded for navigation purposes was ascertained.

For a depth of 20 fathoms or less a handline was used with a lead weighing about nine pounds. In the end of it (as in the dipsy lead also) was a cavity filled with lard, so that the character of the bottom—sand, mud or gravel—and its color might be observed. On sailing ships the leadsman stands in the mizzen chains, swings the lead over his head to give it momentum and throws it forward into the water. The line runs through his hands until it reaches bottom, and he tells the depth of the water by the "marks," as the little pieces of rag or leather tied on the line at various measured distances are called. At a length of two fathoms (twelve feet) from the lead are two strips of leather; at three fathoms, three strips; five fathoms, a white cotton rag; seven fathoms, a red woollen rag; ten fathoms, a piece of leather with one round hole in it; thirteen fathoms, three strips of leather; fifteen fathoms, a white cotton rag; seventeen fathoms, a red woollen rag; twenty fathoms, a piece of leather with two round holes. The unmarked fathoms between the "marks" are called "deeps," and whether the depth (for instance) is six fathoms or "and a half six," is left to the leadsman's experienced judgment. The short way of giving the depth would be simply to shout, "two fathoms," "quarter less five," etc. In the noise of the wind and sea, however, it might be difficult for the pilot to tell whether the leadsman said "five" or "nine," or "seven" or "eleven." But if he sings to the tune that goes with it, "By the mark five" or "By the deep nine," the one cannot be mistaken for the other. So the old-time pilots preferred to hear the "long song," calling the deeps or marks; but some sailors either could not or would not sing for any pilot.

The story is told of an Irish sailor who was asked if he could give the long song in heaving the lead. He replied, "Well, sir, I know the tune but I don't know the words." Although the tune without words would not be a perfect performance, he was told to go ahead and do the best he could, which he did. Circling the lead over his head, he made a splendid cast, the line slipping through his hands until the lead struck bottom, whereupon he roared out the tune to the words, "Oh, here's a whole row and another red rag." Not a very self-explanatory statement, a landsman might think, but a pilot or any sailor would know that the depth was seventeen fathoms, as indicated by the words "*another* red rag."

Greenwich Hospital in 1830

As everybody knows, the author Samuel Clemens had for a time been a Mississippi River steamboat pilot. Hence he was necessarily expert with the lead, and his pen name "Mark Twain," being interpreted, means two fathoms. As is sometimes the case with nautical men, whether on a river or at sea, it is said that Mark occasionally used theological terminology out of place, and that his wife, hearing him indulging in this naughty nautical language, burst out by way of rebuke with a repetition of the words he had just uttered. Mark looked at her for a shocked moment and then drawled, "O, Mary, you know the words but you don't know the tune!" An obvious parody of the Irishman's answer in the above story, which no doubt Mark had heard from the pilot who taught him the "long song," and who in turn probably heard it from the pilot who taught him—for it is an ancient classic.

At 3 P.M. the captain came on board at Gravesend, and with cockbilled yards and the jibboom and spanker boom rigged in, we took steam and towed up to London. I have mentioned with reference to Harbor Island, near Japan, Captain Coffin's likening its scenery to the River Thames, and as for the first time I sailed up the English Channel and the London river, I saw the truth of his comparison. The river pilot was an old sea captain and, seeing my interest, he told me many of the places we passed, about which I had heard and read. They were a beautiful sight and I cannot describe my wonder at their charm—the green fields, mansions, castles and, last, the Greenwich Hospital and Observatory, which had been a palace for kings, but was now a nation's shrine, made so by a sailor's coat and vest, Lord Nelson's, which he wore when he fell on the deck of the *Victory* at Trafalgar.

London Dock Basin in 1831

We moored ship at 6 P.M. in London Dock Basin. The captain, as he was leaving the ship, harked back to the refusal-to-scrub-paint episode. He said, "All you men of the starboard watch that will go over the side and scrub paint before you leave can come down day after tormorrow and get your wages." His hope was, apparently, that we would be timid enough to comply, rather than take the chance of forfeiting wages on complaint being made that we had refused to obey orders. But nobody paid any attention to the threat that was back of his words. As soon as the decks were cleared up all hands went ashore—I to the Sailors' Home in Welles Street, to board.

The captain's complaint, I think, was justified and we would have had the worst of it if it had been pressed. But the men were aware that the sugar and flour, and perhaps the lime juice and vinegar, had not been dealt out just as the law said it should be, and London is a ticklish place to trifle with sailors' rights. "Old Ballantine," as he was called, was in those days a famous police magistrate, severe against real offenders, but with a very humane feeling for the underdog. Decent sailors regarded him as their protector. If one complained to him of any wrong, he would have the captain and all hands up before him, and if everything on the voyage had not been done according to Act of Parliament, he would slap a fine on the ship. Captain Banes knew "Old Ballantine" too well to give anyone a chance to complain, so two days later when we went down for our wages we were paid off, and nothing said about scrubbing paint.

— CHAPTER XXII —

A VOYAGE WITH SIX LEGS

July 25th to December 24th, 1848

*T*HE SAILORS' HOME IN WELLES STREET, LONDON, HAD existed for generations before I ever saw it, and I believe it still endures—much enlarged and improved on the model of the houses built by Lord Rowton at King's Cross. It was then a well-regulated, comfortable hostel accommodating about thirty men. No ship's officers lived there. Jack could take his ease in his inn unembarrassed by any superiors in rank. In later years there was a shipping office connected with the home, but at this time that service was rendered by a Mr. Simonds, whose office was nearby in the Minories, Tower Hill. Adjoining the Sailors' Home was the Sailors' Church, and the day after our arrival being Sunday, I turned out and went to Church that morning. It may seem trivial to note such an event but, as is common among seafaring men, I had generally neglected such opportunities and I might as well admit that now I was willing to express in this way the sense of thankfulness which was upon me to be again in a land from which it was easy to sail for home. This I could do any day by working my passage or paying for it. I determined not to do either, and looked every day for a berth. It was so long, however, before I found one that at last the flatness of my purse compelled me to take what came. Meantime I was glad to enjoy a period of sightseeing in this greatest city of the world.

As soon as I was paid off I went to what I was told was the largest shop in London, Moses & Sons, Minories, to fit out with shore clothes. For all I know, that great emporium may be still holding forth at the old stand, or perhaps in the more fashionable shopping district to the west. Whatever its fate, it was then the biggest and best place of the kind I had ever seen, and I stepped out of it equipped in such style, if I could believe the salesman's assurances, as to be taken anywhere for an English gentleman. He must have been mistaken, however. I was anxious only to be taken for what I was, and in the month I spent in London—going to the theatre, visiting museums, art galleries, cathedrals, the Tower and other historic places—no occasion arose to explain myself. In order to get a ship, it was necessary for me to register as a British seaman. When I went to do so, however, I met obstacles. The registration officials declared I was a Yankee. I sincerely wished I was, and told them so, but that I was British American and claimed the rights of a British subject. Evidently my new English clothes deceived no one. When I spoke, it was plain I was not English, for all my h's were where they ought to be and none where they ought not to be. That was suspicious. It could not be supposed that the aspirate was handled differently in unheard of

Barrington, Nova Scotia, where I said I was born, than in the Parish of Bow; so I could not be British and was, therefore, a Yankee. But truth was mighty and finally I received my ticket of registration.

Thus furnished, on August 23rd, with a young English fellow named Stafford who had been my roommate and guide about London, I shipped at Mr. Simond's office for a voyage on the ship *Alceste*, hailing from Yarmouth, Nova Scotia, commanded by Captain James D. Cann to Newport, Wales, Bermuda, and the United States of America. The *Alceste* was lying in Commercial Dock, ready to sail the next afternoon. We put our dunnage aboard and went back to the Home for the night. At 4 P.M. of the 24th the tide suited and we hauled out of the dock, took steam and towed down to Gravesend, anchoring there at 9 P.M. A watch was set which consisted only of Stafford and me, the rest of the crew being drunk. At 5:30 A.M. of Friday, the 25th, we were called to wash decks. The men shipped in London turned out sober enough. Presently four other men came out of the forecastle. None of us who were washing decks had known they were there. Stafford and I had been on deck all night, and the rest were in no condition to observe anything. The spokesman for these others asked the mate if he wished their services. He told them "No," with such emphatic garnishments to that simple word, that we gasped with admiration.

It seemed that we had two crews on board. The men who were strange to us were a set of Saint John, New Brunswick, Irishmen, mere dock-workers and not seamen. They had shipped in Saint John, the vessel's last previous port, for the purpose of getting to England where they had hoped to help along the expected Revolution. By the articles, however, they were to perform a voyage to England and back. Their ignorance of sailors' duties made trouble with the officers, and they became insubordinate. The mate, Mr. John Fields, of Halifax, Nova Scotia, was a fine old disciplinarian. He had been master of a Saint John ship which had been cast away, and he had joined the *Alceste* as mate. When he left here, it was to take command of a ship out of Halifax. His strict and steady hand would have controlled the men, but the familiar "bucko" methods of the captain had roused their determination that Ireland should be free, with the age-old result to the Irish of increasing their oppression. Arrived in London, they found the chance of a revolution had glimmered out and they decided to stay by the ship. Captain Cann was equally resolved to get rid of them and ordered them ashore without their wages. They went up to "Old Ballantine" who heard both sides and, weighing their incompetence against bad treatment, evened matters up by sending them back aboard to complete the voyage. The captain considered this half a victory, since he had not been fined, and continued his efforts to drive them ashore, so far without success. When ready to sail, he shipped another crew, and here we were steering into more trouble.

The cook came along with breakfast and announced it was only for the men who had shipped in London. The Saint John men told us what was the trouble while they shared breakfast with us. The London crew then went to work getting out the jibboom. The Irish spokesman said to the mate, "We are ready to work, sir, whenever you say so, sir." The mate came back, "You go to hell, sir, and if you don't I'll have you arrested; you don't belong here, sir." The Irish then withdrew to the forecastle and stayed there all the morning.

To prevent us from sharing another meal with them, the mate ordered the cook to bring our dinner into the after part of the half-deck house where the two apprentices lived, and we had to eat it there. In the middle of the afternoon the captain came on board with a police officer. All hands were called aft and the captain read our names from the articles, to which each one answered in turn. The captain said, "Officer, the men who have answered to their names on the articles are my crew. Any others that you find on board are stowaways, and I want you to arrest them and take them ashore." Then to us, he said, "Now men, assist this officer in putting those stowaways in the boat."

At that moment the four "stowaways" sprang out of the forecastle, drew their knives and shouted defiance. The captain cried out, "These men are mutineers," and ordered us to help the policeman overpower and throw them into the boat. If we had been at sea, such an order would have called for unquestioning obedience. But the captain had just told the policeman the men were stowaways. Now he said they were mutineers. If that is what they were, then they belonged to the ship, and here we were in port where he could get all the help he needed without calling on us. We had seen no mutinous conduct, not even disobedience of orders in port, but only repeated offers on their part to go to work, and it certainly was not mutiny to refuse to be driven ashore. Our sympathies were not with the captain. Whatever the men were, therefore, we decided to be ringside standees and see what happened.

The policeman attempted to put his hands on one of the stowaway-mutineers, who promptly knocked him down and jumped on him. One of the 'prentice boys jumped on that fellow, and then a second stowaway or mutineer (as you please) jumped on him. For a little while it was as pretty a mix-up, over and under, as I ever kept out of. The mate came arunning with an old horse pistol, ready to use either end of it. He snapped it twice harmlessly and then concluded it would make a magnificent club. With the butt he charged the squirming bundle of men and laid out three of them, including one of the 'prentice boys whose head accidently got in the way. That was all. The bobby scrambled to his feet and went ashore, the pilot came aboard, the tide suited, and we got under way. The wind was ahead, east northeast, and we had to beat. Ten miles down the river we anchored, set a watch and hoisted a light. The captain called the four men aft and offered to pay them off if they would go ashore. They agreed to do so if he would pay them three months' extra wages. This he refused to do, so we had them as shipmates all the way to Newport, Wales.

What with calms and head winds, it took us four days to work down to Margate, and twenty-four hours later we anchored in the Downs. The captain again offered the Saint John men their wages and discharge, and they again refused. They told us in the forecastle it was their intention to sue the captain when we reached Newport. Apparently the captain suspected this and had been trying to head it off. So there they were. "Old Ballantine" had told them they could stay, and they bided their time, living in the forecastle but performing no duty. Fortunately we were not in an English ship, for they had excellent appetites, and the rules of "Eat all you can" did more to keep trouble away than all the Acts of the British Parliament.

Such perversity of winds on a short voyage I had never seen. After beating from Gravesend to the Downs, the wind went from east northeast to west southwest, a heavy blow, and we beat down Channel for four days, during which we carried away the main-topgallant mast over the side. This did not cause much delay, for we had a good crew and in little more than two hours we had cleared away the wreck, set up a new topgallant mast and set the topgallant sail again. At 9 A.M. on September 2nd we doubled Cape Cornwall, the wind was again east northeast, and we were a week beating up the Bristol Channel to the mouth of the river Usk. At 8 A.M. of Monday, September 4th, we were eight miles west northwest of Lundy Island. From that time we frequently spoke the Bristol pilots, but as long as there was reasonable room to tack and a chance of a fair wind, we sailed her alone. At 6 P.M. of the 5th it was fine but still head wind. Night was too near, and the English and Welsh shores too close aboard on either hand, to take any more risk. The captain accepted a pilot, who tacked ship to the north and at 10 P.M. we came to anchor under the Welsh shore. There could be no mistake; I was in a Nova Scotia ship with a native captain and mate, for that breed never takes a pilot unless they are sure they need one.

With a pilot in charge, the captain expanded enough the next day to notice, while I was sailmaking, that I had lost three fingers, and to ask how and where. I told him, "On board a Saint John whale ship." To his further question, "What ship?" I answered, "The *Athol*, Captain Coffin." "Oh," he said, "he belongs in Barrington. He had his wife with him." He said he also knew Captain Joseph Kenney of Barrington (Captain Kenney's home was on Cape Sable Island), of the whale ship *James Stewart*, and I admitted that I did too. That ended the conversation. It would not have been sailor etiquette for me, unasked, to say that the men and the lady spoken of were my relatives and that I was from Barrington also; and it would be unheard of for a captain to sustain a personal conversation with a foremast hand. I was grateful for the interview, slight as it was. It was the first time I had spoken to anyone who knew any friends of mine since I had bade farewell to Captain Coffin and his wife in Sydney, and that seemed as long, long ago, as it was far, far away. I actually felt that I was drawing near home.

With the mate, Mr. Fields, the distance created and kept by difference in rank was more easily bridged. I liked him from the first. He called me "Dan" instead of "Doane," and after he knew my first name, I was still familiarly "Dan" to him. At 6 A.M. of September 7th, the Newport pilot boarded us and took over from the Channel pilot. At 9 we entered the mouth of the Usk, the wind blowing right down the river. We had two hours of flood tide, in which we tacked to and fro and when the ebb made, we anchored. At 4 P.M. the ship was dry on the mud, kept upright by props which had been placed as the tide receded, and we commenced cleaning her bottom. When the flood tide sent us aboard, the mate gave each of us a glass of brandy. As I received mine, I bowed and, with a sweep of the hand to the heart, said, "Here's to your good health, sir, on my birthday." He inquired, "Where were you born?" "Nova Scotia, sir." "Here's to a fellow countryman," he replied, and down the hatch flowed ardent spirits which burned to sincere friendship during the six months we were together.

It was six miles from the mouth of the river up to Newport. The wind continued ahead, and we kedged the ship all the way, beginning on the 7th and completing it on the 12th, six miles in six days. On the 9th we parted our hawsers and had to anchor. The four Saint John men were set ashore and went up to town. The captain also went to town that day. We remained at anchor until he returned on Monday, the 11th. He hailed the ship from the bank, and I was sent to bring him off in the boat. He asked if there was a man aboard named "Doane." I told him that was my name. He said, "Then you have a brother here, Captain of a Shelburne, Nova Scotia brig." No further explanation was given or sought. It was plain that the captain had met my brother Martin, told him there was a man aboard the *Alceste*, who had been with Captain Coffin in the *Athol*, and my brother, presumably, had remarked that a brother of his had sailed on the *Athol* from Saint John, and naturally he wondered if the man on the *Alceste* would know anything about him.

At six o'clock I had leave from the mate to go ashore. I walked up to town and had no difficulty in finding the brig *Rose*, of which my brother Martin was master and my nephew, Thomas Doane, second mate. We sat up until midnight talking. My brother strongly advised me to go home, a counsel which was most acceptable, and here was an opportunity. The *Rose* was ready to sail for Boston. Going in her depended upon obtaining my discharge from the captain of the *Alceste*. It would be easy to ship another man in Newport, he had done his best to get rid of the four Irishmen—I had a vision of being in Barrington by Christmas.

On Tuesday morning, September 12th, the weather was thick and rainy. Our breakfast on the *Rose* was shortened by a woman with a child in her arms falling into the dock. They got pretty wet but Tommy Doane and I took

Newport, Wales, about 1850

the boat and picked them up safely. In the afternoon the weather had what the English call "bright intervals"—the sun shining between showers. Tommy and I walked down the path by the river and watched the *Alceste* warping up. At 9 P.M. she got into the dock and I went aboard. I asked the captain for my discharge so I could go home in the *Rose*. I offered to pay back the advance of wages I had received in London and to ship a new man in my place. Captain Cann kindly refused to let me go. With equally kind feelings for him, I sent some clothes and my South Sea specimens and curiosities to the *Rose* and watched her sail at 4 P.M. of the 13th, a sight which I had to muster all my stoicism to enjoy.

It was some comfort that the next day the captain was summoned to court by the four men from Saint John, and he went to town with the log book and the second mate as a witness. The case lasted two days and ended with a fine laid against the ship of two hundred and fifty pounds, including the men's wages and costs. A court bailiff was put on board and an advertisement to all the world nailed to the mast that the ship was under arrest until the fine was paid. We were allowed, however, to go under the chute and load coals. This took only a few days, and we were then ready to sail for Bermuda except for the notice on the mainmast and the old bailiff. Meantime, on the 16th, the brig *Margaret* of Yarmouth, Nova Scotia, sailed loaded with coals for Bermuda. Our captain went away, nobody knew where, and did not return until the first of October. All the crew, except Stafford, a man named Morris and I, ran away before his return. We who were left enjoyed ourselves, especially the second mate, Mr. Gilbert. The bailiff had a very pretty daughter, who came on board to see her father and perhaps to see who else was there, and the second mate fell in love with her. During the captain's absence their romance was beautiful. On October 3rd the captain paid the money to release the ship and picked up a pretty poor crew in Newport. The old bailiff left, the paper was torn down from the mainmast, we sailed on the 4th and the second mate had to say farewell to his sweetheart. If he did not keep all his parting promises to her and she never saw him again, all the better for her.

With a river pilot in charge, we took steam and towed out to Penarth Roads where, the wind blowing strong to the westward, we anchored. In that operation we had a sample of the mate's temper. He was out on the forecastle head, holding a club hammer with which to loosen the cat-stopper, when a man shipped in Newport gave him a back answer. In a flash the mate threw the hammer with good aim at his head. The man dodged and the hammer struck the windlass bitt, denting the hard oak an inch deep. Sailors' thoughts do not linger over what might have happened, but the new hands, thus early in the voyage, got the idea that obedience and respect for the officers of the ship would be best. With that object lesson in discipline before them, it was deplorable that the captain should then demean himself before us all.

The weather being the same the next day, we remained at anchor and the captain ordered a man named Brown and me to row him aboard another ship lying in the Roads. Her captain got in our boat, we rowed them to Cardiff, and they went ashore, ordering us to wait for them. Brown and I spent the day agreeably enough and at midnight went in search of the two captains. We found them in a poor state for navigation, helped them down to the boat and put them aboard their respective ships. The night was dark and the strong west wind was still blowing. The captain turned all hands out, ordered the chain hove short and the topsails set, intending to get under way, when the mate came on deck and with gentle but firm persuasion put the captain to bed. We then paid out the chain, clewed up the sails, and all was quiet again.

On the morning of the 6th, the wind had hauled northwest. We got under way and reached down the channel on the starboard tack, took a pilot at 9 A.M., discharged him at 2 P.M., and at 6 P.M., Lundy Island bore west by south, distant eight miles. We were again at sea, where sailors can lead decent lives, uncontaminated by the wicked people who live on shore.

The voyage to Bermuda gave us the usual variety of fair weather and foul—rather more foul than fair—and the ship was kept under all the sail she would carry. On October 19th we saw the island of St. Mary's, one of the Azores, bearing northwest by north, distant fifteen miles. I quote the entry in my journal for the next day:

> Fri. 20th. Strong gales attended with rain from Southeast. Steering west. Gale increases. At 4 P.M. took in F., M. and Mizzen topgallant sails, two-reefed the topsails and furled the crossjack course, two hands at the wheel. At 6 P.M. the wind shifted suddenly to west by south which took the ship aback. Boxed her off and braced the yards, larboard tacks on board. A heavy sea and heavy showers of rain. The wind moderates gradually.

A few days later we were subjected to a violent tempest.

Loud roars the dismal thunder,
The rain in deluge pours,
The clouds are rent asunder
By lightning's vivid powers.

Entrance to West Bute Dock, Cardiff, Wales, in 1849

A heavy squall cleared up the weather and we set all sail, heading by the wind southwest by west, starboard tacks on board. Then the wind hauled more to the eastward, we took a pull at the weather braces and set studding sails, the ship's course west. The breeze freshened to a strong gale and the old ship "walked the water like a thing of life."

> *See with what swan-like grace she seems to glide*
> *O'er the bright bosom of the silvery tide*
> *Unfurled in proud array her snow-white sails*
> *To woo the influence of the favoring gales.*

Alas! In the days to which I have survived there is nothing upon the ocean to which such words can apply. The glory has departed. But even at the height of the sailing era, the poetry that was at the heart of sea life, which gave to the rudest sailor a depth of nature not generally found on land, was frequently obscured by the happenings on board incident to wind and weather and the strain on the ship's tackle and the tempers of the officers and men.

October 26th commenced with gentle breezes from east southeast, after several days of strong gales that had carried away half of our studding sail booms. One of them—the main-topgallant—had come unlashed and fallen, going through the mainsail and overboard. Because of these losses we could carry studding sails only on one side. The bad weather had wearied us with reefing, taking in and resetting sails day and night, and the watch below were taking their deserved rest. Before going to breakfast, the morning watch had shifted the studding sails from one side to the other, where they would do the most good. Shortly after the forenoon watch came on deck, the captain called all hands to shift the studding sails back again. The watch which had just gone below refused to turn out, saying it was unnecessary and they needed sleep. Immediately the captain's bucko spirit leaped up and a knock-down argument was imminent. The mate, however, intervened, not exactly on the side of the men, but he would not help to punish those who had done their best under difficulties, when they were pushed needlessly beyond limits. By a few words—"Now men, we have done well in bad weather, don't let's spoil a fine day," and then sharpening his tone, "Come, turn to and obey the captain's orders"—he led all hands out of trouble. They were ready to defy the captain, whom they detested, but the studding sails were shifted according to his whim, because of their wholesome respect for the mate. We were kept busy all day, some rattling down the shrouds and others painting ship until 6 P.M., when the wind hauled to the southeast with squalls of rain, which was very bad for the paint—a heavenly retribution on the captain's unreasonableness in "making" work for tired men.

As the voyage progressed, the ship developed a serious leak, making increasing quantities of water and keeping all hands at the pumps for hours at a time—the most irksome work that a sailor is ever required to do. It is only in an emergency, as when the pumps get out of order and the carpenter must repair them before the ship is waterlogged, that Jack pumps with a will.

On Saturday, November 4th, we saw the first flying fish; one flew on board for the captain's dinner. At this time of year "flying fish weather" frequently changes to a heavy gale. Through the forenoon the wind was hauling gradually from southwest. By noon it had hauled around to east northeast, and we set the studding sails, course west. At 2 P.M. the wind shifted north northeast in a squall and all hands were called to shorten sail. We had taken in the mizzen royal, topgallant sail and crossjack course, the main royal and topgallant sail and the fore royal when the fore-topgallant sheet parted and unrove out of the topsail yard. As the clew swung forward, the frazzled end of the sheet flew out and caught around the fore royal stay. We lowered the topgallant sail down but, with the sheet caught, we were unable to haul up the weather clew, which was slatting away out of reach, ready to split any moment. I went up to the royal masthead and got out on the stay. It shook so from the surging of the sail that I was afraid to go down.

Mr. Fields was watching me. Seeing me start down the stay, he yelled, "Come back, Dan, don't go down there—Down on deck with you, I say." I thought, however, I would tell him why I did not do as he said when I got on deck again—if I ever did. I pulled out my sheath knife, got my legs around the stay and slid down. The stay was shaking so that though my teeth were well rooted I had to clench them to keep them in my mouth. The mate kept hailing, "Hold on, boy, hold on." I sawed away with the sheath knife on the rope until it was cut through, and then slid down the stay to the jibboom. When I came in on deck the mate shook me by the shoulders and said, "What a man you are, Dan, I never expected to see you come down alive. Why didn't you come down when I told you to?" "Well," I said, "I was afraid you'd send somebody else up there, and if he did what I didn't dare do, I'd be forever ashamed of myself." The ship being made all snug aloft, we spent two hours at the pumps, and then damned the rest of the dog watch, the strong gales from north northeast and a heavy sea from north northwest.

Bermuda Dockyard in 1857

On Tuesday, November 14th, at 7 A.M., we saw the island of Bermuda bearing west northwest, distant fifteen miles. At 1 P.M., the ship was within four miles of the land, the Mount Hill lighthouse bearing west. We tacked ship to the east southeast, and at 4 P.M. a pilot boarded us, the lighthouse bearing northwest, distant six miles. At 3 P.M. of the 15th we came to anchor in four fathoms of water, half a mile west of the Dockyard. The voyage from Newport had taken forty-two days, not counting the eleven days after we were ready for sea, that we lay in Newport waiting for the captain to turn up. Here we found the brig *Margaret* of Yarmouth, Nova Scotia, which had left Newport while we were loading. She had arrived a day or two before us, having taken sixty-four days to make the passage. Neither the *Alceste* nor the *Margaret* was setting a record for quick voyages.

The captain went ashore and brought off six letters for the crew—none for me. Of course I did not expect any, for no one at home knew where I was. But worse than that, the mate of the *Margaret* came aboard, and when I made certain inquiries he told me that the young lady in Little River in whom I was interested had given me up and was soon to be married to a young Yarmouth sea captain. Well, she was a beautiful girl, much sought after, and I had been away for three and a half years. I had written to her, but such postal systems as then existed were so haphazard that she had not heard from me. So what else could be expected? I could only think of her with kindness and wish her happiness. It was no pleasure to see the men reading letters from their friends and I tried to shake off my feelings by gazing around the harbor.

There was much to admire, especially the dockyard with its solid stone dock. The three convict hulks that floated there, however, crowded with prisoners, made me think I had nothing to complain about. One of those prisoners was the famous John Mitchell, Irish Nationalist and editor of the *Nation*. The rising of his party in 1848 was unsuccessful, he had published some articles which the Crown authorities considered too patriotic, and he was now serving a long sentence for sedition. Escape from the dockyard hulk was thought to be possible and for greater security he was soon secretly removed to Norfolk Island, off the coast of Australia. He was an eminently popular hero among the Irish in America, who after several years learned where he was imprisoned. They fitted out a schooner which sailed to Norfolk Island, rescued John Mitchell and brought him to New York. There, as author and journalist, he spent the rest of his life, devoted to the cause of Irish independence. While we lay in Bermuda we frequently saw him taking his daily exercise, strongly guarded, on the deck of his prison.

It was no less than providential that the Saint John men, who had made Captain Cann pay through the nose to get rid of them, left us in Newport. If they had been on the *Alceste* in Bermuda, and seen John Mitchell walking up and down the deck of his prison hulk, they would certainly have been fired to storm the dockyard unaided in an attempt to rescue him. In later years I became acquainted in New York with one of the participants in the Norfolk Island expedition, Thomas Brennan, the sort of man who would be picked for such an adventure. Mitchell himself wrote a lively account of his whole prison experience, entitled *Jail Journal*, but his scholarly style could not vie with Brennan's spunyarn narration of the escape from Norfolk Island.

For several days we were busy unbending sails and stowing them in the sail room. We sent down the main-topgallant yard to refit the rigging and bands, and sent it up again. We also filled in time scrubbing paint and repairing sails. Periodically we pumped by the hour. On the 17th, the West Indies mail steamer *Forth* arrived on her way to St. Thomas. We hauled alongside of her on the 18th and worked for four hours (until 8 P.M.) coaling her and then swung off to our anchor. On Sunday morning, the 19th, we were called at six o'clock to pump ship and then to haul alongside the *Forth* and complete coaling her. We all refused to work on the coal on Sunday, when on well-regulated ships only necessary work was required. The captain offered us two dollars if we would do so. But our sailor devotion to the day of rest could not be purchased. We hauled off from the steamer and spent the day washing and holy-stoning decks, loosing and furling sails and sundry other jobs which the captain's charitable nature invented for us. The brig *Margaret* discharged coal all day. Her captain, like ours, was a professed church member, but when a dollar was to be made both conveniently forgot their profession of the purpose of the Sabbath. By five o'clock Monday morning we were alongside the steamer *Teviot* (which had arrived in the night) and worked for twelve and a half hours coaling her, then to the pumps and supper, "and so to bed," which shows that if it was not righteousness, neither was it laziness that had caused us to decline both work and wages on Sunday.

A near view of the Dock did not make it more attractive. We lay in it for three weeks discharging coals. To merchant sailors it was like a prison, nothing but soldiers and convicts to be seen. We were not allowed to speak to them nor they to us. On December 1st, HMS *Wellesley*, Admiral Cochran, arrived and moored off the Dockyard, and HMS *Scourge* hauled into the camels and moored with her jibboom over our taffrail. On the 2nd the *Margaret* hauled out of the camels and anchored in the stream, ready to sail for Yarmouth, Nova Scotia. I sent two letters home by her mate, but not one to the fair lady who had preferred not to await my return, lest it disturb her peace of mind. On December 4th the West Indian mail steamship *Great Western* arrived. We hauled alongside and discharged coals into her all day and the next. Our shipmate Brown had a fiddle, and the two evenings that we were alongside the *Great Western* the whole crew of the *Alceste* was invited on board to dance with the passengers. Between dances one or another of the talented passengers would sing.

We withdrew at 9 P.M., all but Brown, who remained to play for the passengers in the saloon, where they danced until two o'clock in the morning. On December 7th, the *Great Western* sailed for England, having on board a great quantity of cochineal and two million pounds sterling in dollars.

Discharging coal is work that leaves its mark on a man by the end of the day, no matter how white he was in the morning, and bathing facilities in the forecastle did not exist. We did the best we could with buckets of salt water, which was only partly satisfactory. It was a great delight on Sundays when no "work up" jobs were thought out for us, to take the ship's boat, with Stafford for company, outside the harbor and dive for sea fans, shells and coral. In my youth we were taught that going in swimming on Sunday was wicked, but in spite of early training I think it would benefit anybody who has been shovelling and hoisting coal for a week to take a swimming lesson on Sunday.

We finished discharging cargo on December 12th, and the Scotch brig *Alice Haviland* took our berth. We hauled over to the ballast wharf, where first we washed the ship and then started ballasting. For this work we divided into two gangs. Each gang had a cart which would hold a ton, each cart had a tongue, each tongue a crossbar on the end of it, and each Jack tar was transformed from a sailor to a Jack donkey, hauling ballast rocks and stowing them on board. Comparatively, the convicts had a soft job. When Sunday came we were a weary crew, and Stafford and I were glad to be let take the boat and, after a short swim, sail over to the town of Hamilton, which lies across the Great Sound and up a little harbor hemmed in with islands, about five miles from the Dockyard. The winter resort business in Bermuda was then quite undeveloped, and no passenger ship being in port at the time, we were almost the only strangers in town. It was a neat, clean, substantial little town, its British air softened by the semi-tropical climate, but it was a dull place in which to linger. We ended our stroll by buying some fruit and spent the rest of the day sailing among the really beautiful islands, returning to the ship at dark.

On Wednesday, the 20th, the brig *Micmac* of Liverpool, Nova Scotia, Captain Sponagle, arrived from Antigua loaded with cement for the Dockyard. On the 23rd, with the help of two men from the *Micmac*, we got all the sails bent and furled. On Sunday morning, the 24th, in a strong northwest gale, with a hawser out astern, we cast off our moorings, set the topsails, let go the hawser, hoisted the jib and sailed out, anchored in four fathoms of water about a mile from the shore and a hundred yards from the flagship, intending to sail the next day. In the afternoon two convict passengers came on board to go to the United States. America was "the home

S.S. *Great Western*

of the free" and a fine place for convicts out of jail, whose entry and subsequent careers were the concern of nobody. It was certainly also "the land of the brave," for its people were not yet afraid of the consequences of wholesale unregulated dumping of hordes of humanity upon their shores. That the country has stood up in spite of the indiscriminate immigration which has existed so long is a certificate to the vitality of its democratic institutions.

Such reflections, if I had had them, would have lightened the gloom of Christmas Eve, but I was too miserable to think of anything but present misery—alone and far from home, which I had been trying to reach for the past year but with no prospect of soon being there. The word-of-mouth news that had reached me was not pleasant. My only comfort was in the thought of my aged parents' love, and I shut out other memories. No use to hang up my stocking. So in a verminous, evil-smelling forecastle, with a last "God bless father and mother," I slept.

— CHAPTER XXIII —

A CARGO OF COTTON

December 25th, 1848 to June 27th, 1849

*B*ANG! BANG! BANG! BEAT A BELAYING PIN ON THE FORE-castle door, and the mate's piping voice at daylight wel-comed in the Christmas morn—"Turn out, men, and wash decks." "Damn your decks! this is Christmas, we want to go to church," groaned one of the men, not loud enough for the mate to hear, and the feet of all hands (if you know what I mean) landed on the floor, ready to celebrate the day in ship fashion. The decks washed, we got tackles on the yards and hove the boats in, then loosed the topsails, to the tune of the mate for some of us—"Bear a hand, there!"—"Look at that fellow going up the rigging like a sick bear!"—"Hurry up, or I'll light you up with a rope lantern!" At 10:30 A.M. all hands manned the windlass, we got under way and beat down to the point by Fort Catherine. There the ship mis-stayed and ran aground. We put out a kedge and warped her off, came to anchor and let her lay for the night. A merry, merry Christmas, with few thoughts and fewer prayers on land "for those in peril on the sea" or in foreign ports.

After kedging off on Christmas Day, we cut the hawser and buoyed the kedge. The next day when we looked for the kedge the current had swept the buoy under water. We searched for two hours and then went ashore by the Fort, got some holystones and took them on board, picking up the kedge on our way. In the afternoon a gale was blowing from northeast, so we let go the starboard anchor and lay where we were until Thursday, the 28th. The wind had then hauled to the southwest, which was favorable. At 1 P.M. we two-reefed the topsails, weighed anchor and proceeded to sea, bound for Savannah. The pilot left at 4 P.M. Baffling squalls and heavy rain prevailed throughout the night. We tacked ship four times. She was very lightly ballasted and on a lee shore—not a very comfortable situation, considering the reefs which lie all about those islands.

The voyage to Savannah took eleven days of stormy weather. I quote my journal entry for New Years Day:

Monday, Jan 1st, 1849. First part strong gales attended with rain. Course west by south, wind east. Set fore and main-topmast studding sails. At 8 A.M. parted studding sail halyards and fore topgallant sheet, also the slings of the main yard. All hands at work taking in sail and repairing slings. At noon had the yard refitted and furled main course. Ends with strong gales and rainy weather. All hands to supper wet and cold after working all day.

Pure ill nature was all that any of us felt at the end of that holiday. Two days later we were somewhat placated by a dinner of roast pig. Three years' experience of the cooperative methods of a whale ship had perhaps made me too critical of the hard fare and hard routine of merchant ships. Work caused by the frequent emergencies of a voyage, however perilous, and a well-regulated routine, are matters of course; but experienced sailors are quick to observe any departure from seamanlike methods and to judge their officers accordingly. Criticism of the captain of the *Alceste* was almost a daily theme in her forecastle, for although an ordinarily good navigator, he was frequently unreasonable and erratic in his orders. I have mentioned his whimsical shifting of the studding sails to no purpose. In a variable wind he would tack ship to take the benefit of a slight change, and by the time steerage way was gained, the wind would veer, so that no advantage was obtained. Again, we had to holystone the decks frequently, especially on Sunday, and on this run to Savannah he ordered the decks to be varnished. To holystone and then varnish would be proper enough, but he directed that both operations proceed together. Now, the process of holystoning creates a chowder or thick soup of sand, wood pulp and water on the deck, which the rolling or pitching of the ship spreads about until it is dowsed and squeezed out through the scuppers. Imagine then, the unavoidable mess made by holystoning and varnishing, both at the same time, and the opinion held forward of a captain who would give such orders.

On January 4th we took a cast of the lead and struck soundings, 30 fathoms and sandy bottom. We hove the lead every half hour through the night, with soundings varying from 25 to 30 fathoms. On the 6th, at 11 P.M., we saw Tybee Lighthouse bearing west northwest, distant twelve miles. At nine o'clock Sunday morning, the 7th, a Savannah pilot came aboard and at 11 A.M. we came to anchor between the Light and Fort. Next morning we sailed up to an anchorage abreast of Four Mile Point. Here we were beset by boarding house runners offering to take us ashore and ship us in other ships at forty dollars a month. Their disinterested efforts, however, met with no reward. The captain went ashore, and our two convict passengers left us to commence their apprenticeship as American citizens. I wonder if either of them became perhaps a policeman or an alderman.

On the 10th we were ready for sea and started to sail down the river, but with the ebb tide, the strong breeze and the narrow channel, we ran aground on the bank. When the tide flowed we kedged off and proceeded down the river to Five Fathom Hole, where we anchored at 11 P.M. Next morning in a strong gale we beat down the river under topsails and courses, and anchored abreast the Fort. The captain and pilot had a sharp row because we had not got out of the river. At 5 P.M. we headed the topsail yards, ready for morning; but on the 12th, the gale continuing ahead, we did not get under way. We improved the time by going ashore for oysters, which the cook served up to us at our expense—a relief from salt beef and bread washed down with "coffee" made from parched peas. It is small wonder that an old sailor's digestion should remain good, for he never eats enough to hurt him.

On Saturday, the 13th, north at 6 A.M. with a fine breeze from north by east, we hove the anchor short, set the topsails and waited for the tide to turn. At 9 A.M. we weighed anchor and proceeded to sea, bound for Apalachicola;

Opposite:
Florida and the Bahamas

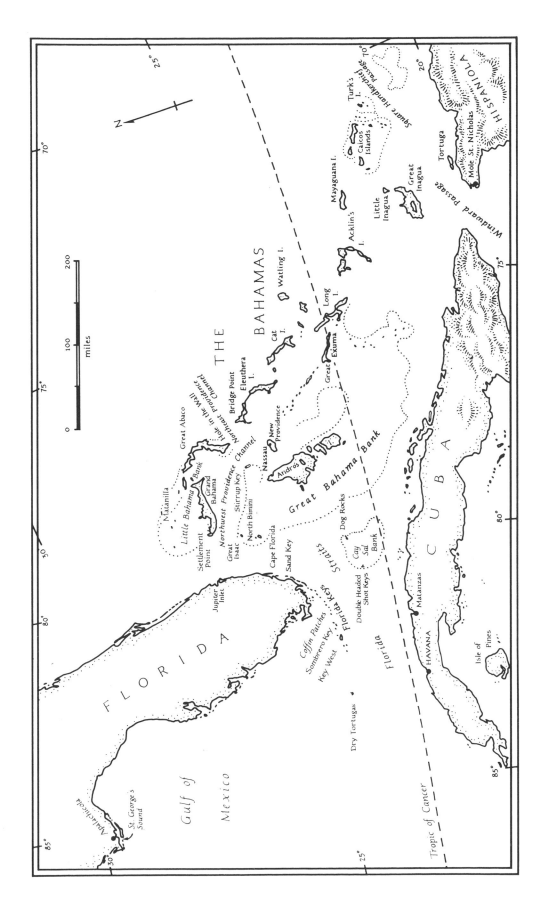

at 1 P.M. we crossed the bar and backed the mizzen topsails to put off the pilot. The captain refused to pay him, so he called the boat and two other pilots came aboard to arbitrate. They settled it among them and left the ship, and we braced forward the yards and stood our course, southeast by south. While we were getting the anchor on the rail and stowing chains below, one of the men thought he was wiser than the mate and offered a suggestion, contrary to orders. For answer the mate threatened to smash his brains out and, remembering the dent in the windlass bitt, the man wisely hastened to do as he was told.

Mr. Fields was indeed a hard old ticket, but he was also a very accomplished seaman and a gentleman, considerate of those in a crew who tried to do their best. I spent many spare minutes on the voyage grafting a cover on the captain's spyglass, and while I was doing so Mr. Fields would often come and talk with me.

It was as good as a play to see and hear the old man tell his stories. Tall and straight he was, raw boned and with long arms, white hair and the kind of blue eyes that you see in old sailors, glowing with his young memories. Compelling our admiration, who would not leap to obey his commands, or, if wrong-headed enough to rebel, who would dare to disobey? He won my lasting affection and esteem and in his long life he must have made a host of friends. Only a scoundrel could be his enemy, and he was that to all scoundrels.

Apalachicola, as everyone knows, is a port on that stretch of the Gulf of Mexico coastline which extends westerly from the peninsula of Florida. To get there from an American Atlantic port, in these days, perhaps the usual course is to sail down the coast, through the Straits of Florida and around into the Gulf. The Straits of Florida, which lie between the Florida coast and the Bahamas, are nowhere more than sixty miles wide. Through them runs the Gulf Stream at the rate of two to four and a half miles an hour, its axis being much nearer the Florida shore than to the Keys and Banks on the Bahama side of the Straits. Even to this day, the western side of the Little Bahama Banks, from Matanilla down to Settlement Point on the western end of Grand Bahama, has no navigational aids, and the current near the Bank sets strongly toward it.

Ships taking this route, therefore, will generally keep near the Florida coast as far south as Jupiter Inlet, and then keep away southeasterly until they make the Biminis. From that point, along the edge of the Great Bahama Bank until it trends too far easterly to be regarded, are scattered Keys from eight to fourteen feet high, sufficient to serve as landmarks and departure points. From North Bimini steering southwesterly past the Dog Rocks and Double Headed Shot Keys, a ship will be out of the strength of the stream current and can then, if bound for Havana, shape a course for that port, or, if bound into the Gulf, haul across the Stream and pick up the land anywhere from Key West to Tortugas.

In 1849, however, and for many years afterwards, the comparatively few lighthouses along this inside route caused it to be almost completely shunned by sailing masters. The favorite route for ships bound to the Gulf, and the one taken by the *Alceste*, was to cross the Gulf Stream to its eastern limits, then sail south and to the east of Great Abaco, into the Northeast

Abaco Light

Providence Channel and through the Hole in the Wall, a passage about twenty-five miles wide between Eleuthera and Abaco, into the Northwest Providence Channel, and up that Channel west by north, approximately 160 miles, around Great Isaac, a hill of coral sand forty feet high, into the Straits of Florida. The ship will then be a few miles north of Bimini, and from that point the courses will be the same as described above for the inside route.

For five days out of Savannah we made a southeasterly course with moderate southwesterly winds, carrying all the sails we could muster. At 5 P.M. of January 18th, with the wind north northeast, the course was changed to southwest by south to take us into the Northeast Providence Channel. We carried fore and main-topmast studding sails on the starboard side until 3 A.M. of the 19th. Then the wind hauled to east northeast and we shifted the studding sails over to the port side and set topgallant studding sails. At 7 A.M. we passed the brig *Undine* from Charleston, U.S., bound for Matanzas, Cuba. While passing her, the fore-topmast studding sail halliard parted. We hauled down the sail, rove a new halliard and set it again. By 4 P.M. a strong gale was blowing and we still carried studding sails, when all hands were called to shorten sail. Every man jumped to it with a will. Anxious glances had shot back and forth between officers and crew that afternoon of rising gusts and white-capped combers. When at times the ship yawed wildly under the over-press of topgallant studding sails carried in a strong gale, some of us wondered if the demijohn of "corn licker" which went to the captain's quarters just before sailing from Savannah had lost its cork. Knowing winks were all that anyone risked in reply. But if the imp was out of the bottle, it was responsible for the over-strain of sail, spars and rigging which had been punishing the ship, and only,

> *The sweet little cherub that sits up aloft*
> *To watch o'er the life of poor Jack*

kept us from adorning a beach of the Bahamas with a pile of splintered Nova Scotia spruce plank and spars. A sea captain in port can with great dignity "take the sun" through the bottom of a glass tumbler, but at sea, foreward or aft, rum and salt water are a treacherous mixture.

We took in the light sails, two-reefed the topsails and hauled close to the wind on the port tack. I ventured to ask the mate the reason for this manoeuvre. He merely said the captain did not like to run for the Hole in the Wall at night. At 9 P.M. we laid the main-topsail to the mast and lay hove to until daylight. To anchor was impossible because of the great depth of water in the Channel, everywhere more than 1700 fathoms. There was no lighthouse in those days to mark either side of the entrance to the Hole in the Wall. At six o'clock in the morning of the 20th the wind was still strong east northeast, and all hands were called to make sail. The man who was loosing the main-topgallant sail cried out, "Land O, on the starboard beam!" We were then seven miles northeast by north of Bridge Point, the north end of Eleuthera.

It may be said by those competent to express an opinion that a shipmaster who runs for an unmarked entrance to a difficult channel, with a strong following gale, until nightfall is close upon him, and then takes the precaution of heaving to to await daybreak, and in the morning finds his ship right where he would have placed her if he could have picked her up in his hands and set her down again, is either a star navigator or (in plain sailor language) has had "the devil's own luck!" Yet I state but the facts, "which the same I would rise to maintain." What the mate's opinion was of such reckless carrying of sail, he imparted to no one, unless possibly to the captain himself long before we hauled by the wind. His advice, if offered, was obviously disregarded, and I know he spent a most anxious night. That at daylight we found ourselves marvelously safe would not mend his shattered confidence in the captain, and from that day a strained relation was increasingly noticeable between them. As for the crew, matters of navigation were out of our sphere and we had little conception at the time of the peril which had passed us by. Even if we had known, sailors (as I may have said before) never waste thought upon what might have been.

As soon as sail was set, the course was given west by north, which with the breeze still strong from east northeast would take us up the Northwest Providence Channel. The more of that water we covered before dark the better. We set the studding sails to starboard and at 10 A.M. sent the royals. By 1 P.M. Stirrup Key bore southwest, distant eight miles. At 10 P.M. we were around Great Isaac and in the Straits of Florida. We had made the run in sixteen hours, an average speed of at least ten knots. Keeping on down the Straits, we passed the Double Headed Shot Key Light at 11 P.M. on Monday, the 22nd, and no further vagaries of navigation occurred on the voyage. Every day, however, the leak which has been referred to increased. On the 22nd, the pump did not suck after five hours of continuous pumping. Day and night we pumped for two hours in every watch. Hateful as swinging away at the pump brakes was, it was more wearisome in the watch below to hear the sound of pumping; it got on our nerves. Yet a worse annoyance was the noise made by the cook in grinding the peas for our breakfast coffee. Sailors are notorious growlers about their food, no matter how good it is. If the salt beef is lean, they scoff at it as "mahogany"; if there is any fat, they will trim it and throw the fat overboard. But if a captain wants his crew to run away at the next port, thus forfeiting their wages, he has only to humbug them on their tea and coffee. Whether that was the captain's intention or not, some of us thought so. Our tea was "water bewitched," and at breakfast the cook would jokingly sing out, "Come get your coffee, Jack, for the peas are boiled." The discontent bred by such trifles would have been driven away if a storm had compelled us to risk our lives on deck or aloft; but it was fine weather with a fair wind until we reached port.

On January 25th we got up thirty fathoms of chain, lifted the anchors off the rails and into the shoes, and at 2 A.M. of the 25th we hove to until daylight. A cast of the lead gave twenty-three fathoms. At 6 A.M. the leadsman in the chains saw the land ahead. At 8 A.M. we hauled by the wind, and at ten o'clock the pilot boarded us. As he was doing so I was sent to heave the lead, and the line caught around my head and took my cap overboard, in I do not remember what depth of water. At 11 A.M. we anchored in St. George's Sound, about fifteen miles from Apalachicola. The captain took the launch with a man to bring her back, and went to town. When the launch returned, it and the other boats were hoisted up to the after part of the mainmast, so the crew could not run away in the night. Apalachicola at this period was an important outlet for the rich crops of the "deep South," an ambitious rival of Mobile and New Orleans. Ships were arriving and clearing every day while we were there, most of the cargoes going to England. The Civil War, the coming of steam, railroads and other causes, perhaps chiefly the shoal water of St. George's Sound—which necessitated long slow miles of lightering from town to anchorage—in a few years lost to this thriving port its large export trade, and now it is seldom heard of in the outside world.

At noon on Saturday, the 27th, I went in the boat to town for the captain. He told me he had a freight of cotton for the ship, at five-eighths of a penny per pound, for Liverpool, Great Britain. Without attempting any accurate calculation, it can be estimated that to fill a 700-ton ship with cotton, the weight of the cotton would be about one-third of the gross tonnage, or 233 tons; and at five-eighths of a penny, the freight would amount to about £1,370, or upwards of $6,500. It looked to be a fairly profitable enterprise for the owners after all ordinary expenses were paid. At least the deduction for sailors' wages and maintenance would be ridiculously small; yet "who would not sell a farm and go to sea?"

This cargo would come down from town on lighters. The interval of several days before its arrival gave an opportunity to do some work necessary for the rest and comfort of the men in the forecastle—the massacre of as many as possible of that well known little pest called by the learned *Cimex lectularius*—but popularly known by another name which I need not advertise on this page. This red raid finished, and no freight yet alongside, I was glad to be one of the three seamen whom the captain and second mate took in the jollyboat oystering. I was sorry the mate was not of the party, but he and the captain were now on terms of the most formal civility, and very little of that. With a grappling we raked up out of the shallow water a straptub full of oysters (which were a most welcome delicacy served to all hands at supper); then we went ashore to bathe and for a walk among the oaks and pines.

On Tuesday, January 30th, the first lighterload of cotton, 170 bales, came alongside and the work of discharging ballast and loading cotton commenced. In those days the steam-compressed bales that are now familiar were unknown. The cotton was pressed on the plantations with hand screws into bales considerably larger but not more than two-thirds the weight of those of the present day. To stow as many as possible into a ship, they were pressed into place with the aid of screws operated by the different loading gangs. The work was somewhat similar to stowing wool in the Colonies, only the cotton was packed in much more tightly. The ballast was gradually discharged as the ground tier was laid. When that was completed, the hard work of jamming, squeezing, crowding and mashing the bales into every

Cimex lectularius is the scientific name of the common bedbug.

Apalachicola, Florida, in 1837

corner went on until the hold and between-decks were packed as hard as four men in each gang could screw them. The mate and second mate each had charge of a gang. A stevedore from town bossed the third and had general charge of the loading.

If the back pressure of the cotton were as great as that exerted against it in stowing, no ship's frame could stand it; she would simply split open. But though there was some strain on the ship, the leak which had been so vexatious had diminished since we were at anchor, and an hour's pumping night and morning kept her free. The rest of the day, from six o'clock to six, we stowed cotton, accompanying the work with the worst din that the singing of all hands could make. Each gang had its own music, often singing a different song with different words and tune: *Oh, Heave Around Cheerily; Come Roll Me Over; Blow, Why Don't You Blow, Ah Ho; Jimmy King and Julie Handy, Gal a Dandy; Tom Has Gone Away*; and other classics. Listening at the hatchways when the three gangs were driving home their sets, the sound was like that of an old-fashioned prayer meeting with saints and singers all singing, or like a schoolroom full of boys when the master is out. You could not understand a word of it, but it put life into everyone and facilitated teamwork.

It took us nearly six weeks to load. The hold and between-decks being crammed full, thirty bales of cotton were stowed in a house which the carpenter had built on deck for the purpose, and still, of our 1,333 bales there were fifty-five left, which had to be carried on deck and tended to make the ship very cranky. Meantime the same howling hubbub was going on in numerous other ships at anchor near us. The sound from them, softened by the distance, was more pleasing than our own raucous voices at close range. Of the other ships I remember only two, the *Commodore* of Saint John, New Brunswick, and the *Saksusa* of Wiscasset, Maine.

Involved in the routine of work during this period, several things happened that meant much at the time. The second mate was rather slow-minded. His second thoughts led him to do things when too late, which should have been done sooner or not at all. In his gang was a sailor named Harry, a West of England man shipped at Newport, who was a great bully and constantly insolent to the second mate. A dozen times, a word or an act of authority at the right moment would have saved the situation, but the second mate always let the chance slip. One morning when our noisy work was in full swing, some action of Harry's, which no one in the other gangs saw, exasperated the second mate beyond endurance. Instead, however, of resenting it at once, he let it pass until it seemed to be a closed incident. Then, while Harry with the others was bawling his loudest, *Blow, Why Don't You Blow?*, the second mate stepped up behind him and struck him under the ear. Harry went sprawling, the song stopped, and at its sudden cessation all hands from the two other gangs swarmed around, wondering what had happened. By the time a word of explanation had circulated Harry got up, rubbing the side of his head, and meekly went back to his place in the gang. Work was at once resumed at full volume of voice and muscle, but in everyone's mind was the thought that a blow had been cowardly struck and as cowardly yielded to. If the boats had not been hauled up to the mast that night, I think the whole crew would have run away before morning, the general discontent was so aggravated by this event which was equally disgraceful to both participants.

On February 17th, at the end of a hard day's work, a sudden violent gale sprang up and all hands were called to let go the port anchor. It was very dark; the large globe lantern held by the mate could not be seen through the rain, and the lightning was blinding. As the anchor dropped it caught in the bobstay, and I climbed down on it to clear it. A flash of lightning played around the anchor, sending out sparks as from an anvil. It blinded me at once, which did not matter much in the dense darkness. Rubbing my eyes with iron-rusty hands did them no good. We got the anchor cleared, paid out forty fathoms of chain, and all was snug for the night, but I could not see for an hour afterwards. Then I could not endure the light of the forecastle lamp and had to tie a handkerchief over my eyes. My head was giddy all night, and the next morning the racket of voices in the hold had no help from me, the least exposure to light was so painful. The mate came to inquire, "Dan, what can I do for you?" and answered himself by bringing some brandy and bathing my eyes with it, neat. One application proved that the remedy was worse than what was the matter, my head felt as if it was in a straw bonfire. Good old mate, like the kind father whipping his son, it hurt him as much as it did me. A long day of sitting around blind-folded helped most, and I went to work the following day; but for a week or more daylight or lamplight was intensely painful.

A few days before we finished loading, while we were heaving at our screws on a heavy set, singing *Tom has Gone Away*, the heel of the samson post gave way and struck Tom Morris on the leg. This disabled him for further work at stowing cotton. The following day the mate fell down the hold with a crowbar in his hand. The distance was not great, and he fetched up on a pile of cotton, so the accident would not have been serious but for the crowbar with gave his shin a painful wound, and he was unable to stand for several days. Morris was in the stevedore's gang, to which I also belonged. Due to the mate's accident, his gang was without a leader, and the stevedore put me in charge of it, thus leaving his own gang with only two men, Strafford and Brown. They worked on deck, while the second mate and I finished off the hold. The captain stayed up in town, and the work went on much better without him.

On Saturday, March 3rd, the decks were full of cotton and there was no room below to put it. It would have to be carried on deck somehow, but that was a problem for the following week. We hoisted a bucket in the rigging, a signal for the water boat, which came and supplied us with water. We filled the four water-butts alongside the forward house and renewed their lashings. A few tierces we stowed in the "eyes" of the ship above the chain lockers. Everywhere else in the hold, cotton was king. Nevertheless, water was vital, and we stowed two hogsheads in the main hatchway. Then we caulked, tarpaulined and battened the hatches. On Sunday the mate made his first appearance on deck since his accident. Grin-and-bear-it had been his only remedy, but he was much better. I spent the day with Stafford and the 'prentice boy Charlie Cook, of Yarmouth, sailing about the bay and cruising in the woods along the shore. We had a gun, but did not fire it. Any game that may have been around must have seen us first. We visited the spot where the carpenter had cut down trees for studding sail booms; we would be carrying studding sails on both sides whenever possible going home. They were rafted alongside the following day and also four new spars from town. When they were hoisted aboard, we stowed cotton between them and lashed it down. A few remaining bales were stowed in the long boat. The daily washing down decks would now be confined to the poop and topgallant forecastle, everywhere else being covered with cotton. It was a very heavy deckload, and we were leaking badly again—not a nice prospect for a spring crossing of the North Atlantic.

On Friday the 9th, we put a new heel lashing on the jibboom and got the ship ready for sea. At 3 P.M. the captain came on board and hoisted a flag for a pilot, but none came. It was a Friday, of course, but if a captain wanted to sail on that day of the week, I never heard that a pilot would hesitate to take him to sea. Be that as it may, next morning the pilot was aboard by eight o'clock, we hove up the anchor and made sail in exactly twenty-five minutes. Everything went with a will and a song, for this would be the last passage to complete the voyage. At 9 A.M. we were over the bar, the pilot left us and we set fore- and main-topgallant and topgallant studding sails. The wind was west and very moderate, course south southeast. As the ship had a slight list to port, we shifted the port chain amidships to trim her—which gives some idea of how cranky we were, owing to the deckload.

For nine days we held our southerly course with fine weather and light airs or calms. At 1 P.M. of Sunday, March 18th, with the hot sun shining, the weather calm and clear, all hands were sitting about the deck when our attention was attracted to a bright star overhead. It caused a stir among us, for it was a strange phenomenon, enough to rouse the superstitions that always lurk in sailors' minds. By nightfall it was of course below the horizon, and we could not compare its brilliance with other stars, but it must have been brighter than any known star or such things would be of daily occurrence. We had nothing else to do but talk about it, and many odd theories were advanced and discussed, which could not all have been correct. But astronomers themselves, though they have recorded similar apparitions from time to time for centuries, do not agree upon the why or wherefore, so our ignorance was as respectable as theirs. A light easterly breeze wafted us down to the westward of Tortuga Bank, heading south, and in the afternoon of the 19th we were in the Gulf Stream current, wind east southeast, ship heading northeast.

Warm nights gave every encouragement to sleep on deck, or on the deckload, the cotton bales being more comfortable than the alternative, a "donkey's breakfast" stuffed into a bunk in the forecastle. But a stronger urge was the red army of insect foes to whom, so long as we could run, we would never surrender. I never saw such a prolific breed, before or since, in my long experience with such cattle. Reduce their numbers by organized executions to the lowest possible terms, and in a few days their population was reaching toward the limit of the food supply. The children of one day were the grandfathers of the next. We vacated the forecastle in their favor, to wait until cool weather in the North Atlantic should compel them to lie dormant and enable their victims to do the same. Every two hours we were obliged to pump to keep the water from the cotton. Between times we were busy setting up the rigging and putting on chafing gear. One whole day, except for the time at the pumps, we spent seizing on scotchmen to the rigging. This sounds like an act of concerted violence against a race that would be likely to resent such treatment; but there was no resistance. A scotchman (with a small s) is merely a pad of old canvas and ropeyarn tied to a stay or other rope to prevent chafing, the name being a delicate allusion to the reputed indebtedness of the Scotch to the Duke of Argyle.

Thursday morning, March 22nd, was fine, the wind southeast by south, course northeast by east, all hands employed shifting the braces end for end, so that the wear on them would come in new places. The land was in sight; we were somewhere between Key West and Cape Florida. On a little island we noticed a schooner ashore with a signal hoisted in her rigging. One look assured us that she was a Nova Scotian; we would not pass her by. We hove to, put out a boat, and the mate with four men, including myself, rowed in alongside of her. She proved to be from Yarmouth, Nova Scotia, bound home from Matanzas, loaded with molasses. The mate introduced me to her captain as a Nova Scotian. When he heard my name he blushed and showed embarrassment. The vessel had gone ashore in the night and worked so far in that they were unable to heave or haul her afloat. They had recognized us as a Nova Scotia ship and wanted to be reported. They intended to discharge cargo on the beach—a few hogsheads would be enough—until she floated, then resume their load and proceed. With twenty-four hours of fine weather they could do it. Before we returned to the ship the schooner's captain called me aside and bashfully confessed that he had married the young lady to whom I have several times referred, and he asked my forgiveness! Of course, he was unaware that I had heard the news in Bermuda, and I think it was fortunate I had. If it had come as a bolt from the blue it might have covered me with as much confusion as he suffered himself. I mustered all the gallantry of manner that I could and offered him my congratulations.

Diversion for my thoughts on returning to the ship was furnished when an unusually large shoal of porpoises and dolphins came around the ship. I took the captain's grains, went out to the martingale, and in five darts caught five of them. These two sea mammals are much alike, the name dolphin being properly applied to the bottle-nose variety, but both are very generally called porpoises. Both yield a certain amount of oil, the rendering of which kept the cook, with his limited facilities, busy for two days. The flesh of the dolphin is the more palatable, quite like fresh young pork, and we all enjoyed dolphin steaks for supper. That evening about nine o'clock, we passed two ships with their lights hoisted to the mizzen peaks. Whether it was to help them keep in company through the night, or some signal to the shore, I have no idea.

The 23rd commenced with light airs from southeast by east, the land bearing northwest by west, the ship by the wind, starboard tacks aboard, getting nearer and nearer in with the land. At 3 A.M. all hands were called to tack ship, but she would not come about and, wind and current being onshore, she drifted in to the reef. She did not strike heavily, but with every roll kedged farther and farther in. We clewed up the sails, hoisted out a boat and ran out a kedge with 120 fathoms of line, hove her off afloat, let go the starboard anchor and ran out another length of line. Then we hove up,

kedged out again and anchored in thirteen fathoms of water to wait for a steering breeze. At daylight it was still calm and by six o'clock there were nine boats alongside, ten men in each, asking if we wanted assistance. They were wreckers from Key West. The schooners to which they belonged were anchored at various distances with their sails up, like so many gooneys waiting in the slick to leeward of a whaleship.

A light breeze sprang up in the afternoon and we got under way, heading northeast, but it was so moderate and the breeze right on shore that we only ranged along the reef. The water began to shoal and we tried to tack ship, but again she mis-stayed. We braced around the foreyard and squared the after-yards, but she would not luff on the other tack and kept going in on the reef. We let go the anchor, paid out thirty fathoms of chain and brought her up in five fathoms of water. We furled the sails to wait for a breeze off the land, tried the pumps and found the leak had increased. That night there was heavy thunder and lightning but no wind or sea. I think we must have been in the neighborhood of Sombrero Key or the Coffin Patches; but there were then no lights or buoys in that vicinity to distinguish one key or shoal from another. The wreckers came on board several times in the evening and kept hovering around; the captain had a good night's sleep, but the mate kept watch all night. There was plenty to keep him awake. Constant work at the pumps was necessary for we were making two feet of water per hour, and ninety men were around us in boats, anxious to turn our condition to their profit. The wreckers' calling was an honest one, but full of temptations which we were not certain they were able to resist.

The early morning of the 24th was calm and cloudy with heavy thunder and lightning. At nine o'clock there was a light breeze from northeast by east. We were underway by 9:30, all sail set, bound for Key West. Whatever might be thought as to responsibility for our running ashore, no one could question the captain's judgment that it was imprudent to proceed on his voyage with such a leaky ship. The skipper of one of the wreckers came aboard, and our captain engaged him to go down to Key West ahead of us and report our coming. We had a strong breeze by 3 P.M. At 3:30 the ship struck heavily three times on a shoal but did not stop. We tried the pumps but found no increase in the leak. In the latter part of the day there were heavy squalls, thunder and lightning. At 8 P.M. we took in light sails, reefed the topsails and ran down under short sail. At midnight we backed the mainyard and let her lay till daylight.

Sunday, March 25th brought squally weather, thick and rainy. At 5 A.M. we made sail and stood in for the land. At 6 we saw a small schooner standing for us and we hauled aback. It was the wrecker we had sent down to Key West. Her skipper came on board with a Mr. Brown, who was the French and Spanish Consul at Key West. The wrecker recommended Mr. Brown to our captain as his agent, and I think the introduction was a fortunate one for the ship's interests, for not all the acquaintances of Key West wreckers were as honorable and capable as Mr. Brown. At 7 A.M. a Key West pilot came aboard and took us into port, and at 2 P.M. we anchored in five fathoms of water about half a cable's length from one of the wharves. The captain and Mr. Brown went ashore, and with the mate's permission, Stafford, Morris and I took a walk about town.

Key West in 1849 was a clean little town with a very West Indian appearance. The houses had cupolas on top of them as lookouts for wrecks. There were many fine little shops kept by Spaniards, Frenchmen and a few Yankees. Wrecking, however, was the chief support and absorbing occupation, engaging some forty schooners. Whenever a wreck was reported

Key West, Florida, about 1835

everybody went wrecking. It was even said, and perhaps some believed it, that the bedtime prayer of the little children, instead of "Now I lay me," was "God bless papa and mamma and send us a wreck before morning." But I have heard the same story about the children on the South Side of Cape Sable Island, Nova Scotia. The inhabitants of every locality where wrecks are frequent are credited with making capital of the dangers to navigation with which Nature has endowed their coasts. The establishment of numerous lighthouses, lightships and buoys along the whole North American coast has greatly reduced such perils. Letting bygones be bygones, therefore, no reason now exists, from Key West to Cape Race, why parents may not teach their children to pray for the family welfare without invoking disaster upon us poor miserable sailors.

At high water, which came at midnight, we ran a hawser ashore and hauled the ship in until she grounded forty feet from the wharf. The captain came early with several men, and a survey was held. The inspectors recommended that the cargo be discharged and the ship hove down and caulked. They went ashore and the captain with them. We discharged the deckload, got all the spars off the deck and towed them ashore. While we were heaving the ship up to the wharf the captain came aboard, drunk. He began to quarrel with the mate, who at first took the abuse with the patience due to a drunken man. The captain's outrageously foul and insulting language at last drew from the mate a scathing word-portrait of the captain, which we all recognized as fitting him to a T and we felt grateful to the mate for it. Our satisfaction, however, was cut short when we heard the mate say he would do no more duty. He went to his cabin and in a few minutes walked ashore. Later a drayman came and took away his belongings.

A gloom came over us all, for we held the mate in such high regard as well might be the pride of any ship's officer. Exacting and peremptory in his orders, he never failed to commend anyone for doing well, and he had won the loyalty of every man forward. His long tolerance and forbearance toward his weak-willed, overbearing superior, and his stepping into an emergency and handling it as if acting under orders, displayed a magnanimity which we had to admire, much as we felt (and undoubtedly he did too) that it was misplaced. We all wanted to desert on the spot. The reason we did not was that Key West is a rather small island; hiding on it for very long was impossible; if caught, we would be put in jail until the ship sailed, when we would be dumped aboard and compelled to complete the voyage. Men in other employments (except the army and navy) could break their contracts and walk out without penalty. We merchant sailors were considered so indispensable to commerce that, if we refused to perform our articles, punishments ranging from death to imprisonment and loss of wages actually earned could be heaped upon us, often without trial. We felt compelled, therefore, for the time being to dissemble our love for the captain and bide a better opportunity. Sulkily, we hauled the ship within twenty feet of the dock, built a stage and commenced discharging and storing the cotton.

The captain, second mate and four men—Stafford, Boyd, Williams and I—went to the British Consul's office to swear to a note of protest against the winds and waves which, as the document claimed, had caused disaster to the ship and cargo. Perhaps it did protest too much against the mild elements, but the men told their story accurately and substantially as given here. The damage was made a matter of general average and the loss would fall on the underwriters.

Getting the cargo out occupied a full week. Thirty men were hired from shore to assist in unloading and to caulk the top sides. Working in the hold, shirtless, dripping with sweat, I took every opportunity to come up for air. The strong breeze on deck gave me a sudden check and I caught a violent cold—chills, fever, faintness, headache and inside-outness of stomach. For four days I lay in my bunk, with no attention, food or medicine except some pepper tea, which the cook prescribed. On March 30th Mr. Fields came aboard to see me. He told me he was going home to Halifax. He had met the captain ashore and recommended me to him as second mate when a vacancy should occur by the expected promotion of the present incumbent to first mate. I realized his kindness but was too weak and light-headed to act as if I cared. Remembering the painful bath of brandy he had put on my eyes in Apalachicola, I did not—nor did I need—ask him to do anything for me now. Seeing the state I was in, he thought of the sailor's chief remedy, and at his request the steward brought me a dose of castor oil, the first and only medicine (except the pepper tea) that I had taken since leaving home. In the words of President Lincoln, "Those that like that sort of thing, that's the sort of thing they like," but if Mr. Fields had anointed my eyes with the oil when they were blinded by lightning and given me the brandy now, it would have been pleasanter and perhaps as beneficial. We shook hands in friendly farewell, and as he walked ashore I lamented that I could not follow him.

I never saw Mr. Fields again, but heard later that soon after reaching home he went to sea again as master of a Halifax schooner to the West Indies. He was then aging, and must have made his last landfall long ago. Many ships' officers have sailed in and out of my horizon. None combined such passionate energy with gentleness, ability and unselfishness as did this Bluenose sailor, John Fields.

> *Of long experience in the naval art,*
> *Blunt was his speech and naked was his heart;*
> *Alike to him each climate and each blast,*
> *The first in danger, in retreat the last.*

Life on board the *Alceste* was now a good deal disorganized. The captain was ashore making noble efforts to cure his droughty disposition—or indisposition; the mate was gone, and no one had any respect for the second mate's authority. The crew went ashore and returned, or failed to return, drunk or sober, when they pleased. Nor did it matter much. Mr. Brown was practically in control, discharging and storing cargo, selling enough to pay wages and expenses, and in general acting for the interests of all concerned. The captain's infrequent appearances were more disturbing than his absence. He came to see me the day after the mate's call, but I was in no condition, and certainly neither was he, to talk business. The smell of bad liquor had no more than faded from the forecastle after he left than there was trouble on deck. He tried to take charge of the gang of laborers who were unloading ballast, and soon had them so enraged that they all knocked off and went ashore. Their foreman found Mr. Brown, who tactfully invited the captain to a conference in a quiet room up the street over a better than ordinary brand of refreshment. It was so good that we saw no more of the captain for ten days.

On Sunday, April 1st, I was much better, though still weak and without appetite for the ships's rations. Key West has an excellent fish market. I toddled up there and bought half a dozen fresh fish. The steward gave me some pork and potatoes and resigned from the galley in my favor. He flattered me, however, by watching while I made a chowder such as I had been taught to make for the gallant companions of those two gallant craft, the *Favorite* and the *Two Sons*, when first I went to sea. The steward served it to all on board—four of us forward and the second mate aft. It was the first meal I had eaten in four days and the best for many more months, for it made me think of the old shores and the old home and the old familiar faces. The next day I felt well enough to join those of the crew who were not off on a spree, heaving out the ballast preparatory to careening the ship, as recommended by the inspectors. This was the fourth time we had handled that ballast, over and over again. It was hard work and half a day of it was all I could then stand. At noon I cleaned up, put on my shore togs and went ashore. Soon three more of the men followed my example, leaving the hired laborers to discharge the ballast without our practised assistance. We played billiards and rolled tenpins until dark, had tea together, and then two of our number went in search of more perilous adventures. Stafford and I went aboard at seven o'clock. Hearing distant thunder, we put out more fasts to the wharf, to keep the ship (with so much ballast out) from capsizing if a squall should come up.

Without leadership, we were like the Children of Israel before they had a king, "Every man did that which was right in his own eyes," coming, going as we pleased. Seldom were more than four of us on board at a time. When one did turn up after a spree ashore he would be of little use for a day or two, half crazy from the cheap but potent liquor for which the Key West bars were famous. With such unsteady help we unshackled the boat davits, unbent and made up the sails and stowed them in a store-room belonging to Mr. Brown, lashed the blocks and rove the falls for heaving down the ship, and took the second mate's belongings and all our chests and clothes up to a house at the head of the wharf hired for us by Mr. Brown, where we were to live while the ship was being repaired.

The first night we were in our new quarters, two of our men, Harry and Dick, who had been ashore on French leave for two weeks, came in. Every well-found sailor has a wooden chest in which he keeps his possessions. Others carry their kit in a bag, If a man is a "Geordie"—a North British sailor—his poverty is respected because expected. To express personal independence there is an old forecastle saying, "Every man on his own chest and a Geordie on his bag." But for other than Geordies, a bag marks a man as inferior. These two were the only ones who had come aboard at Newport with bags instead of chests. They liked not the rest of us, and we returned their dislike. Now, stone-broke and shabby after their long carousal, they had forfeited wages and clothing in the *Alceste* and had shipped on a wrecker which was sailing for the reefs in the morning. No one of us would prevent them from taking their clothes away, and we wished them good luck civilly enough as they walked up the street with their bags.

On April 6th about thirty men came, clapped on to the capstan and hove the ship keel out. Then the caulkers, eight of them, commenced to caulk the bottom, while our three boys scraped the pitch and painted her with marine paint. Caulkers' wages were three and four dollars a day. That was excellent pay for those days, higher than in Northern shipyards. Two wrecks had been brought in since we came. There was plenty of work the year round. If I turned over in my mind the idea of joining the craft, I dismissed it. There was not a chance of obtaining my discharge and I had no intention of running away from my wages. The expectation of promotion did not bother me—I would leave ship as soon as the voyage ended, unless she chartered for home. Home was were I longed to go, and staying by the ship was the likeliest way of reaching home. All other ambition was at bay.

I took three men, Stafford, Morris and Boyd, and went to work in the store loft mending sails. One of the crew had to stand watch at night aboard the ship, usually Stafford or I, because with all the others, the bar room being always open, the question would be, Who would watch the watch? Until the side of the ship that was first hove out was caulked, she had to be pumped twice a day. To do this, a spare pump was let down the main hatch into the bilge with the upper end leaning over the coaming.

Sunday, April 8th, was a beautiful day, clear and cool with a fresh Northwest breeze. By 5:30 all hands were bathing, shaving and changing to clean clothes to keep the day of rest. There is great truth in the old saying that "cleanliness is next to godliness,"—it is often salvation. As the ex-slave Fred Douglas said, "Black a man's boots and he will keep out of mud." And it was a Boston lady of high degree who said, "There is a satisfaction in being well dressed which the world cannot give or take away." To obtain as much benefit as possible away from temptation, therefore, the second mate and I, dressed in our Sunday best, went fishing. We rigged up the ship's boat, took some hooks and lines, and had a pleasant sail among the reefs and islands, catching groupers enough to give all hands a "fish fry" for supper. The grouper is an important local article of food, red and in appearance half way between a sea bass and a codfish. In the evening I went to the Episcopal Church. The beauty of the liturgy was agreeable, and the sermon was calculated to do anybody good. The first lesson was the fourth chapter of Hosea, and the text was its seventeenth verse, "Ephraim is joined to idols: let him alone." I paid close attention, for the subject was what any sailor needed to hear, and when I got home I repeated nearly every word of it to the second mate. I even remember the gist of it to this day, but there is an old locution, "Shoemaker, stick to your last," and it is an equally good rule, "Sailor, stick to your course."

Something sent the captain down aboard the next day, like the man from the tombs, clothed and in his right mind. The old jest might well have been entered in the log, "Captain sober all day." He had an interview with the second mate, and afterward with me. He told me the second mate was now mate, that I could consider myself second mate from this time, and that we would agree on the wages before we sailed. I did not like this half-way method of settling matters, but as I was going in the ship anyway I assented.

After explaining this new status to the crew, the captain went ashore again, off on another week's battle with his great Enemy. All the foremast hands had been on their spree and got over it; but perhaps their comparative sobriety was because their money was spent, while the captain was able to charge up his extraordinary expenses to general average.

All the men, except Harry and Dick, who had deserted to go wrecking, were back at work, and things were going better. The mate took from three of the men who had been mending sails, leaving Morris, the best man with palm and needle, on board. All the others were set to scraping pitch off the bends and painting the hull and masts. On April 16th we righted the ship and then hove her keel-out on the other side, to make a finish of the caulking. This would be a short job as only the bilge strakes on the side just hove out remained to be done. But we had no more than belayed the heaving-down falls when our false keel dropped off. We towed it ashore and examined it. It had been badly split and splintered by the ship's running ashore and striking several times afterward while sailing down to Key West. That had wrenched it loose from the through-and-through bolts which reached through keelson, main and false keel, headed up though they were over iron washers at each end. The damage necessitated making and bolting in place a new false keel, involving unexpected and very unwelcome delay.

The best way to endure delay, and most other annoyances, is to keep busy and seek recreation. Working at the sails in the loft occupied the time of half of us, the other half being on leave on alternate days. Dancing to Brown's fiddle enlivened the evenings and attracted spectators from other ships. The mate and I went sailing and fishing Sunday mornings, and in the evening attended church. At the Methodist Church the girls kept looking at us, instead of paying attention to the sermon as they ought. Perhaps some of them winked at us, but of course we took no notice! We went once to a Negro church. The singing was wildly emotional. The sermon and prayers were seriously meant and brought forth much humming and many loud Amens. One petition, that when this hard and suffering life was over the Lord would send down a big alligator to take us all up to Heaven together, was met with approving shouts of "Hurry Lord!" and like excited outcries from men and women whose very souls they did not dare call their own. Though not in favor of going to Heaven in the way requested, I think I obtained as much spiritual elevation on that occasion as ever came my way in church. But I have been to church so few times that I have no right to make comparisons.

The last few Sundays we were at Key West, three or four of our men went to church as steady as deacons. Having had their run of rum and other shore evils, they were ready to behave on land as well as they were obliged to do at sea. All healthy men are full of human spirit. Kept corked up too long, they effervesce when released. The misfortune of sailors is that when they expand ashore the land-sharks get them. Once out of the hands of such scavengers, then their fine qualities appear in all the strength developed by the hard discipline of the sea.

A Boston brig loaded with molasses was towed in, a wreck, and moored at the wharf alongside of us. Her cargo was discharged in order to put some new planks in her bilge. When a cask was landed on the wharf it was immediately surrounded by a crowd of boys and girls, baling and licking and carrying off the molasses in pails, pans and even bottles. The children were the progeny of a peculiar people from Nassau, Bahama, called "Conchs," who lived in a section of the town called after them "Conchtown." Whether white blood or black predominated among them it would be hard to tell; they had no prejudices against one or the other. They had all the instincts of born wreckers and were as persistent around a molasses cask as a swarm of flies. When completely daubed with molasses from head to foot they would jump overboard, dart around in the water like so many polliwogs, and then resume their depredations, with none to let or make them afraid.

With the repairs completed, the ship righted and moored, the work of reballasting commenced. That old familiar ballast, we recognized each lump of it as we handled it again for the fifth time! The sight of it must have made our lads homesick, for three of our best men deserted and sailed to the reefs on a wrecker. Harry and Dick had joined that free and easy fraternity without causing any regrets, but those who now remained so missed these others that they were sorry they had not gone also. Four more wrecks had just occurred, and their sails, rigging and cargoes were sold here, to the great enrichment of the wreckers. This raised visions of easy money and added to the discontent. Even common laborers earned $2.50 a day, four times as much as able seamen's wages.

We were now living aboard the ship again. The prodigal captain had returned, perhaps because no more cargo need be sold after the repairs were finished, thus cutting off his extra supply. The cotton remaining in store had to be stowed again in the old noisy way. Any gang of laborers could hoist cargo out of a ship, but so few cargoes were ever re-loaded that stevedores were unknown in Key West. The 'longshore workers knew nothing about trimming a ship to the right relative draft forward and aft. The captain, therefore, on Monday, April 23rd, agreed to pay me an increase of five dollars a month as second mate and, in addition, a dollar a day while loading and a bonus after arrival in Liverpool, if I would take charge of stowing the cotton. I consented and a few days later signed the articles. I might as well say that the old rascal (I am sorry the word carries more than a Pickwickian sense) never paid either the per diem or the bonus. The agreement was merely by word of mouth, made independently of my duties as second mate, and therefore not entered in the articles. There was no witness, the captain's word to a stranger was as good as mine, and keeping it depended on how much respect he had for it. Any seamen can have peremptory justice in all civilized ports for breach of any agreements within the articles; but it would be idle to sue the captain on this outside agreement.

I went immediately to work with two gangs, four men in each, reloading the cotton. Soon the mate, who had plenty else to do, came professing to be the stevedore and that I was his foreman. Well, the dignity of being boss stevedore was not much, but it was a responsibility which I would not resign until relieved by superior authority. We had no trouble about it. I was a little firmer than he had ever noticed before, and soon demands upon his time kept him busy with other work. The captain hired four men from shore to take the place of the five who had run away. These went to work on the cargo, and the mate took four sailors from the loading gang and set them to bending sails. When Sunday came we went to church together like close friends. The captain, for once, had a good excuse for not going to church One of the 'prentice boys had run away and got on board a wrecker. To leave him to his fate would be the ruin of a fine youngster. The captain hired a pilot boat and went after him, took him back and put him in jail. A good day's work, for, rescued from his foolish adventure, the boy made the voyage with us and, warned by the captain's horrible example, developed in a few years into a successful Bluenose shipmaster.

We finished loading on May 10th, put on the hatches and caulked them down, and at high water hauled the ship into the stream. Here we lay for five days getting ready for sea. The boss carpenter, Mr. Brown, who had superintended our repairs, engaged passage for himself and wife to go to Liverpool with us. Among the things which they were taking to their new home, they sent on board ten sea turtles, two dozen fowls, an eagle, an alligator and a three-legged dog. Of the cotton held out for sale to pay ship's expenses, eleven bales were not sold. These we towed alongside and stowed in the fore hold. That increased the ship's draft forward, and after getting to sea we had to stow the chains in the after hatch to bring her in sailing trim.

On the 14th the captain shipped a full complement of men, a fine looking lot of sailors. They had been cast away on Sand Key in a ship from New York bound for New Orleans. One of them I had met in Sydney, New South Wales, when he was sailing master of a whaleship. He had come home and was off again sailing deep water, while I had been wandering from one foreign land to another and must go through many thousand miles more of stormy seas before raising my native shores. The thought drove me to my little cabin where I wrote the cheerfullest letter I could contrive to my dear parents. Due to the imperfect postal service of that day, it never reached them. If it had, they would have thought I was the happiest sailor afloat. The new men were all in good spirits, glad to be out of the trap into which the wreck of their ship had cast them. The old hands, however, appeared more discontented than ever. Two of them, my old London chums, Stafford and Morris, I talked into good humor. It would be a shame if the disgust for everything connected with the *Alceste* which had been growing on them should lead them to desert just as we were about to sail for home.

The repairs to the ship had not made the forecastle any more attractive, and all the crew slept in hammocks under an awning forward. On the morning of May 14th at six o'clock, the order was passed to masthead the topsail yards and get under way. When the men mustered aft we found that two—Brown and Boyd—had run away during the night. They had gone into the unoccupied forecastle, taken their own clothes, ransacked the chests of the others, choosing what they liked, stolen a compass, chronometer and sextant from a schooner lying near us, hoisted sail on a sloop which they had found unwatched, and gone to sea. They were already out of sight. Whatever became of them, who knows? They could not go wrecking, for Key West wreckers, though capable of looting castaway ships, would not tolerate thieves who stole from themselves. Havana was the nearest port they could make, and the few friends they had among us could only hope they went there and found a vacant berth. Excepting the captain, we did not think of them as escaped criminals, but we would miss Boyd's gloomy grumbling and the lively tones of Brown's fiddle. The captain went ashore to pick up a couple of men to take their places. He returned at nine o'clock with one man and our two passengers. We weighed anchor immediately and proceeded to sea under full sail, the wind light and baffling.

We made the run to Liverpool in forty-four days. The first day out a violent squall with thunder and lightning split the flying jib, and we had to take in the light sails and two-reef the topsails. For a week the wind was swinging all round the compass, the shifts coming with heavy squalls, and our progress up the Florida Straits was cautious and slow. The mate soon showed his unfortunate capacity for doing the wrong thing. The cabin boy, William, was bringing a potful of hot tea from the galley to the cabin when the light breeze from east southeast died out and suddenly changed to southwest by south in a squall. Everything slacked up and then set taut with a bang, which carried away a studding sail boom. The boy gave a startled look aloft, tripped over something and went sprawling. While all hands were aloft clewing up topgallant sails, the mate exercised his new authority by giving the poor chap a ropes-ending for spilling tea on deck.

One of our early duties was to fit up some spare water-casks for sea turtle pens and fill them with water. The turtles and the rest of the little menagerie were cared for by Mr. and Mrs. Brown, and they all arrived safely in England. Out of the Straits with more room to port and to starboard, we made good time for several days. On May 27th, course northeast, with a strong breeze veering from southeast to south by west and back again, we made ten knots for twelve hours, during which time we carried away the main royal back stay and had to take in the royal. By June 4th we were on the Banks of Newfoundland, wind northeast, course east. For several days we experienced the usual fog which those who live there have to endure, during which a man was kept stationed to ring the ship's bell every three minutes, and two men were forward on lookout for fishermen and ships bound east.

On the 6th the footrope of the main-topsail (a sail which the captain had bought at auction in Key West) parted and the sail split from foot to head. We unbent it and set a new topsail. Later we made the old one into studding sails. At 8 A.M. we saw three ships and a brig ahead of us bound east. At 1 P.M. we passed several schooners and a French brig at anchor fishing. We lowered a boat and sent her aboard one of the schooners to buy some fresh fish. At 8 P.M. we spoke our old friend, the brig *Margaret* of Yarmouth, Nova Scotia, Captain Hilton, from St. Andrews, New Brunswick, for Liverpool. She had left Newport a few days after we arrived there, bound for Bermuda. We fell in with her again in Bermuda, and I sent home two letters by her. Now we had caught her in mid-ocean on her passage to Liverpool.

On the following day we saw a great number of French barques and brigs, and Yankee and Provincial schooners, fishing. None of these craft had any flag flying, and if it be asked how we knew the French from other nationalities, the first answer is that only Frenchmen go fishing in square riggers. But sailors can usually distinguish ships of different nationalities by little pecularities of spars and rigging or design of hull. At 3 P.M. we hauled aback the main yard and tried for fish, with all the lines out that we had. At the first sound I caught the biggest codfish I ever saw—just the ordinary luck of the poorest fisherman.

A modern whaleman would have been cheered, after we got underway

again, by the sight of a large school of sulphur-bottom whales, which we sailed through. But in those days that species, the largest and richest in oil and baleen of all the whales, went unmolested by man. As is sometimes said of the inhabitants of a certain beautiful American city who have the undeserved reputation of being slow, "They like snails but they can't catch them." So the huge sulphur-bottom, protected by his speed and wariness, entirely escaped the "wood and blackskin" methods of that period and was preserved to be a victim of the long-range artillery devices of the present day steam whalers. That night we saw a great number of vessels' lights—all fishermen at anchor.

Clear of the Banks and well to the northward, for several days we took a series of westerly gales, which required active work aloft. So, a hundred years earlier, Falconer described our situation. The mate and I alternated at night with eight hours on deck and four below, except that one midnight, as the moon rose, riding higher and higher, racing through heavy clouds, all hands were called to reef the courses. Only the master, asleep, knew nothing about it. With an able crew, he was satisfied to leave the handling of the ship at night to his officers, confident that they would call him when circumstances required that he take over responsibility. And on the whole, the ship sailed better with the captain asleep. Throughout one twenty-four hours she averaged ten and a half knots, and the next, nine knots. Then the wind moderated to a full breeze.

On Saturday, June 23rd, we made five degrees difference of longitude in twenty-four hours, averaging ten and a half knots. The following day, by an observation at 4 P.M., we were twenty miles south of Cape Clear and sixty miles to the westward. On the 25th at 6 A.M. we made Cape Clear bearing east by south, distant fifteen miles. At noon we were abreast the Old Head of

Kinsale, and at 6 P.M. Cork Lighthouse bore north northwest, distant ten miles. At eight o'clock the island of Ballycotton bore north, and the daylight was still strong when we saw the Highlands of Dungarvan raising their blue heads above the clouds. Waterford Hook Light bore north, distant ten miles, at five the next morning; at noon we passed the Tusker and steered away from Holyhead with a strong breeze from west by north.

Being a Nova Scotia ship it was yet too early for a pilot. At midnight we saw Holyhead Light bearing east by south, distant fifteen miles. At 3 A.M. saw the Skerries, and at 8 A.M. a Liverpool pilot boarded us. We rigged in the jibboom and got the anchors off the rail and at noon came to anchor off Brunswick Dock, where the captain went ashore. The hands were employed getting up fenders and hawsers.

— CHAPTER XXIV —

SAILOR HOME FROM THE SEA

June 28th to October 12th, 1849

WE HAULED INTO BRUNSWICK DOCK ON JUNE 28TH, WHERE we were all paid off and the crew discharged. The only ones who remained by the ship were the mate, second mate (myself), the cook, and the three boys. The captain persuaded me not to take my discharge by holding out hopes of a charter to Halifax or Boston, which would be within a few days of home. He then went ashore, to be gone much longer than we thought he would be. I bade Stafford and Morris goodby with genuine regret, for we had been congenial shipmates and real friends for the past year. But that is the way with sailors. The truest maxim of their lives is, "The best of friends must part," and friendships are severed as swiftly as the wake of a ship is obliterated in a following sea.

In the afternoon, by order of the consignees, we hauled out of Brunswick Dock and into Albert Dock, and the next day discharge of the cargo commenced. For that work the Dock Company furnished everything—the blocks, falls and men—and we who belonged to the ship had nothing to do with it but look on if we wanted to. Our job was to unbend and stow away the sails, send down yards, overhaul lifts, footropes and brace-blocks, and send them up again, and generally to get the ship as spick-and-span as possible and keep her so. We boarded and lodged ashore, the mate and I being allowed a pound a week for that purpose. All hands had to be out of the dock gates at 5 P.M., not to enter again until six o'clock next morning. The Albert was an import dock, one of the largest in Liverpool at that time, named for Prince Albert, the husband of Queen Victoria. My readers will recall that I was in Liverpool in June, 1844, in the old brig *Thomas Edwards*, Captain John Kendrick, at the time Prince Albert laid the first stone in its construction, and that I did not know what all the celebrating was for until it was over.

In addition to overseeing the house-cleaning, the mate and I alternated in taking account of the cargo as it was hoisted out. While at this work, the foreman stevedore brought me a gun which he had found stowed away under the deck beams among the cotton. I gave him half a crown for it, which was a fair market price, under the circumstances. He could do nothing with it. The dock keepers would not allow him to take it ashore, so it was just as if he had found the ship's anchor. I never saw another gun like it. It was a double-barrelled, muzzle-loading rifle of Dutch make, and a remarkably straight shooter. Discussing with the mate how it came to be on board the *Alceste*, we concluded that the men who ran away the night before we sailed from Key West had probably bought it in a junk shop in that port—a catch-all for strange objects from the ships of all nations—and stowed it away where it was found, and that they were in some way prevented from taking it with them in their hasty flight.

That old matchlock from that time went with me on every voyage I made until I retired from the sea forty-two years later. I have hunted wild cows with it in the forests of Venezuela, and shot crocodiles with it in South American rivers. On one occasion it saved my life in a mutiny which, with the assistance only of the cook, I was fortunate enough to quell. That occurred one night during the American Civil War, on a ship anchored at Lower Quarantine, New York Harbor, after our arrival from Maracaibo. I did not shoot anybody, but when the fight was over I had to bandage the head of the ringleader. It was damaged in the match between us, he armed with a capstan-bar and I with the old rifle, used as a club because it was not loaded. The stock was badly splintered in the struggle, but I had it carefully repaired by a New York gunsmith. I still treasure it as a keepsake.

Nowadays people, including sailors, are better than they used to be; but in those long years ago sailors did not always obey all the Acts of Parliament, especially those against smuggling, and I have some regrets (feeble ones) that I was no exception in that respect. I am certain that I never took a false Custom House oath in my life, but I have already related how in Halifax I helped to carry gin ashore for the captain of the *Thomas Edwards*; and how I performed a similar volunteer service for the captain of the *Alceste*— during his absence—in taking Key West cigars ashore through the dock gates. This was not an easy thing to do, as everyone was searched at the gates to prevent that kind of enterprise. In spite, however, of all their precautions, I passed out with about two thousand cigars a day during the time that the cargo was being discharged. I shall not tell how, lest on the one hand it tempt others to try the same method, and on the other enable some bright inspector to catch them at it.

A week passed and the Fourth of July with it, which was celebrated by day with a great display of bunting on the American shipping, and in the evening with fireworks, which are the Yankee safety-valve for high pressure patriotism. We were too much worried over the captain's absence, however, to take any interest in our neighbor nation's holiday. This was the seventh day since we had seen him, and we could give no answer to the daily inquiries for him. For all we knew, a serious accident might have befallen him or, as we strongly suspected, he might be pursuing a kind of pleasure which his responsibilities should have led him to shun. Whatever the cause, it was an interference with my plans for going home. Our feelings were relieved on the 5th of July when at four o'clock a boy handed me a note from the captain, asking me to come and see him at a house in Bridge Street.

The place where I found him was decent but seedy, and the captain was a sight to behold—his face unshaven, scratched and scabby, one eye swollen shut and as black as somebody's big fist (or was it a door that he ran into?) could make it. His linen was filthy. The suit of clothes he had on when he went ashore was gone. He was now dressed in the shabbiest outer garments that the slums of Liverpool could boast. I asked him no questions, and he offered no explanations. He gave me a letter to deliver to the mate and asked me to send the steward to him in the morning. Two days later he came aboard, a very presentable shipmaster who had been ashore on business. Meantime we had finished unloading, hauled out of the Albert Dock and on to the Queen's Dock gridiron, where some caulking and graving was done. Then we hauled into King's Dock and moored close to the dock gates. The captain's visit to the ship was brief, only to gather up some papers, and then he left for London to attend a lawsuit, informing us that he would be back in about four weeks.

It seemed to be the fate of the *Alceste* to lie idle in dock half of her life, instead of sailing the seas. My only interest in her was the hope that she would get a freight to an Atlantic port in North America, and this delay was exasperating. No other chance came for some time or I would have jumped at it. But day after day wages went on, and the idea of leaving them behind for the benefit of the owners (one of whom was the esteemed captain) and paying my passage home was too repugnant to be entertained. The alternative was to wait and use the time as well as possible. We kept the boys from idleness, scrubbing the ship outside and in with soap and water, painting her inside, mending sails in the between-decks, hauling taut the ropes and squaring the yards by lifts and braces until she was the finest ship in port. At four o'clock we would knock off for tea, a leisurely English habit which our too great idleness prompted us to adopt.

The mate and I during this time succeeded in keeping amicable if not cordial relations. He seemed to realize, as everyone else did, that he was a poor excuse as a mate, and it made him morose and suspicious. It did not keep him, however, from sleeping half of every day, or walking importantly about in the afternoon inspecting the work that had been done. Since the cargo was out we had slept on board, our meals ashore costing fourteen shillings a week, leaving six shillings apiece out of our allowance of a pound a week. This surplus we paid to the night watchman hired by the ship, for over-time service, so that we were free not only to go to the theatre in the evening, but to spend the long daylight hours after supper seeing the sights and fashions. I enjoyed a number of afternoons at the hotel frequented by the officers of the Halifax mail steamship, playing billiards with them. On Sunday mornings the mate and I went regularly to a Presbyterian church. The accent of the old white-haired Scottish preacher reminded me of my childhood friend, Mr. John Wilson, and of the home I longed to see.

No frigate of any navy was ever in better trim than we kept the *Alceste* without and within. The day we finished scraping and varnishing the hold beams, when the mate woke up and inspected them, he had no criticism to make, although we received no praise.

So July and half of August slipped away, with not a word from the captain. One afternoon ashore I met Benjamin Banks, of Barrington, and went to the theatre with him. He had left his ship and was going to Halifax as passenger in a brig which was about to sail. After saying farewell and sending remembrances home by him, I was as restless as the fly of an ensign. It was too late to consider clearing out and paying my passage to Halifax, for by this time the tailor, the theatre and other amusements ashore had too greatly affected my purse and there could be no pay day until the captain returned.

August 13th was a rainy day. After dinner the mate went to sleep and the boys asked me if they might go ashore for the afternoon. Instead of waking the mate and referring their requests to him, I gave them permission. When he woke up he inquired for the boys and I told him I had let them go ashore. He flew into a petty rage and swore he would give them a licking when they came back. I thought his anger was more at me for exceeding my authority than against the boys, and had no unnecessary words with him. It continued to rain, the boys came back in good time and turned in.

The following day was fine and I set the boys at shifting the sails in the between-decks to air them and keep the rats out of them. The mate came down with a reef-earing and commenced to lay it about the boys' shoulders, shouting, "I'll teach you to go ashore without asking me!" I told him to stop it, that I was the one who had given them leave, and if he wanted to lick anyone to tackle me. Puffing out his stomach more than his chest, he turned to me and said, "I've a great mind to do so." Whatever his great mind was, I knew his small mind had so such intention, and in a moment he began to beat the boys again. Getting between him and them, I told him to stop or I would stop him, and I offered to take off my jacket and let him whip me in their stead. I meant what I said when I said it, but he appeared to have no confidence in my word. He would not trust me with my jacket off, for he went to his cabin, dressed and went ashore, where he stayed all day and night.

The mate returned in the morning, and the captain with him. Evidently they had met ashore and discussed the late unpleasantness, for the captain called the boys into the cabin. Then he invited me to a private interview and asked if I had given the boys leave to go ashore. I told him I had and that I would not let the mate beat them for doing so, and if he or the mate had any objections I would take my discharge as soon as he could give it to me. I hoped he would do so. One word of disapproval from him would have brought on an explosion that might have sent me to jail. Captain Cann sensed the heat lightning in the atmosphere and changed the subject. He proceeded to talk of many things, Nova Scotia shipping in particular, and the quills of the fretful porcupine in my bad disposition slowly subsided. The conversation turned to the subject of the next voyage. The captain said he had partly engaged a charter for Calcutta and that he would increase my wages if I would go with him. I told him if he went to any of the British North American provinces or to the United States, I would go, but not to Calcutta, and he could discharge me now if he wished. After a few more words I consented to wait and see, and returned to the work of the day.

Ten tedious days followed. There was little to do about the ship, the captain was not on board, and it suited the mate and me to keep out of each other's way. On Saturday, August 25th, the captain sent for me to come up to his hotel—quite a different place from the dingy den I had found him in almost two months before. He had chartered the ship for Calcutta, and offered me five pounds a month to go another voyage. I declined politely but firmly and asked for my discharge. We talked things over a few minutes, but seeing I was of the one mind, determined only upon going home, he said he would be aboard in the afternoon. When I got back to the ship the mate was looking very sulky. He started to give me orders. I told him I was not on duty but only waiting for the captain to come and give me my discharge. The mate asked me why I was leaving. I said, "One thing, I want to go home, and another thing, you and I would not agree on another voyage, and I think I know what is best." He tried to make some friendly advances, hoped I would forget the little clash we had had, but my mind was on other things and I kept what may have seemed a disagreeable silence. The situation was relieved by the arrival of the captain. I signed off the articles in his cabin. He paid me the few pounds, shillings and pence that were due and gave me the long desired discharge paper.

With a sense of deliverance I left the *Alceste*, realizing how much better off I was than the poor fellows who deserted in Key West, or than Mr. Fields as he walked ashore in that isolated port of broken ships. Alone, without boat or oars, four thousand miles from home, a glance at the forest of masts in port showed the slender spars of many American ships, with here and there the less graceful rigs of others which said as plainly as words could speak that the letters "N.S." were painted under the name of their port of hail. Among them there must be one that would take me home. I felt that home was near— and dear. Just a little thoughtful, but confident, I walked up to the hotel which I have mentioned as the resort of the officers of the Halifax mail boats. There at tea I met a Mr. Mackie, mate of the Halifax barque *Adelaide*. He told me they were loading for Halifax and would sail in a few days. They had all their officers but wanted a crew, and he said he would speak to the captain for me. Nothing could be done about it, however, until Monday morning.

My last Sunday in Liverpool was a dull one. The watched pot is slow to boil. But the long day and night ended, and on Monday morning I went on board the *Adelaide*, Samuel Jolly, master, and shipped before the mast for a round voyage to Halifax and back to Liverpool. I would not take the risk of asking to sign on only for Halifax, but when I gave my residence as Barrington, Nova Scotia, I think the captain knew as well as I did that I was bound home and no farther. One of my new shipmates was a Halifax man Tom Reed, who had come out mate of a barque—the same one that Ben Banks had left. Tom had never been in Liverpool before and I, as an old resident for nearly two months, thought it my duty to show my countryman around. Locking my small funds in my chest aboard the *Adelaide*, I obtained a half-month's advance note, which I cashed—one pound, ten shillings, or say $7.50. Reed did the same, and thus well heeled, we strolled through the city, saw some of the fashions, visited the Zoological Gardens, had tea and a game of billiards at our favorite hotel, and went to the theatre in the evening.

But pleasure seeking on a pound and a half apiece could not last long, and we were glad to be told that the *Adelaide* would haul out of the dock on the morning tide, Thursday, the 30th. We were on board early. We got the ship ready for sea and hauled her to the pier head, and at 10 A.M. took steam and towed outside of the Rock. It rained all day and we had the hardest drilling that I ever got in my life. At 8 P.M. we had everything to rights, set the watch and shifted our wet clothes. The only note I have in my journal of the voyage, aside from the routine work, is that at 9 P.M. of the day we sailed we passed the Halifax mail steamer for Liverpool under full sail, with studding sails set alow and aloft.

At that period steamships, to outward appearance, were little else but full-rigged sailing ships with paddle wheels and a smokestack. Now sails are as rare as paddle wheels on the ocean. I am convinced, however, that it would still be of advantage in bad weather for the finest merchant steamship afloat to be able to show some canvas, if only a few stout staysails, to ease the strain on the engines. In my own last years at sea in an American coasting steamer, after a stormy voyage during which we had carried away most of our few sails, I requisitioned new ones. The owners objected to the expense, arguing that the other ships of the line were not letting their sails blow away as I did. My answer was, "You compare my repair bills with the others, and if you don't think I rate a new set of sails, you can take even the masts away from me." The hint appeared to be sufficient, for the new sails were furnished, and bent; and until my last landtacks were boarded I never ran under bare poles as long as canvas would remain in the bolt ropes.

The voyage to Halifax was made in twenty-six days—a very good passage. On Tuesday, September 25th, 1849, at 3 A.M. we saw Sambro Light bearing northwest by west, distant fourteen miles. We took in the mainsail, backed the yards and got a sound. At 4 A.M. we took on board a Halifax pilot, and at ten o'clock anchored off Halifax town in eight fathoms of water, north of George's Island. Old Halifax never gave me the same thrill, before nor since. I wanted to go right ashore, but it was not until the following afternoon that we could haul into the wharf. We cleared up the decks in a hurry, and again and at last I stood upon the land that I was born in.

I went up to Mr. Sanders' boarding house, where I met Captain Bell, with whom I had sailed when he was mate of the *Reindeer*. He was about to sail for the West Indies and asked me to go with him as mate. I was pleased with the offer, but declined it because of my anxiety to go home. "Hello, Uncle Ben," said a voice behind me, and turning, I saw my nephew Hervey Doane (or "Harvey," as the lady he married several years later renamed him). He was five years younger than I, just turned twenty-one, and going ahead rapidly in his chosen career—following the sea. On my next voyage to sea we were shipmates, he as mate and I second mate with my brother Martin as master, in the Shelburne brig *Ambassador*. On my last voyage under the British flag, in the barque *Josephine* from Philadelphia to Buenos Aires, and

Sambro Light in 1873

thence to Mauritius with a load of mules, Hervey was master and I was mate. We were closer friends than brothers, and he had more of my admiration than any other man since my brother Nehemiah's death. He was very successful in his calling and, possessed of excellent business ability, had an important part in the development of the transportation business by sea and by land in his native province. Hervey and I sat up nearly all night. He had to do the answering while I asked questions about everybody and everything that had happened at home in the last four years—lots of which he did not know, as he had been away to sea himself most of that time.

At the first opportunity I went down aboard the *Adelaide* and asked the captain for my discharge without wages. I can see no reason why he refused, but he did. The ship would save the expense of paying what I had earned, it was easy to ship a whole crew in Halifax, and dropping me off the articles would not be detriment to anyone. He did not insist that I remain on board; he simply chose, knowing the circumstances, to retain the right to put me in jail if he wanted to, and if he could catch me, and compel me to go back to the ship to Liverpool as a foremast hand. Naturally, I was equally determined, as I had been when I signed articles on the *Adelaide*, to let nothing interfere with my going home. Politely as my temper would permit, I bade Captain Jolly good morning. It was also good-bye, as he well knew.

Walking along the waterfront, I met Captain Jesse Smith of Barrington and his partner, Mr. John A. Knowles, with whom I had gone coasting ten years previously in the schooner *Two Sons*. We greeted each other cordially. He had just arrived from Barrington in a little schooner, which was lying at Tobin's Wharf, loading for home. Captain Jesse exclaimed, "Why, Ben, the last time I saw you was that Election Day when Dick Hitchens and I tried to take you back to the Town House for spiking the cannon." "Yes, Captain," I said, "and now I'm running away again, but this time I want you to help, instead of trying to catch me." I told him the present situation, and he entered heartily into the plan.

Late that evening Hervey and I took a boat and went aboard the *Adelaide*. The second mate was on watch, but whatever he may have thought or known, he acted as though he believed I had been discharged and made no attempt to stop us from lowering my chest into the boat and following it ourselves over the side. We rowed aboard of Captain Jesse, who was waiting for us, and as he stowed the chest away in his own little cabin, "There," he said, "there'll have to be a fight before anyone but you takes that chest out of here." I could have hugged him for his friendly, risky co-operation. All I had to do now was keep out of sight, if possible, until Captain Jesse was ready to sail. But I was pretty sure that Captain Jolly was really conniving at my escape, though he would not consent to it, and I was certain of it a few days later when, as Hervey and I were returning from a walk, we met the captain head and head in the street. He passed us without a wink of recognition. He must have known by that time that I had taken all my belongings out of the ship, and yet he was sensible enough not to care. I therefore had no more anxiety on that score.

But a more fateful, though unforeseen, experience was pending than had ever yet befallen me, which made risk of arrest and imprisonment, by comparison, trifling matters.

There were two branches of the Doane family in Barrington, which on Cape Cod six generations previously had a common origin. One branch lived at the Head of Barrington Harbor, the other at Barrington Passage. For distinction, they were spoken of as "the Doanes at the Head" and my own family, "the Doanes at the Passage." Captain Hervey Doane (of the "Head" branch), who for some years had been a so-called "pilot" of a Cunard mail steamer, was at this time keeping a Sailor's Home in Halifax. He sent me an invitation to call, and I did so, dressed in my best shore togs. His daughter Cordelia ushered me in. She was a beautiful young woman, soon to be the bride of Captain Gilbert Shaw, who had succeeded his prospective father-in-law as a pilot of the Cunard Line. Miss Cordelia spoke to a younger lady, whom she called Maria, and introduced me to her cousin, Miss Knowles. She identified this young person as the daughter of Mr. John A. Knowles of Barrington. Mr. Knowles had been co-adventurer with Captain Jesse Smith in the *Two Sons*, with me as their cook and foremast hand, and at their homes I had boarded in alternate weeks between coasting trips.

Naturally enough, time had made a great change in Miss Knowles' appearance. Ten years before, when I was making hay or at other farm work in her father's fields, or doing chores for her mother, she was a romping child playing with an elder brother or "little- mothering" her younger sisters. She was now a woman grown, startling in beauty, which I should only fail in trying to describe. Perhaps I stared too hard, for she blushed and looked amused as she led me upstairs to the living room—the dining room, kitchen and reception room for the boarders being on the first floor. By the time she had asked me to be seated, while she went to call her aunt and uncle, I was in a new heaven and a new earth, transported with all those emotions which have baffled expression of all lovers and all poets of all time. If I ever had the opportunity would I dare tell this lovely girl that I loved her? Well, love found a way—but this is not a love story. Two and a half years later we were married and were supremely happy.

I spent a pleasant evening at Captain Doane's and was asked to call again, a privilege which I did not neglect. On Sunday, my nephew Hervey and I went to church. Whether by accident or not, it was the very church I wanted to be preached to in, for Miss Knowles was there with her uncle's family. On Monday, October 8th, Captain Jesse's schooner had finished loading and would sail the next day. In the afternoon I made a farewell call at the Sailor's Home, and to my delight Miss Knowles consented to take a walk with me. Those were the days when a ten-mile walk was not unusual. We walked around Pleasant Point Fort and up the Northwest Arm and back to her uncle's house—by which time, though nothing was settled, I was not discouraged.

On October 9th at 7 A.M., in Captain Jesse's little schooner, with a fine breeze from the northeast, we made sail from Tobin's wharf. At ten o'clock we passed Sambro Island, and by noon we were fairly off St. Margaret's Bay. Eagerly I watched the familiar landmarks—Cross Island a mile away on the port hand, and the Highlands of Aspotogan lifting far to the northwest. Soon Ironbound and the Ovens would be abeam, and the LaHave, where we would anchor for the night. The wind, however, hauled northwest and freshened, the schooner's sails began to tear and split, and we wore ship and

Maria Knowles (1831-1864)

put back for the Chimney Corner or Sambro Basin, where we anchored. At noon on the 10th we had finished repairs and were under way, the wind northeast but fine, and at 4:30 we anchored in LaHave. At 4 A.M. of the 11th we were under way again and proceeded slowly up the shore. At noon we were off Port L'Hebert, the breeze moderate from north northeast, and at 6 P.M. we were abeam of Shelburne Light.

Captain Jesse, when navigator of the *Two Sons*, as I well knew, took no chances with the open sea but made a harbor every night, and I fully expected we would anchor in Shelburne until morning. He suggested instead that the continued northeast wind might end in a gale, and if we kept going all night we might make Barrington ahead of it. I think, however, the dear old man wanted to give me the pleasure of being home early next day. I immediately offered to stand watch all night. I could not have slept anyway, for as we came nearer home I was more uneasy than they that watch for the morning.

At midnight we were off Port La Tour. At 4 A.M. we rounded Baccaro Point and were fairly in Barrington Bay. I was below dressing for shore when we ran aground at 5:20 about forty feet from Mr. Robertson's wharf.

Going up on deck, I saw again in the growing light the many places familiar to me all my boyish days—stirring memories which at black moments on distant seas and shores had made me long to see them again. Suddenly a feeling came over me that I cannot reasonably explain. Those memories were pleasant dreams. Dreams are real until the dreamer wakes. Actually to see again the people and the places with which they were associated was to wake, and I would rather keep the dreams. If there had been in that little port a ship bound away on a long voyage, I would gladly have joined her and sailed again without going home. There was no such escape and, crushing such thoughts, I got into the boat and went ashore.

No one would be up at that hour with the expectation of meeting Captain Jesse. It was time for him to be in, but the natural place to think of him, since he had not arrived the day before, was in some nearby harbor getting under way. But there we were, and there on the wharf to prove it were the Robertson boys—or men, all of them now. I met Gabriel first, then William, then Robert and last, Tommy, my constant pal in our childhood's far-off days—or they seemed far-off then for he was wearing a beard, a dignity that I had not yet assumed. They would not detain me, except with a word of welcome, and I started off toward the old house. I met no one on the road, it was too early, for which I was glad. If anyone had failed to recognize me it would have hurt me to feel that I was a stranger. The little brooks and the birds in the alders by the roadside startled me to joy with their familiar sound and movement. Coming in sight of the house, I saw an old lady wearing a white cap come out of the front door. She stood and watched me until I passed the gate. Oh, it was my mother, and she did not know me! What countless days she had watched passersby to see if an absent loved one had returned and would open the gate. But I had passed by, and she must still wait, her heart sinking with hope deferred.

My brother Martin's gate was just beyond. I went in there, and his wife, Jane, answered my knock. She did not know me. She asked if I was one of her brothers, and several others of her relatives. Then I spoke, and she called my name. Jane ran and called my mother to come and see a visitor who had dropped in. In a moment Mother entered and sat down but did not see me. I took her hand and said, with not too firm a voice, "Mother!" She stood up and said, "Who is it? Is it possible—is it possible? My son, Benjamin!" and her arms were around me. In came my youngest sister, Irene, who knew me and spoke my name. We all went up to the old house and in a few minutes my father came in. He shook my hand and welcomed me home and thanked God we had met once more. Breakfast was ready, and before we sat down my eldest brother entered. He had just arrived from Boston and anchored his vessel in the Back of the Island Channel. So we all had breakfast together. My brother Martin (who was home while a new vessel was building for him in Shelburne) had that morning gone into the woods hunting and did not return until four o'clock. Whatever work was laid out for the day was all postponed, and we spent the time companying with each other.

The young people of the neighborhood called in force the following evening. The first were Tommy Robertson and his sister Maria. The big east room was crowded. Some said they would not have known me if they had not been told, others that they would have recognized me anywhere, even my ashes if I had been burned. Which proves once more that all people do not see alike. Many of these young friends were engaged to be married, and during the evening the hope was expressed that I would soon be in that happy state. I replied, "Then it will have to be to the prettiest girl in all Barrington." That led to a discussion as to what young lady answered that description. Several names were mentioned, showing that none of them was the unanimous choice, but Daniel Sargent settled the matter with, "I think the most beautiful girl in Barrington is Maria Knowles." They all broke into applause, and even Dan's fiancée gave her approval.

No one present, of course, knew of my state of mind regarding the young lady so honored, but the unexpected verdict affected me so that my sister Irene observed it, and I was sure she had guessed my secret. This she admitted to me that night after the guests were gone, and said she hoped my suit would be successful after Miss Knowles returned home. Dear loyal-hearted sister Irene, I owe her more than I can ever repay for her faithful lifelong devotion.

— AFTERWORD —

*T*HE YEARS WHICH FOLLOWED THE CLOSE OF THIS RECORD have seen swift changes in ships and shipping and life at sea. With the vanishing of sails, the sailor and his peculiar skill are obsolete, and the word "sailor" is a figure of speech. The communities on this side of the Atlantic where he was bred have lost their occupation and changed into summer resorts, to which in his declining years he furnishes an element of what is called quaintness. When the last survivors are gone—and they are going fast—life under sail can only be guessed at from reading the old log books and journals they have left, and the published lives of a few mariners. It cannot be reproduced in fiction, even if competently written.

Happily, the story of the clipper ships is to some extent preserved; in less degree, that of New England's wooden ships and iron sailors has been told. The Maritime Provinces of British North America—now a part of Canada—merit a place in that saga, but it has not been recorded. The modest ambition of these pages is to give a glimpse of one tiny Nova Scotian port from whence many sailors hailed, and some notion of the life they led. I could tell it only as it touched myself. The experiences here written down were tame and commonplace compared with scores of other Barrington boys of my time who sailed deep water. Many of them ended their careers early in life, off soundings; many attained to high rank in their calling, expert navigators, shrewd manager-owners in command of ships bearing the mysterious letters "N.S." on their name-boards, and in which they sailed the Seven Seas. Hard-headed, hard-fisted, they had to be. Their integrity was inborn. None ever ceased to love the "rocks and rills" among which they were born. From childhood they were all grounded in the rugged virtues of defying danger and despising comfort, skilled in the art of carrying sail—every man a sailor:

Who smiled at fortune, scoffed at fate,
And risked his life to save his mate.

Benjamin Doane about 1860

EPILOGUE

Maria Knowles Doane and son, Benjamin Hervey, shortly before Maria's death

EXCEPT for a short trip to Saint John to settle the account for his whaling voyage, Benjamin Doane spent the next six months at Barrington. In the spring of 1850 he signed as second mate on the newly built brig *Ambassador* of Shelburne, Nova Scotia. During the next two years while she sailed primarily between New York and Europe, he became mate and ultimately master of the vessel. He returned to Barrington in early March of 1852.

Soon smitten with gold fever, he began planning a trip to Australia with a group of young Barrington men. Determined not to go alone, he asked his fiancée, Maria Knowles, to accompany him. She consented and they were married on March 18, 1852. The Australian mining expedition proved to be a "flash in the pan." The voyage never got underway because many investors became reluctant to risk capital in the venture. In 1853 he sailed his last voyage under the British flag on the barque *Josephine* of Liverpool, Nova Scotia.

Shortly thereafter, Benjamin and Maria Doane emigrated to New York where they became American citizens, so that Benjamin could fulfill his ambition to become the master of an American vessel. He signed as a mate on a vessel in the coffee trade between New York, Columbia and Venezuela. Unable to become master of one of this firm's vessels, he joined a smaller firm in the same trade and assumed command of one of their vessels.

Benjamin and Maria had four children between 1855 and 1863, one of whom, Caroline, died in infancy. On July 23, 1864 Maria died leaving Benjamin with the three children, Eva, Francis and Benjamin H., whom he subsequently sent to live with his older sister, Irene, in Barrington. Benjamin continued his seafaring life, but shortly after the conclusion of the American Civil War the firm which employed him went bankrupt. Unable to secure command of another vessel and unwilling to become a mate, he stayed ashore.

Late in the 1860s he returned to sea as a master of a side-wheeler which he sailed from New York to Jacksonville, Florida. From the early 1870s to 1890 when he retired from the sea, he commanded a number of coastal vessels running along the eastern seaboard of the United States. Most of these years were spent aboard the Clyde Line steamers, *Benefactor*, *Regulator* and *Cherokee*. The latter he commanded following her launch in 1886 until he retired in 1890.

In preparation for retirement, he purchased land in Plainfield, New Jersey in 1885 and built a house and barn. Here he spent his retirement living with his daughter, Eva, and her husband Joseph Hervey Doane. When Joseph Hervey became terminally ill, Benjamin moved in 1916 to his son Francis's residence in Bayonne, New Jersey. There he died on August 17, 1916, three weeks before his 93rd birthday.

Captain Benjamin Doane in retirement

WHALES ENCOUNTERED

Scale: 1″ = 40′

Blue whale

Fin whale

Sperm whale

Right whale

Humpback whale

Pilot whale

VESSEL RIGS

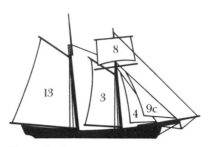

Topsail schooner

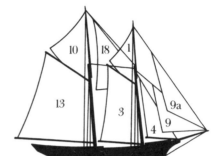

Schooner

1. Fore gaff topsail
2. Fore royal
3. Fore sail
4. Fore staysail
5. Fore spencer
6. Fore topgallant
7. Fore topmast staysail
8. Fore topsail
9. Jib
9a. Jib (flying)
9b. Jib (outer)
9c. Jib (inner)
10. Main gaff topsail
11. Main royal
12. Main royal staysail
13. Main sail
14. Main spencer
15. Main staysail
16. Main topgallant
17. Main topgallant staysail
18. Main topmast staysail
19. Main topsail
20. Mizzen or crossjack
21. Mizzen gaff topsail
22. Mizzen royal
23. Mizzen royal staysail
24. Mizzen staysail
25. Mizzen topgallant
26. Mizzen topgallant staysail
27. Mizzen topmast staysail
28. Mizzen topsail
29. Spanker

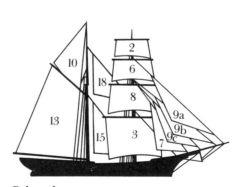

Brigantine

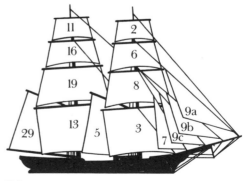

Brig

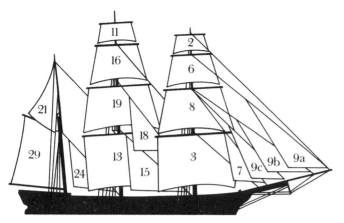

Barque

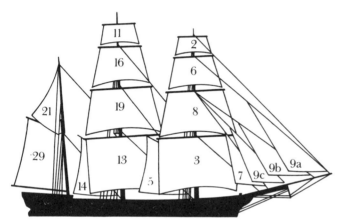

Barque with fore and main spencer

Ship

VESSELS ENCOUNTERED

THIS LIST provides additional information about most of the vessels mentioned in this book and is intended to place Doane's encounters with these vessels in an historical context. Although we have been continually impressed with the historical accuracy of Doane's recollections, the rig and port of registry given by him do not, in some cases, coincide with the official sources we have consulted. This is attributable either to the usual changes in a vessel's rig and port of registry or to lapses in Doane's recollection or recording. Unfortunately the identification of a few vessels was not possible due to inconclusive evidence in the book or to the lack of extant or readily available sources.

The port registers for Halifax, Liverpool, Shelburne and Yarmouth, Nova Scotia; St. Andrew's and Saint John, New Brunswick; and Charlottetown, Prince Edward Island, provided information on the locally owned vessels, many of which Doane served aboard. For those wishing further information, the appropriate microfilm copies of these registers can be viewed at the Dalhousie University Archives and Public Archives of Nova Scotia in Halifax; The New Brunswick Museum in Saint John, New Brunswick, and the Public Archives of Prince Edward Island in Charlottetown, P.E.I.; or collectively at the Public Archives of Canada in Ottawa.

Port registers for Liverpool and London, England can be consulted at the Public Records office, Kew, Richmond, Surrey, England.

Information relating to the American whaling vessels was taken from Alexander Starbuck's *History of the American Whale Fishery*, which provides an annual listing of vessels departing from American ports. *Lloyd's Register of Shipping* and *The Record of American and Foreign Shipping* for the appropriate dates provided information relating to British and American vessels respectively. All are available at various museums, archives and libraries. References to *The Whalemen's Shipping List*, December 26, 1846 was provided by Mystic Seaport Museum, Connecticut. Extant copies of journals kept by sailors aboard some of these American whaling vessels gives another perspective on their encounters with the *Athol*. These are available, as cited, at the Kendall Whaling Museum, Sharon, Massachusetts and the New Bedford Whaling Museum, New Bedford, Massachusetts. In the case of American whaling vessels the dates of the voyage on which Doane encountered them are given.

Published sources and their abbreviations are as follows:

DANFS *Dictionary of American Naval Fighting Ships,* Volumes 1-3, (The Naval Department, Washington, D.C., 1959, 1963 and 1968).

HASN *The History of the American Sailing Navy* by Howard I. Chapelle, (W.W. Norton and Company Inc., New York, 1949).

HAWF *History of the American Whale Fishery* by Alexander Starbuck in Report of the United States Commission of Fish and Fisheries for 1875-76. Part IV, (Government Printing Office, 1878).

MS *Merchant Sail*, Volumes 1-6 by William A. Fairburn, (Fairburn Marine Educational Foundation Inc., Center Lovell, Maine, 1945-55).

NAS *North Atlantic Seaway*, Volumes 1-5 by N.R.P. Bonsor, (David & Charles, Newton Abbot, U.K., 1975).

SRN *Ships of the Royal Navy: An Historical Index* by J.J. College, (David & Charles, Newton Abbot, U.K., 1969).

For the purposes of brevity the following abbreviations were used:

L - Length

LR - *Lloyd's Register of Shipping*

RAFS - *Record of American and Foreign Shipping*

Reg - Registered at

Page numbers in italics refer to the first mention of that vessel in *Following the Sea.*

Adelaide barque 278 tons L. 100.5.' Built Rustico, P.E.I., 1845 by Joshua Dourong. Master (1846): William Jolly.
Owners (1846): Black Brothers & Co.
Reg: Charlottetown, #63, 1845; Halifax, #70, 1846.
Page 227

Adrianna [*sic*] *Addrianah* schooner 36 tons L. 50.7'. Built Yarmouth, N.S., 1841 by John Crosby. Master (1841): John Crosby. Owners (1841): Foster Crosby, John Crosby, Nathan Huestis (?) and Marcus Ring.
Reg: Yarmouth, #19, 1841.
Page 20

Alceste ship 559 tons L. 122.6'. Built Salmon River, N.S. 1847 by Benjamin Killam. Master (1847): James Dane Cann. Owners: Benjamin Killam Sr., Benjamin Killam Jr., and James Dane Cann.
Reg: Yarmouth, #55, 1847.
Page 187

Alice Haviland, possibly *Alice Haviland* schooner 181 tons L. 80.5'. Built Grand River (East) P.E.I., 1841 by Murdock MacLeod. Master (1849): C. Williams. Port: Dumfries, Scotland.
Reg: Charlottetown, #55, 1841.
LR 1848, lists her destined voyage from Clyde to Trinidad.
Although a direct connection between the *Alice Haviland* mentioned by Doane and the one appearing in *Lloyd's Register* is not possible, given the information in this book, it is improbable that another vessel called *Alice Haviland* registered in Dumfries was on this route at the same time.
Page 197

Ambassador brig 191 tons L. 89.4'. Built Shelburne, N.S., 1850 by William Muir. Master (1850): Martin Doane. Owners: William Muir, Martin Doane and James Muir.
Reg: Liverpool, N.S., #4, 1850.
Page 228

Arnolda ship 360 tons. Master: David U. Coffin. Port: New Bedford, Mass. Voyage: 1844-48.
HAWF pp. 408-9.
Page 107

Athol ship 398 tons L. 107.5'. Built Saint John, N.B., 1845 by William and James Lawton.

Master (1845): James Doane Coffin. Owner: Charles Cole Stewart.
Reg: Saint John, #40, 1845.
Page 49

Balenor, [*sic*] probably *Balaena* ship 301 tons. Master: Dexter. Port: New Bedford, Mass.
Voyage: 1845-49.
HAWF pp. 420-1.
The Whalemen's Shipping List December 26, 1846 reports *Balaena* off Galapagos on
May 10, 1846.
Page 98

Benefactor steamer 844 tons L. 179.6'. Built Chester, Pa., 1870. Port: New York. Master
(1872-79): T. Jones. Owner: William P. Clyde & Co.,
RAFS 1872-1890.
Page 236

Bermondsey barque 507 tons L. 110.7'. Built Whitby, U.K., 1841. Master (1846): Banes. Owner:
Wilson & Co.
Reg: London, U.K., #381, 1841
LR 1847 lists her destined voyage from London to Sydney, Australia.
Page 167

Boy of Warren probably *Boy* ship 252 tons. Master: Barton. Port: Warren, R. I. Voyage: 1843-46.
HAWF pp. 402-3.
Page 98

H.M.S. Bramble cutter 161 tons L. 71' 10 guns. Launched Plymouth Dockyard, 1822. Survey
vessel in 1842. Lent to Colonial Department 1853 as diving bell vessel at Sydney,
Australia.
SRN p. 87.
Page 163

Bride schooner 58 tons L. 55.6'. Built Barrington, N.S. 1841 by Joshua Nickerson. Master
(1841): Israel L. Crowell; Owners: Israel L. Crowell, Thomas Crowell, Joshua
Nickerson, Nehemiah Nickerson and Isaac Nickerson.
Reg: Halifax, #33, 1841.
Page 49

Brisk brigantine 80 tons L. 65'. Built Shelburne, N.S., 1842 by William Muir. Master (1842):
Martin Doane. Owner (1842): William Muir.
Reg: Halifax, #154, 1842.
Page 27

Canmore barque 292 tons L. 93.6'. Built Saint John, N.B., 1843 by William & Richard Wright.
Master: (1843) Donald Bannerman. Owner: James Malcolm.
Reg: Saint John, #70, 1843.
Page 128

Cartecheria barque Glasgow. We are unable to identify her.
Page 175

Catawba ship 355 tons. Master: Coleman. Port: Nantucket, Mass. Voyage: 1843-47.
HAWF pp. 400-1.
Journal of the *Catawba* (Journal #46, Kendall Whaling Museum) states that on Friday,
February 27, 1846 "spoke *Athol* of St. John Lat. 47.57. Long. 75.05."
Page 86

Charlotte probably *Charlotte* barque 643 tons L. 127.6'. Built St. Mary's Bay, N.S., 1835 by
Charles Everett. Master (1835): George C. Hunt. Owner (1845): James Kirk.
Reg: Saint John, N.B. #39, 1835.
LR 1845 lists her destined voyage from London to New Brunswick.
Although a direct connection between the *Charlotte* mentioned by Doane and the one
appearing in *Lloyd's Register* is not possible, given the information in the book, it is
improbable that another vessel called *Charlotte* was on this route at the same time.
Page 52

Cherokee steamer 2,557 tons L. 269'. Built Philadelphia, Pa., 1886. Port: New York. Master
(1887-1890): Benjamin Doane. Owner: William P. Clyde & Co.
RAFS 1886-1891.
Page 236

Chili ship, 291 tons. Master: H.H. Ricketson. Port: New Bedford, Mass. Voyage: 1845-48.
  HAWF pp. 420-1.
  Page 85

Christopher Mickel [*sic*] *Christopher Mitchell* ship, 387 tons. Master: Enoch Ackley. Port:
  Nantucket, Mass. Voyage: 1845-1848.
  HAWF pp. 426-7.
  Page 78

Columbia ship 212 tons L. 83'. Built North River, Scituate, Mass., 1773.
  Together with the sloop *Lady Washington*, the *Columbia*, John Kendrick, Master,
  sailed from Boston, September 30, 1787 and arrived at Vancouver Island on August 16,
  1788. They were the first American vessels to round Cape Horn.
  MS Vol I pp. 500-3.
  Page 22

Commodore probably *Commodore* ship 686 tons L. 130' built Wilmot, N.S., 1846 by Aaron
  Eaton. Master: Joseph Prichard. Owners: Gilbert T. Roy, Aaron Eaton and Joseph
  Prichard.
  Reg: Saint John, #11, 1846.
  This is the only vessel of this name and rig appearing on the Saint John port register at
  this time.
  Page 207

U.S.S. Congress frigate 1,867 tons L. 179' 50 guns. Launched Portsmouth, N.H. 1841. As the
  flagship of Commodore R. Stockton, she was despatched to the Pacific Ocean in
  October 1845 and called at Honolulu, Hawaii, in June 1846.
  DANFS Vol. II, pp. 163-4.
  Page 95

Duchess privateer. Bristol. We are unable to identify her further.
  Page 110

Duke privateer. Bristol. We are unable to identify her further.
  Page 110

Eagle schooner 45 tons L. 51.9'. Built Barrington, N.S. 1837 by Herman Nickerson. Master
  (1837): Moses Crowell. Owner: Obediah Wilson, Sr.
  Reg: Halifax, #139, 1837.
  Page 16

U.S.S. Erie sloop of war 509 tons L. 117'11" 18 guns. Launched at Baltimore, Md., 1813, she
  was stationed in the Pacific Ocean 1845-48.
  DANFS Vol II, p. 363.
  Page 118

Euphrates probably *Euphrates* barque 368 tons. Built Sunderland, U.K. 1845. Master:
  R. Wilson. Port: London, U.K.
  LR 1848 lists her destined voyage from London to Calcutta, India.
  Although a direct connection between the Euphrates mentioned by Doane and the one
  appearing in *Lloyd's Register* is not possible given the information in this book, it is
  improbable that another vessel called *Euphrates* was on this route at the same time.
  Page 180

Expedition We are unable to identify her.
  Page 180

Fanny probably *Fanny* ship 367 tons. Built Island of Guernsey, 1840. Master: High. Port:
  Liverpool, U.K.
  LR 1846 lists her destined voyage from Liverpool, U.K. to Lima, Peru.
  Although a direct connection between the *Fanny* mentioned by Doane and the one
  appearing in *Lloyd's Register* is not possible given the information in this book, it is
  improbable that another vessel called *Fanny* was on this route at the same time.
  Page 95

Favourite schooner 38 tons L. 50.1'. Built Barrington, N.S. 1828 (Builder not given). Master
  (1838): Thomas T. Crowell. Owners (1838): Thomas Crowell and Israel Lovitt Crowell.
  Reg: Halifax, #80, 1828; #169, 1838.
  Page 8

Formosa ship 450 tons. Master: L. Briggs. Port: New Bedford, Mass. Voyage: 1844-49.
> HAWF pp. 408-9.
> *Page 118*

Forth steamer. We are unable to identify her.
> *Page 196*

Garland probably *Garland* ship 243 tons. Master: Crowell. Port: New Bedford, Mass.
> Voyage:1846-49.
> HAWF pp. 434-5.
> *Page 118*

Gem brig 115 tons L. 71.8'. Built Guysborough, N.S., 1841 by James Gosbee. Master (1841):
> Benjamin Doane. Owners (1841): Winthrop Sargeant and Benjamin Doane.
> Reg: Halifax, #111, 1841.
> *Page 20*

George probably *George* ship 273 tons. Master: McCleeve. Port: New Bedford. Voyage: 1843-47.
> HAWF pp. 398-9.
> *The Whalemen's Shipping List,* December 26, 1846 reports *George* off Paita (Payta),
> on August 2, 1846.
> *Page 98*

George possibly *George* brig 234 tons L. 93.3'. Built New London, P.E.I., 1847 by William Bell.
> Master (1849): Hogan. Owner (1849): J. Hogan.
> Reg: Charlottetown, #69, 1847.
> *LR* 1849 lists her destined voyage from Liverpool to Newfoundland. Although it is
> impossible to link this *George* with the one sighted by Doane, she is the only vessel so
> rigged listed as sailing between England and Newfoundland at that time.
> *Page 180*

George Holmes possibly *George Home* barque 441 tons. Plymouth, U.K. 1809. Master: Distant.
> Port: London, U.K.
> *LR* 1847 lists her destined voyage from London to South Seas. This is the only vessel of
> this name listed by *Lloyd's Register* as sailing in the area at that time.
> *Page 130*

George Porter probably *George Porter* ship 285 tons Master: E.A. Arthur. Port: New Bedford,
> Mass. Voyage: 1843-47.
> HAWF pp. 398-9.
> *Page 98*

Grapeshot barque 345 tons L. 120'. Built New London, Conn., 1853.
> William Poole eluded authorities and found passage to Europe on the steamer *Isabella
> Jewett.* The American government chartered the *Grapeshot* and sailed in pursuit,
> leaving port a day after the steamer, which was scheduled to call at Fayal, one of the
> Azores. *Grapeshot* sailed for that port and was waiting for the *Jewett* when she arrived.
> MS Vol. V., p. 3150.
> *Page 60*

Great Britain steamer 1,016 tons L. 322'. Built Bristol, U.K., 1843.
> She was the first steamer with a screw propeller to cross the Atlantic, sailing from
> Liverpool, U.K., on July 26, 1845 and arriving at New York on August 10.
> NAS Vol 1, p. 60-6
> *Page 82*

Great Western steamer 1,340 tons L. 212'. Built Bristol, U.K. 1836-37.
> She was the first steamer designed specifically for the trans-Atlantic service. In 1847 she
> was owned by the Royal Mail Steam Packet Company.
> NAS Vol. 1, p. 60-6.
> *Page 196*

Henry ship 346 tons. Master: William Brown. Port: Nantucket, Mass. Voyage: 1844-48.
> HAWF pp. 412-3.
> *Page 118*

Henry barque 262 tons. Master: Lind. Port: Salem, Mass. Voyage: 1845. Sold at Tahiti.
HAWF pp. 430-1.
Journal of barque *Henry* of Salem 1845-47 (New Bedford Whaling Museum) states that on Saturday, May 2, 1846 "at 4 p.m. spoke the Athol of St. Johns [*sic*]. 10 months, 200 sperm."
Page 92

Herrold American whaler, probably *Herold:* insufficient evidence to distinguish her from among the three vessels of the same name on voyages at this time.
Herold ship 262 tons. Master: Luce. Port: Fairhaven, Mass. Voyage: 1844-47. HAWF pp. 412-3.
Herold ship 274 tons. Master: George Stewart. Port: New Bedford, Mass. Voyage: 1845-48. HAWF pp. 422-3.
Herold ship 241 tons. Master: Barker. Port: Stonington, Conn. Voyage: 1845. Sold at Rio de Janeiro, 1848. HAWF pp. 430-1.
Page 116

Hoquaw [sic] *Honqua* ship 399 tons. Master: Brown. Port: New Bedford, Mass. Voyage: 1846-49.
HAWF pp. 434-5.
Page 145

Hudson barque 511 tons L. 115.3′. Built Parrsboro, N.S., 1846 by James L. Chubbuck. Master (1846-49): William Pines. Port (1846): Liverpool, U.K.
Reg: Halifax, #120, 1846, Liverpool, U.K. #262, 1846.
LR 1847 lists her destined voyage from Liverpool to Sydney, Australia.
Page 165

Iris ship 311 tons. Master: G.B. Spooner. Port: New Bedford, Mass. Voyage: 1843-47.
HAWF pp. 398-9.
The journal of the *Iris,* New Bedford, 1843-47 (New Bedford Whaling Museum) states that on Thursday, June 11, 1846 "at daylight saw whales. Lowered struck and killed. To the S.E. the ship *Athol.* Caught one at 9 p.m." Lat. 5.37 Long. 104.50.
Page 99

James Allen ship 355 tons. Master: Harvey Shearman. Port: New Bedford, Mass. Voyage: 1844-48.
HAWF pp. 408-9.
Page 118

James Stewart ship 386 tons L. 109.5′. Built Saint John, N.B., 1833 by George Thomson. Master (1845): Joseph Kenney. Owner: Charles Cole Stewart.
Reg: Saint John, #43, 1833.
Page 52

Jane schooner 48 tons. L. 53′. Built Barrington, N.S., 1829 by Obediah Wilson, Jr. Master (1837): Joseph Wilson. Owners (1837): Obediah Wilson, Sr., Obediah Wilson, Jr., and Israel L. Wilson.
Reg: Halifax, #139, 1829.
Page 20

Japan ship 332 tons. Master: Valentine S. Riddell. Port: Nantucket, Mass. Voyage: 1845-49.
HAWF pp. 426-7.
The journal of the *Japan,* Nantucket, 1845-49 (New Bedford Whaling Museum) states that on Tuesday, May 5, 1846, "at 6 p.m. spoke ship *Athol,* Coffin of St. John's [*sic*], N.B. in running across her stern she caught aback and steered into us and stove the L. boat and the boat over the stern gammed till 9 o'clock."
Page 93

Java ship 294 tons. Master: Lucas. Port: Fairhaven, Mass. Voyage: 1845-49.
HAWF pp. 424-5.
Page 82

John A. Rob ship 279 tons. Master: Winslow, Port: Fairhaven, Mass. Voyage: 1845-49.
HAWF pp. 424-5.
Page 125

John Adams ship 268 tons. Master: F.A. Mason. Port: New Bedford, Mass. Voyage: 1844-48.
    HAWF pp. 408-9.
    Page 118

Joseph Maxwell ship 302 tons. Master: Perry. Port: Fairhaven, Mass. Voyage: 1843-1847.
    HAWF pp. 400-1
    The journal of the *Joseph Maxwell,* Fairhaven, 1843-47, (Journal #124 Kendall
    Whaling Museum) states that on Saturday, December 26, 1846 "comes in pleasant
    spoke the *Athol* of st. john's [*sic*]."
    Page 118

Josephine barque 267 tons L. 108.5'. Built LaHave, N.S., 1852 by Nathan Randall. Master
    (1852): Hervey Doane. Owner: Maklon (?) Vail.
    Reg: Liverpool, N.S., #8, 1852.
    Page 228

Josephine ship 397 tons. Master: Hedges. Port: Sag Harbour, N.Y. Voyage: 1846-49.
    HAWF pp. 442-3.
    Page 146

Lady Washington sloop 90 tons L. not available. Together with ship *Columbia,* the *Lady
    Washington,* Robert Gray, Master, sailed from Boston, September 30, 1787 and arrived
    at Vancouver Island on August 16, 1788. They were the first American vessels to round
    Cape Horn.
    MS Vol. I, pp. 500-3.
    Page 22

Lottery brig. We are unable to identify her.
    Page 34

Marco Polo ship 1,625 tons L. 184.1'. Built Saint John, N.B. 1851 by James Smith. Master
    (1852): James N. Forbes. Owner: Black Ball Line.
    Reg: Saint John, #35, 1851.
    After an extremely short passage from Liverpool, U.K. to Australia and back in 1852,
    she was proclaimed the fastest ship in the world.
    Page 174

Margaret schooner 61 tons L. 55.9'. Built Yarmouth, N.S. 1845 by William Jenkins. Master
    (1845): Benjamin Hilton. Owner: Nathan Weston.
    Reg: Yarmouth, #37, 1845
    Page 191
    Some confusion exists regarding this vessel. In an earlier version of the manuscript she
    is referred to as the brig *Margery* of Yarmouth. This reference was changed to *Margaret*
    in the later version. Both names are listed in the Yarmouth register, with Hilton's
    associated with them. The vessel Doane refers to is probably the brig *Margery* since
    according to the Yarmouth *Herald,* December 4, 1848 she arrived at Bermuda on
    November 15 from Newport. Subsequent issues of the Yarmouth *Herald,* May 14 and
    July 23, 1849 state she arrived at St. Andrew's from Boston and later sailed to Liverpool,
    U.K.

Margery brig 127 tons L. 79'. Built Jordan River, N.S. 1847 by Hugh R. MacKay. Master (1847):
    George C. Wyman. Owners: Benjamin Ellenwood, Jacob Hilton, James McNutt,
    Freeman Crosby and George C. Wyman.
    Reg: Yarmouth, #25, 1847.
    Page 191, see Margaret

Margaret Rait barque 308 tons L. 99'6". Built Saint Andrew's N.B. 1831 by George Walker.
    Master (1844): James D. Coffin. Owner: Charles Cole Stewart.
    Reg: Saint John, #72, 1832. Saint Andrew's, #2 and #14, 1832.
    Page 49

Menker [*sic*] *Menkar* ship 371 tons. Master: Norton. Port: New Bedford, Mass., Voyage: 1845-48.
    HAWF pp. 422-3.
    Page 118

Micmac brigantine 128 tons L. 81.6'. Built Broad Cove, N.S., 1847 by Benjamin and Martin Rynard. Master (1847): Stephen Sponagle. Owners: Benjamin D. DeWolf and James DeWolf.
Reg: Liverpool, N.S., #19, 1847.
Page 197

Minerva Smith [*sic*] *Minerva Smyth* ship 335 tons. Master: Crocker. Port: New Bedford, Mass. Voyage: 1845-48.
HAWF pp. 422-3.
Page 88

Nassau probably *Nassau* ship 408 tons. Master: Weeks. Port: New Bedford, Mass. Voyage: 1846-1850.
HAWF pp. 436-7.
A vessel called *Nassau* is not listed as sailing from Sag Harbour during this period. The only *Nassau* listed is the one departing from New Bedford.
Page 146

Nye probably *Nye* ship 211 tons. Master: R. F. Pease. Port: New Bedford, Mass. Voyage: 1844-48.
HAWF pp. 410-1
The journal of the *Nye,* New Bedford, 1844-48 (Journal #293, Kendall Whaling Museum) states that on Tuesday, May 26, 1846: "Light breezes from the N. steering S.S.W. at 6 p.m. pick up a boat and crew from ship Athol of St. John's [*sic*], N.B. George Porter has another boat and crew they were lost while chasing whales. The current taking their ship to the North in a calm North head bearing east dist. 15 miles." It also states that on Friday, May 29 "At 3 p.m. the Athol got her men. At 4 headed to the South."
Page 98

Ocean schooner 48 tons L. 49'. Built Barrington, N.S. 1825 by James Kenny. Master (1825): Nehemiah Doane. Owners: Nehemiah Doane, Harvey Doane, Thomas Doane, Jonathan Knowles and James Kenny.
Reg: Halifax, #70, 1825.
On July 15, 1850 Nehemiah Doane wrote to the Register of Shipping at Halifax, stating that "said schooner [Ocean] sailed from Halifax, N.S. about 22 February 1829 for the British West Indies and has not since been heard of."
Page 5

Pacific ship 385 tons. Master: Hoxie. Port: New Bedford, Mass. Voyage: 1844-1848.
HAWF pp. 410-1.
Page 118

Pearl possibly *Pearl* barque 361 tons. Built Sunderland, U.K., 1842. Master: Chalmers. Port: London.
LR 1847 lists her destined voyage from London to Montreal, Quebec.
It is not possible to make a direct connection between the vessel encountered by Doane and the *Pearl* listed in *Lloyd's Register,* but she is the only vessel by that name which is listed as sailing from London to Quebec at that time.
Page 180

Phinney possibly *Phenix* ship 323 tons. Master: Perry Wilson. Port: Nantucket, Mass. Voyage: 1844-48.
HAWF pp.412-3.
Since no vessel with this name is listed among American whalers, it is possible the *Phinney* of Nantucket encountered by Doane was actually the *Phenix* of Nantucket which was on the whaling grounds at the same time.
Page 121

President ship 293 tons. Master: John C. Brock. Port: Nantucket, Mass. Voyage: 1842-1847.
HAWF pp. 390-1.
The *Whalemen's Shipping List,* December 26, 1846 reports *President* off Galapagos on May 1, 1846.
Page 98

H.M.S. Rattlesnake ship 6th rate 503 tons L. 114' 28 guns. Launched at Chatham Dockyard, 1822, she was used as a survey ship in 1845.
SRN p. 474
Page 163

Regulator steamer 847 tons L. 165′ Built Chester, Pa., 1869. Port: New York. Master (1884-87): Benjamin Doane. Owner: William P. Clyde & Co.
RAFS 1870-1888.
Page 236

Reindeer brigantine 82 tons L. 64′4″. Built Shelburne, N.S., 1832 by Enos Churchill. Master (1832): Enos Churchill. Owners (1833): William B. Hamilton and James M. Hamilton.
Reg: Halifax, #142, 1832, #211, 1833.
Page 32

Robert Edwards ship 356 tons. Master: N. Burgess. Port: New Bedford, Mass. Voyage: 1845-48.
HAWF pp. 424-5.
Page 107

Rose brigantine 128 tons. L. 77′. Built Shelburne, N.S. 1847 by William Muir. Master (1847): Martin Doane; Owners: William Muir and James Muir.
Reg: Halifax, #169, 1847.
Page 190

Russell barque 302 tons. Master: J. O. Morse. Port: New Bedford, Mass. Voyage: 1845-49.
HAWF pp. 424-5.
Page 86

Samuel Adams possibly *Samuel and Thomas* barque 191 tons. Master: Swift. Port: Provincetown, Mass. Voyage: 1844-1846.
HAWF pp. 416-7.
Since no vessel with this name is listed among American whalers, it is possible that Doane encountered the *Samuel and Thomas* of Provincetown. She would have been 10 months out at the time Doane met with her.
Page 79

Saksusa Wiscasset, Maine. We are unable to identify her.
Page 207

Sarah barque 286 tons. Master: Rice. Port: Warren, R.I. Voyage: 1845-49.
HAWF pp. 428-9.
Page 142

Sarah ship 370 tons. Master: Purrington. Port: Mattapoisett, Mass. Voyage: 1846-48.
HAWF pp. 436-7.
Doane mentions meeting a *Sarah* of New Bedford. HAWF does not list a vessel named *Sarah* as sailing from New Bedford during this period. Doane probably met with one of the above vessels.
Page 142

Sarah Francis ship 301 tons. Master: Hiller. Port: Fairhaven, Mass. Voyage: 1843-47.
HAWF pp. 400-1.
Page 100

H.M.S. Scourge sloop 1,128 tons L. 190′. Launched Portsmouth Dockyard, U.K., 1844.
SRN p. 495.
Page 196

Sheffield ship 579 tons. Master: White. Port: Cold Spring, N.Y. Voyage: 1845-49.
HAWF pp. 432-3.
Page 146

Spartan ship 333 tons. Master: Nehemiah C. Fisher. Port: Nantucket, Mass. Voyage: 1843-47.
HAWF pp. 400-1.
Page 118

Spermaceti probably *Spermaceti* barque 411 tons L. 115′2″. Built Deer Island, N.B. 1834 by William Cummins. Master (1847): E. Moon. Owner (1847): Nichols & Co.
Reg: St. Andrew's, N.B., #29, 1834.
LR 1847 lists her destined voyage from Plymouth to Quebec. Although a direct connection between the *Spermaceti* mentioned by Doane and the one appearing in *Lloyd's Register* is not possible given the information in this book, it is improbable that another vessel called *Spermaceti* was on this route at the same time.
Page 180

Teaser schooner 26 tons. L. 48.5'. Built Barrington, N.S. 1837 by Gamaliel Kenny. Master (1837): John Knowles. Owners (1840): Jesse Smith Jr., and John Robertson. Reg: Halifax, #178, 1837.
Page 15

Teviot steamer. We are unable to identify her.
Page 196

The Thomas Edwards brigantine 102 tons L. 65'. Built Clare, N.S. 1839 by Ansitin [?] Therio. Master (1843): Nehemiah Crowell. Owners (1843): Nehemiah Crowell, John Robertson, James Keith, Michael Wrayton, Israel L. Wilson, Thomas Crowell, John Crowell, Gamaliel Kenny, William Robertson Jr. and Robert Robertson. Reg: Halifax, #244, 1839.
Page 38

Thomas Perkins U.S. transport ship. Port: Boston. Master: James P. Arthur. We are unable to identify her further.
Page 118

Tomitan barque 428 tons. Built Greenock, U.K., 1839. Master: Turner. Port: Glasgow, U.K. LR 1849 lists her destined voyage from Clyde to Singapore.
Page 179

Triton ship 300 tons. Master: Spencer. Port: New Bedford, Mass. Voyage: 1846-50. HAWF pp. 436-7.
Page 125

Two Sons schooner 32 tons L. 43'. Built Digby, N.S., 1829 by Joseph Young Jr. Master (1829): Joseph Young Jr. Owners (1836): Jesse Smith Jr., and John Robertson. Reg: Halifax, #93, 1829, #159, 1836.
Page 12

Undine brig. We are unable to identify her.
Page 204

Union probably *Union* barque 327 tons. Built Sunderland, U.K., 1835. Port: London, U.K. LR 1849 lists her destined voyage from London to Port Phillip, Australia. Although a direct connection between the *Union* mentioned by Doane and the one appearing in *Lloyd's Register* is not possible, given the information in the book, it is improbable that another vessel called *Union* was on this route at the same time.
Page 179

Victoria schooner 45 tons L. 54'. Built Barrington, N.S., 1839 by Herman Nickerson. Master: (1839) Martin Doane. Owners: (1839) Isaiah Nickerson, Ebenezer Nickerson, Herman Nickerson, Martin Doane, Scott Nickerson, John Nickerson, Alfred Nickerson, Zacheus Chatwyne and Phineas Nickerson. Reg: Halifax, #31, 1839.
Page 16

H.M.S. Victory ship 2,142 tons L. 186', 100 guns. She was launched at Chatham Dockyard, U.K., 1765 and rebuilt in 1801. Currently she is drydocked at Portsmouth Dockyard, U.K. SRN p. 593.
Page 184

Volga [*sic*] *Wolga* barque 285 tons. Master: Luce; Port: Fairhaven, Mass. Voyage: 1846-52. HAWF pp. 436-7.
Page 155

U.S.S. Yorktown sloop of war 3rd class 566 tons L. 117'7", 48 guns. She was launched at Norfolk Yard, Virginia in 1839. HASN pp. 402 and 502.
Page 59

H.M.S. Wellesley ship 1,746 tons L. 176', 74 guns. She was launched at Bombay Dockyard, India in 1815. SRN p. 607.
Page 196

LIST OF ILLUSTRATIONS

CHAPTER XXIII
Page 203
Abaco Light
From *Sailing Directions To Accompany The Chart Of The Gulf Of Mexico And Islands Of Haiti, Jamaica, Cuba, The Bahamas, Caribbees & C.* James Imray & Son, London, 1874.

Page 206
Apalachicola, Florida, in 1837
Courtesy of The Florida State Archives, Tallahassee, Florida.

Page 211
Wreckers at work
From *Harper's New Monthly Magazine* vol. XVIII, no. CVII, April 1859. Courtesy of The Historical Association of Southern Florida, Maimi, Florida.

Page 212
Key West, Florida, about 1835
Courtesy of The Historcial Association Of Southern Florida, Miami, Florida.

Page 221
Head of Kinsale about 1835
From Hall, Mr. and Mrs. S.C., *Ireland, Its Scenery, Character, Etc.,* 3 volumes (London, n.d.) c. 1835. Courtesy of Neville Elwood, Halifax.

CHAPTER XXIV
Page 228
Sambro Light in 1873
Courtesy of The Maritime Museum of the Atlantic, Halifax.

Page 231
Maria Knowles
Courtesy of Dr. Benjamin K. Doane, Halifax.

AFTERWORD
Page 235
Benjamin Doane
Courtesy of Dr. Benjamin K. Doane, Halifax.

EPILOGUE
Page 236
Maria Knowles and son, Benjamin Hervey
Courtesy of Dr. Benjamin K. Doane, Halifax.

Page 237
Captain Benjamin Doane
Courtesy of Dr. Benjamin K. Doane, Halifax

WHALES ENCOUNTERED
Pages 238-239
From Scammon, Charles M., *The Marine Mammals of The North-Western Coast of North America, described and illustrated: Together with an account of the American Whale Fishery.* John H. Carmany and Company, San Francisco, 1874.

VESSEL RIGS
Pages 240-241
Drawn by Graham McBride, curatorial Assistant Maritime Museum of the Atlantic, Halifax and enhanced by Etta Moffatt, Nova Scotia Museum, Halifax.

Glossary
of
Nautical & Whaling Terms

This Glossary has been prepared for the ordinary reader rather than for those readers who either have or desire specialized knowledge. Both of the latter groups would perhaps be better served by consulting a more extensive dictionary of nautical terms.

aback	the position of the sail when the wind blows on its forward side, pushing it back against the mast; the sail acts as a brake or drives the vessel backward
abaft	toward the stern relative to some other position on the vessel
abeam	a location or direction at right angles to the fore-and-aft line of a vessel
able seaman	an experienced sailor who performs all regular duties on deck and aloft on a sailing vessel
aft	at or toward the stern of a vessel
aft oar	the stroke oar nearest the stern of a whale boat. The stroke oarsman sets the rhythm for the rest of the crew
after hatch	the opening into the hold nearest the stern of a vessel
after quarter	a vessel's side from its middle to its stern
after sails	the sails attached to the yards on the mast nearest the stern of a vessel
after thwart	the seat nearest the stern of an open boat
afterguard	the captain and officers whose accommodations are in the after part of a vessel
afull	describes sails that are filled with wind so that the vessel is driven forward
aloft	any place above the deck, in the rigging, on the yards or on the mast of a vessel
alow	near or on the deck
amidships	in or toward the middle of a vessel
anchor watch	the crew on duty while a vessel is at anchor
anchorage	the area in a harbour set aside for vessels to lay at anchor
apprentice boy	a youth bound to serve at sea for a period of training to qualify to become an officer
articles (Articles of Agreement)	the documents signed by the captain and each crew member stating their duties, conditions of service and pay during a voyage or a stipulated period of time
astern	— any point behind a vessel — to move backward
athwartships	lying across the width of a vessel
awning	a tent-like covering over part of a vessel's deck for protection against the sun and rain
back	to cause a vessel to move backward by adjusting the sails so the wind strikes them from the forward side, or by pushing rather than pulling on the oars
back a sail or a yard	to position the sail so the wind blows on its forward side

backstay	a heavy rope leading from an upper mast to a point on the vessel's side behind the mast; provides support for topmasts, topgallant masts, royal masts and skysail poles
backwater	to drive a boat backward by pushing the oars in the opposite direction to which they are usually pulled
baffling around	sailing without progress against a current or in light variable winds
balance reef	to reduce the area of a fore-and-aft sail set to the wind by reefing the sail diagonally from the lower forward corner to a midpoint on the outside edge
balanced sail	a sail that has been reefed or partially taken in to reduce the sail area exposed to the wind
bale	— a wire handle — to remove water from a boat
baleen	the fibrous plates attached to the upper jaw of certain types of whales that filter food organisms from sea water
ballast	heavy material placed near the bottom of a vessel to maintain proper stability
bands of a yard	iron hoops around a spar or yard to which other rigging is attached
bare poles	describes the masts of a sailing vessel when all its sails have been taken in during a storm or heavy gale
barge	a large boat aboard a naval vessel for use by the ship's crew
bateau	in northeastern North America, a long, double-ended, flat-bottomed boat with flared sides
batten down	to secure the openings on the deck and sides of a vessel in expectation of stormy weather
beam	— the part of a vessel's frame that runs from side to side and on which the deck is laid — the width of a vessel's hull at its widest point
beam ends	describes a vessel that has rolled so far to one side that her deck is nearly vertical and remains in that position
bear up	to sail closer to the direction from which the wind is coming
bearing	the direction of an object from the viewer's position
beat	sailing in the direction from which the wind is coming by a series of alternate tacks or changes in direction across the wind
before the wind	sailing with the wind blowing directly from behind
belay	to make a rope secure by wrapping it around a cleat or belaying pin in a figure 8 pattern
belly (of a sail)	the main part of a sail that bulges when the wind fills it
bend	— to attach a sail to a yard, boom, gaff or stay — to tie one rope to another
bends	the thickest planks on the side of a vessel from the waterline upward
between decks	the space between two decks on a vessel
bight	a loop of rope or chain
bilge	the inside of a vessel's hull from the keel to the point where her sides rise vertically
bilge strakes	the outside planking on the hull at the bilge
blanket piece	a 2- to 4-foot wide strip of blubber cut from a whale in a spiral direction and raised with heavy tackle; its length varies from 10-25 feet
blasted	a whale in an advanced stage of decomposition
block	a device consisting of one or more grooved pulleys mounted in a casing and used to achieve mechanical advantage
blowhole	the nostrils of the whale, situated on top of the head
blubber	the fat of a whale or other sea mammal from which oil is rendered
board the fore tack	to pull down and secure the lower forward corner of the foresail after bringing the vessel closer to the direction from which the wind is coming
boarding	bringing a blanket piece on board a whaleship

boarding knife	a sword-like knife used to cut a hole in the blanket piece to insert a blubber hook or toggle
boards (tacks)	time spent sailing in one direction, *e.g.*, short boards means a vessel changed direction frequently
boat-header	the crew member who mans the steering-oar and maneuvers the whale boat until the whale is struck with a harpoon. He then changes place with the boat-steerer and goes forward to lance the whale
boat spade	a tool resembling a spade or large chisel used to chop the flukes of a whale during the chase
boat steerer	the crew member who harpoons the whale and then goes aft to steer the whale boat until the whale is killed
boathook	a sharp, pointed metal hook with a wooden handle used to hold a boat alongside or push it off
boat's head	the bow of a boat
bobstay	a heavy chain, rope or iron rod attached to the stempost of a vessel just above the water line and leading to the end of the bowsprit
boiling	in whaling this refers to rendering oil from whale blubber
bold water	deep, navigable water close to shore
bollard	a heavy post of wood or iron attached to the edge of a wharf or to the deck of a vessel to which mooring lines are secured
boltrope	rope sewn to the edge of a sail for added strength
bomb lance	an explosive projectile on the head of a harpoon fired from a whale gun to kill a whale
booby hatch	a movable wooden structure fastened to an open hatchway and fitted with a framed glass window to permit access and light below deck
boom	a heavy spar to which the bottom of a fore-and-aft sail is attached
bousing	sailing vigorously with sails and rigging taut
bow	the forward end of a vessel
bow boat	the whale boat carried closest to the bow on the port side of a whaleship
bow oar	the oar located nearest the bow on the port side of a whale boat
bows	the outside forward end of a vessel
bowsheets	a platform at the bow of a small boat that provides structural support and is sometimes used as a seat
bowsprit	the large spar projecting forward and slanting upward from the stem of a large sailing vessel
box her off	to change a vessel's course by adjusting her forward sails so the wind strikes them on the forward side, thus driving the vessel backward and away from the wind
boxhauling	the technique used to put a square-rigged vessel on a new tack in a confined area or in rough weather. First the head of the vessel is brought into the wind; the wind then blows on the front of the forward sails, pushing the vessel backward, and the helmsman steers her in a complete semi-circle until she is heading in the opposite direction; the sails are then positioned so the vessel can begin her new course
brace	a rope or tackle attached to the end of a yard and running to the deck; used to swing the yard around into a new position
brace aback	to position the sails on a vessel so the wind strikes them from the forward side
brace block	a block attached to the end of a yard through which the brace or rope is passed to enable the yards to be re-positioned
brace forward	to position the sails on a vessel so the wind strikes them from the back side, enabling the vessel to get under way
brace the yards	to re-position the yards by hauling on the braces or ropes that control their position, thus swinging them around. This is done to change the vessel's direction or to use the wind more effectively
breach	the leap of a whale partially out of the water

broad on the bow	the position of an object that is located four points (45°) or more of the compass from the fore-and-aft line of a vessel, looking forward
broadside	the side of a vessel above the water line
bulkhead	any upright partition or wall separating the various compartments on a vessel
bulwarks	the portion of the hull planking above the deck that in rough weather helps to keep the deck dry and prevent deck cargo, fittings or crew from being washed overboard
bumpkin	a short boom projecting from each side of the vessel used to spread the lower corners of the square foresail
bunghole	the round opening in a cask or barrel at its widest point
bunk	a built-in wooden bed aboard a vessel
bunt	— the main body of a square sail that billows out when it catches the wind — the portion of the yard over which the bunt of the sail is wrapped as the sail is being furled or gathered up
buntline	one of several ropes attached to the bottom of a square sail; they lead to the mast directly above the yard and from there down to the deck where they can be hauled to gather the sail up to the yard
buoy	a floating marker
buoyed the anchors	marked the position of the anchors with floating markers
burden, burthen	the cargo-carrying capacity of a vessel
by the wind	sailing as near as possible to the direction of the wind with the vessel's sails full
cabin	a room on board a vessel
cable length	in Doane's time, probably 120 fathoms or 720 feet
camel	— a float or raft placed between a vessel and a wharf to protect the side of the vessel — a floating watertight structure placed alongside a vessel to enable her to float in shallow water
can buoy	a cylindrical buoy
cap	— a band or collar, usually of metal, fitted around the upper end of a mast so that it can be extended by fitting the bottom of another mast on top of it — the metal band around the end of a spar
capstan	a vertical drum revolving on a spindle used to haul on a rope or anchor cable
careen	to lay a vessel on one side so the other side can be repaired below the water line
carpenter	the crew member responsible for the upkeep of the decks, boats and other wooden parts of the vessel
carry away	to break off or wash away
case	the cavity on the upper left side of the head of a sperm whale that contains clear oil
cat the anchor	to hoist the anchor to the cathead
cat-stopper	a short piece of chain on which the anchor is hung from the cathead
cathead	a heavy piece of timber or iron projecting from each side of a vessel near the bow, and fitted with pulleys on which the anchor is lifted from the water and supported before being stowed
caulk	to drive oakum or other fiber into the seams of a vessel's planking to prevent it from leaking
caulking iron	a broad flat chisel for driving oakum into the seams of planking
caulking mallet	a wooden mallet with a long head used to strike a caulking iron
ceiling	the planking fastened to the inside of a vessel's frame or ribs
centerboard	a movable metal or wooden plate enclosed within a watertight casing in the bottom of a boat. It is lowered during sailing to prevent the boat from being pushed sideways by the wind
chafing gear	pieces of mats and canvas fastened to various places on a vessel's spars or rigging to prevent damage caused by the chafing of rope or wood

chain pendant	a length of chain attached to the end of a yard, sail or masthead and with a metal ring or pulley fastened to its free end. A rope passed through the ring or pulley controls a distant piece of rigging
chain strap	a length of chain passed through a hole in the whale's head to hoist part of the head aboard
charter	to hire or lease a vessel
chock	a u-shaped opening in the gunwale of a whale boat through which the tow-line runs when fastened to a whale
chronometer	a dependable clock used in navigation
claw off shore	to work away from shore by sailing against the wind using a series of short tacks
cleat	— a strip of wood or metal fastened to another surface to strengthen or prevent slippage — a block of wood with a hole drilled in it large enough to receive the handle of an oar. Cleats were fastened to the bottom of whale boats at the feet of each crew member so their oars could be secured while they were occupied with other tasks — a wooden or metal fitting with a single or double horn around which a rope can be wrapped in figure 8 fashion
clew	the lower corners of a square sail or the aftermost point of a fore-and-aft sail
clew up	to haul the clews of a square sail up to the yard before the sail is furled
close reefed	a sail reduced in size to its last set of reef points to present as little of its canvas to the wind as possible
clumsy cleat	a notched plank near the bow of the whale boat used by the boat-steerer to steady himself during the capture of a whale
coaming	the raised piece of wood or iron around a hatchway or deck opening to strengthen the deck in the area of the opening and prevent water from coming inboard
coaster	a vessel involved in the coasting trade
coasting trade	the commerce at sea between the ports of one country
cockbill	to raise one end of a yard so that the yard is at an angle to the deck; sometimes necessary if a vessel is in close quarters at dockside
coign, quoin	a wedge used to keep casks from rolling
colors (ships)	an ensign or flag flown to indicate a vessel's nationality
come about	to steer a vessel into and across the wind which then acts on the other side of the vessel to allow her to sail in a new direction
come into the wind	to sail so close to the wind that it strikes the sail from the forward side
come to	to sail closer to the direction from which the wind is blowing
come to the wind	to sail or steer closer to the direction from which the wind is blowing
companionway	a stairway leading from the deck to a cabin below
con	to direct a helmsman in steering a vessel
cooler	a copper or iron tank into which the oil is first bailed after being rendered from the blubber
cooper	the crew member responsible for making and repairing barrels and casks
copper sheathing	copper sheets fastened to the bottom of the hull for protection from fouling and ship-worm
course	— the direction in which a vessel is steered — the sail attached to the lowest yard of each mast of a square-rigged vessel
covering board	a wide plank laid along the edge of the upper deck to cover the ends of the deck beams where they join the tops of a vessel's frames or ribs
crab capstan	a small portable capstan
cranky	the sailing quality of a vessel when it is top heavy
cross quartering the bows	appears to refer to the whale's movement across the bow of the whale boat at about a 45° angle
cross sea	a choppy sea in which the waves are running in different directions

cross the yards	to hoist the yards aloft and secure them in position across the masts
crossjack	the square sail spread on the lowest yard of the mizzenmast of a 3- or 4-masted ship or 4-masted barque
crosstrees	the part of the wooden framework on a vessel that supports the platform attached to the mast where the upper and lower masts meet
crown piece	the strip of blubber just in front of the whale's eye
crowsnest	a barrel or hoop lashed to the fore or main masthead of a whaling ship from which a lookout is kept for whales
crutch	a piece of oak about 2 inches square and 18 inches high shaped like a three pronged fork at the top and fastened to the gunwale of the whale boat near the bow. The poles of the first and second irons are kept in it ready for use
cutter	a single-masted fore-and-aft rigged vessel
cutting in	removing the blubber from the whale
cutting in gangway	a platform projecting from the side of the whaleship on which the whalemen work cutting the blubber from the whale
dart a lance	to plant the blade of the lance in a whale
davits	a curved or straight-armed crane for hoisting and lowering boats
deadeye	a flat circular block of hardwood grooved around its circumference and pierced with three holes; used in pairs to secure the ends of the rigging supporting the lower masts to the side of the vessel
deadlight	— a wooden shutter for a cabin window or side port — a heavy piece of glass inserted in the deck for lighting
dipsy lead (deep sea lead)	a lead weight of 30-50 pounds attached to a rope of 60 fathoms or more marked at various depths by distinctive markings; used to measure the depth of water below the hull
disbursements	the money paid by a shipmaster or shipowner's agent for voyage necessities such as port charges, cash advances to crew, repairs and provisions
ditty-bag	a small canvas bag used by seamen to hold sailmaking gear and personal belongings
dog watch	a 2-hour evening watch on board a vessel. The first is from 4-6 P.M., the second from 6-8 P.M.
double (a point of land)	to sail a vessel around a point of land so that when completed the point is between the vessel and her original position
double-reefed	a sail that has been shortened by taking it in to the second band of reef points
doublings (of the mast)	the overlapping parts of a lower mast and an upper mast
draft	the depth of water a vessel requires to float freely
drawback	the act of inhaling (for whales)
driving	being carried helplessly by the force of the wind and sea
drogher	a sea-going sailing barge
duck trousers	pants made from strong cotton or linen
duff	a stiff flour pudding, often containing raisins or currants, boiled in a cloth bag
dunnage	loose pieces of wood or other material placed under or around cargo in a vessel's hold to protect it from bilge-water, leakage from other cargo and condensation
earing, earring	*see* reef earing
East Indiaman	a sailing vessel that made voyages to India or the East Indies
eight pounder	a cannon that fired shot weighing eight pounds
embayed	a sailing vessel when it is unable to sail seaward against strong wind or current in a land-locked bay
ensign	a flag or banner

eye splice	a loop at the end of a rope made by splicing the end back into the rope
eyes of the ship	the bow of the ship, so called because the hawse-pipes, through which the anchor cables pass, resemble eyes
falls	the rope passing through one or more sets of pulleys that are used as a hoisting rig or tackle
false keel	a heavy plank fastened to the bottom of the main keel of a wooden hulled vessel designed to take the chafing when a vessel goes aground or into a dry dock
fan out	to slacken the ropes controlling a fore-and-aft sail when the wind is blowing strongly from the side of the vessel in order to ease the pressure on the sails
fasts	the lines holding a vessel to a wharf
fathom	a measure of length equalling 6 feet, a little less than 2 meters
felucca, feluca	a type of small vessel found in Mediterranean waters on the Portuguese and western Spanish coasts
fenders	anything acting as a buffer or bumper to protect a vessel's sides from chafing against a wharf or another vessel
fetch up	to reach a destination by sailing
fid	a hardwood pin tapered to a point and used to open the strands in splicing rope
fill away	to resume course after the sails have been flapping in the wind
fin (of a whale)	a whale's flipper
fin-chain	a chain attached to a whale's fin to hold it fast to the side of the whaleship
first mate	the officer next in command to the captain
fish the anchor	to hoist and secure the anchor on deck
fitting out	to equip a vessel with the necessities for the next voyage
fittings	the permanent equipment for a vessel
Flemish eye	a particular type of fancy loop made at a rope's end by splicing the end back into the rope
fluke chain	a chain attached to the flukes of the whale to hold it fast to the whaleship
flukes	the horizontal tail fin of a whale
flush deck	the main deck of a vessel, all on one level
fly (of an ensign)	the outer or free end of a flag
flying jib	the outermost triangular sail set on the rope leading from the bowsprit up to one of the mastheads
footrope	a strong rope extending along and suspended under a yard; sailors stand on the footrope when handling the sail
fore	located at or near the front of a vessel
fore-and-aft	running lengthwise, from stem to stern, parallel to the keel
fore-and-aft rig	any rig consisting of fore-and-aft sails only
fore-and-aft sail	any sail that is set running lengthwise on a vessel
fore royal stay	the heavy rope running from the end of the jibboom to a point near the top of the fore royal mast, which is the upper part of the foremast
fore-topgallant stay	a heavy rope or wire running from the end of the jibboom to the fore-topgallant mast, which forms part of the foremast
forecastle	a structure near the bow of the vessel or immediately behind the foremast that provides accommodation for the crew
foremast	the mast located closest to the bow of a vessel
foresail	— the lowest sail on the foremost mast of a sailing vessel — a small fore-and-aft sail attached to a removable mast located near the front of a whale boat

forward	at or toward the front of the ship
foul	to snarl or tangle
founder	to sink after being filled with water
four-pounder	a small cannon which fires shot weighing four pounds
fourth mate	officer fourth in line of command from the captain
fresh breeze	a comparatively stiff wind with a velocity of 17 to 21 nautical miles per hour
freshen	describes a wind beginning to increase in velocity
frigate	three-masted, square-rigged naval vessel with a battery of about 40 guns
furl	to gather up a sail, roll it over a yard, boom or stay and secure it with gaskets
gaff	— a tool that has a wooden handle with a hook at one end — a spar that spreads the upper edge of a fore-and-aft sail
gaff topsail	a sail set above the gaff
gale	a strong wind blowing at a velocity of about 30 to 50 nautical miles per hour
galley	a vessel's kitchen or cooking house
gallied	frightened
gamming	visiting from one whaling ship to another
gangway	an opening in a vessel's rail that allows passengers and cargo to pass through
gasket	a small line or canvas strip for securing a sail to its yard, boom or gaff after it is furled
general average	a marine insurance term for the adjustment that is made after part of a ship's cargo has been sacrificed to save the whole, so the loss will be shared proportionally by the owners of all cargo carried by the vessel
globe lantern	a lantern with a spherical or round-shaped glass protecting the flame
good billet	a relatively easy job
good offing	to get well clear of the land
good rap full	describes sails filled with wind
goose-winged	to spread one side only of a square sail, especially a topsail or a course by securing the weather half of the sail to the yard and spreading the lee side of the sail
grains	a harpoon
grappling (grapnel)	a small anchor consisting of a shank and four or five claws or curved flukes
grave	to clean barnacles from a vessel's bottom and apply a protective coating of tar, pitch and resin
great-circle sailing	a method of navigating a vessel on a long voyage along the shortest distance between the point of departure and the point of arrival. Navigators accomplish this by calculating a series of approximations to an imaginary great circle around the earth's circumference laid out along the course they intend to sail
gridiron	a floor of parallel timbers laid crosswise near the bottom of a seawall so the hull can be repaired at a low tide
gripes	canvas bands or straps used to secure a whale boat to its cradle on the whaleship
grog	an unsweetened drink of liquor and water
ground tier	the bottom layer of a cargo of barrels, boxes etc.
gunwale	the heavy plank on the upper edge of a vessel's side
guy	a rope, wire or chain to steady or support a spar
hail	to speak or call out
half-deck house	the crew's accommodation located between the mainmast and after cabin
half-watch	refers to the practice on whale ships of having only one-half the normal watch on duty

halliard (halyard)	a single rope, or rope in combination with blocks and tackle, used to hoist or set a sail
hard down	describes the wheel fully turned to the leeward side of the vessel
hard tack	a thick hard biscuit
harpoon	a barbed spear with a rope attached used to attack whales, either thrown by hand or shot from a gun
hatch	a deck opening into the hold of a vessel
haul	— to pull, drag or tug on a rope — to alter a vessel's course — the wind hauls when the direction from which it blows changes in a clockwise fashion, *e.g.*, from west to north
haul up	— to bring up — to alter a vessel's course toward the wind — to come to a halt
hawser	any length of heavy rope or wire used for mooring or towing a vessel
head	— the forward part of a vessel — the top of the mast
head and head	two vessels approaching each other
head sea	waves running in the opposite direction to a vessel's course
head the yards	to adjust the yards in a certain direction
headstay	a rope running forward from the foremast to the foreward part of the hull, bowsprit or jibboom
heave	to draw, pull or haul on a rope
heave down	to pull a vessel over on its side so the other side can be inspected, cleaned and repaired as required
heave down blocks	large blocks used to pull the vessel over on its side
heave her short	to haul on an anchor cable until the vessel is almost over the anchor, in preparation for getting under way
heave the lead	to determine the depth of water beneath a vessel using the deep sea lead
heave to	to stop a vessel by adjusting some of the forward sails so that the wind strikes them on the foreward side thereby counteracting the push of the aftersails
heel lashing	a rope or chain lashing securing the inner end of the jibboom to the bowsprit
heeled over (listing)	a vessel leaning over to one side due to the wind or the shifting of cargo or ballast
helm	a wheel or tiller used to steer a vessel
hemp	the plant *Cannabis sativa* whose fibers are used to make strong rope
high latitude	a great distance north or south of the equator
hitch	a knot, loop or noose by which a rope is made fast to another object
hitches of a harpoon	the knots that attach the rope to a harpoon where the iron head meets the wooden shaft
hogshead	a large cask or barrel whose capacity is 52.5 Imperial gallons
hold	the entire cargo space below the deck of a vessel
hold beam	the widely spaced beams running the width of a vessel
hold water	the command to oarsmen to set the blades of their oars vertically in the water and at right angles to the boat to stop the boat from moving forward
holystone	a block of soft sandstone used with water to scour wooden decks
hooker	a derogatory word for an old clumsy vessel
hounds	the lowest part of the wooden framework that supports a platform attached to the mast where an upper and lower mast meet
hove	*see* heave

hulk	the hull of a dismantled, disabled or old vessel unfit for sea
hull	the body of a vessel excluding deck structure, spars, rigging and machinery
iron	a whaler's term for harpoon
jib	a triangular sail set on a rope leading from the bowsprit to the top of the fore-topmast
jibboom	a spar attached to and forming an extension to the bowsprit
jig tackle	a small tackle composed of a double and single block, or two single blocks for general use aboard ship
jollyboat	small workboat carried on a larger vessel and used to carry out ship's business while in port
junk	— a fibrous tissue containing oil lying below the case in the head of a sperm whale — old rope that can be unravelled and reused for many different purposes aboard ship, such as making gaskets, mats, swabs and oakum — a sailing vessel common to Japanese and Chinese waters characterized by a flat bottom and a high stern with two or three masts carrying batten-stiffened four-sided sails
kedge	to move a vessel by pulling on the line attached to a small anchor, also called a kedge
keel	main structural member or "backbone" of a vessel
keelson	a heavy piece of timber laid parallel to the keel and bolted through the vessel's frames or ribs to the keel for structural strength
keep off	to sail a vessel away from the direction of the wind or any object in sight
keep to	in sailing, to continue in a position or on a course
keeping to the wind	to continue sailing close to the wind
knot	a measure of a vessel's speed equal to one nautical mile, or 6080 feet, per hour
laid the sail to the mast	*see* aback
lance	a long, sharp-pointed, spear-like instrument with keen cutting edges and a recovery line attached; used to kill a whale after it has been harpooned
lantern keg	a keg in a whale boat used to store a lantern, candles and foodstuffs in case of an emergency
lanyard	— a piece of rope or cord for fastening or holding an object — the rope passed through deadeyes to attach the lower ends of rigging to the sides of a vessel
lanyard hitch	a knot or hitch used to secure the end of a lanyard
larboard	the port side of a vessel, i.e., the left side if one is looking forward
larboard boat	the whale boat located nearest the stern on the port side and used by the first mate
lashing	a general term used for any small rope, chain or wire used to fasten one thing to another
lateen sail	a large sail shaped like a right angle triangle, whose longest side is attached to a yard; the end of the yard is angled at 45° downward toward the front of the boat
lay	— a whaleman's share of the profits of the voyage — to place or put in position
lay to	*see* heave to
lee	the sheltered side, protected from wind and sea
leeshore	a nearby shore on the lee side of the vessel, *i.e.*, the shore onto which the wind is blowing
leeway	— the difference between the course steered and that actually sailed — the angle of drift caused by wind or current
liberty man	an enlisted man granted shore leave
lie to a wharf	a vessel occupying a berth next to the wharf

lifts	a rope or chain extended from a mast to each end of a yard or boom as a support or means of lifting the spar
light	having little weight, strength or size
light airs	unsteady, faint puffs of wind
lighterage	the transportation of goods to and from large vessels in the harbor via barges called lighters
loggerhead	a bollard or post in the front end of a whale boat for holding the line after a whale is harpooned
long boat	a strongly constructed boat carried on board a vessel and used to transport supplies and people to and from the vessel
long-footed swell	the undulation of the sea after a gale characterized by a long trough between the crest of the waves
long splice	a splice in which the rope is unlaid 18 to 24 times the diameter of the rope, thus making a stronger splice
loose	to let go or slacken
luff	— the forward edge of a fore-and-aft sail — to sail closer to or turn a vessel's head toward the wind
lugsail	a four sided sail hoisted on a yard and often used on small boats
main	attached to or rigged from the mainmast, *e.g.*, the main topsail
main keel	the main structural member or "backbone" of a vessel
main tack	Doane refers to riding a whale "like a new main tack," meaning to follow it very closely
mainboom	the spar to which the bottom of a fore-and-aft mainsail is fastened
mainmast	the tallest mast, usually second from the bow of a vessel
mainsail/main course	the lowest sail set on the mainmast of a vessel
make	to arrive at, or sight a place or position
make sail	to raise the sails when getting under way or spread more canvas for greater speed
man-of-war	a large naval vessel ready for active hostilities
manila	fiber from *Musa textilis,* a Philippine species closely related to the banana, and used for making rope
marline spike	a tapering, pointed steel tool 12-24 inches long used for separating strands of rope or wire when splicing
martingale	part of a vessel's rigging supporting the jibboom
mast	a verticle spar of wood that supports a vessel's yards, booms and gaffs
mast rope	a line used for hoisting or lowering an upper mast
masthead	the upper part of the mast
masthead the topsail yard	to hoist the topsail yard into position for the topsail to be set
mate	the officer next in command to the captain of a vessel who assists in navigating and commanding it. Depending on its size, a vessel could have two to eight mates, distinguished by first, second, third, and so on, to indicate seniority
mate's watch	the crew assigned to work under the command of the first mate; also known as the port watch
meridian time	meridians are the lines of longitude; when the sun passes an observer's meridian, the time is reckoned to be 12 noon
middle latitude sailing	a method of navigating east or west that projects approximate courses and distances by assuming that the area being sailed across is a flat surface. This method involves averaging the latitudes of the place the vessel has left and to which she is bound
midship	located near the middle of a vessel
midship boat	the whale boat located second from the stern on the port side of a whaleship and commanded by the second mate when pursuing whales; also called the waist boat

midship oar	the oar on a whale boat located second from the stern on the starboard side
mincing horse	a bench about 2 feet long, 6 to 8 inches wide, used on a whaling ship; pieces of blubber cut from the blanket piece are laid on it lengthwise, flesh side downward, and cut or scored into thin slices with a mincing knife
mincing knife	a knife about 30 inches long with a handle at each end; used to mince blubber
mis-stay	to fail to come about from one tack to another. After a vessel gets its head to the wind, it comes to a standstill and begins to fall back to its original course
mizzen	attached to or rigged from the mizzen mast
mizzen chains	a stout length of chain fastened to a vessel's hull and used to secure the lower part of the shrouds to the side of the vessel. When Doane said that he was "in the mizzen chains," he was actually standing on the channel, a small timber platform which spread the chains out from the side of the vessel
mizzen topsail	the second sail from the deck on the mizzenmast
mizzenmast	third mast from the bow of a vessel having three or more masts
mizzentop	the platform at the head of the lower mizzenmast
monkey-rope	a lifeline tied to a man's waist while he works in a hazardous position over a vessel's side
moored	to secure a vessel to a wharf or anchors
mooring bitts	a pair of stout wooden or iron posts around which a heavy rope is turned to secure a vessel
mooring pipe	a heavy casting fitted into the side of a vessel; mooring ropes are passed through it to secure a vessel to a wharf
netting	probably refers to ropework in the form of a net secured to an opening in the rail of a vessel; it is supported by vertical posts or stanchions
nettles	a thin line made into short lengths used for other general purposes aboard a vessel
nipper	a thick band or mitten with a reinforced palm used to protect the hand when hauling lines
northing	in sailing, the distance sailed toward north
officer of the watch	the officer in charge of the watch and responsible for navigating the ship in the absence of the master
offing	the distance separating the vessel from shore or another vessel
paid off	discharged with pay at the end of a voyage
painter	a length of rope permanently secured to the bow of a boat for mooring or towing
pantile	a biscuit, or hard tack
parallel sailing	navigating along a given latitude or sailing true east or west
parao	probably refers to a type of large double-ended, flat-bottomed boat with flared sides
parrel of the yard	a fitting usually resembling a collar that attaches a yard to a mast so that the yard can be hoisted or lowered
pawl	a short piece of metal that pivots on one end so it can drop into notches on a wheel to stop the wheel from turning
pawl bitt (post)	a heavy post to which the pawls on a windlass are attached
pay	— to run a mixture of melted pitch and resin into the caulked seams between a vessel's planking — to allow a line to run out
peak	— to raise upright — the upper and outer corner of a gaff, lug or lateen sail
peak halliard (halyard)	a single rope or tackle used to hoist the outer end of a gaff and hence the peak of a sail
pendant	see chain pendant

piggin	a small wooden bucket with one long stave used as a handle
pipe	a large cask
pitch	— a dark residue obtained by distilling coal tar or other petroleum products — the motion of a vessel when its bow and stern rise and fall alternately with the waves
plane sailing	a navigational practice used to simplify the calculation of courses and distances; assumes that the surface being sailed is flat
planksheer	*see* covering board
point	one of the 32 divisions of a compass, each equalling an arc of 11¼°
poop deck	a raised deck located at the stern of a vessel
port	the left side of the vessel if one is looking forward
port tack	the direction being sailed when the wind is blowing from the port side of the vessel
port watch	*see* mate's watch
pratique	permission granted to a vessel by port medical authorities to have contact with the shore
press gang	a group of seamen, commanded by a naval officer, which captured and forced men into the naval service
privateer	a privately owned vessel authorized by a country to destroy or capture merchant and naval vessels from another country
pump	a mechanical device used to pump water from the hold of a vessel
pump brake	a pump handle
put back	to return or turn back
put the helm down	to turn a vessel's wheel away from the wind in order to bring the head closer to the wind
quadrant	a navigational instrument used to determine the position of a vessel by measuring the altitude of heavenly bodies in relationship to the horizon; a quadrant measures up to 90°
quarter	the rounded part of a vessel's side; located near the back where the side meets the stern
quarter-watch	one-quarter of a vessel's crew on watch duty
quartering of the yard	the portion of a yard extending from the middle to about half way out from either side of the mast
rack	to bind together the ropes on a tackle with a smaller rope to prevent them from moving
rail	an open fence-like structure along the sides of a vessel
rank sheer	a sudden change in direction
ratline stuff	small, three-stranded tarred hemp line
ratlines	ropes across a vessel's shrouds forming a series of steps so that crew can climb aloft
rattling down the shrouds	installing new ratlines on the shrouds
reach ahead	to move ahead very slightly
re-copper	replace copper sheathing on the bottom of a vessel
reef	to take in part of a sail so that less canvas is exposed to the wind
reef earing	a short piece of rope secured to the corner of a sail and used for raising or reefing it
reef gear	a small tackle used in reefing sails
reef points	short pieces of rope fitted in a row across a sail so the sail can be reduced in size
reeve	to pass the end of a rope or chain through a block or deadeye
render	to ease a rope through a block or deadeye, or wrap it around a windlass
rib	a vessel's frames
rigged in	to bring a spar aboard a vessel and lash it in place

rigger	tradesman who installs all the gear and fittings of rope and wire on a vessel
rigging	a vessel's masts, yards, booms, other spars and all the rope used to support masts, set or take in sails, and hoist or lower booms, yards and other spars
right ahead	straight ahead
right astern	directly behind
right the ship	to bring a vessel that is heeling over on her side to her normal position
roaring forties	an area of the oceans between the latitudes 40° and 50° south, characterized by strong westerly winds
roll	the tilting movement of a vessel from side to side
rope yarn	a yarn or thread comprised of a number of fibers loosely twisted together; several rope yarns make up a strand of rope
rove	*see* reeve
row lock (oarlock)	a u-shaped swiveling crutch in which an oar is placed for rowing
royal backstay	a rope or stay leading down from the royal mast to a vessel's side behind the mast
royal mast	the upper part of the topgallant mast on which the fourth sail from the deck is set
royal sail	a square sail set on the royal yard above the topgallant sail; usually the fourth sail from the deck
royal yard	the yard attached to the royal mast
rudder	a vertical flat piece of wood or metal mounted to the stern of a vessel under water and used for steering
rudder head	the upper or inboard part of the rudder
rudder post	the heavy upright timber at the stern of a vessel to which the rudder is attached
run afoul	to become entangled in
running bowline	a slip knot made at the end of a rope
running rigging	rigging used to adjust, hoist or lower the yards and to set and take in sails
sail loft	a large open room used for sailmaking
sail room	an area in a vessel to store spare sails and other similiar gear
sailing trim	describes a vessel loaded or ballasted to sail as efficiently as possible
salt horse	salted beef
sampan	a plank-built, flat-bottomed boat found in the waters off China, Japan, the East Indies, and Malayasia
samson post	short, sturdy piece of timber in the hold of a vessel that is placed between the keelson and a deck beam
scotchman	a wrapping of canvas or rope, attached to the rigging of a vessel to reduce chafing
scud	to sail in a strong wind, with few or no sails set
scull	to propel a boat with a single oar over the stern by moving the oar from side to side
scupper	an opening in the side of a vessel for carrying water off the deck
scuttle	to sink a vessel intentionally
scuttle butt	a large covered cask kept on deck to hold drinking water for the crew
sea room	space at sea needed to manoeuvre a vessel
second dog-watch	the watch between 6 and 8 P.M.
seize	to fasten or bind with small cordage
seizing	the turns of thin cordage used to bind, lash or fasten one object to another on a vessel
send down	to lower an object to the deck
send up	to raise an object aloft

set	— to spread a sail to the wind — to appoint a watch
set up (rigging)	to draw or pull rigging taut
seventy-eight pounder	a large cannon that fires shot weighing 78 pounds
sextant	a navigational instrument used to determine the position of a vessel by measuring the altitude of heavenly bodies in relationship to the horizon. A sextant can measure up to 120°
shake	describes sails that shiver or flap when a vessel sails too close to the direction from which the wind is blowing
shallop	a small two-masted vessel driven by oars or sails
shape a course	to steer a vessel toward a particular destination
sharp by the wind	to sail at an acute angle to the direction from which the wind is blowing
sheave	a disc or wheel grooved around its circumference and set into a block, mast or yard as a roller over which a rope travels; a pulley
sheer	to swing or swerve from the original course
sheer plank	*see* covering board
sheet	a tackle, single rope or chain leading from the lower corner of a sail and used to set or re-position it
ship	— to bring supplies or equipment aboard — a sailing vessel with three or more masts, each of which carries square sails
ship oars	to bring the oars inboard
shiver	to shake or flutter; a vessel's sails shiver when it sails close to the wind or heads into the wind
shoal	an area of shallow water
shoes (for anchor)	rounded blocks of wood temporarily fitted to the anchor flukes to prevent damage to the deck of a vessel
short splice	a splice made by unlaying the strands of rope about 12 times the diameter of the rope and marrying them to form a short bulky splice
shorten sail	to reduce the spread of sails by reefing or taking them in
shroud	one of a set of strong ropes extending from the sides of each masthead to the sides of a vessel to support the masts
skylight	a framed deck structure with windows to allow light and ventilation below
slack line	to ease off or loosen a line
slat	to flap about
slings	ropes or chains that are attached to the center of a yard and support it when the yard is raised or lowered
sloop	a single-masted fore-and-aft rigged vessel
sloop of war	a relatively small naval vessel usually rigged as a brig or ship
slop-chest	a supply of personal necessities kept on board a vessel for sale to the crew
slush	fat collected from a ship's galley to lubricate the masts
smack	a small, fore-and-aft rigged sailing vessel used principally in the fishery of Great Britain
snatch block	a block with a hinged opening at the top to enable a rope to be placed directly over its sheave without passing it through the hole in the block
snub (a line)	to hold a line taut
snug alow and aloft	describes a vessel that, in preparation for bad weather, has had its upper masts and yards sent down, topsails close-reefed and all movable items secured on deck and aloft
sound the water	to measure the depth of water
sounding	describes a whale diving, usually after it has been harpooned

southing	distance made to the southward
spade	a cutting instrument shaped like a broad chisel and used for removing blubber
spade pole	the handle for a spade
spanker	a triangular or four-sided fore-and-aft sail that is the lowest and aftermost sail on a brig, barquentine, barque, ship or 3- to 5-masted schooner
spar	a general term for a boom, mast or yard
spar deck	in Doane's time, referred to all of the main deck
speak a ship	to hail or communicate with another vessel
spencer	a triangular or four-sided fore-and-aft sail set behind the lower foremast in a brig or brigantine and behind the lower fore and main masts in a barque, barquentine or ship
spermaceti	a waxy yellowish to white oily wax extracted from the spermaceti organ in the head of a sperm whale
splice	to join a rope end with any part of the same or another rope by interweaving the strands
sprit	a small spar that extends from the mast near the foot of a sprit sail diagonally across the sail to its top outside corner. It is used to spread the sail to the wind
sprit sail	a four-sided fore-and-aft sail used in small boats
squall	a sudden strong wind often followed by rain or snow
square away	to alter a vessel's course so she sails in the same direction the wind is blowing
square sail	a rectangular sail set from a yard mounted at right angles across the mast
squaring off the ratlines	to attach ratlines on the shrouds so that they are lined up horizontally and parallel to each other
stakeboat	an anchored boat showing a flag for use as a turning point in yacht racing
stanchion	an upright post for supporting a deck, rail or other structure
stand	— to sail in a specific direction — to maintain a relative position — to perform a certain duty
stand a masthead	to serve as lookout at the top of a mast
standing rigging	the fixed rigging that supports masts, bowsprit and jibboom and includes shrouds, backstays and stays
starboard	the right side of a vessel if one is looking forward
starboard boat	the whale boat situated on the starboard side of the whaleship and used by the captain or fourth mate
starboard tack	the direction being sailed when the wind is blowing from the starboard or right side of a vessel
starboard watch	the part of the crew assigned to the watch commanded by the captain or second mate
start	to loosen or break free
stay	a heavy rope used to support a mast in a fore-and-aft direction
staysail	a triangular sail spread from a stay
steerage	passenger accommodation on the lower deck
steering gear	the arrangement of tackle used to control a vessel's rudder
steering-oar	a long oar placed over the stern of a boat for use as a rudder
stem	the foremost timber in a vessel's frame
step	a socket in which a mast or stanchion is set to keep it in an upright position
stern	the after end of a vessel
stern all	a command to a boat's crew to row backward
sternboard/sternway	backward movement
sternpost	the heavy upright timber attached vertically to the keel at the back of a vessel. The rudder is hung on this timber, so it is frequently called the rudder post

sternsheets	a platform at the stern of a small boat that provides structural support and is sometimes used as a seat
steward	the crew member responsible for the domestic needs of the crew
stove in	describes a vessel's planking that is badly crushed or broken inward
stow	to pack away, lash in place or secure
strake	one row or strip of planking on a vessel's hull
strap	— a narrow strip of flexible material for temporary holding or securing — a piece of rope with the ends spliced together to form a loop and used to attach a tackle to another object
strip	to remove or send down sails and running rigging
struck down (to the hold)	to lower cargo into the hold and stow it away
studding sail	a four-sided sail set in light winds by using a portable, temporary extension to each end of a yard
studding sail boom	a spar rigged at the end of a yard to spread a studding sail
studding sail covers	snug-fitting coverings made of light canvas to protect studding sails from weather
swamped	decribes a vessel filled with water
sway up	to throw one's weight on a rope while hoisting an upper mast, yard or sail in preparation for releasing it so it can be sent down to the deck
sword mat	a mat woven from unravelled rope strands and used as chafing gear
tack	— the lower forward corner of a fore-and-aft sail — the lower corner of a square sail closest to the wind — any rope or fastening that secures the lower corner of a square sail closest to the wind — the act of changing the direction of a vessel so the wind blows on the opposite side — the direction that a vessel is heading relative to the direction from which the wind is blowing; a vessel is sailing on the port tack when the wind is blowing from the port side — the distance and duration sailed on either a port or starboard tack
tack and half tack	an alternating series of long and short tacks
tackle	a set of blocks in which rope or chain is used to gain mechanical advantage. Collectively a number of sets of blocks make up a vessel's tackle
taffrail	the rail around a vessel's stern
tauten	to haul tight
telegraph	probably refers to signalling with flags
tender	describes a vessel that is top heavy and thus unstable
thigh board	a notched plank near the bow of a whale boat used by the boat-steerer to steady himself during the capture of a whale
three-fold purchase	a tackle of two blocks, each one having three sheaves
three-reefed sail	a sail that has been reduced in size by securing its third row of reef points to the yard or boom
thwart	one of the planks that extend crosswise in an open boat for lateral stiffening and often used as a seat
tideway	a channel followed by a tide or current
tie, tye	a chain attached to the middle of a yard and used for raising and lowering it
tierce	a cask with a capacity of 42 Imperial or 50 U.S. gallons
toggle	a piece of wood or metal fitted crosswise in the end of a rope or a chain for the purpose of quickly engaging or disengaging with a link, ring or an eye
tom	a piece of timber used to brace cargo so that it will not shift while at sea
top hamper	— a vessel with too much gear aloft thus making her unstable — the upper masts, spars and rigging of a vessel

topgallant breeze	a strong breeze suitable for setting topgallant sails
topgallant forecastle	a raised deck on the extreme forward end of a ship to accommodate the crew
topgallant mast	the mast set above the topmast
topgallant sails	the sails set to the yards attached to the topgallant mast
topmast	the mast set above the lower mast, *i.e.*, the second mast aloft from the deck
tops	a platform at the lower masthead on a square-rigged vessel; serves to spread the topmast shrouds and as a working platform for the crew
topsail	the sails set on the yards attached to the topmast
topsides	the outer surface of the hull above the waterline
trades (trade winds)	the winds blowing in an almost constant direction and found over several regions of the ocean, *e.g.*, the northeast and southeast trade winds of the tropical and subtropical latitudes in the Atlantic and Pacific Oceans
travelling wheel	a type of ship's wheel mounted on top of the tiller that controls the rudder. When turned, the wheel moved (travelled) with the tiller. As the wheel was mounted behind the rudder post, the helmsman turned it in the opposite direction to that normally turned on vessels of that era
traverse sailing	a type of navigation in which a vessel's actual course and distance is found by combining the results of the courses and distances of a succession of alternate tacks
treenail	a round wooden peg used to fasten planking to the side of a wooden vessel
trestle-trees	strong pieces of wood fixed fore-and-aft at each side of a mast to form the foundation of a platform attached to a mast where an upper and lower mast meet
trick at the helm	a regular shift spent steering a vessel
trim	— to adjust the sails or yards — to adjust a vessel's floating position by moving ballast or cargo in the hold
trough of the waves	the hollow between the waves
truck (of the mast)	a rounded block of wood fastened to the extreme upper end of a mast, usually fitted with a sheave to enable flags to be hoisted
truss	a strong iron pivot attaching the middle of the lower yard to the lower mast, thus allowing it to be braced as required
try out	to melt oil from whale blubber
trypot	a large pot for melting blubber
tryworks	the brick structure over which pots filled with blubber are heated
tub oar	the oar just forward of the steering-oar on the port side of a whale boat; so named because it is the oar nearest the tub holding the tow line attached to the harpoon
tun butts	large casks of varying capacity
turn	a single wind of a rope around a capstan, belaying pin, bollard or cleat
turn in	to secure a shroud, stay or other rigging by passing its end around a deadeye or other similar device and then lashing it back
two-reefed sail	one that has been taken in or reduced in size by securing its second row of reef points to the yard or boom
typhoon	a term used in the Far East to describe a cyclone or severe storm with winds up to 130 miles per hour
unbend	to detach or remove from a secure position
under the lee	a location off the sheltered side of a vessel
unlay	to unravel the strands of a rope
unreeve	to haul a rope or chain out of a block, deadeye or other similar device
unship	to remove or detach from a vessel

unstep	to remove from its step or slot, *e.g.,* to unstep a mast
upper deck	the uppermost continuous deck on a vessel
upper works	all the parts of the hull on deck
variation (of the compass)	the difference between true north and magnetic north
victualing	the provision of food for a vessel
waif	— a buoy or float fastened to the end of a harpoon line as a marker to claim a dead whale — a flag at the end of a sharp stick marking the carcass of a whale
waist boat	*see* midship boat
wales	*see* bends
warp	— a heavy rope or hawser used in mooring or shifting a vessel — to move a vessel in a harbour by hauling on warps attached to anchors or bollards
watch	a period of duty, usually four hours, to which part of the crew is assigned
waterway	thick planking at each side of the vessel set slightly below the level of the deck to form gutters that carry off water to the scuppers
ways	a slightly inclined track made from smooth-faced timber; a vessel slides on it when being hauled out of the water or being launched
wear	to steer a vessel onto another tack by turning the head of the vessel away from the wind instead of across the wind
weather	toward or lying in the direction from which the wind is blowing
whale boat	a sharp-sterned open boat about 25 feet long, manned by 5 oarsmen and an officer and used for capturing whales
whip	a rope passed through a single block and used for hoisting
windlass	a winch installed near the bow and used to raise the anchors or to warp a vessel when in harbor
windlass bitts	one or two short strong posts of wood or iron fastened to the deck to which the windlass is secured
windward	in the direction from which the wind is blowing
wing	the part of the hold nearest to either side of a vessel
wrecker	one who salvages goods, cargo and equipment from stranded or wrecked vessels
yard	a spar attached at its midpoint to a mast
yardarm	the last one-quarter of the yard's length at each end
yaw	to swing wildly off course